Chronic Schizophrenia and Adult Autism:
Issues in Diagnosis, Assessment, and Psychological Treatment

Johnny L. Matson, Ph.D. is Professor of Psychology and Director of the Clinical Psychology program in the Department of Psychology at Louisiana State University in Baton Rouge, Louisiana. He is the author of 20 books and over 200 journal articles and book chapters on developmental disabilities and chronic emotional problems. Further he is the editor of the journal *Research in Developmental Disabilities* and has served on the editorial boards of a number of journals including *Behavior Therapy, Journal of Applied Behavior Analysis, Journal of Clinical Child Psychology, Scandinavian Journal of Behavior Therapy, Mental Retardation, Behavior Modification, Journal of the Multihandicapped Person and Exceptionality.* He has been president of the mental retardation and developmental disabilities division of the American Psychological Association, president of the the psychology division of the American Association on Mental Retardation, consultant to the Presidents Committee on Mental Retardation, the National Institute of Mental Health and the U.S. Justice Department.

Chronic Schizophrenia and Adult Autism:
Issues in Diagnosis, Assessment, and Psychological Treatment

Johnny L. Matson, Ph.D.
Editor

Springer Publishing Company
New York

Springer Publishing Company, Inc.
536 Broadway
New York, NY 10012

89 90 91 92 93 / 5 4 3 2 1

Chronic schizophrenia and adult autism : issues in diagnosis,
    assessment, and psychological treatment / Johnny L. Matson, editor.
        p. cm.
    Includes bibliographical references.
    ISBN 0-8261-6020-4
    1. Schizophrenia., 2. Autism. I. Matson, Johnny L.
    [DNLM: 1. Autism—diagnosis. 2. Autism—therapy.
3. Schizophrenia—diagnosis. 4. Schizophrenia—therapy. WM 203
C551]
RC514.C484 1981
616.89'82—dc20
DNLM/DLC
for Library of Congress   89-21631
                                                                    CIP

Printed in the United States of America

Contents

Preface

Autism and chronic schizophrenias have been two of the central topics of interest for psychologists, psychiatrists, and educators for many years. Much has been written, and a good deal of clinical and basic research has been conducted. But with autism, the focus has traditionally been on children, the problems they display, and how they are treated. Treating adults with autism has only infrequently been a topic to consider in clinical research and in books. The same problem is apparent in the literature on schizophrenic clients. Much has been done in pharmacotherapy with persons who evince acute episodes that incapacitate them for short periods. When these short periods occur several times, the client is described as having chronic schizophrenia. However, many clients evince extreme symptoms, without remission, over many years. This latter group differs markedly from the other groups of schizophrenic persons.

This book was developed as a means to describe the problems, possible assessments and interventions for adult autistic people and the most chronic schizophrenic clients. It became apparent, in working with these patients and in reviewing the research conducted to date, that although the means by which extreme problem behaviors develop may differ, the deficits that are evident and the treatments used are really quite similar. Both groups had marked social, verbal, and self-help deficits. Both groups responded marginally to psychotropic medications and often were functioning, from an adaptive standpoint, as if they were mentally retarded. Marked improvements in these skill areas and the hope that at least sheltered workshop or competitive employment with supervision could be planned are focal points in treatment planning. Our book, then, is an effort to describe how these clients, who are very difficult to treat, may benefit from systematic evaluation and a range of therapeutic procedures. The volume highlights the major changes and improvements in quality care for such populations, with an emphasis on the considerable potential these highly involved clients have for positive change of their problem behaviors.

JOHNNY L. MATSON

Contributors

Alan Bellack, Ph.D.
Medical College of Pennsylvania at EPPI
Philadelphia, PA

Edward G. Carr, Ph.D.
Department of Psychology
SUNY at Stony Brook
Stony Brook, NY

David Coe
Department of Psychology
Louisiana State University
Baton Rouge, LA

Mark Durand, Ph.D.
Department of Psychology
SUNY at Albany
Albany, NY

Roger C. Katz, Ph.D.
Department of Psychology
University of the Pacific
Stockton, CA

Christian Lemmon
Department of Psychology
University of Mississippi
University, MS

Ramasamy Manikam
Department of Pediatrics
Johns Hopkins Medical School
Baltimore, MD

Johnny L. Matson, Ph.D.
Department of Psychology
Louisiana State University
Baton Rouge, LA

John R. McCartney, Ph.D.
School of Social Work
University of Alabama
Tuscaloosa, Al

Kim T. Mueser
Medical College of Pennsylvania at EPPI
Philadelphia, PA

Floyd O'Brien, Ph.D.
Department of Special Education
University of the Pacific
Stockton, CA

N. Jennifer Oke, M.A.
Department of Psychology
University of California—San Diego
San Diego, CA

Bertram O. Ploog, M.A.
Department of Psychology
University of California—San Diego
San Diego, CA

Janet S. St. Lawrence, Ph.D.
Department of Psychology
Jackson State University
Jackson, MS

Laura E. Schreibman, Ph.D.
Department of Psychology
University of California—San Diego
San Diego, CA

Nirbhay N. Singh Ph.D
Department of Psychiatry
Medical College of Virginia
Virginia Commonwealth University
Richmond, VA

1

A Historical Overview of Autism and Schizophrenia

Ennio Cipani and Floyd O'Brien

ABNORMAL BEHAVIOR

Today we speak of abnormal behaviors as mental disorders when they generate distress, disability, and increased risks of death, pain, and losses of important freedoms (APA, 1987). People with the disorders of autism and schizophrenia portray such debilitating abnormal behaviors that they typically remain dependent on others to provide even a meager existence. In our current culture, they usually depend on mental health agencies for medical, psychological, and social support.

In earlier cultures, people suffering with autism and schizophrenia may have depended on shamans, churches, or other agents selected by the culture to accommodate those with such abnormal behaviors (Alexander & Selesnick, 1966). These selected agents were sanctioned by their respective cultures to provide special practices to people who exhibited abnormal behaviors (cf., Lahey & Ciminero, 1980; Ullman & Krasner, 1969).

In a general sense, cultures determined which abnormal patterns were acceptable, beneficial, or harmful, using only subjective criteria. Thus, some cultures determined an abnormal pattern to be beneficial, and other cultures considered it harmful. Also, some cultures considered the abnormality beneficial during one era and harmful during some other time (Lahey & Ciminero, 1980). Yet the abnormal behavioral patterns of people with autism and schizophrenia are so severe that it has been rare for cultures to consider them beneficial or even tolerable.

The abnormal behaviors portrayed by people with autism and schizophrenia have been noted throughout history. Disturbances in affect, impairment in the content and form of verbal behavior, stereotyped behaviors (rituals), hallucinations, asocial tendencies, and delusions, for example, were noted in the earliest of cultures (Alexander & Selesnick, 1966). However, classifying these into clinical entities occurred only recently. The clinical entities (syndromes) of autism and schizophrenia need definition for the reader to know what we mean by the terms. Thus, we begin with a historically recent event, the defining of schizophrenia and autism.

SCHIZOPHRENIA IDENTIFIED
Early Description of Schizophrenia

Schizophrenia was first described in treatises published in 1809 by two physicians, John Haslam, an Englishman and Philippe Pinel, a Frenchman. Pinel's term for the disorder was slightly changed to dementia praecox by Kraepelin in 1896 (Calhoun, 1977) and continued to be the popular term until 1911, when Bleuler changed it to schizophrenia.

Bleuler described schizophrenia as a disorder consisting of four abnormal patterns of behavior: disturbances in association and affect, ambivalence, and autism (Salzinger, 1980). By disturbances of *association*, Bleuler referred to the propensity for people with schizophrenia to speak of matters with such "loosening of associations" as to make their verbalizations incomprehensible (e.g., "I like the sun . . . but his feet, and we knew . . . were the birds?"). By disturbance in *affect*,

Bleuler referred to the display of emotions that were inappropriate (e.g., giggling when being asked a neutral question, crying when hearing a funny story, or laughing when hearing of a tragedy). By *ambivalence*, Bleuler was referring to the rapid changes people with schizophrenia made in behavior and verbal evaluations of specific events (e.g., saying, "I love cabbage" while sitting down to eat and, before taking the first bite, getting up and saying, "I've got better things to do than eat"). Finally, *autism* referred to a tendency to be inward-directed, self-centered, and to behave in an asocial manner (e.g., mumbling and pointing skyward while being told to shush during a religious ceremony). Since this early description of schizophrenia by Bleuler, many others have been provided (cf., Singh & Katz, this volume), culminating in our present definition of schizophrenia.

Current Definition and Diagnostic Criteria of Schizophrenia

A source of a currently popular definition of schizophrenia is the revised third edition of the *Diagnostic and Statistical Manual of the American Psychiatric Association* (DSM-III-R). This description of schizophrenia includes characteristic psychotic symptoms, a duration of at least 6 months, and a deterioration in self-care, social, and occupational functioning (APA, 1987). The characteristic psychotic symptoms included bizarre delusions, prominent hallucinations, and specified disturbances in affect, verbal behavior, and psychomotor patterns (described below).

Bizarre delusions or prominent hallucinations must occur during the active phase of the disorder. But some people with schizophrenia portray no indications of delusions or hallucinations (Torrey, 1983). For such persons to be diagnosed with schizophrenia, they need to display any two of the following: incoherence or marked loosening of associations, flat or grossly inappropriate affect, and catatonic-type disturbances in psychomotor behavior (APA, 1987). It is noted that "no single feature is invariably present or seen only in Schizophrenia" (p. 188). Also, because any of these symptoms may exist as a feature on another disorder (e.g., schizoaffective disorder), DSM-III-R requires that other, similar disorders be disconfirmed.

The various psychotic symptoms portrayed by people with schizophrenia are discussed in DSM-III-R. Hallucinations are considered to be disturbances in perception. The most common involve hearing voices they believe to be coming from outside their bodies but that are heard only by them. Voices that run a commentary on the person's ongoing behavior are typical. Most dangerous are those voices that command the person to do something. Visual, tactile, and gustatory hallucinations are also occasionally reported.

Delusions are considered to be disturbances in the content of verbal behavior or thought. These involve explanations of events that most people in the culture would consider to be entirely impossible. Common ones involve persecutory delusions like being spied on, others planning to do them harm, or all family members lying about them. The authors of DSM-III-R discuss several delusions that are more typical in schizophrenia than in other psychotic disorders: thought broadcasting (one's thoughts are broadcast to others as they occur), thought withdrawal (one's thoughts have been erased or otherwise taken away), and faulty attribution (one's thoughts and actions are attributed to external forces imposing them).

In addition to these disturbances in the *content* of verbal behavior, disturbances in the *form* of verbal behavior (thought) are also typical of schizophrenia. We discussed one common example earlier—loosening of associations. This disturbance is portrayed by the speaker's shifts between topics that are unrelated or by shifts between remarkably different frames of reference, often to such an excess that the message is incoherent. Poverty of content is another example of a disturbance in form. In poverty of content, the speaker provides a sufficient amount of speech, but because the speech is remarkably vague, overgeneralized, or repetitive, it conveys little information. Neologisms, clanging, and blocking are other disturbances in the form of verbal behavior noted in schizophrenia.

Flat or grossly inappropriate affect are considered to be disturbances in emotions—affect being the observable behaviors expressing the experienced feeling (APA, 1987). Affect is said to be flat when the speaker presents little variation in tone, facial expressions, or mannerisms regardless of the topic. Affect is said to be inappropriate when inexplicable outbursts occur and when the affect is inappropriate for the content (e.g., laughing when speaking of painful events).

Finally, DSM-III-R provides a discussion of disturbances in psychomotor behavior. People with schizophrenia may hold to a rigid posture (catatonic rigidity). They may remain impervious to environmental events (catatonic stupor). Without provocation, they may display excited motor movements (catatonic excitement). They may assume bizarre, statuesque postures (catatonic posturing). Finally, they may resist attempts to get them to move (catatonic negativism).

These, then, are the characteristic psychotic symptoms that must occur for the diagnosis of schizophrenia. Either bizarre delusions or prominent hallucinations must occur during the active phase. Otherwise, any two of the following must occur: flat or grossly inappropriate affect, marked loosening of associations or incoherence, and psychomotor disturbances of the catatonic type. These disturbances must be present for at least 1 week (unless successfully treated) to confirm an active phase of schizophrenia (APA, 1987).

The criterion of 6-month duration must include the active phase but may also include prodromal and residual phases. A prodromal phase involves a substantial deterioration in functioning that precedes an active phase. A residual phase may follow the active phase. (A diagnostician must rule out mood disturbance or substance abuse for the impaired function in both prodromal and residual phases.) Another criterion for denoting prodromal and residual phases is that two of the following must occur:

marked social isolation
marked impairment as worker, student, or homemaker
markedly peculiar behavior
marked impairment in grooming
flat or grossly inappropriate affect
marked lack of initiative, interests, or energy
digressive, vague, overelaborate, or circumstantial speech
poverty of speech
poverty of content of speech
odd beliefs that influence overt behaviors
unusual perceptual experiences

This, then, is the current definition of schizophrenia; these are the current diagnostic criteria. The essential features of schizophrenia are characteristic psychotic symptoms, a deterioration in function from a prior level preceding the disorder, and a duration of disturbance lasting at least 6 months.

AUTISM IDENTIFIED

The term *autism* was used for a disorder identified nearly 40 years after schizophrenia was first described. Kanner (1943), who defined the disorder, studied 11 children who portrayed a pattern of behaviors he called "early infantile autism." He noted the following common behavioral patterns: (a) withdrawal of contact with people, (b) obsession with maintaining sameness, (c) affectionate relationship with objects, (d) adaptive potential in some same-age peer tasks, and (e) autism or dysfunctional use of language. Kanner also noted that the onset of the disorder was before 2 years of age.

The 1943 description of autism by Kanner marked the beginning of the study of autism as a distinct disorder. Yet autism was considered by most to be an early form of schizophrenia (Goldfarb, 1961; Mahler, 1952; Ritvo, 1976). Although Eisenberg and Kanner (1956) convincingly argued that autism was a condition distinct from schizophrenia—neither delusions nor hallucinations were evident in autism—the authority of earlier writers (especially Bender) maintained the notion that the different types of psychosis resulted from differing times of onset of the same schizophrenic process (Werry, 1972). Gradually, the disorders were increasingly considered to be distinct.

The gradual acceptance of the notion of two distinct disorders had a partial setback in 1961, when a group of British physicians known as the British Working Party (BWP) listed nine criteria for the diagnosis of childhood psychosis. In retrospect, it appeared that the BWP compiled this list from Kanner's description of autism and, by using less specific language, allowed for the inclusion of all forms of childhood psychosis. Worse still, the BWP chose the term "schizophrenic syndrome of childhood" (Werry, 1972).

The nine criteria of the BWP were incorporated as the basic symptomatology for childhood psychosis in the classification system of the Group for the Advancement of Psychiatry (GAP) in 1966 (Werry, 1972). The GAP system is especially noted for attempting to classify the various disorders within a developmental context. In the GAP system, for example, "early infantile autism" is included in the category of "disorders of infancy and early childhood" (Werry, 1972).

Defining the disorder within a developmental context was further extended by the National Society for Autistic Citizens (NSAC), whose criteria became dominant during the late 1970s. NSAC provided the following criteria: (a) signs and symptom onset prior to 30 months of age; (b) disturbances of developmental rate; (c) unresponsiveness to sensory stimuli; (d) disturbance of speech, language, and cognitive capability; and (e) disturbance relating to people, objects, and events (Ritvo & Freeman, 1978). This and countless other descriptions were provided, evaluated, and modified, ultimately culminating in our present definition of autism.

Current Definition and Diagnostic Criteria of Autism

Presently, the DSM-III-R (APA, 1987) provides a widely accepted definition of autism. The disorder occurs within the category "Disorders Usually First Evident in Infancy, Childhood, or Adolescence." Even further emphasizing the developmental nature of the definition. DSM-III-R classified autistic disorder as a "Pervasive Developmental Disorder."

The diagnostic criteria include onset of the autistic disorder during infancy or childhood. The essential features that define the disorders are three:

1. Impairment in social interaction.
2. Impairment in communication and imagination.
3. Restricted repertoire of activities and interests.

The authors of DSM-III-R operationalized the extent to which these essential features must be portrayed. They did so by listing 16 items to exemplify the essential features: 5 for impairment in social interaction, 6 for impairment in communication and imagination, and 5 for restricted repertoire of activities and interests (see Table 1.1). The criteria for the diagnosis of autistic disorder includes confrontation of more than 7 of the 16 items, with more than 1 item for impairment in social interaction and at least 1 item for both impairment in communication and imagination and restricted repertoire of activities and interests.

For diagnostic purposes, the autistic disorder is defined as a disorder with an onset in infancy or childhood that involves impairment in social interaction and in communication and imagination and a restricted repertoire of activities and interests. The diagnostician must also confirm that these items are abnormal for the person's level of

Table 1.1 Essential Features of Autistic Disorder

Impairment of social interaction

Lacking awareness of others or their feelings
Impaired imitation
Abnormal social play
Lacking normal patterns of seeking comfort when distressed
Gross impairment in making friends with peers

Impairment in communication and imagination

Lacking babbling, facial expression, gestures, or speech
Abnormal eye contact, posture, gestures, and other aspects of nonverbal
    communication
No imaginative activity (e.g., playacting of adults, animals, and fantasy
    characters)
Marked abnormalities in the form or content of speech
Marked impairment in initiating and sustaining conversation

Restricted repertoire of activities and interests

Stereotyped behaviors
Preoccupation with parts of objects or attachment to unusual ones
Marked distress over trivial changes in the environment
Unreasonable insistence on sameness in performing routines
Generally restricted range of interests and preoccupation with one narrow
    interest

Adapted from DSM-III-R (APA, 1987).

development and must specify if the onset was during childhood (after 36 months of age).

Many people who were diagnosed with autism during recent years will be unlikely to satisfy this definition. The authors of DSM-III-R note that many infants and children will portray qualitative impairments in social interaction and communication skills but will fail to meet the strict criteria for autistic disorder, schizophrenia, or other similar disorders. For them, DSM-III-R provides a diagnosis entitled "Pervasive Developmental Disorder Not Otherwise Specified." The authors of DSM-III-R allude to the possibility that this diagnosis may include even more people than does the autistic disorder category. Regarding the discussion to follow, readers may consider our use of "autism" to include both pervasive developmental disorders (i.e., autistic disorder and not otherwise specified).

These are the defining characteristics of autism and schizophrenia. (Criteria for diagnosis are more fully analyzed in Singh & Katz, this volume.) Our historical overview, however, will begin prior to the development of diagnostic classification systems.

HISTORICAL PERSPECTIVES

Differing perspectives of mental disorders have been prominent in different cultures and periods (cf., Calhoun, 1977; Kazdin, Bellack, & Hersen, 1980; Lahey & Ciminero, 1980; Ullman & Krasner, 1969). No one perspective totally dominated during a given era. However, during each period, one of the competing perspectives was dominant. The perspectives we chose for our overview are supernatural, biological, psychodynamic (mental), and behavioral because they proved to be the most dominant themes in history relating to people with mental disorders.

Supernatural Perspective

Primitive people left no writings. However, artifacts (e.g., skulls with holes and instruments for creating them) and written documentation of later cultures generated speculation that mentally ill people were treated by making passageways in their skulls for demons to escape (Calhoun, 1977; Ullman & Krasner, 1969).

The earliest written documentation of disorders was included in the cuneiform clay tablets of Hammurabi, written circa 2000 B.C. (Alexander & Selesnick, 1966). These early writings document supernatural explanations that were provided to understand disorders. For example, one goddess was believed to cause disease through eight assistant theists who each specialized in causing different syndromes. Priest physicians treated the physical illnesses with assistance from their preferred god. Lay physicians battled insanity in concert with their preferred god against the demon Idta and her sorcerers, who used concoctions, ceremonies, and the evil eye to cause insanity. The treatments typically involved incantations, animal sacrifices, and sour searching.

Similarly, ancient writings of India and Egypt (i.e., Ramayana, AyurVeda, Ebers papyrus, and Edward Smith papyrus) implicated supernatural entities as causes of dysfunctional behavior (Alexander & Selesnick, 1966; Ullman & Krasner, 1969). For example, the authors of India classified the demons causing delusions into seven categories (Alexander & Selesnick, 1966).

In ancient Greece, supernatural powers were thought to emanate from the gods. Even as late as circa 400 B.C., Plato had divided the

"Divine Madness" into categories, depending on which god was causing the problem (Lahey & Ciminero, 1980). The Greeks treated illnesses in sanctuaries they built for their god of healing (Ullman & Krasner, 1969).

Authors prepared many documents describing disorders and their treatments in supernatural terms during the Middle and Dark ages. Of special note is the Christian *Malleus Maleficarum* (The Witches Hammer) circa 1480 (Alexander & Selesnick, 1966). At a time when plagues had killed half of the population of the Christian cultures, women in towns near monasteries were being harassed by sexually promiscuous monks. The status quo was being threatened, and the church found a scapegoat—women. The clergy argued that women stirred men's passions; therefore, they must be the carriers of the devil. The prescribed methods of determining who were witches included looking for hallucinations, delusions, and ritualistic behaviors. Although many people were persecuted as witches during the Middle and Dark ages, most witch burnings occurred following the Renaissance (Torrey, 1983). Hundred of thousands of women and children were burned at the stake (Alexander & Selesnick, 1966). Many of them were mentally ill. Besides witch burnings, moral treatments included cutting crosses in the skin, continuous repetition of prayers, purges of the body with emetics and laxatives, yelling prayers directly into ears, and torture to get the devils to leave the bodies (Alexander & Selesnick, 1966; Torrey, 1983).

Moral treatments were more humane when provided by Arabs, who thought the invading spirits were good (Alexander & Selesnick, 1966). They provided care for mentally ill people in residential settings, thereby initiating institutionalization. The Arabs built an insane asylum in Baghdad in 705 and one in Cairo in 800. By 1270, they had built two more, and their influence in Spain was responsible for the building of one in Valencia, circa 1409 (Alexander & Selesnick, 1966).

Biological Perspective

Some biological issues were entertained during years when the supernatural perspective was prominent. For example, the Edward Smith papyrus mentioned earlier presented the first written description of the brain and recognized this organ as the site of mental function. However, an elaborate perspective arose as late as the seventh and sixth centuries B.C., when the Greek philosophers introduced rationalism to understand nature (Alexander & Selesnick, 1966). This secular perspective replaced the supernatural one with a presumption that natural phenomena have natural causes. The biological perspective was applied to understanding and treating physical illnesses, and by circa 425 A.D., Hippocrates had applied this secular tradition to the mental disorders (Lahey & Ciminero, 1980; Ullman & Krasner, 1969). In doing so, he initiated the conflict among social agents responsible for the mentally ill that has continued even to the present. If the disorders are of supernatural phenomena, the religionists and philosophers should be societal agents. If the disorders are of natural phenomena, the physicians and natural scientists should be in charge (Kazdin, 1980). (See Calhoun, 1977, for examples of the use of supernatural treatments in recent times.)

Hippocrates explained disturbances of behavior as resulting from an imbalance of four bodily fluids (humors): bile (black and yellow), blood, and phlegm. A good balance of these resulted in normal behavior. Too much black bile caused depression; too much yellow bile caused irritability (Lahey & Ciminero, 1980). His treatments included diet, exercise, hygiene, sweating, bathing, purgatives, and bloodletting. Hippocrates explained hysteria as being caused by the misplacement of a woman's uterus. Therefore, he used smoke to invade the vagina, which was thought to cause the uterus to return to its proper place. Hysteria in men was caused by a wandering spleen (Alexander & Selesnick, 1966). Hippocrates' views were still dominant in medicine 500 years after his death, and his theory remained virtually unchanged for the following 1,300 years (Lahey & Ciminero, 1980).

Methods of biological treatments (e.g., diet, exercise, and hygiene) merged with earlier moral treatments (e.g., prayer, fasting, and torture) in continuing the movement of institutionalization. In London, this merger was enhanced when the Bethlehem Hospital (Bedlam) for physical illnesses changed to serving mental disorder in 1407 (Grun, 1979). Public hospitals expanded prolifically throughout Western Europe and the United States during the 18th and 19th centuries. These institutions typically served mentally ill people and the poor. Dorothea Dix led a movement in the United States to establish hospitals to treat only mental disorders (Golann & Eisdorfer, 1972). Her efforts accounted for the establishment of at least 30 state hospitals (Matson & LaGrow, 1983). Optimism arose for moral and biological treatments, but the results generated pessimism, leaving the hospitals as human warehouses for segregating people with mental disorders (Matson & LaGrow, 1983).

The biological perspective remains active in the study and treatment of schizophrenia and autism (cf., Bellack, 1984; DeMyer, 1979). Although a highly controversial topic, the role of heredity has occupied a prominent position within the biological perspective. Genetic explanations for the etiology of autism were provided by Rimland (1964). Earlier, Kallmann (1953) had demonstrated that schizophrenia is more probable the more closely related one is to a person with schizophrenia (suggesting genetic influence). However, evidence to the contrary exists. DeMyer (1979) reported that of 11 persons with autism who had identical twins, only 4 of the twin siblings also had autism. Similarly, other research reviews indicated that identical twins of people with schizophrenia had a 35 to 38% chance of also having schizophrenia (Liberman et al., 1984). That nearly as many (100 − 58 = 42%) or more identical twins do not have autism or schizophrenia demonstrates that heredity is insufficient as a sole explanation for the etiology of these disorders.

Other alternative biological explanations for these disorders have been advanced and researched. Liberman et al. (1984) reviewed some studies showing anatomical abnormalities of the brains of persons with schizophrenia and concluded that these abnormalities may be related to schizophrenia in some. Even if it could be demonstrated that these abnormalities were not caused by psychopharmacological treatment, the explanation would not apply to some of the people diagnosed with schizophrenia who are without these abnormalities. DeMyer (1979) reviewed neurobiological impairments in autism, and Liberman et al. (1984) reviewed psychophysiological abnormalities in schizophrenia. Both concluded that the issues deserve continued study, but no one explanation is sufficient to describe the disorders.

The biological perspective has been enhanced in the last four decades by the research on medication. The psychopharmacological literature provides much evidence to support the dopamine hypothesis (Davis & Gierl, 1984) as an explanation for the patterns in schizophrenia. The accidental finding of the antipsychotic effects of chlorpromazine led investigators to discover what chlorpromazine did to produce this effect. The dopamine hypothesis suggested the relevant activity: blocking the neurotransmitter dopamine at postsynaptic membrane receptor sites in the central nervous system. All drugs that are known to reduce psychotic patterns produce this physiological effect. Conversely, similar drug compounds that do not block dopamine have no antipsychotic effects. Additionally, when drugs that increase dopamine at receptor sites are given to normal people in large doses, they produce psychosis-like symptoms. Although this and other considerable evidence seemingly supports the theory that schizophrenia is an impairment of the dopamine system, the evidence remains inconclusive (Davis & Gierl, 1984).

Many studies on the action of similar drugs in people with autism have provided negative results (e.g., Campbell, Fish, Shapiro, & Floyd, 1971), although some small-sample studies reported benefits (e.g., Fish, Campbell, Shapiro, & Floyd, 1969). More recently, researchers have reported positive results with fenfluramine (Campbell et al., 1986; Ritvo, Freeman, Gellor, & Yuwiler 1983). Should fenfluramine continue showing beneficial results in well-designed studies, we would suggest that researchers begin investigations as to why. Such investigation could capture sufficient evidence to provide a hypothesis for autism like the dopamine hypothesis for schizophrenia.

Psychodynamic Perspective

The psychodynamic perspective was developed by Sigmund Freud (1856–1939), who began investigations within the biological tradition (Boorstin, 1983). His early notions regarding the mental disorders were that they resulted from impairments in the nervous system, usually the brain (Ullman & Krasner, 1969). After a visit with Charcot, Freud began popularizing the idea that patterns of behavior dysfunction are signs of mental illness (Szasz, 1961).

Like Hippocrates earlier, Freud began with limited observations and concluded with an elaborate theory that explained all maladaptive behavior patterns. This psychodynamic perspective is one in which behavioral patterns are interpreted as symptoms of subconscious processes (e.g., conflicts, repressions, and fixations) produced by immaterial, mental structures (i.e., id, ego, and superego). The ramifications of Freud's work on the study of schizophrenia and autism are twofold. First, by considering behavior to be symptomatic of mental illness, Freud delayed the study of behavior in its own right. Second, his theories, like those of Hippocrates, appeared to explain maladaptive behavior, thereby impeding the further study of autism and schizophrenia.

Psychoanalytic interpretation of etiology regarding schizophrenia and autism utilized mental constructs such as cathexis (emotional investment) of the object world and its private representation, ego insufficiency or disintegration, and so on (Calhoun, 1977). The theory also provided a substantial rationale for blaming the families of mentally ill people for the disorders. In 1948, Fromm-Reichmann described the mothers of people with schizophrenia as being cold, domineering, rejecting, and overprotective—the schizophrenogenic mothers (Calhoun, 1977). Similarly, Eisenberg and Kanner (1956) reported that the mothers of autistic children were "highly intelligent, obsessive, and emotionally frigid" (p. 561). Such mothers were portrayed as "emotional refrigerators" (Bettleheim, 1967).

Strict classical psychoanalysis was seldom prescribed as treatment for people with schizophrenia or autism for several reasons. Adults with such disorders could not effectively engage in the treatment because of their withdrawal from reality (Gomes-Schwartz, 1984), and their deficits in cognitive coherence (McNeil, 1970). However, the parents of children with autism were encouraged to enroll in long-term psychoanalysis. The results were discouraging (Eisenberg, 1956; Sullivan, 1976). Similar discouraging results were obtained by the many offshoots of psychoanalysis that were provided to people with schizophrenia (Gomes-Schwartz, 1984).

Behavioral Perspective

Pavlov (1927) studied the etiology and modification of behavior in its own right. Skinner (1938) added to Pavlov's respondent, reflexive model the concept of the operant—a behavior influenced by its consequences. These researchers provided a perspective in which behavior is the primary dependent variable and environmental events the independent variables.

Lindsley (1956), one of Skinner's students, demonstrated that people with schizophrenic disorders could respond to operant principles in a laboratory experiment concerned with simple operant responses. In 1962, Ferster and DeMyer demonstrated the same with autistic children. Further, in a classic paper on behavior modification, Ayllon and Michael (1959) reported a successful application of operant conditioning in treating the behavioral dysfunctions of several hospitalized patients with schizophrenic disorders. Wolf, Risley, and Mees (1964) similarly applied operant principles to ameliorate several disorders (e.g., self-injurious behaviors, refusal to wear glasses, and inappropriate mealtime skills) of an autistic child. Later follow-up showed continuing improvements (Wolf, Risley, Johnston, Harris, & Allen, 1967). Thus, within the short span of about 35 years, the behavioral perspective was systematized and successfully applied to ameliorate problems commonly found among people with schizophrenia and autism.

Ayllon and Azrin (1965) undertook the administrative responsibility of directing a behavioral treatment program for women with schizophrenic disorders in a state hospital. Although concerned with reducing the maladaptive behaviors of these women, Ayllon and Azrin designed a system for providing positive reinforcement (reward) for the performance of adaptive behaviors by their clients. They argued that the bizarre symptoms noted in these disorders are no more important than the deficits in adaptive functioning that people with schizophrenia display (Ayllon & Azrin, 1968). They named their treatment "the token economy" because they provided reinforcers to their clients in the form of metal tokens that the clients could later exchange for "backup reinforcers," including activities, consumables, rentals, and about anything else the clients would request that would be ethical and not detrimental to their treatment (O'Brien, Azrin, & Henson, 1969).

Visitors to the token economy ward reported that these chronic patients tended to display fewer bizarre behaviors than similar patients on other wards (Ayllon & Azrin, 1968). Yet the selection method assured that only "difficult patients" would be received as residents in this unit. It was later demonstrated that these patients displayed fewer bizarre behaviors because the bizarre behaviors were "functionally displaced" by the increased adaptive behaviors the token economy generated (O'Brien & Azrin, 1972b).

A most impressive demonstration of the behavioral perspective applied to autism was conducted at the University of California at Los Angeles (UCLA) under the direction of Ivar Lovaas. Twenty children were selected, all of whom demonstrated severe problems that had earlier been shown to reflect a poor prognosis (Kanner &

Eisenberg, 1956; Rutter, 1966). Half were mute; the others were echolalic. The program successfully treated a variety of behavioral dysfunctions, including self-injurious behaviors (Lovaas & Simmons, 1969), stereotyped behaviors (Lovaas, 1977), and echolalia and language deficits (Lovaas, 1969, 1977).

A follow-up study was conducted from 1 to 4 years after the children with autism were transferred to other settings (Lovaas, Koegel, Simmons, & Long, 1973). The children showed continued improvement when they were transferred to homes where the parents or care providers were trained in behavior analysis. Those transferred to institutions and other settings where traditional treatments were used lost some of their gains. More recently, Lovaas (1987) demonstrated that early intervention with the behavioral perspective resulted in about half of the children with autism approaching normalcy.

Following Ayllon and Azrin (1965), others instituted similar token economy programs for hospitalized persons with schizophrenic disorders (Magaro, Talbott, & Glick, 1984). At about the same time, some began describing a ward system called milieu therapy—"highly-structured, highly-organized, highly-expectant milieu that stresses adaptive skills" (Magaro et al., 1984, p. 205). Paul and Lentz (1977) completed the most thorough outcome study of treatments for people with schizophrenia and demonstrated that a version o f the token economy was more effective than either the standard hospital programs or milieu therapy.

Others followed Ayllon and Azrin in directing treatment to developing adaptive behavior, especially social skills, in people with schizophrenia (Hersen & Bellack, 1976). In their elaborate review of the many facets of social skills training, Morrison and Bellack (1984) present a history of its progress and refinements.

Within the behavioral perspective, treatments have not been designed for the general disorders (e.g., autism and schizophrenia). Rather, treatments are designed for specific behavioral excesses and deficits. (For reviews of these behaviors, see Matson & McCartney, 1981, for autism and other developmental disabilities; Bellack, 1984, for schizophrenia; and Durand & Carr, this volume). The excesses and deficits to be treated are selected on the basis of the extent to which they will increase reinforcers or decrease punishers for the clients living in normal community environments (cf., Ayllon &

Azrin, 1968; Brown et al., 1979). Examples include treatments for decreasing self-injurious behaviors (Augustine & Cipani, 1982; Lovaas, Schaeffer, & Simmons, 1965; Matson, Stevens, & Smith, 1978), self-stimulation (Foxx & Azrin, 1973a; Matson & Stephen, 1981; O'Brien, 1981; Rincover, 1978), inappropriate sexual advances (Polvinale & Lutzker, 1980), and echolalia (Lovaas, 1977). Examples of treatments for overcoming deficits include those for language (Barton, 1970; Garcia, 1974; Gobbi, Cipani, Hudson, & Lapenta, 1986; O'Brien, Azrin, & Henson, 1969; Wheeler & Sulzer, 1970), toileting (Foxx & Azrin, 1973b), classroom/instructional skills (Koegel, Dunlap, & Dyer, 1980; Koegel, Russo, & Rincover, 1977), mealtime behaviors (O'Brien & Azrin, 1972a), housekeeping (Bauman & Iwata, 1977), laundry (Cuvo, Jacobi, & Sipko, 1981), safe pedestrian skills (Matson, 1980a; Page, Iwata, & Neef, 1976), transportation skills (Neef, Iwata, & Page, 1978), preventing home accidents (Matson, 1980b), vocational skills (Bellamy, Sowers, & Bourbeau, 1983; Gold, 1973; Rusch & Mithaug, 1980), and job-finding methods (Azrin, Flores, & Kaplan, 1975).

The impetus for a community model of behavioral treatment can also be found in societal, legislative, and judicial forces in the 1960s, 1970s, and 1980s. During the 1960s period of social change, there arose a grater concern for handicapped people (Matson & LaGrow, 1983). For people with schizophrenia, the need to remain institutionalized was substantially reduced with the demonstrated efficacy of pharmacological treatments (Davis & Gierl, 1984), and people with autism were provided relief from the shackles of the psychodynamic perspective that explained the cause of autism but offered no effective treatment.

Legislation, court activity, and the popularity of a general treatment principle promoted a focus on treating people with mental disorders in the community. The treatment principle known as normalization provided for developing normal behaviors in as normal an environment as possible and became popular with many professionals and care providers, especially those working with developmentally disabled people (Wolfensberger, 1972). Large state hospitals and other institutions were housing many mentally ill and developmentally disabled people with little pretense of providing adequate treatment (cf., Fontana, 1980). Judicial inquiry brought in Alabama mandated that people have a right to effective treatment in the least restrictive of settings (Wyatt v. Stickney, 1972). Finally, legislation (e.g., Public Law 94-142 and Section 504 of the Handicapped Act) further prescribed that all citizens have the right to the least restrictive (most normal), effective treatment that can be provided. These added to the deinstitutionalization movement that had been earlier initiated in response to the bad press regarding conditions in the institutions. From 1955 to 1977 the number of patients in state hospitals decreased from 559,000 to 160,000 (Sharfstein, 1984). Preparing hospitalized patients for discharge along with those mentally disabled people already in the community resulted in treatment that was more focused on developing normal community skills.

Adults and adolescents with disabilities face the same life-style problems that confront their nonhandicapped peers: to find meaningful work, to reside outside their parents' homes, and to continue the development of skills initiated in high school (Bellamy & Horner, 1986; Israel, 1976). However, unlike their nonhandicapped peers, adults with disabilities seldom have the skills needed to function independently under these conditions. Despite incentive programs such as the Targeted-Jobs Tax Credit and federal laws prescribing vocational habilitation for people with handicaps (e.g., The Rehabilitation Act, Section 504; The Developmental Disabilities Assistance and Bill of Rights Act), many adults with autism and schizophrenia remain unemployed (Bellamy et al., 1983).

Behavioral techniques have been developed that make possible supported employment of people with severe disabilities. Several projects have utilized a methodology that includes (a) focus on teaching skills that lead immediately to employability, (b) use of the best training techniques available in the target site, and (c) long-term follow-up of placement (Bellamy et al., 1983). One of the most successful training and placement efforts has been at the University of Washington's Food and Service Vocational Training Program, where 30 individuals with severe disabilities were placed in competitive employment for at least 6 months (Bellamy et al., 1983). The findings of this and other research support the contention that people with severe disabilities can learn to perform meaningful work (Bellamy, Inman, & Yeates, 1978; Bellamy, Peterson, & Close, 1975; Cuvo, Leaf, & Borakove, 1978; Gold, 1973; Horner & McDonald, 1982; Rusch & Mithaug, 1980).

In addition to an emerging behavioral technology for the training of technical work-related skills, researchers in the vocational training field have developed successful strategies for training in ancillary behaviors required in the work environment. Social survival skills for job maintenance, following instructions, grooming skills, and attendance, are skills of paramount importance in job maintenance (Rusch, 1983). Research has demonstrated the efficacy of techniques that develop a host of relevant social behaviors needed in the work environment (Rusch & Mithaug, 1980; Sowers, Rusch, Connis, & Cummings, 1980).

SUMMARY

Currently, the biological and behavioral perspectives appear to be the most promising in regard to autism and schizophrenia, whereas the supernatural and psychodynamic are on the wane. Education and treatment approaches continue, with a focus on the community. The transition from school to adult life is receiving increasing attention. Supported employment is currently targeted for increased funding at the state and national level. A continued push for early intervention is plausible in both the mental health and developmental disabilities fields.

Advocacy for people with disabilities has also steadily increased. With psychodynamic parent-blaming generally in disrepute (Donnellan, 1985), parents, professionals, and civil libertarians have joined in advocacy for autism in the National Society for Autistic Citizens (NSAC). Through political and court actions, they garnered increased resources for treatment and research (especially in education) for youngsters with autism. Parent and professional groups such as NSAC, the American Association on Mental Retardation (AAMR), and the Council for Exceptional Children (CEC) continue to press for the rights of people with severe disabilities to live in the mainstream of society.

Similar attempts for people with schizophrenia have been sporadic, but recently the Alliance for the Mentally Ill (AMI) has begun to show growth and effectiveness (Torrey, 1983). The public is being bombarded with the fact that somewhere between 250,000 and 3 million Americans are living in cities, without homes ("News from Earth," ABC Television, December 26, 1988), and that an estimated 40% of these people are mentally ill and receiving no care or treatment. Others depend on Social Security disability insurance, Medicaid, and Medicare for the financial support to exist, typically living in nursing or community care homes and receiving inadequate treatment services. The demonstrated efficacy of the behavioral perspective is many years ahead of the provision of services. The needs are two: (a) obtain more money from government for research into causes and treatments for these disorders and (b) obtain sufficient money for providing the treatments that have been demonstrated effective. This requires government lobbying. Furthermore, some professionals and the Alliance for the Mentally Ill have accepted the challenge. This promises a better quality of life in the future for persons with autism and schizophrenia than is currently available or was provided them previously.

ACKNOWLEDGMENTS

The authors wish to express their appreciation to Dr. Gary Lavigna for his helpful comments on parts of this manuscript.

REFERENCES

Alexander, F. G., & Selesnick, S. T. (1966). *The history of psychiatry: An evaluation of psychiatric thought and practice from prehistoric times to the present*. New York: Spectrum.

American Psychiatric Association. (1987). *Diagnostic and statistical manual of mental disorders* (3rd ed. rev.). Washington, DC: Author.

Augustine, A., & Cipani, E. (1982). Treating self-injurious behavior: Initial effects, maintenance and acceptability of treatment. *Child Behavior Therapy, 4*, 53–69.

Ayllon, T., & Azrin, N. H. (1965). The measurement and reinforcement of behavior of psychotics. *Journal of the Experimental Analysis of Behavior, 8*, 3357–384.

Ayllon, T., & Azrin, N. H. (1968). *The token economy*. New York: Appleton-Century-Crofts.

Ayllon, T., & Michael, J. (1959). The psychiatric nurse as a behavioral engineer. *Journal of the Experimental Analysis of Behavior, 2*, 323–334.

Azrin, N. H., F lores, T., & Kaplan, S. J. (1975). Job-finding club: A group-assisted program for obtaining employment. *Behaviour Research and*

Therapy, 13, 17–27.

Barton, E. S. (1970). Inappropriate speech in a severely retarded child: A case study in language conditioning and generalization. *Journal of Applied Behavior Analysis, 3,* 299–307.

Bauman, K. E., & Iwata, B . A. (1977). Maintenance of independent housekeeping skills using scheduling plus self-recording procedures. *Behavior Therapy, 8,* 54–64.

Bellack, A. S. (Ed.). (1984). *Schizophrenia.* Orlando, FL: Grune & Stratton.

Bellamy, G. T., & Horner, R. H. (1986). Beyond highschool: Residential and employment options after graduation. In M. E. Snell (Ed.). *Systematic instruction of persons with severe handicaps* (3rd ed., pp. 491–510). Columbus, OH: Charles Merrill.

Bellamy, G. T., Inman, D. P., & Yeates, J. (1978). Workshop supervision: Evaluation of a procedure for production management with the severely retarded. *Mental Retardation, 16,* 317–319.

Bellamy, T., Peterson, L., & Close, D. (1975). Habilitation of the severely and profoundly retarded: Illustrations of competence. *Education and Training of the Mentally Retarded. 10,* 174–186.

Bellamy, G. T., Sowers, J., & Bourbeau, P. (1983). Work and work-related services: Post school options for students with severe handicaps. In M. E. Snell (Ed.), *Systematic instruction for the moderately and severely handicapped* (2nd ed., pp. 490–502). Columbus, OH: Charles Merrill.

Bettleheim, B. (1967). *The empty fortress: Infantile autism and the birth of the self.* New York: Macmillan.

Boorstin, D. J. (1983). *The Discoverers.* New York: Random House.

Brown, L., Branston, M. B., Hamre-Nietupski, S., Pumpian, I., Certo, N., & Grunewald, C. A. (1979). A strategy for developing chronological age appropriate and functional curricular content for severely handicapped adolescents and young adults. *Journal for Special Education, 13,* 81–90.

Calhoun, J. F. (1977). *Abnormal psychology.* New York: Random House.

Campbell, M., Fish, B., Shapiro, T., & Floyd, A., Jr. (1971). Imipramine in preschool autistic and schizophrenic children. *Journal of Autism and Childhood Schizophrenia, 1,* 267–282.

Campbell, M., Perry, R., Polansky, B. B., Deutsch, S. I., Palij, M., & Lukashak, J. (1986). An open study of fenfluramine in hospitalized young autistic children. *Journal of Autism and Developmental Disorders, 16,* 495–506.

Creak, E. M. (1963). Childhood psychosis. *British Journal of Psychiatry, 109,* 84–89.

Cuvo, A. J., Jacobi, E., & Sipko, R. (1981). Teaching laundry skills to mentally retarded adults. *Education and Training of the Mentally Retarded, 16,* 54–64.

Cuvo, A. J., Leaf, R. B., & Borakove, L. S. (1978). Teaching janitorial skills to the mentally retarded: Acquisition, generalization, and maintenance.

Journal of Applied Behavior Analysis, 11, 345–355.

Davis, J. M., & Gierl, B. (1984). Pharmacological treatment in the care of chronic schizophrenia. In A. S. Bellack (Ed.), *Schizophrenia* (pp. 133–173). Orlando, FL: Grune & Stratton.

DeMyer, M. K. (1979). *Parents and children in autism.* New York: Random House.

Donnellan, A. M. (1985). Introduction. In A. M. Donnellan (Ed.), *Classic reading in autism* (pp. 1–10). New York: Teachers College Press.

Eisenberg, L. (1956). The autistic child in adolescence. *American Journal of Psychiatry, 112,* 607–612.

Eisenberg, L., & Kanner, L. (1956). Childhood schizophrenia. *American Journal of Orthopsychiatry, 26,* 556–566.

Ferster, C. B., & DeMyer, M. A. (1962). A method for the experimental analysis of the behavior of autistic children. *American Journal of Orthopsychiatry, 32,* 89–98.

Fish, B., Campbell, M., Shapiro, T., & Floyd, A. (1969). Comparison of trifluperidol, trifluoperazine, and chlorpromazine in preschool schizophrenic children: The value of less sedative antipsychotic agents. *Current Therapeutic Research, 11,* 589–595.

Fontana, A. F. (1980). Mental illness and the mental hospital. In A. E. Kazdin, A. S. Bellack, & M. Hersen (Eds.), *New perspectives in abnormal psychology* (pp. 472–491). New York: Oxford University Press.

Foxx, R. M., &Azrin, N. H. (1973a). The elimination of autistic self-stimulatory behavior by overcorrection. *Journal of Applied Behavior Analysis, 6,* 1–14.

Foxx, R. M., & Azrin, H. H. (1973b). *Toilet training the retarded: A rapid program for day and night-time independent toileting.* Champaign, IL: Research Press.

Garcia, E. E. (1974). The training and generalization of a conversational speech form in nonverbal retardates. *Journal of Applied Behavior Analysis, 7,* 137–149.

Gobbi, L., Cipani, E., Hudson, C., & Lapenta, R. (1986). Developing "spontaneous requesting" among children with severe mental retardation. *Mental Retardation, 24,* 357–363.

Golann, S. E., & Eisdorfer, C. (1972). Mental health and the community: The development of issues. In S. E. Golann & C. Eisdorfer (Eds.), *Handbook of community mental health* (pp. 3–17). New York: Appleton-Century-Crofts.

Gold, M. W. (1973). Research on the vocational habilitation of the retarded: The present, the future. In N. R. Ellis (Ed.), *International review of research in mental retardation,* (Vol. 5, pp. 97–147). New York: Academic Press.

Goldfarb, W. (1961). *Childhood schizophrenia.* Cambridge, MA: Harvard University Press.

Gomes-Schwartz, B. (1984). Individual psychotherapy of schizophrenia. In A. S. Bellack (Ed.), *Schizophrenia* (pp. 307–336). Orlando, FL: Grune &

Stratton.

Grun, B. (1979). *The timetables of history—new updated edition*. New York: Simon and Schuster.

Hersen, M., & Bellack, A. S. (1976). A multiple-baseline analysis of social skills training in chronic schizophrenics. *Journal of Applied Behavior Analysis, 9,* 239–245.

Horner, R. H., & McDonald, R. S. (1982). A comparison of single instance and general case instruction in teaching a generalized vocational skill. *The Journal of the Association for the Severely Handicapped, 7,* 7–20.

Israel, M. L. (1976). Educational approaches at the Behavior Research Institute, Providence, Rhode Island. In E. R. Ritvo, B. J. Freeman, E. M. Ornitz, & P. E. Tanguay (Eds.), *Autism: Diagnosis, current research and management* (pp. 239–271). New York: Spectrum.

Kallman, F. J. (1953). *Heredity in health and mental disease*. New York: W. W. Norton.

Kanner, L. (1943). Autistic disturbances of affective contact. *Nervous Child, 2,* 217–250.

Kanner, L., & Eisenberg, L. (1956). Notes on the follow-up of autistic children. In P. H. Hoch & J. Zubin (Eds.), *Psychopathology of childhood* (pp. 227–239). New York: Grune-Stratton.

Kazdin, A. E. (1980). Basic concepts and models of abnormal behavior. In A. E. Kazdin, A. S. Bellack, & M. Hersen (Eds.), *New perspectives in abnormal psychology* (pp. 7–32). New York: Oxford University Press.

Kazdin, A. E., Bellack, A. S., & Hersen, M. (Eds.). (1980). *New perspectives in abnormal psychology*. New York: Oxford University Press.

Koegel, R. L., Dunlap, G., & Dyer, K. (1980). Intertrial interval duration and learning in autistic children. *Journal of Applied Behavior Analysis, 13,* 91–99.

Koegel, R. L., Russo, D. C., & Rincover, A. (1977). Assessing and training teachers in the generalized use of behavior modification with autistic children. *Journal of Applied Behavior Analysis, 10,* 197–205.

Lahey, B. B., & Ciminero, A. R. (1980). *Maladaptive behavior*. Glenview IL: Scott, Foresman.

Liberman, R. P., Marshall, B. D., Maeder, S. R., Dawson, M. E., Nuechterlein, K. H., & Doane, J. A. (1984). The nature and problem of schizophrenia. In A. S. Bellack (Ed.), *Schizophrenia* (pp. 1–34). Orlando, FL: Grune & Stratton.

Lindsley, O. R. (1956). Operant conditioning methods applied to research in chronic schizophrenia. *Psychiatric Research Reports, 5,* 118–153.

Lovaas, O. I. (1969). Behavior modification: Teaching language to psychotic children [Instructional film, 45 min., 16 mm, sound]. New York: Appleton-Century-Crofts.

Lovaas, O. I. (1977). *The autistic child: Language development through behavior modification*. New York: Irvington.

Lovaas, O. I. (1987). Behavioral treatment and normal educational and intellectual functioning in young autistic children. *Journal of Consulting and Clinical Psychology, 55,* 3–9.

Lovaas, O. I., Koegel, R. L., Simmons, J. Q., & Long, J. S. (1973). Some generalization and follow-up measures on autistic children in behavior therapy. *Journal of Applied Behavior Analysis, 6,* 131–166.

Lovaas, O. I., Schaeffer, B., & Simmons, J. Q. (1965). Building social behavior in autistic children by the use of electric shock. *Journal of Experimental Research in Personality, 2,* 143–157.

Lovaas, O. I., & Simmons, J. Q. (1969). Manipulation of self-destruction in three retarded children. *Journal of Applied Behavior Analysis, 2,* 143–157.

Magaro, P. A., Talbott, J. A., & Glick, I. (1984). The inpatient care of chronic schizophrenia. In A. S. Bellack (Ed.), *Schizophrenia* (pp. 193–218). Orlando, FL: Grune & Stratton.

Mahler, M. S. (1952). On child psychosis and schizophrenia: Autistic and symbiotic infantile psychosis. *Psychoanalytic Study of the Child, 7,* 286–305.

Matson, J. L. (1980a). A controlled group study of pedestrian skill training for the mentally retarded. *Behaviour Research and Therapy, 18,* 99–106.

Matson, J. L. (1980b). Preventing home accidents: A training program for the retarded. *Behavior Modification, 4,* 397–410.

Matson, J. L., & LaGrow, S. J. (1983). Developmental and physical disabilities. In M. Hersen, V. B. Vanhasselt, & J. L. Matson (Eds.), *Behavior therapy for the developmentally and physically disabled* (pp. 3–24). New York: Academic Press.

Matson, J. L., & McCartney, J. R. (Eds.). (1981). *Handbook of behavior modification with the mentally retarded.* New York: Plenum Press.

Matson, J. L., & Stephen, R. M. (1981). Overcorrection treatment of stereotyped behaviors of adult retardates. *Behavior Modification, 5,* 491–502.

Matson, J. L., Stevens, R. L., & Smith, C. (1978). Treatment of self-injurious behavior with overcorrection. *Journal of Mental Deficiency Research, 22,* 175–178.

McNeil, E. B. (1970). *The psychoses.* Englewood Cliffs, NJ: Prentice-Hall.

Morrison, R. L., & Bellack, A. S. (1984). Social skills training. In A. S. Bellack (Ed.), *Schizophrenia* (pp. 247–279). Orlando, FL: Grune & Stratton.

Neef, N. A., Iwata, B. A., & Page, T. J. (1978). Public transportation training: In vivo versus classroom instruction. *Journal of Applied Behavior Analysis, 11,* 331–344.

O'Brien, F. (1981). Treating self-stimulatory behavior. In J. L. Matson & J. R. McCartney (Eds.), *Handbook of behavior modification with the mentally retarded* (pp. 117–150). New York: Plenum Press.

O'Brien, F., & Azrin, N. H. (1927a). Developing proper mealtime behaviors of the institutionalized retarded. *Journal of Applied Behavior Analysis, 5,* 389–399.

O'Brien, F., & Azrin, N. H. (1972b). Symptom reduction by functional displacement in a token economy. *Journal of Behavior Therapy and Experimental Psychiatry, 3,* 205–207.

O'Brien, F., Azrin, N. H., & Henson, K. (1969). Increased communications of chronic mental patients by reinforcement and response priming. *Journal of Applied Behavior Analysis, 2,* 23–29.

Page, T. J., Iwata, B. A., & Neef, N. A. (1976). Teaching pedestrian skills to retarded persons: Generalization from the classroom to the natural environment. *Journal of Applied Behavior Analysis, 9,* 433–444.

Paul, G. L., & Lentz, R. J. (1977). *Psychosocial treatment of chronic mental patients: Milieu versus social learning programs.* Cambridge, MA: Harvard University Press.

Pavlov, I. P. (1927). *Conditioned reflexes.* (G. V. Anrep, Trans.) New York: Dover.

Polvinale, R. A., & Lutzker, J. R. (1980). Elimination of assaultive and inappropriate sexual behavior by reinforcement and social-restitution. *Mental Retardation, 18,* 27–30.

Rimland, B. (1964). The etiology of infantile autism: The problem of biological versus psychological causation. In A. M. Donnellan (Ed.), *Classic readings in autism* (pp. 84–103). New York: Teachers College Press.

Rincover, A. (1978). Sensory extinction: A procedure for eliminating self-stimulatory behavior in autistic and retarded children. *Journal of Abnormal Child Psychology, 6,* 695–701.

Ritvo, E. R. (1976). Autism: From adjective to noun. In E. R. Ritvo, B. J. Freeman, E. M. Ornitz, & P. E. Tanguay (Eds.), *Autism: Diagnosis, current research and management* (pp. 3–6). New York: Spectrum.

Ritvo, E. R., & Freeman, B. J. (1978). National society of autistic children definition of the syndrome of autism. *Journal of Autism and Childhood Schizophrenia, 8,* 162–167.

Ritvo, E. R., Freeman, B. J., Geller, E., & Yuwiler, A. (1983). Effects of fenfluramine on fourteen outpatients with the syndrome of autism. *Journal of the American Academy of Child Psychiatry, 22,* 549–558.

Rusch, F. R. (1983). Competitive vocational training. In M. E. Snell (Ed.), *Systematic instruction of the moderately and severely handicapped* (2nd ed., pp. 503–523). Columbus, OH: Charles Merrill.

Rusch, F. R., & Mithaug, D. E. (1980). *Vocational training for mentally retarded adults: A behavior analytic approach.* Champaign, IL: Research Press.

Rutter, M. (1966). Prognosis: Psychotic children in adolescence and early adult life. In J. Wing (Ed.), *Early childhood autism* (pp. 83–99). London: Pergamon Press.

Salzinger, K. (1980). Schizophrenia. In A. E. Kazdin, A. S. Bellack, & M. Hersen (Eds.), *New perspectives in abnormal psychology* (pp. 244–270). New York: Oxford University Press.

Sharfstein, S. S. (1984). Sociopolitical issues affecting patients with chronic schizophrenia. In A. S. Bellack (Ed.), *Schizophrenia* (pp. 113–132). Orlando, FL: Grune & Stratton.

Skinner, B. F. (1938). *The behavior of organisms*. New York: Appleton-Century-Crofts.

Sowers, J. A., Rusch, F. R., Connis, R. T., & Cummings, L. E. (1980). Teaching mentally retarded adults to time-manage in a vocational setting. *Journal of Applied Behavior Analysis, 13*, 119–128.

Sullivan, R. C. (1976). Current trends in services for autistic persons in the United States: An overview. In E. R. Ritvo, B. J. Freeman, E. M. Ornitz, & P. E. Tanguay (Eds.), *Autism: Diagnosis, current research and management* (pp. 291–298). New York: Spectrum.

Szasz, T. S. (1961). *The myth of mental illness*. New York: Hoeber-Harper.

Torrey, E. F. (1983). *Surviving schizophrenia*. New York: Harper & Row.

Ullman, L. P., & Krasner, L. (Eds.). (1965). *Case studies in behavior modification*. New York: Holt.

Ullman, L. P., & Krasner, L. (1969). *A psychological approach to abnormal behavior*. Englewood Cliffs, NJ: Prentice-Hall.

Werry, J. S. (1972). Childhood psychosis. In H. C. Quay & J. S. Werry (Eds.), *Psychopathological disorders of childhood* (pp. 173–233). New York: John Wiley & Sons.

Wheeler, A. J., & Sulzer, B. (1970). Operant training and generalization of a verbal response form in a speech-deficient child. *Journal of Applied Behavior Analysis, 3*, 139–147.

Wolf, M. M., Risley, T., Johnston, M., Harris, F. R., & Allen, K. E. (1967). Application of operant conditioning procedures to the behaviour problems of an autistic child: A follow-up and extension. *Behaviour Research and Therapy, 5*, 103–112.

Wolf, M. M., Risley, T., Mees, H. L. (1964). Application of operant conditioning procedures to the behaviour problems of an autistic child. *Behaviour Research and Therapy, 1*, 305–312.

Wolfensberger, W. (1972). *The principle of normalization in human services*. Toronto: National Institute on Mental Retardation.

Wyatt v. Stickney, 344 F. Supp. 387 (M.D. Ala. 1972).

2

Theories of Schizophrenia and Autism

John R. McCartney

The syndromes of autism and schizophrenia have received a bewildering amount of attention in their relatively short scientific histories. The literature in both areas is voluminous and increasing at a rapid pace. Theories that organize all or meaningful parts of this data, that are testable, and that stimulate systematic research efforts are very important to logical progress in such areas. This chapter attempts to summarize some of the major theories and theoretical dimensions in schizophrenia and autism, an ambitious undertaking considering the undulating nature of the literature in both areas.

The reader may feel that theories of autism and schizophrenia cannot be adequately discussed in the same chapter. Autism and schizophrenia are now generally considered to be distinct disorders (e.g., Rutter, 1978). However, there is much overlap in theory development in the areas, with many similarities in the types of factors considered to be important and the kinds of arguments that have divided researchers. Since the two syndromes were considered to be at least in the same family of disorders for three decades or so, this is not surprising. Indeed, there continue to be theorists with lingering suspicions that schizophrenia and autism are simply different manifestations of the same underlying disorder (e.g., James & Barry, 1980). Many researchers and theorists tacitly accept this by using data interchangeably from subjects diagnosed in childhood as having schizophrenia and autism.

OBSTACLES FOR THEORY DEVELOPMENT
Territoriality

Territoriality has been common in the history of theory development in both autism and schizophrenia. As an example, in the United States the psychoanalytic influence has been strong; and during the middle third of this century, theories of that orientation were relatively predominant. The result was a heavy emphasis on the effect of aberrancies in the mother-child and/or family-child relationship in producing behavioral deviance. Theorists of this orientation often did not seriously consider the theories or findings from a stricter biological orientation, and vice versa (Rosenthal & Kety, 1968). Because of this rigidity in theoretical camps, little interaction between perspectives occurred, delaying the valuable contribution of theories that postulate multiple factors as being important in explaining these complex syndromes (Zubin & Spring, 1977).

Oversimplification

Many researchers have approached these disorders as if a single, rather easily identified deficiency could explain them. Because the formal identification of these disorders is fairly recent, this single-shot approach is understandabie, but it is not very logical considering the complexity of the syndromes. This problem has been more common with the biologically oriented investigator, who has looked for the single neurochemical defect or brain neuropathology related to autism or schizophrenia. Fortunately, multifactorial approaches are becoming more common and appear to hold more promise for progress.

Confusion and Lack of Detail in Diagnostic Indicators

Replication of results is a necessity for theory confirmation or disconfirmation. Obviously, attempts at replication are severely compromised if the target population is different from study to study, which is frequently the case in the literature on these disorders. In many cases the subject samples have had obvious differences, and conflicting results have been common.

An even more basic problem is the failure to adequately specify the diagnostic criteria used in a research program. Ritvo, Rabin, Yuwiler, Freeman, and Geller (1978) found that most studies of biochemical factors in autism, a particularly popular area of research in the last 15 years or so, failed to adequately specify the diagnostic criteria used in selecting subjects. This seriously compromises an entire area of research.

Subgroups

A problem inherent in these syndromes is that even in cases where specific, accepted diagnostic criteria are used, subgroups based upon symptomology and etiological indicators are common. An investigator may find several different patterns of etiological indicators in various subgroups of the same subject sample. Conflicting results between studies may often be caused by this heterogeneity, and the development of theories is delayed.

NATURE VERSUS NURTURE

The old heredity-environment debate has raged in schizophrenia and autism, as implied above. Just as in general psychology, theorists have argued about the degree to which heredity or the environment is responsible for the genesis of these disorders (Rosenthal & Kety, 1968). The dichotomy is not a clean one, however. Some theorists postulate that both biological and environmental factors play a role (Despert, 1971). Even within this latter group there are divisions; some feel that heredity plays a primary role, with the environment affecting the particular symptomatic expression of the disorder. Others feel that environmental factors play the major role, though natural factors may interact to some degree.

Fortunately for progress in the field, the nature-nurture debate has abated in recent years, although the controversy is still alive and well (DeMyer, Hingtgen, & Jackson, 1981). Theorists seem to be less concerned about supporting a particular philosophy and more willing to consider evidence from a variety of orientations.

BASIC MODELS

The many different theories of autism and schizophrenia cannot be comprehensively reviewed in a single chapter. Entire volumes have been devoted to the theories of schizophrenia alone (e.g., Shapiro, 1981). A more practical goal here is to give the reader a general feel for the types of theories that have influenced and are currently influencing the field. Therefore, the following pages provide a selective summary of the many theories. The theories chosen for discussion are some of the most influential and productive in autism and schizophrenia. One or two others have also been included for their overall dominance in the field of psychopathology rather than in autism or schizophrenia per se. In each case the basic evidence supporting the general theory area is presented, followed by a short discussion of the problems in that theory area. Finally, an example of one theory will be discussed in each area, with the examples approximately equally divided between theories of autism and schizophrenia.

Genetic Models

Earlier in this century, the genetic view was a primary one on the nature side of the nature-nurture controversy, particularly among etiological theories of schizophrenia (Strauss & Carpenter, 1981). Of course, in the early part of this century, when the formal study of schizophrenia was beginning, genetics played a dominant role in a number of areas. In more recent years the genetic viewpoint has moderated to include other factors as important to the expression of schizophrenia. Most theorists subscribe to a general "diathesis-stress" model, for example, in which the diathesis is a constitutional predisposition to the syndrome, and the stress is environmental events that interact with the diathesis to produce the syndrome. The diathesis is not considered sufficient to produce the syndrome in the absence of environmental stressors. In the view of some, the softening of the genetic position has facilitated the integration of data from various viewpoints and improved the heuristic value of the genetic approach (Strauss & Carpenter, 1981).

Genetic researchers began to find evidence for the inheritability of schizophrenia as early as 1916 (see Gottesman & Shields, 1982 for a review). In the 1920s studies of twins began to establish compelling evidence for a genetic component in schizophrenia. These studies compared the degree of concordance in monozygotic twins, in which at least one member was affected, with the concordance rate in dizygotic twins and found a higher rate of concordance in monozygotic twins. However, since the concordance rates were less than 100% for identical twins, it was clear that inheritance was not the necessary and sufficient factor for schizophrenia. Further, twin studies confound the heredity-environment issue, in that not only do identical twins share the same genetic material, but their environments may be more similar than those of nontwins.

Adoption studies, in which persons with similar genetic material are reared in different environments, began in the 1960s to resolve the heredity-environment issue (Gottesman & Shields, 1982). One version of the studies involves comparing adopted children of schizophrenic mothers with children who remained with their schizophrenic mothers. Results typically show similar rates of schizophrenia in both groups, indicating that the environment is not sufficient to explain the occurrence of schizophrenia.

In family studies the occurrence of schizophrenia in family members with varying degrees of similarity in genetic material is examined (Gottesman & Shields, 1982). If genetics plays a part in the etiology of schizophrenia, siblings should have higher rates of schizophrenia than is found in first cousins, for example, because of a greater amount of similar genetic material. This is the basic pattern of results.

Although the results of studies using the above techniques have provided almost indisputable evidence supporting a genetic component in the etiology of schizophrenia, the particular mode of transmission has not been determined (Farone & Tsuang, 1985).

In autism there has not been a heavy emphasis on genetic theories, at least relative to schizophrenia. This is perhaps because of the emphasis on parenting factors in the early years after the formal identification of the syndrome and because of the rarity of autism, making it difficult to obtain samples of sufficient size.

Coleman and Gilberg (1985) report a very small number of genetic studies (twin and family studies with autistic subjects). The data seem to suggest a large inheritance factor in the etiology of autism. The twin studies (e.g., Folstein & Rutter, 1978) have shown a much higher concordance rate for autism in monozygotic twin pairs than in dizygotic twin pairs and a higher rate of autism in the relatives of autistic persons than in the general population (e.g., Coleman & Rimland, 1976). Coleman and Gilberg (1985) as well as Ritvo et al. (1985) conclude that the data seem to support an autosomal recessive model of inheritable autism.

Theory example:

The multifactorial-polygenic-threshold theory (e.g., Farone & Tsuang, 1985; Gottesman & Shields, 1982) is presently a prominent theory in the genetics of schizophrenia. It appears to support the family prevalence data in schizophrenia better than a single-major-locus model does (Farone & Tsuang, 1985). In the single-major-locus model a specific pair of genes is postulated as necessary for the transmission of schizophrenia. However, since the data do not follow the standard Mendelian pattern, several adjustments have to be made to the model to improve its correspondence with the data (Farone & Tsuang, 1985). In the multifactorial-polygenic-threshold approach, a specific, single locus for the critical gene pair is not hypothesized. Genes at many different loci combine to produce a liability for schizophrenia (Gottesman, McGuffin, & Farmer, 1987). The affected genes are relatively common and have a cumulative effect. The individual who has more of them will be more likely to suffer from schizophrenia. As in most modern genetic theories, the model also includes environmental factors as being partially responsible for the development of schizophrenia. If the individual's liability for schizophrenia exceeds a certain threshold, including genetic and environmental components, then schizophrenia will be expressed (Farone & Tsuang, 1985).

Biochemical Models

Biochemical theories of schizophrenia and autism postulate that some chemical within the bodily fluids contributes to the occurrence of the disorder. Typically, the suspect chemical is a brain neurotransmitter, such as dopamine, serotonin, or epinephrine. This approach was initiated by the discoveries that various chemicals, such as LSD, could produce hallucinations, a primary symptom of mental illness. It was noted that the hallucinogens were sometimes similar in chemical makeup, or at least bore some relationship, to brain neurotransmitters (e.g., Osmond & Smythies, 1952). Hence, it was logical to postulate that some problem with brain neurotransmitters was responsible for various mental disorders, particularly if hallucinations or other florid symptoms were involved. Most evidence for current biochemical theories is pharmacologic in nature (Strauss & Carpenter, 1981). The drugs that have been most effective in treating the symptoms of both schizophrenic and autistic individuals have been drugs that affect the action of one or more of the neurotransmitters or the action of some aspect of the neurotransmitter system. As will be seen below, although the last 20 or so years have brought many attempts, no more direct evidence has consistently been found. Researchers have investigated many isolated biochemical deviations, or possible deviations, with very disappointing results. This might be expected because the extreme variability in these syndromes makes it unlikely that a universal biochemical deviation will be found. As early as 1959, Kety criticized the previous biochemical research and suggested promising areas of systematic research, rather than the piecemeal type so common in the area. Haracz (1982) also noted the tendency in early biomedical research in schizophrenia to attempt to isolate relatively simple factors as possible causes of schizophrenia. Because this approach has been basically unsuccessful in generating compelling information, he concluded that the time has come for the development of more complex theories that include the influence of other important biological as well as environmental factors.

Theory example:

The most influential biochemical hypothesis in schizophrenia is the dopamine hypothesis. This hypothesis, first appearing in 1963 (Carlsson & Lindquist), predicts that there is some hyperactivity along dopaminergic neuronal pathways in the central nervous system (Strauss & Carpenter, 1981). This is the result of either the release of too much dopamine at the synapse, the hypersensitivity of the postsynaptic dopamine receptors, or other errors in the use or inhibition of dopamine within the system (Crider, 1979). The theory was derived primarily from pharmacologic drug action; that is, psychotic symptoms can be produced by dopamine agonists, and antipsychotic drugs, which are effective in improving many of the symptoms of schizophrenia, inhibit dopaminergic transmission (Strauss & Carpenter, 1981).

The striking success of the antipsychotic or antischizophrenic drugs makes a dopamine-type hypothesis very compelling, but there are a number of problems with the dopamine hypothesis as an etiological theory. First, the exact action of the antipsychotic drugs is not known. Their action may not be as simple as the inhibition of dopaminergic transmission. They may affect multiple areas of brain operations (Strauss & Carpenter, 1981). Another problem is that there is no direct evidence of the dopaminergic system's hyperactivity (Crider, 1979), and the more definitive *in vivo* experiments are very difficult, if not impossible, to perform. More peripheral measures (e.g., measuring chemicals in cerebrospinal fluid) may not be valid indicators. Performing autopsies on the brains of schizophrenic patients is also an inadequate method because abnormalities may reflect changes correlated with but not causing schizophrenia (Strauss & Carpenter, 1981).

As Haracz (1982) has indicated, the dopamine hypothesis has generated a great deal of research; however, the best evidence supporting the hypothesis still continues to be the indirect body of evidence showing the effectiveness of the antipsychotic drugs. Attempts to document increased levels of dopamine, or some hyperactivity or hypersensitivity along the dopaminergic pathways, have not been consistent or specific in their results.

One of the major contemporary areas of research into the dopamine system in schizophrenia has been stimulated by evidence for an increased number of postsynaptic dopamine receptors in the brains of schizophrenic patients (Seeman, 1985). Some controversy has developed over whether this increase has been an artifact of taking neuroleptic medication or a problem that predates the use of neuroleptics and is a result of the disease *per se* (e.g., MacKay, Bird, & Spokes, 1980). However, Seeman (1985) has reported several reasons that he thinks the elevation is a legitimate finding unconfounded with the administration of neuroleptic medication.

Neurophysiological Theories

Theories of the function of the nervous system and how it relates to behavior are common in schizophrenia and autism. There is an abundance of research examining these groups on a great variety of measures, including galvanic skin resistance, electroencephalograms (EEGs), evoked potentials, eye movements, and arousal. As might be expected, schizophrenic and autistic subjects are different from control subjects on many of these measures, but again, perhaps reflecting the complexity of the syndromes involved, the results are not consistent and few firm conclusions can be drawn. Strauss and Carpenter (1981) list several reasons for this confusion, including the state rather than trait characteristics of many of the variables, the low correlations among some of the variables thought to be measures of the same basic factor (e.g., heart rate, respiration, and galvanic skin resistance), and the great performance variability of schizophrenic and autistic subjects on psychophysiological measures. James and Barry (1980) report that the literature on psychophysiological measures with autistic subjects is replete with failures to adequately specify subject characteristics, limited reporting of medication regimens, and failures to include appropriate control groups, such as a mentally retarded group to control for the effect of mental age.

A wealth of differences between "psychotic" children (autistic, schizophrenic, and others) and normal children were noted in James and Barry's (1980) review. Abnormal or borderline EEGs were some of the earliest findings. This has been true for conventional waking EEGs, the rapid eye movement phases of EEG sleep, and average evoked responses to sensory stimuli. Measures of cardiovascular activity—specifically, heart rate, heart rate responsivity, vasometer responses, and respiratory reactivity—have also shown differences. From all of this, James and Barry (1980) tentatively concluded that psychotic children have a neurophysiological hyperreactivity to stimulation in comparison to normal subjects.

In a review of psychophysiological studies with schizophrenics, Holzman (1987) found research documenting eye movement abnormalities, differences in sensory evoked potentials, and differences in electrodermal responsiveness, and other abnormalities, Schizophrenic subjects appear to suffer from a generalized deficit when it comes to psychophysiological measures.

Theory example:

Ornitz (1985) has proposed a neurophysiological theory of autism, which he calls a brainstem-diencephalic hypothesis. From clinical observations he proposes that one of the dominant, if not predominant, symptom clusters in autism is sensory modulation and motility deficiencies, which involve, among other things, failing to respond to stimulation, excessively seeking out certain types of sensory input, and stereotypic behavior such as hand flapping. Since these behaviors are probably mediated at the level of the brainstem and nearby diencephalic structures, Ornitz suggests that these areas are primary in the neurophysiology of autism.

If the above notion is correct, three areas of functioning related to the brainstem-diencephalic region should be affected in the autistic subject (Ornitz, 1985): autonomic responses, brainstem auditory evoked responses (BAER), and vestibular responses. In the case of autonomic responses, there is evidence for increased heart rate variability in autistic subjects in comparison to normal subjects, as well as a failure to habituate respiratory responses to stimulation, providing an autonomic link to the sensory modulation deficit. As the BAERs, the findings have not been consistent, although there appear to be subgroups of autistic subjects that exhibit a deficit in brainstem transmission times.

The primary area in which Ornitz (1985) has found supportive evidence for brainstem-related pathology in autistic subjects is the vestibular reflex, specifically vestibular nystagmus. Clinical descriptions (Ornitz, 1978) have suggested abnormalities in various behaviors related to equilibrium, such as fearfulness of being spun around or lifted or, in contrast, excessive rotating and whirling while playing. In a very sophisticated study of vestibular nystagmus, Ornitz (1985) was able to experimentally verify the clinical impressions of abnormal vestibular nystagmus in autistic children.

The above evidence strongly implicates a brainstem-diencephalic lesion or deficiency in autism. Ornitz (1985) further suggests that the language-cognitive symptoms that appear to predominate in the middle childhood and teenage years of autism, suggesting pathology in the cortical mechanisms, are secondary to the brainstem-diencephalic difficulty. The actual root mechanism(s) affected may be the autistic subject's inability to "make sense out of sensation" (Ornitz, 1985), which leads to the deficiencies in other more sophisticated processes such as language and social relatedness.

Information-Processing Theories

Information-processing theories are closely related to neurophysiological theories in that some of the neurophysiological measures are simply assumed to be more basic indicators of the same phenomena, or at least closely related indicators. It is common to intermingle the discussion of the more peripheral, psychological measures of attention, memory, perception, and the like with the electrical activity measures of the neurophysiologist (e.g., Holzman, 1987); and there are many correlations between these sets of measures. However, they will be discussed separately here.

The behavior of schizophrenic and autistic persons provides many examples of what appears to be faulty processing of information from the environment. Kraepelin and Bleuler both recognized an impairment in attention in their early descriptions of schizophrenia (Cutting, 1985). The distorted reality of the florid schizophrenic may be explainable as some sort of abnormal information processing (Bernheim & Lewine, 1979). The language deficiencies common to autistic subjects may result from a deficit in one or several basic processes, such as perception, attention, or memory. Many theorists have recognized these possibilities in both schizophrenia (e.g., McGhie & Chapman, 1961; Shakow, 1979; Silverman, 1964) and autism (e.g., DeMyer, 1971; Hermelin, 1976).

Theory example:

Beginning in the 1940s Shakow began a research program with institutionalized schizophrenic subjects that led to his theory of segmental set (see Shakow, 1979, for a review of his theory). He studied the performance of schizophrenic subjects relative to that of nonschizophrenic subjects, in a reaction-time paradigm. For example, the subject might be asked to press a button when he heard a bell and release it when he saw a light. The speed with which the subject released the button after the presentation of the light was the primary dependent variable; and the interval between the bell and the light, the preparatory interval, was a primary independent variable. Shakow found that not only were the schizophrenic subjects slower than nonschizophrenic subjects in most reaction-time tasks, but the length of the preparatory interval and the pattern of preparatory intervals within a series of trials had different effects on the reactions times of the schizophrenic and normal subjects. His group also found that the schizophrenic subjects performed relatively better in tasks in which the experimenter maintained control as opposed to one in which the subject had more autonomy. The performance of the normal subjects was just the opposite: they performed better in the more autonomous tasks.

The basic tenets of Shakow's (1979) theory of segmental set are as follows. First, the segmental set of schizophrenic persons, as opposed to the adaptive generalized set of nonschizophrenic persons, produces a slowness, or lack of readiness to respond, perhaps because of inability to filter out irrelevant and distracting stimuli. Second, the schizophrenic person also has a tendency to respond in idiosyncratic ways no matter what the task. He is overwhelmed by irrelevancies.

Family and Parenting Theories

Perhaps at least partially because of the influence of psychodynamic theory and learning theory in the middle third of this century, the effects of the parents and family upon behavior was emphasized during the same period. It was during this time that Fromm-Reichman (1948) discussed the role of the "schizophrenogenic" mother in producing schizophrenic children. When Kanner (1943) first formally identified the syndrome of autism, he coined the term "refrigerator mother" to describe the cold, rejecting style of the rather intelligent mothers he found to be common in families of autistic children. In fact, parents and families, especially mothers, were often blamed for the faulty development of their children during these postwar years.

In autism, the tendency to accuse parents of producing extreme behavior in their children began to change in the 1960s. Rimland (1964) wrote a scorching critique of the faulty-parenting notion, asserting that, among other things, the increased incidence of autism in the twin sibling of autistic individuals and the relationship of known organic disease to some cases of autism provided strong disconfirming evidence. Since Rimland's article appeared, faulty-parenting theories have been basically refuted by the experimental evidence (e.g.,

Cantwell, Baker, & Rutter, 1978; DeMyer et al. 1981; McAdoo & DeMyer, 1978). DeMyer et al. (1981) reported on a number of findings from the 1970s that did severe damage to the faulty-parenting theories, including Cox, Rutter, Newman, and Bartak's (1975) results showing that the parents of autistic children were similar to control group parents in emotional warmth and sociability, and the findings of DeMyer et al. (1972) that the infant care practices of the parents of autistic children did not differ from those of the parents of normal children in infant acceptance, warmth, nurturing, feeding, and so on. No evidence was found that the parents of autistic children exhibited any of the negative characteristics attributed to them by the theorists of faulty parenting.

In the family and parenting literature on schizophrenia, a primary initial concept was that of the "schizophrenogenic" mother advanced by Fromm-Reichman (1948). Actually, this domineering, aloof, rejecting mother was viewed as often being paired with a passive, immature father who failed to exert a normal "fatherly" influence (Bernheim & Lewine, 1979). The families were also viewed as exhibiting a defective pattern of communication, called the "double-bind" (Bateson, (1972), in which the developing child is given mixed signals. For example, the mother may give the child verbal indications that she wants the child to display affection toward her yet give nonverbal signals rejecting affection from the child.

The family and parenting hypotheses in schizophrenia have generally gone the way of those same notions in autism, at least in regard to the theories that postulate abnormal parenting as a primary etiological factor (Bernheim & Lewine, 1979; Waxler, 1975). As Cutting (1985) puts it, "One is inclined to dismiss the whole issue as causally irrelevant, and regard the few consistent findings (maternal overprotection, paternal dominance, peculiar parents, deviant family communication of one kind or another) as secondary to bringing up a preschizophrenic child" (p. 119).

Theory example:

Bettelheim's (1967) theory of autism proposes that for several possible reasons (e.g., pain or discomfort, misperception) the preautistic child perceives that his mother has rejected him/her and begins to withdraw from him/her and the world. This withdrawal creates feelings of incompetence or frustration in the mother, who, in turn, responds in a negative fashion, perhaps with anger or indifference. This creates further discomfort and/or anxiety for the child, who continues to withdraw, not only from his mother but also from the environment altogether. As this cycle continues, the individual loses all contact with reality, and his personality fails to develop. All energy is expended shielding out the hostile and/or anxiety- producing outside world. The lack of language or disturbed- language characteristic of the autistic child is viewed as the autistic individual's negation of himself and others (Levinson & Osterweil, 1984).

A major problem with Bettelheim's theory, as well as with many other theories in this class, is that the supporting evidence is primarily anecdotal in nature. Many of Bettelheim's concepts are basically nonobservable. And from the evidence presented above, there is simply no documentation for any deficiency in infant care practices in parents of autistic children that might lead to withdrawal on the part of the child.

Psychodynamic Theories

Any discussion of psychopathology in the 20th century must include the psychodynamic viewpoint, if for no other reason than its general influence upon psychology and psychiatry. Actually, the family and parenting theories of autism and schizophrenia discussed above were heavily influenced by psychodynamic theory.

Clear theoretical formulations of schizophrenia, particularly of an etiological nature, are seldom found in the psychoanalytic literature (Shapiro, 1981). Freud did not discuss schizophrenia in any comprehensive way, and his clinical experience with schizophrenic patients was limited. In the early stages of his work he apparently believed that schizophrenic persons were not appropriate for psychoanalytic treatment, and this apparently served to limit the development of psychodynamic theories of schizophrenia during the early part of this century (Shapiro, 1981).

A basic formulation in psychoanalytic theory is that the schizophrenic person has a weak ego (Bellak, 1970), that aspect of the mind or psychic apparatus that deals with the environment and includes the sense of self. It mediates between the environment and the other two aspects of the mind, the id and superego, by developing defense mechanisms such as denial, repression, isolation, projection, sublimation, and reaction formation (Robinson & Robinson, 1965). Thus, in schizophrenia, the ego defenses may be weak, leading to a loss of contact with reality and disturbed ego functions, such as reality testing, judgment, sense of reality, regulation and control of drives, and so on (Bellak, 1970). Of course, as is common in most psychoanalytically oriented theories, the basis of the disturbance is formed in infancy or early childhood; so when stresses occur later in life (adolescence and young adulthood in schizophrenia), the individual regresses to the early, faulty stage of development.

A major weakness of psychoanalytic theory is its inferential, retrospective method. Many of the concepts, particularly those concerning infants and young children, are difficult, if not impossible, to test; and many of them are inconsistent with well-established notions concerning early cognitive development (Shapiro, 1981).

Theory example:

Goldstein (1978) has attempted to integrate the rather disjointed psychodynamic literature regarding schizophrenia into a clear theoretical formulation. He uses the various concepts of Mahler (1970), Hartmann (1953), Arlow and Brenner (1969), and other influential psychodynamic theorists.

The mother-child interaction within the first few months of life is viewed as the critical aspect. The symbiotic relationship between the mother and the child fails to resolve appropriately, and the child's concept of himself as an individual is either not formed or poorly formed, leading to defective or nonexistent ego boundaries. This leads to subsequent problems in superego formation as well. These defects are observable almost immediately, but the severe symptoms of schizophrenia do not appear until later. The schizophrenic episode is produced by an upsurge of libidinal (sexual) and/or aggressive drives in adolescence or young adulthood that cannot be handled by the defective ego and/or superego, and the exact manner of the decompensation will depend upon the type of deficit that originally developed during the early mother–infant interaction.

The primary criticism of this theory of psychopathology, as well as of others in the psychoanalytic tradition, is the failure to provide empirical evidence for the concepts and processes postulated. These theories must be considered speculative in nature until empirical research supporting them is forthcoming.

Learning Theories

Learning or behavioral theories have not had the serious influence in autism and schizophrenia of the more biologically oriented theories. Bellack (1986) discusses some of the reasons that behaviorally oriented therapists have not taken a greater interest in schizophrenia, and at least one of these reasons probably applies to learning theorists as well: the significant evidence that schizophrenia has a strong biological component. In regard to learning theories of autism, Levinson and Osterwell (1984) assert that the syndrome of autism often appears too early in infancy for the operation of learning principles to have played a part in its genesis and that the success of behavioral treatments does not necessarily lend any etiological significance to learning principles. However, though relatively rare and in spite of the pessimistic attitudes of many, learning theories of autism and schizophrenia do exist and may include both etiological and descriptive theories.

One of the early etiological learning theories in this area was formulated by Adolph Meyer (1948). He proposed that schizophrenia is the result of learning increasingly abnormal behaviors. Others have proposed this operation or dysfunction of many basic learning mechanisms in the genesis of schizophrenia and autism, including the failure to develop appropriate secondary reinforcers, the sparse reinforcement of any and all behaviors, the extinction of appropriate social behavior coupled with the reinforcement of gradually increasing levels of maladaptive behavior, and direct reinforcement of deviant patterns of behavior modeled by parents. Learning theories are similar to psychodynamic and family parenting theories in that they often imply that the critical factor in the genesis of the disorder is the parent-child interaction. However, the theories differ in their explanatory concepts and in the implication as to who is or is not to blame.

Etiological theory example:

Ferster (1961) has proposed that autistic behavior can be the result of intermittent reinforcement and extinction effects. For example, he suggests that much of the child's appropriate social behavior may be weakened by the parents' failure to respond or their inconsistent responses, such as in the case of the ill, depressed, or otherwise preoccupied parent. If this lack of reinforcement is pervasive enough, the total extinction of some appropriate behaviors can result. Another factor that operates is the development of the child as a conditioned aversive stimulus for the parent because caring for the child interferes with behaviors the parent finds rewarding (e.g., social events, work). Therefore, less and less time is spent responding to the child, accelerating the weakening of appropriate behaviors in the child.

Ferster (1961) also suggests that the tantrum behavior in some autistic children is actually differentially reinforced by the parents. Parents who do not reinforce more appropriate behaviors may respond with attention or other rewards to tantrum behavior because of its aversiveness, therefore strengthening the likelihood of tantrums. With further exposure to the tantrums, the parents may be less likely to respond to low-magnitude tantrums, so the child then begins to emit higher-magnitude tantrums that are sufficient to elicit a response. This shaping process continues until the high-magnitude tantrums becomes a very likely response in the child's repertoire.

Ferster (1961) goes on to suggest that the lack of parental responsiveness impedes the development of the conditioned and generalized reinforcers necessary for the development of more complex chains of behavior.

Although this is not a comprehensive summary of Ferster's theoretical arguments, it will serve to illustrate his basic approach to the development of autistic behavior. As is common in behavioral approaches, he isolates some of the basic components of autism and describes how they might develop by using learning principles. The main criticism of Ferster's approach is that it is only descriptive in nature, as he freely admits (Ferster, 1961). He quite accurately contends, however, that the variables he uses are potentially manipulatable and directly observable. In subsequent work (Ferster & DeMyer, 1961, 1962) he demonstrated that autistic children do respond to techniques based upon learning principles.

Descriptive theory example:

Descriptive theories attempt to outline some of the characteristics of the current behavior of schizophrenic or autistic persons and not typically concerned with etiology (Salzinger, 1973). There are a number of such theories related to basic learning concepts such as drive arousal, stimulus processing, attending responses, and conditioning.

Ullmann and Krasner (1969) contend that a basic deficit in schizophrenic individuals is in attending to social stimuli. Appropriate attending is viewed as an operant behavior that has been extinguished through the schizophrenic person's experiences with the environment.

Much of the bizarre behavior of such persons is conceptualized as resulting from not attending to the same stimuli that normal people attend to and thus responding in an unexpected manner. The apathy often seen in the behavior of some schizophrenic persons at various times may result from their failure to react to stimuli that others find

important. Using the same basic concept, Ullmann and Krasner explain the occurrence of numerous behaviors common in schizophrenia.

CURRENT INFLUENTIAL THEORIES

The sections above sketched some of the major theory areas in autism and schizophrenia and briefly discussed some sample theories from each area. The following section discusses two recent theories—one for autism and one for schizophrenia—that appear to be particularly influential in guiding contemporary research efforts in each area.

Cognitive-Language Theory of Autism

The basic deficit in autism has been a source of disagreement since the syndrome was formally conceptualized by Kanner (1943). Although Kanner vacillated somewhat over the years, his basic orientation was that the root deficit in autism was a social one (Rutter, 1983). However, since the 1970s cognitive disorders have been viewed as primary in autism (DeMyer et al., 1981). There are theorists who continue to espouse the notion that the social withdrawal, or lack of social relatedness, deficit is the basic disorder in autism. For example, Fein, Pennington Markowitz, Braverman,, and Waterhouse (1986) have recently proposed a neurophysiological theory based upon their contention that the social symptoms are the basic problem in autism. However, as Fein et al. admit, their approach is contrary to the general trend in autism.

Rutter (1968, 1979, 1983) has been the leading spokesman for the importance of the cognitive deficits in autism. As he wrote in 1983, "it is being argued that, in some respect, the cognitive deficit constitutes the core of autism; . . . and that it is likely to underlie many of the autistic features" (p. 516).

Rutter (1983) uses several types of evidence to argue for the preeminence of cognitive factors over social factors in autism. For example, he suggests that if the social symptoms are primary and thus responsible for intellectual deficiencies in autism, then virtually all autistic children would be expected to perform in the mentally retarded range on IQ tests; but a significant number of them do not. He also supports his argument that social functioning does not determine intellectual functioning with evidence showing that the intellectual functioning of autistic persons does not improve with improvements in social involvement. Positive suggestive evidence that the cognitive deficit underlies the autistic syndrome is presented by Wing and Gould (1979). They found that as IQ goes down, the risk of autism increases; and Rutter (1970) and Lotter (1978) have found that IQ is a potent predictor of future adjustment in autistic individuals.

Although the evidence above favors the cognitive deficit hypothesis of autism, it does not help in identifying the specific cognitive deficit(s) that may be primary in autism. In a series of studies comparing developmentally dysphasic and autistic children, Rutter and his collaborators (Bartak, Rutter, & Cox, 1975; Boucher, 1976; Cantwell et al., (1978) present evidence that the primary deficient process is language. The autistic children were not impaired relative to the dysphasic children in nonverbal skills and articulation, but they were deficient relative to the dysphasic children in measures of language understanding and measures of though processes that required verbal skills, imaginative play, the use of gestures, and social communication. The autistic children also displayed more deviant language.

Rutter (1983) feels that the evidence supports his assertion that cognitive deficits, specifically language-related cognitive deficits, underlie the syndrome of autism. He suggests that further understanding of the cognitive disorder(s) could facilitate normal development in autistic children.

Vulnerability Theory of Schizophrenia

Zubin and Spring (1977) proposed this theory of schizophrenia to stimulate progress in the field. They suggested that research utilizing the other theoretical approaches in the field was losing steam and that a new approach that was an amalgam of the other classic approaches to schizophrenia (e.g., genetics, learning, biochemical, neurophysiological) handled much of the data already generated and offered some new, helpful insights.

The basic concept in vulnerability theory is that everyone has some degree of susceptibility that, under the right conditions, can be expressed as schizophrenia (Zubin & Spring, 1977). Drawing from the two basic types of etiological theory—the internal biological (e.g., genetic) and the social-psychological-environmental (e.g., learning theory)—two major components of vulnerability are proposed: inborn and acquired. The variables that contribute to the inborn component are the genetically acquired attributes of the organism, such as its neurophysiology. Examples of the variables that contribute to the acquired component are pre- and perinatal trauma, disease, and family life experiences. The combined contribution of the inborn and acquired factors that the individual experiences determines the degree of vulnerability. An episode of schizophrenia is triggered when an event produces a crisis that exceeds the individual's vulnerability threshold. The individual who has had a number of contributing inborn and/or acquired factors (low vulnerability threshold) will be more likely to experience an episode of schizophrenia when exposed to critical life events than will the individual with fewer contributing inborn and/or acquired factors (high vulnerability thresholds).

The model makes yet other predictions. For example, it suggests that schizophrenia is primarily an episodic syndrome rather than a permanent debilitating condition. As Zubin and Spring (1977) point out, there is increasing evidence that schizophrenic episodes are temporary in most cases. They emphasize Bleuler's (1974) longitudinal data, which found that only 10% of the cases resulted in permanent debilitation, and most subjects suffered only one acute episode of schizophrenia. Others had several intermittent episodes but lived most of their lives in the community. The vulnerability hypothesis suggests that schizophrenic episodes are time-limited. When the critical event and the subsequent crises it may trigger are resolved, the schizophrenic episode ends.

The vulnerability hypothesis has stimulated research in the reliable vulnerability "markers" in schizophrenia (Zubin & Steinhauer, 1981). These markers are defined as trait characteristics of schizophrenic or preschizophrenic persons, indicating the existence of low vulnerability. According to Zubin and Spring (1977), the markers might come from all of the classic models of schizophrenia, such as dopamine levels from the biochemical area, evoked potential characteristics from neurophysiology, acquisition abnormalities from learning theory, and so on. Identification of markers could lead to valuable information concerning the prediction of schizophrenic episodes and the identification of low-vulnerability individuals.

The full research program Zubin and Steinhauer (1981) suggest has three aspects: (a) the identification of vulnerability markers, (b) the study of low-vulnerability individuals longitudinally to determine the kinds of crises that trigger schizophrenic episodes, and (c) the use of the knowledge from the first two studies to prevent schizophrenic episodes.

CONCLUDING COMMENTS

This literature is so diverse that drawing conclusions is challenging. Both autistic and schizophrenic individuals show a large number of differences when compared to control groups, and may of the differences have been expanded into either an etiological or a descriptive theory. The result is a massive literature in both autism and schizophrenia, which is difficult to integrate because of the variety of concepts involved.

It is possible to see some trends concerning the relative influence of biological versus psychosocial factors. In autism, the trend is away from psychosocial causes such as faulty parenting and toward biological factors as important in the genesis of the disorder. As DeMyer et al. (1981) put it, "As we begin the 1980s, all but a few researchers hypothesize that autism is an organic disorder involving the brain" (p. 432). Considering Rutter's (1983) discussion of the primacy of cognitive-language deficits, the basic effect of this organic deficiency may be on the development of language.

In schizophrenia there have been numerous trends in the relative influence of biological versus psychosocial factors. Currently, the literature appears to be moving away from a fairly predominant biological emphasis in the theories of schizophrenia to theories that take an interdisciplinary approach to the problem. Such theories recognize that an exclusively biological approach has not been totally successful in explaining the genesis of or the behaviors in schizophrenia and that there is strong evidence for the effect of psychosocial factors. The theories of Zubin and Spring (1977) and Strauss and Carpenter (1981) reflect this shift. A similar integrative approach with autism is also being considered.

The parochialism that permeated the field in years past has fortunately given way to a recognition by many theorists and researchers that a disjointed approach has been counterproductive (Rosenthal, 1968; Zubin & Spring, 1977). Researchers have begun to listen to the arguments of the other camps, and more enlightened research and theories have been the result. If this trend continues, greater and greater strides toward the understanding of these complex disorders will be made.

REFERENCES

Arlow, J. A., & Brenner, C. (1969). The psychopathology of the psychoses: A proposed revision. *International Journal of Psychoanalysis, 50*, 5–14.

Bertak, L., Rutter, M., & Cox, A. (1975). A comparative study of infantile autism and specific developmental receptive language disorder: I. The children. *British Journal of Psychiatry, 126*, 127–145.

Bateson, G. (1972). *Steps to an ecology of mind*. New York: Ballantine.

Bellack, A. S. (1986). Schizophrenia: Behavior therapy's forgotten child. *Behavior Therapy, 17*, 199–214.

Bellack, L. (1970). The validity and usefulness of the concept of the schizophrenic syndrome. In R. Cancro (Ed.), *The schizophrenic reaction* (pp. 41–58). New York: Bruner/Mazel.

Bernheim, K. F., & Lewine, R. R. J. (1979). *Schizophrenia: Symptoms, causes, treatments*. New York: W. W. Norton.

Bettelheim, B. (1967). *The empty fortress*. New York: Free Press.

Bleuler, M. (1974). The long-term course of the schizophrenic psychoses. *Psychological Medicine, 4*, 244.

Boucher, J. (1976). Articulation in early childhood autism. *Journal of Autism and Childhood Schizophrenia, 6,* 297–302.

Cantwell, D., Baker, L., & Rutter, M. (1978). A comparative study of infantile autism and specific developmental receptive language disorder: IV. Analysis of syntax and language function. *Journal of Child Psychology and Psychiatry, 19,* 351–362.

Carlsson, A., & Lindquist, M. (1963). Effect of chlorpromazine or haloperidol on formation of 3 methoxytyramine and normetanephrine in mouse brain. *Acta Pharmacologia, 20,* 140–144.

Coleman, M. K., & Gilberg, C. (1985). *The biology of the autistic syndromes.* New York: Praeger.

Coleman, M., & Rimland, B. (1976). Familial autism. In M. Coleman (Ed.), *The autistic syndromes* (pp. 175–182). Amsterdam: North-Holland.

Cox, A., Rutter, M., Newman, S., & Bartak, L. (1975). A comparative study of infantile autism and specific developmental receptive disorder II. Parental characteristics. *British Journal of Psychiatry, 126,* 146–159.

Crider, A. (1979). *Schizophrenia: A biophysiological perspective.* Hillsdale, NJ: Lawrence Erlbaum.

Cutting, J. (1985). *The psychology of schizophrenia.* London: Churchill Livingston.

DeMyer, M. (1971). Perceptual limitations in autistic children and their relation to social and intellectual deficits. In M. Rutter (Ed.), *Infantile autism: Concepts, characteristics, and treatment* (pp. 81–96). London: Churchill.

DeMyer, M., K., Hingtgen, J. N., and Jackson, R. K., (1981). Infantile autism reviewed: A decade of research. *Schizophrenia Bulletin, 7,* 388–451.

DeMyer, M., Pontius, W., Norton, J., Barton, S., Allen, J., & Steele, R. (1972). Parental practices and innate activity in normal, autistic, and grain-damaged infants. *Journal of Autism and Childhood Schizophrenia, 2,* 49–66.

Despert, J. L. (1971). Reflections on early infantile autism. *Journal of Autism and Childhood Schizophrenia, 1,* 363–367.

Farone, S. V., & Tsuang, M. T. (1985). Quantitative models of the genetic transmission of schizophrenia. *Psychological Bulletin, 98,* 41–66.

Fein, D., Pennington, B., Markowitz, P., Braverman, M., & Waterhouse, L. (1986). Toward a neurophysiological model of infantile autism: Are the social deficits primary? *Journal of the American Academy of Child Psychiatry, 25,* 198–212.

Ferster, C. B. (1961). Positive reinforcement and behavioral deficits of autistic children. *Child Development, 32,* 437–456.

Ferster, C. B. & DeMyer, M. K. (1961). The development of performances in autistic children in an automatically-controlled environment. *Journal of Chronic Diseases*, 13, 312–345.

Ferster, C. B. & DeMyer, M. K. (1962). A method for the experimental analysis of the behavior of autistic children. *American Journal of Orthopsychiatry*, 32, 89–98.

Folstein, S., & Rutter, M. (1978). A twin study of individuals with infantile autism. In M. Rutter & E. Schloper (Eds.), *Autism: A reappraisal of concepts and treatments* (pp. 219–241). New York: Plenum Press.

Fromm-Reichman, F. (1948). Notes on the development of treatment of schizophrenics by psychoanalytic psychotherapy. *Psychiatry*, 11, 263–273.

Goldstein, W. (1978). Toward an integrated theory of schizophrenia. *Schizophrenia Bulletin*, 4, 426–436.

Gottesman, I. I., McGuffin, P., & Farmer, A. E. (1987). Clinical genetics as clues to the "real" genetics of schizophrenia. *Schizophrenia Bulletin*, 13, 23–47.

Gottesman, I. I., & Shields, J. (1982). *Schizophrenia: The epigenetic puzzle*. Cambridge: University of Cambridge Press.

Haracz, J. L. (1982). The dopamine hypothesis: An overview of studies with schizophrenic patients. *Schizophrenia Bulletin*, 8, 438–469.

Hartmann, H. (1953). Contribution to the metapsychology of schizophrenia. In R. S. Eissler, A. Freud, H. Hartman, & E. Kris (Eds.), *The psychoanalytic study of the child* (Vol. 8, pp. 177–198). New York: International Universities Press.

Hermelin, B. (1976). Coding and the sense modalities. In L. Wing (Ed.), *Early childhood autism: Clinical, educational, and social aspects*, (2nd ed.), (pp. 135–166). Oxford: Pergamon Press.

Holzman, P. S. (1987). Recent studies of psychophysiology in schizophrenia. *Schizophrenia Bulletin*, 13, 49–75.

James, A. L., & Barry, R. J. (1980). A review of psychophysiology in early onset psychosis. *Schizophrenia Bulletin*, 6, 506–525.

Kanner, L. (1943). Autistic disturbances of affective contact. *Nervous Child*, 2, 217–250.

Levinson, B. M., & Osterweil, L. (1984). *Autism: Myth or reality?* Springfield, IL: Charles C. Thomas.

Lotter, V. (1978). Follow-up studies. In M. Rutter & E. Schloper (Eds.), *Autism: A reappraisal of concepts and treatment* (pp. 475–495). New York: Plenum Press.

MacKay, A. V. P., Bird, E. D., & Spokes, E. G. (1980). Dopamine receptors and schizophrenia: Drug effect or illness? *Lancet*, 2, 915–916.

Mahler, M. (1970). *On human symbiosis and the vicissitudes of individuation* (Vol. 1). New York: International Universities Press.

McAdoo, W. G., & DeMyer, M. K. (1978). Research related to family factors in autism. *Journal of Pediatric Psychology*, 162–166.

McGhie, A., & Chapman, J. (1961). Disorders of attention and perception in early schizophrenia. *British Journal of Medical Psychology*, 34, 103–115.

Meyer, A. (1948). Fundamental conceptions of dementia praecox. In A. Lief (Ed.), *The common-sense psychiatry of Adolf Meyer* (pp. 184–192). New York: McGraw-Hill.

Ornitz, E. M. (1978). Neurophysiologic studies. In M. Rutter & E. Schloper (Eds.), *Autism: A reappraisal of concepts and treatment* (pp. 117–139). New York: Plenum Press.

Ornitz, E. M. (1985). Neurophysiology of infantile autism. *Journal of the American Academy of Child Psychiatry*, 24, 251–262.

Osmond, H. & Smythies, J. (1952). Schizophrenia: A new approach. *Journal of Mental Sciences*, 98, 309–315.

Rimland, B. (1964). *Infantile autism*. New York: Appleton-Century-Crofts.

Ritvo, E. R., Rabin, K., Yuwiler, A., Freeman, B., & Geller, E. (1978). Biological and hematologic studies: A critical review. In M. Rutter & E. Schloper (Eds.), *Autism: A reappraisal of concepts and treatment* (pp. 163–184). New York: Plenum Press.

Ritvo, E. R., Spence, M. A., Freeman, B. J., Mason-Brothers, A., Mo, A., & Marazita, M. L. (1985). Evidence for autosomal recessive inheritance in 46 families with multiple incidences of autism. *American Journal of Psychiatry*, 142, 187–192.

Robinson, H. B., & Robinson, N. M. (1965). *The mentally retarded child: A psychological approach*. New York: McGraw-Hill.

Rosenthal, D., & Kety, S. (1968). Forward. In D. Rosenthal & S. Kety (Eds.), *The transmission of schizophrenia* (pp. ix–xx). London: Pergamon Press.

Rutter, M. (1968). Concepts of autism: A review of research. *Journal of Child Psychology and Psychiatry*, 9, 1–25.

Rutter, M. (1970). Autistic children: Infancy to adulthood. *Seminars in Psychiatry*, 2, 435–450.

Rutter, M. (1978). Diagnosis and definition. In M. Rutter & E. Schloper (Eds.), *Autism: A reappraisal of concepts and treatment* (pp. 1–25). New York: Plenum Press.

Rutter M. (1979). Language, cognition, and autism. In R. Katzman (Ed.), *Congenital and acquired cognitive disorders* (pp. 247–264). New York: Raven.

Rutter, M. (1983). Cognitive deficits in the pathogenesis of autism. *Journal of Child Psychology and Psychiatry*, 24, 513–531.

Salzinger, K. (1973). *Schizophrenia: Behavioral aspects*. New York: John Wiley & Sons.

Seeman, P. (1985). Brain dopamine receptors in schizophrenia. In M. N. Menuck & M. V. Seeman (Eds.), *New perspectives in schizophrenia* (pp. 71–80). New York: Macmillan.

Shakow, D. (1979). *Adaptation in schizophrenia*. New York: John Wiley.

Shapiro, S. A. (1981). *Contemporary theories of schizophrenia: Review and synthesis*. New York: McGraw-Hill.

Silverman, J. (1964). The problem of attention in research and theory in schizophrenia. *Psychological Review, 71*, 352–379.

Ullman, L. P., & Krasner, L. (1969). *A psychological approach to abnormal behavior*. Englewood Cliffs, NJ: Prentice-Hall.

Waxler, N. (1975). The normality of deviance: An alternate explanation of schizophrenia in the family. *Schizophrenia Bulletin, 14*, 38–47.

Wing, L., & Gould, J. (1979). Severe impairments of social interaction and associated abnormalities in children: Epidemiology and classification. *Journal of Autism and Developmental Disorders, 9*, 11–29.

Zubin, J., & Spring, B. (1977). Vulnerability—a new view of schizophrenia. *Journal of Abnormal Psychology, 86*, 103–126.

Zubin, J., & Steinhauer, S. (1981). How to break the logjam in schizophrenia. *Journal of Nervous and Mental Disease, 169*, 477–492.

3

Etiology, Incidence, and Prevalence Of Chronic Schizophrenia and Adult Autism

David Coe and Johnny Matson

Increasingly, studies have shown a life-span developmental sequence for schizophrenic and autistic persons who exhibit symptoms of these disorders throughout their lifetimes, whereas remission occurs in others (e.g., Bleuler, 1978; DeMyer et al., 1973; Kolakowska et al., 1985). Factors that distinguish those who improve from those who do not may be important clues for understanding and treating these conditions. The present volume is an attempt to synthesize what is now known about chronic schizophrenia and adult autism. To date there has been little integration of this research despite a number of similarities in both symptoms and treatments of these disorders. Integration of this sort, however, may help researchers and clinicians recognize similarities in, as well as distinctions between these disorders, thus spurring further advances in knowledge and intervention.

Reviewing research and theories concerning the origin and frequency of chronic schizophrenia and adult autism is not the easiest of tasks. Many studies in the past have employed definitions of schizophrenia and autism that are vague or idiosyncratic, therefore limiting integration and interpretation of findings (Lotter, 1978; World Health Organization [WHO], 1979). A second problem confronting those interested in such conditions is the small number of long-term follow-up studies. This problem is especially acute in the autism literature, where few studies of adults who exhibited autism in childhood are available. For these reasons, any conclusions made at this point concerning the long-term courses of schizophrenia and autism must be considered preliminary. We feel, however, that some general conclusion or at least some constructive statements of ignorance can be made.

This chapter consists of four major sections. It begins with a brief survey of descriptions of chronic schizophrenia and adult autism, followed by a section devoted to reviewing research and theories of etiology. The third part of the chapter discusses research related to both incidence and prevalence. A general summary and discussion are presented in the fourth and final section. Our discussions of etiology and frequency both begin with consideration of the literature on schizophrenia and autism in general. This approach was followed because in many respects our present knowledge of chronic schizophrenia and adult autism represent mere elaborations or refinements of current understanding (or lack thereof) of these more general classifications. With autism, for example, research on the etiology of adult autism, as opposed to forms that eventually remit, has not yet progressed beyond a discussion of factors related to prognosis. The latest word on adult autism is largely the latest word on autism in general.

In the case of population frequencies of chronic schizophrenia and adult autism, there are two relevant sets of studies to consider. One consists of studies on the incidence and prevalence of schizophrenia and autism in general. The other class relates to work on prognosis and outcome for these populations. Therefore, to determine population frequencies of chronic schizophrenia and adult autism, one has to look first at the literature on schizophrenia and autism in general and then draw on outcome studies to identify subsets from these populations. This approach is perhaps less than ideal but is necessitated by the small number of published studies.

HISTORICAL OVERVIEW AND DEFINITIONS OF CONCEPTS

It has been recognized since Kraepelin and Bleuler that many schizophrenics exhibit permanent impairment and deterioration (Bridge, Cannon, & Wyatt, 1978). Kraepelin originally argued that the disorder he called dementia praecox essentially involved progressive deterioration. Years later, however, he admitted that with a minority of cases there was improvement (Kraepelin, 1913). Eugen Bleuler also thought that the prognosis for schizophrenia was poor but argued that remission was possible (Bleuler, 1930). Classification of schizophrenia on the basis of outcome was suggested by Langfeldt in 1939 (cited by Rettersol, 1968); he proposed a distinction between schizophrenia and schizophreniform disorders. Schizophreniform disorders, Langfeldt (1939) claimed, differed from schizophrenia in that a relatively good prognosis was evident. Typically, there was an acute onset and discrete precipitating factors. Conversely, schizophrenia exhibited an insidious onset and a chronic course.

Within several years of Langfeldt, several others suggested similar dichotomizations of good and poor prognosis for schizophrenia cases. Sullivan (1940) proposed that dementia praecox and schizophrenia were unrelated disorders. Several years later, Bellak (1948) suggested a distinction between classic dementia praecox and schizophrenia, which had a better prognosis. Outcome of several subtypes of schizophrenia was the subject of a paper by Holmboe and Astrup in 1957, and Stephens and Astrup (1963) and Vaillant (1964) published seminal papers addressing factors relating to the prognosis of schizophrenia.

As the study of schizophrenia has expanded, the issue of chronicity has assumed increasing importance because of its bearing on type and effectiveness of treatment and the effects the condition has for the long-term care of more recalcitrant clients. Today, the American Psychiatric Association's (APA) *Diagnostic and Statistical Manual*

(DSM-III-R, 1987) contains separate classification categories for both acute and chronic forms of schizophrenic disorders. Similarly, Matson (1985) has recently proposed that chronic schizophrenia might be further divided into acute–chronic and chronic–chronic schizophrenia. Acute–chronic schizophrenia refers to a form of schizophrenia that although long-term only periodically produces expression of psychotic symptoms. These isolated episodes are separated by periods during which the affected individual functions almost normally. The chronic–chronic form of schizophrenia does not show lasting or even periodic phases of total remission. Psychotic symptoms are virtually always evident. In contrast to acute–chronic schizophrenia, the set of symptoms that has come to be known as negative symptoms—flattened affect, minimal speech and motivation—are generally more apparent in chronic–chronic schizophrenia than are positive symptoms—hallucinations, delusions, and loosening of thought associations. These notions have proved of interest and are likely to receive more study in the future.

Interest in the long-term course of autism has yet to achieve the level of attention afforded to schizophrenia. Kanner first drew attention to the disorder in 1943. Eisenberg published the first study on outcome 13 years later, reporting a generally poor prognosis (Eisenberg, 1956). In the years since Eisenberg's paper, only a handful of studies related to outcome for autistic children has been published (e.g., Rutter Greenfeld & Lockyer, 1967; DeMyer et al., 1973). The conclusions of these papers echoed those of Eisenberg: most individuals with autism exhibited little improvement, although a small minority apparently achieved normal or near-normal levels of functioning. To date, however, virtually all of the research on autism, a considerable body of literature, has been on children. Fortunately, a number of recent publications have acknowledged and addressed the lives of autistic individuals in the years beyond early childhood. In 1983, Schopler and Mesibov edited a volume specific to adolescent and adult autism. Although presenting a limited amount of information and systematic research, the book identified and discussed many concerns and issues pertinent to autism as a disorder of adolescence and adulthood. In recent years, several studies have looked at the frequency of autistic individuals in groups of mentally retarded adults (Gillberg, 1983a; Lund, 1986). Rumsey and her colleagues have published neurological and in-depth behavioral assessments of men who were diagnosed as autistic in childhood (Rumsey, Andreasen & Rapoport, 1986; Rumsey et al., 1985; Rumsey, Rapoport, & Sceery, 1985). One hopes that these recent papers represent the vanguard for future research.

It is perhaps with respect to the presence of negative symptoms that comparisons are most constructively made between individuals with schizophrenia and autism. Negative symptoms include (1) lack of responsiveness to others, (2) lack of drive or motivation, and (3) flattened affect. Unlike schizophrenia, individuals with autism do not exhibit hallucinations or delusions. Unlike acute–chronic schizophrenia, chronic schizophrenia and autism do not involve periods of remission. Also schizophrenia generally appears later in life than autism. Table 3.1 briefly summarizes the similarities and differences in acute–chronic and chronic–chronic forms of schizophrenia and adult autism. For illustration purposes, acute schizophrenia has also been included in the table. In the discussion of etiology and population frequency that follows, the reader may find it useful to refer to this table.

ETIOLOGY
Chronic Schizophrenia

Evidence collected to date suggests that transmission of chronic schizophrenia involves genetic inheritance (Gottesman & Shields, 1982). Exactly what is inherited and how this material attains phenotypic expression, however, remains unclear. Early studies conducted in Europe and the United States in the first half of the 20th century concluded that genetics contributed substantially to the expression of schizophrenia (e.g., Rudin, 1916; Essen-Moller, 1941; Kallman, 1946). The results of many of these studies must be considered suspect because blind raters, precise diagnostic criteria, and control for the influence of environmental factors were infrequently used. Later studies have used improved designs and constitute more definitive support for the role of genetics in schizophrenia. Most of these studies have employed criteria for schizophrenia that encompass both what we have described as acute–chronic as well as chronic–chronic schizophrenia. They can be classified into three groups: (1) family studies,

Table 3.1 Similarities and Differences in Various Types of Schizophrenia and Autism

Characteristics	Acute schizophrenia	Acute-chronic schizophrenia	Chronic-chronic schizophrenia	Adult autism
Course	Symptoms may appear in either childhood or adulthood. After a single episode there is apparently complete remission.	Symptoms may appear in either childhood or adulthood. After initial deterioration, recovery of premorbid levels of functioning occurs. Symptoms of schizophrenia reappear on periodic basis through out life of individual.	Symptoms may appear in either childhood or adulthood. Usually age of onset is earlier than for acute-chronic form. Symptoms persist throughout life of individual. Unable to function effectively, the individual requires hospitalization or closely supervised care until death.	Symptoms are evident in early childhood and persist throughout life of individual. Severity of impairment requires hospitalization or closely supervised care throughout life.
Negative symptoms[a]	If present during episode, less prominent compared to positive symptoms.	If present during episodes, less prominent compared to positive symptoms.	Present	Present
Positive symptoms[b]	Present during episode.	Present during episode.	May be present during early course of disorder but eventually less salient than negative symptoms.	Not present.

[a] Lack of responsiveness to others, lack of drive or motivation, flattened affect.
[b] Hallucinations, delusions, loosening of thought associations.

(2) twin studies, and (3) adoption studies (Faraone & Tsuang, 1985; Gottesman & Shields, 1982).

Family studies have involved comparisons of frequency of schizophrenia in the families of schizophrenic subjects with frequencies in the families of appropriate control subjects. The greater the genetic overlap between the schizophrenic subject and a family member, the greater the frequency with which schizophrenia would be expected if transmission is genetic. At present the data is consistent with this pattern (Slater & Cowie, 1971; Tsuang & Vandermey, 1980; Zerbin-Rudin, 1972). Whereas the risk in the general population is approximately 0.86%, the risk for an identical twin is 57.7%. A fraternal twin of the same sex runs a risk of 12%; a parent, 4.4%; and a first cousin, 2.9% (Tsuang & Vandermey, 1980).

Twin studies compare the concordance between monozygotic (MZ) twins with that of dizygotic (DZ) twins of the same sex. In such a comparison major sources of environmental influence—family environment, time of birth, and sex of child—are better controlled for than in other family comparisons. Gottesman and Shield's (1982) review of recent studies conducted in Scandinavia, England, and the United States concluded that concordance in MZ pairs was 46% and in DZ pairs 14%. They also proposed that more severe schizophrenic disorders, such as hebephrenia and catatania, may produce higher concordance rates, a suggestion made by Luxenberger and Kallman, two of the earliest researchers in the area.

Family and twin studies do not constitute definitive proof of a genetic etiology of schizophrenia because they do not necessarily exclude the influence of environmental factors. Individuals raised in the same family are subject to environments of greater similarity relative to the population at large. Higher concordance for schizophrenia in MZ pairs than in DZ pairs, for instance, may be due to the fact that the former group is treated more similarly. Adoption studies that look at the frequency (compared with controls) with which schizophrenia is found in children of schizophrenic parents, when the children are taken from the parents shortly after birth, represents a stronger test of genetic transmission. Heston (1966) conducted one of the earliest studies of this sort. He found that of 47 children born to chronic schizophrenic mothers, 16.6% eventually became schizophrenic. None of the 50 children born to control mothers, on the other hand, developed schizophrenia. A series of more extensive studies has been conducted in Denmark by a group of American and Danish researchers (Rosenthal et al., 1968; Wender, Rosenthal, Kety, Schulsinger, & Welner, 1974). Wender et al. (1974) reported that 18.8% of 69 adopted children of schizophrenic parents were found to be either "probable" or "doubtful" schizophrenics, compared to 10.1% of 79 adopted children of normal parents. This study also compared children who were born to normal parents and were adopted by schizophrenic individuals to children who were born to schizophrenic parents and later adopted by normal individuals. In this case, too, children born to schizophrenic parents subsequently became schizophrenic with greater frequency then those born to normal parents—18.8% and 10.7%, respectively. This difference, however, was not statistically significant. Wender et al. (1974) noted that the difference might have been more substantial with the use of larger numbers of subjects and more careful psychiatric diagnoses.

Although it appears that transmission of schizophrenia involves genetic inheritance, this inheritance cannot totally account for the initial development or later exacerbation and remission of this disorder. This factor is immediately evident in the twin-study data reviewed by Gottesman and Shields (1982). If schizophrenia were purely a matter of genetic inheritance, we would expect 100%, not 46%, concordance among MZ twins. Moreover, a number of environmental stressors as different as obstetric complications (Parnas et al., 1982), viruses (Machon, Mednick, & Schulsinger, 1983), family interaction patterns (Brown, Birley & Wing, 1972; Brown, Bone, Dalison, & Wing, 1966) and stressful life events (Brown & Birley, 1968) have been found to correlate with the appearance and exacerbation of symptoms. The research conducted in England by Brown and his associates, for instance, has demonstrated that the number of comments indicating criticism, hostility, and/or emotional overinvolvement (behavior Brown has called "expressed emotion") made by relatives of patients at the time of admission can be a reliable index of the probability of subsequent relapses. In a typical study, Brown, Birley, and Wing (1972) found that 58% of schizophrenic patients with relatives rated high in expressed emotion relapsed within 9 months of discharge, compared to 16% of schizophrenic patients with relatives rated low in expressed emotion.

In light of this additional evidence concerning the role of genetic, physiological, and psychogenic stressors in schizophrenia, an inter-active model that incorporates both genetic and environmental fac-tors appears most suitable. One of the earliest and most influential of such models is Meehl's diathesis—stressor model (Meehl, 1962). Meehl proposed that the development of schizophrenia involves several processes. First, the individual must inherit a neural inter-grative defect, which Meehl called schizotaxia. The phenotypic expression of schizotaxia he termed the schizotype. If the schizotypal individual has the good fortune to live in a social environment that generates little stress and if he or she also inherits resistance to stress and anxiety, Meehl proposed that this individual will never exhibit symptoms of schizophrenia. The individual who does not inherit resistance to stress and has the misfortune to live in an environ-ment that generates considerable anxiety will, however, eventually develop schizophrenia. Meehl proposed that a schizophrenogenic mother probably was the most important factor in causing the decompensation of a schizotype into a schizophrenic individual. A person who did not inherit schizotaxia, in contrast, could never become a schizotype or develop schizophrenia. In response to environmental stressors this person could develop only a neurotic or character disorder. In short, according to Meehl's theory, the per-son who develops schizophrenia must (1) inherit through genetic transmission a nervous system vulnerable to malfunction under stress, so producing the tangential thought associations characteristic of schizophrenia, and (2) live in an environment stressful enough to precipitate the expression of the neurological defect. The research on expressed emotion provides an example of just how genetic inheritance and environmental stressors might interact to produce initial decompensation and later relapses. The schizotype who has the misfortune to live in a home where he or she is subject to a high level of expressed emotion will eventually decompensate.

The number of studies reporting physiological differences between schizophrenic and other populations continues to grow. What remains to be seen is to what extent these differences are replicated in future studies and actually relate to the disorder's etiology and fundamental properties. Carlton and Manowitz (1983) discussed this issue with respect to evidence concerning the role of dopamine in schizophrenia. The "dopamine hypothesis" of schizophrenia has come to enjoy considerable popularity (Carlton & Manowitz, 1984).

According to this hypothesis, schizophrenia is caused by overactivity of mesolimbic and mesocortical dopaminergic pathways from the ventral tegmental area to the neocortex, limbic cortex, and basal forebrain regions. Most researchers today believe that the dysfunction involved is one of hypersensitive postsynaptic dopamine receptors (Carlson, 1986). Drugs such as chlorpromazine and haloperidol, which alleviate many symptoms of schizophrenia, appear to act by blocking dopamine molecules from attaching to dopamine receptors (Carlson, 1986). Carlton and Manowitz (1983) argued that support for the dopamine hypothesis was still equivocal in nature. They noted that neuroleptics' affinity for competing with dopamine did not always correlate highly with clinical potency (e.g., Creese, Burt, & Snyder, 1976). Changes in receptor sites found in postmortem examinations of deceased schizophrenic individuals, Carlton and Manowitz additionally argued, may reflect the action of previously administered medication and not the actual disorder. Moreover, these sites of increased receptors may not be functionally relevant to the symptoms of schizophrenia.

The relevance of dopamine to some symptoms of chronic schizophrenia has been challenged within the last few years. Crow (1980) has proposed that schizophrenia can be separated into Type I and Type II classes. In Type I schizophrenia, Crow argues, positive symptoms related to disturbance in dopaminergic pathways are exhibited. In Type II schizophrenia predominantly negative symptoms, which may involve structural damage to the brain independent of dopaminergic activity, are exhibited. Type I schizophrenia may precede or coexist with Type II. Crow's two types represent two other dimensions, in addition to the temporal dimension Matson (1985) suggested, a method by which chronic schizophrenia cases can be classified—the extent of positive (Type I) and negative (Type II) symptoms. To date, a number of studies have supported Crow's thesis. Using computerized axial tomographic scans, Johnstone, Crow, Frith, Husband, and Kreel (1976) found that chronic institutionalized schizophrenic patients had significantly larger ventricles than did age-matched controls. Larger ventricles were also correlated with poorer cognitive functions. Johnstone et al. (1978) found a similar inverse relationship between ventricle size and cognitive function, as well as a negative correlation between cognitive function and negative symptoms. However, Williams, Revely,

Kolaskowska, Ardern, and Mandelbrote (1985), it should be noted did not find significant relationships between ventricle size and illness duration, cognitive deficit, or clinical symptoms.

Johnstone, Crow, Frith, Carney, and Price (1978) demonstrated that the therapeutic effect of alpha-flupenthioxe alleviated positive but not negative symptoms of schizophrenia. A similar effect was obtained by Angrist, Rotrosen, and Gershon (1980) using haloperidol. Angrist et al. (1980) also reported that negative symptoms were largely unaffected by administration of amphetamine, in contrast to the effects they observed on positive symptoms.

In summary, the evidence available to date suggests that development of chronic schizophrenia is the product of a number of factors. First of all, the results of a number of studies suggest that susceptibility to schizophrenia is transmitted genetically. The distribution of schizophrenia, however, is such that its expression cannot be based on genetic inheritance alone. Therefore, environmental factors in the form of stress-inducing environments, seem to be a second crucial class of etiological factors. Exactly what is transmitted by genetic inheritance is still unknown. The success of psychotropic drugs that reduce dopamine levels in the brain in controlling symptoms has been taken as evidence that schizophrenia involves excess production of dopamine. The matter is, however, by no means settled. It has been recently suggested that chronic schizophrenia may in fact involve two separate syndromes, one responsible for hallucinations and delusions and one responsible for decreased motivation and withdrawal.

Adult Autism

Many of the early hypotheses concerning the origins of autism were psychosocial in nature. Leo Kanner, who first identified the disorder, vacillated for years between belief in an organic explanation for infantile autism and one centering around pathogenic parental behaviors (Kanner, 1943; cited by Coleman & Gillberg, 1985). Psychoanalytic theorists, such as Mahler (1952) and Bettelheim (1967), insisted that autism was produced by inadequate emotional ties between the child and its mother. Bettelheim (1967) went so far as to attribute the origins of autism to parental pathology, specifically an overpossessive mother who thwarted her child's exploratory behavior (cited by Fein,

Pennington, Markowitz, Braverman, & Waterhouse, 1986). Psychosocial models, however, fell into disfavor in the 1960s. Rimland (1964),
in a landmark work, pointed out many deficiencies in their theoretical approach and proposed a physiological explanation as an
alternative.

The viability of a psychogenic explanation for autism has continued to diminish with time because of lack of confirmatory data
(McAdoo & DeMyer, 1977). DeMyer et al. (1972) compared parents
of autistic children to parents of both normal and brain-damaged,
emotionally immature children. They found no evidence that parents of autistic children were deficient in providing their children
with stimulation or affection. DeMyer et al. (1972) reported that,
in fact, of all three groups of parents, parents of the brain-damaged
children provided the least amount of stimulation, affection, and
physical freedom. Cox, Rutter, Newman, and Bartak (1975) compared mothers of autistic children with normal nonverbal intelligence quotients (i.e., IQs) to mothers of children with severed receptive language disorders. No significant differences in display of
affection or sociability were obtained. Cantwell, Baker, and Rutter
(1977) compared the family interaction patterns of autistic children
with those of dysphasic children. They reported that autistic and
dysphasic children experienced similar amounts of attention from
their families. McAdoo and DeMyer (1978) found that parents of
autistic children produced Minnesota Multiphasic Personality Inventory (MMPI) profiles similar to those of parents whose children
exhibited a range of psychological problems. Only between the two
groups of mothers were any significant differences in average profile obtained, and these occurred for only two scales—Social Introver-
sion (SI) and Correction (K) scales. Mothers of the children who
were not autistic admitted to greater discomfort in social and interpersonal situations, a direct contrast to the once generally accepted
stereotype of the mother of an autistic child as being emotionally
or socially deficient. K scale differences were more ambiguous in
nature. Mothers of autistic children scored higher on this scale. As
McAdoo and DeMyer (1978) pointed out, this could mean (1) the
mothers of autistic children were less apt to admit to problems,
and/or (2) the mothers of nonautistic children had lower self-esteem.
This particular issue remains unsettled. McAdoo and DeMyer (1977)
reviewed many of these studies on parents of autistic children and

concluded that these parents (1) show no more signs of psychological disturbance than do parents of children with nonpsychotic organic disorders or nonpsychotic emotional disorders, (2) exhibit significantly less psychopathology than do parents who are patients in psychiatric outpatient clinics, and (3) display no specific deficits in giving nurturance and stimulation to their children. McAdoo and DeMyer (1977) noted that parents of autistic children often exhibit uncertainty and confusion with regard to the care of their children, but they proposed that these tendencies were understandable in light of the considerable stress engendered by raising autistic children.

Whereas psychosocial models of autism have lost popularity, genetic inheritance has become an increasingly viable explanation within the last 10 years. Folstein and Rutter (1977) looked at concordance rates in 10 monozygotic (MZ) twin pairs and 11 dizygotic (DZ) some sex pairs of which at least one child had been diagnosed as autistic. Four of 11 MZ twins were concordant for autism in contrast to 0 of 10 DZ pairs. Folstein and Rutter also determined concordance among twins for cognitive impairment (i.e., delayed speech, verbal intelligence quotient or social quotient less than or equal to 70, grossly abnormal articulation persisting to age 5 or older, scholastic difficulties requiring special education). Nine of 11 MZ twins proved concordant for cognitive impairment (usually involving language), whereas only 1 of 10 DZ twins was concordant. Ritvo, Freeman, Mason-Brothers, Mo, and Ritvo (1985) located autistic twins through the UCLA outpatient department, referrals, and advertisements in the "Advocate," the newsletter of the National Society of Autistic Children (NSAC). In their study, 22 of 23 MZ pairs and 4 of 17 DZ pairs proved concordant for autism as defined by NSAC and DSM-III criteria. Siblings of autistic individuals may be 50 to 100 times more likely than the average person to exhibit autism (Coleman & Gillberg, 1985). Folstein and Rutter (1977) reported a case of autism in 1 of 33336 siblings (2.8%) of the twins they studied and also severe delays in acquisition of spoken language in 3 of 21 families (14%). They proposed that autism might be genetically linked to a broader range of cognitive disorders, mostly related to delays or disorders in language acquisition. A similar finding was reported by Ritvo et al. (1985). In this study, families of autistic twins gave reports of developmental language problems in 10.7%

of twin siblings (8/78). Epidemiological evidence of this sort, of course, represents only an initial step toward understanding the contribution of genetics to autism, but some additional clues have been accumulating. Gillberg (1983a), for instance, reported the evidence of Fragile X chromosomal abnormality in a set of triplets concordant for infantile autism. The occasional appearance of autistic symptoms in individuals who suffer from phenylketonuria (PKU) indicates that autism could involve interaction between environmental stressors and genetic inheritance (Friedman, 1969; Knobloch & Pasamanick, 1975). These initial findings, based on only a subset of cases, however, admittedly do not tell us whether genetic or environmental stressors alone can induce autism.

A number of studies have in fact found autism to be associated with prenatal and perinatal physical stressors. Torrey, Hersh, and McCabe (1975), for example, found increased levels of midtrimester bleeding in mothers who produced autistic children; and Desmond et al. (1967) and Chess, Korn, and Fernandez (1971) noted symptoms of autism in children exposed to rubella viruses. Additionally, Folstein and Rutter (1977) reported that in 12 of 17 cases of twins discordant for autism, the autistic twin was subjected to biological stress, usually during the perinatal period (e..g., neonatal convulsions, narrow umbilical cord, severed febrile illness). It has been suggested that children who develop autism have deficient immune systems that leave them vulnerable to viruses and other stressors. Stubbs, Ritvo, and Mason-Brothers (1985) noted that parents of autistic children more often shared leukocyte antigens than did control parents. Since offspring of individuals with different immunogenetic backgrounds appear to fare better than those with similar backgrounds, differences at leukocyte antigen sites between parents may stimulate blocking antibodies that protect the fetus and its placenta (Stubbs, Ritvo & Mason-Brothers, 1985). Similarity in leukocyte antigens, Stubbs and his associates proposed, could lead the mother's immune system to attack the entire fetoplacental unit, producing abortion, or attack selected tissue (such as in the nervous system) producing autism.

Although scientists have uncovered a number of promising leads with respect to causes, they do not yet understand what physiological factors are involved in autism. Ornitz (1985) proposed that neurophysiological theories for autism generally take one of two forms. One hypothesis is that autism involves abnormal functioning in the telencephalic region of the brain, in particular the mesolimbic cortex (i.e., temporal lobes and neostriatum). The alternative hypothesis that has gained support is that autism involves dysfunction of the brainstem and diencephalon, in particular the pontine and midbrain reticular formation, substantia nigra, and thalamic nuclei (Ornitz, 1985). The strongest evidence with respect to a telencephalic explanation of autism has come from electroencephalogram (EEG) and evoked potential studies. EEG recordings obtained from some autistic subjects suggest that the disorder may involve abnormal cerebral lateralization (Dawson, Warrenburg, & Fuller, 1982; Small, 1975). Diminished evoked potentials, on the other hand, have been obtained from a small number of subjects (Niwa, Ohta, & Yamazaki, 1983; Novick, Vaughn, Kurtzberg, & Simon, 1980). The brainstem-diencephalic hypothesis has stimulated a search for dysfunctions of physiological and neurological process in these regions. Some researchers have looked at cardiovascular-respiration responses that originate in the brainstem. Cardiac arrhythmia (Hutt, Forrest, & Richer, 1975) and elevation in both peripheral blood flow (Cohen & Johnson, 1977) and heart rate (Kootz & Cohen, 1981) have all been reported in autistic subjects. Vestibular reflexes have been the focus of research by Ornitz (1985), who has proposed that perseveration of nystagmus responses in autistic individuals might reflect abnormal reverberation of neuronal circuits in the brainstem reticular formation. Ornitz (1985) suggested that the telencephalic and brainstem findings might be integrated by conceiving of autism as involving dysfunction of brainstem structures and cortex structures, which are in turn influenced by the brainstem. Coleman and Gillberg (1985) similarly proposed that autism is the product of abnormally functioning dopamine pathways from the brainstem to the cortex. The malfunction of these pathways in the developing child, Coleman and Gillberg suggested, could hinder the development of the mesolimbic and striatal areas through lack of sensory input necessary to stimulate development of these regions during childhood.

What distinguishes those who exhibit various stages of remission from those with more intractable forms of autism remains unclear. Extent of mental retardation appears to be the most reliable prognostic indicator (e.g., DeMyer et al., 1973; Rutter, 1970). Children who are more severely retarded tend to show less substantial remission of symptoms. The most obvious explanation for this is that a higher level of mental retardation is indicative of more extensive brain damage overall. T he reversibility of symptoms after early childhood may in some cases reflect either (1) gradual desensitization to the environment by adventitious or systematic means, (2) development of brain structures that compensate for neurological deficits, or (3) some combination of these two factors. At this point, however, the alternatives are merely speculative. Further breakthroughs in research on the neurological basis of autism and the relationship between environmental history and extent of remission need to occur before scientists can differentiate between the causes of chronic or irreversible forms of autism as opposed to more limited forms.

In conclusion, a lack of evidence for psychosocial causes and a growing amount of evidence for physiological causes of autism have led psychologists to favor physiological explanations for the etiology of autism. To date no single physiological correlate or physical trauma has been reliably associated with this disorder. These results suggest that autism might possibly arise from traumas to which the developing nervous system is vulnerable. Recent papers indicate that autism may be a genetic disorder. Whether genetic inheritance represents a separate pathway for producing autism or produces a nervous system vulnerable to the physical stressors mentioned earlier remains to be seen. Cases that persist largely unchanged beyond childhood years are differentially associated with mental retardation and may represent more severe forms of neurological damage. Little is known, however.

General Summary

At this time, chronic forms of schizophrenia and adult autism both appear to involve a combination of genetic and environmental factors. In the case of schizophrenia, the symptoms usually become evident first in early adulthood, in contrast to autism, which is apparent in early childhood and may actually show signs of remission in adolescence and adulthood. The symptoms of schizophrenia may fluctuate in severity and nature, and they appear to be exacerbated by stress. Autism's symptoms are more stable in course. The development of autism may involve irreversible damage to the developing nervous system that produces permanent impairment rather than vulnerability to malfunction under conditions of stress.

The dopamine hypothesis, which posits excessive action of dopamine or related receptors in neurons running from the tegmental region to limbic and cortex regions, has become a popular model for schizophrenia. Today some feel that the dopamine hypothesis may explain only positive symptoms of schizophrenia (e.g., hallucinations and delusions). Negative symptoms (e.g., withdrawal, diminished affect), which are more evident in chronic than in acute cases of schizophrenia, may arise instead from brain atrophy. This might explain the resistance of many symptoms of chronic schizophrenia to pharmacological treatment and other interventions.

Progress in autism research lags behind that for schizophrenia with regard to understanding the causes of permanent and time-limited forms of these disorders. Indices of prognosis, such as intelligence level and severity of symptoms, are among the only reliable clues scientists presently have for explaining variations in autism. Much interest has focused on explaining autism as a malfunction of the brain in either the telencephalic or brainstem area, and several recent theories have sought to integrate these two general models. Much further research is needed, however. In the meantime, the reader may wish to consult more extensive discussions of the etiology of schizophrenia and autism such as those presented by Cutting (1985) and Coleman and Gillberg (1985).

INCIDENCE/PREVALENCE

In the previous section, explanations and evidence concerning the development of chronic schizophrenia and adult autism were covered. This section reviews research pertaining to the frequency with which both of these conditions are found. This information is important for more than mere record keeping or curiosity's sake. Knowledge concerning the frequency of these disorders in different populations at different times aids researchers in their search for precipitating factors. For example, higher frequency of a disorder in women may suggest that unique aspects of either the female's genetic makeup or environmental stressors to which she is typically subjected may make her more susceptible to developing the disorder.

A disorder that occurs with greater frequency in some countries than in others suggests that differences in genotypes or environment may be responsible and should be the focus of research. Moreover, knowledge concerning the population distribution of disorders allows researchers and clinicians to identify groups and individuals at risk and implement early interventions. Measures of the distribution of disorders in various populations also permits evaluation of the successes and failures of different interventions.

The first part of this section on incidence and prevalence of chronic schizophrenia and adult autism discusses different ways in which population frequency of disorders can be expressed. There are subtle but important differences between the measures used to describe frequency. Depending on the question one is concerned with, one may be more interested in measures of new cases or, alternatively, the prevalence of a disorder once it has appeared. Following this discussion of definitions, data on population frequencies of chronic schizophrenia and adult autism are presented.

Definitions

There are several ways to describe the frequency of a disorder in a particular population. The two most frequently used measures are incidence and prevalence. Incidence refers to the number of new cases of the disorder in question that develop within a specified time period. This index is most commonly expressed as the number of new cases per 100,000 or 1,000,000 of the general population within a given year. Prevalence is the total number of persons now alive who have previously been or are presently afflicted with the disorder. This index is usually expressed as a rate per 1,000 of either the entire population or the population in the age group at risk. Two common ways of expressing prevalence are point prevalence over a year's time. Morbidity risk is a more refined measure of population frequency. This index corrects for the the age of the sample and permits more precise comparison across groups by indicating the probability of contracting a disorder for any individual who lives long enough to be at risk for developing it. Schizophrenia, for example, generally does not develop until an individual attains early adulthood and then may appear at any time during the next several decades. It therefore can be useful to revise population estimates of its frequency to correct for the fact that a portion of the population may not become schizophrenic because they die before they are no longer at risk (Gottesman & Shields, 1982).

Chronic Schizophrenia

Estimates of the incidence and prevalence of schizophrenia vary quite substantially. To what extent these differences across locales and time periods reflect true variation remains uncertain. One explanation is that the differences are merely products of sampling error or differences in diagnostic criteria and/or data collection. Leff (1977), for instance, demonstrated that differences in the frequency with which schizophrenia had traditionally been reported in the United Kingdom and the United States was largely due to differences in diagnostic practices. The study involved comparing the proportion of various diagnostic classifications applied by psychiatrists working at London and New York psychiatric hospitals to that applied by a team of psychiatrists who employed the Present State Examination (PSE) and the eighth edition of the *International Classification of Diseases* (ICD-8). American psychiatrists diagnosed schizophrenia in 61.5% of their hospital sample; English psychiatrists, in 35.1%. Psychiatrists using the same instrument and criteria, however, diagnosed similar proportions of their samples as schizophrenic—29.2% in New York, 33.9% in London. Data related to the numbers of chronic schizophrenic patients may be distorted by yet other means. For example, data collected during the International Pilot Study of Schizophrenia (IPSS) project suggested that the prognosis for schizophrenia in some Third World countries might be better than in some Western countries. Fifty-eight percent of all schizophrenic patients from the Ibadan, India, center had completely recovered 2 years later, in contrast to only 6% of all patients from the Aarhus, Denmark, center (WHO, 1979). One explanation for this is that Third World countries provide more effective assistance to schizophrenic patients. On the other hand, since psychologists at different centers were allowed to make diagnoses according to their own criteria for schizophrenia, it might be that what is called schizophrenia in Third World countries includes less-disturbed individuals than elsewhere. Another issue is representativeness. In Third World countries schizophrenic persons who were more severely and/or chronically disturbed may have been less likely to obtain treatment.

Zerbin-Rudin (1972) has estimated that the median morbidity risk of schizophrenia in the general population is 0.85% based on pooled data from several countries. Estimates of inception rate range from 11 per 100,000 up to 72 per 100,000, and 1-year prevalence rate estimates generally range from 200 to 400 per 100,000 (Cooper, 1978). Schizophrenia appears to afflict men and women with equal frequency, although the mean age of onset in women, 34, is higher than that for men, 27 (Zigler & Levine, 1981). The proportion of schizophrenic patients who remain continuously hospitalized or severely impaired psychiatrically and socially appears to have declined since the time of Kraepelin. Cutting (1985), in a brief survey of earlier outcome studies, noted that 83% of Kraepelin's patients remained severely impaired once stricken, whereas Huber, Gross, Schuttler, and Linz (1980) reported a similar course for only 35% of the patients in their study. However, the number who still require at least periodic hospitalization has not changed considerably since that time (Cutting, 1985). Wing (1982) estimated that approximately two thirds of all schizophrenic patients alternate between acute psychotic phases and remission.

Estimating the percentage of schizophrenic persons who have chronic forms of the disorder is a matter of judgment concerning outcome and symptoms at follow-up. As Manfred Bleuler (1978) rightfully pointed out, there are no definitive guidelines for assessing outcomes, so there could never be an ideal proband for assessment purposes. One must arbitrarily decide what criteria to use and when to carry out assessment, as well as what population of schizophrenic persons to assess. Bleuler proposed that the only reasonable solution was to study the greatest possible number of different types of schizophrenia and compare outcomes. Bleuler's thinking has yet to catch on in the research community, but some preliminary conclusions concerning frequency of chronic schizophrenia can be made.

Outcome and prognosis studies suggest that 20 to 30% of all schizophrenic cases exhibit poor or minimal recovery; another 50% of cases remain active to some extent. Some of the best outcome studies have been conducted in the United Kingdom and Europe, where socialized medical facilities and less mobile populations make such studies easier to conduct than in the United States. Ciompi (1980) reported on the outcome of 289 of an original pool of 1,642 Swiss patients diagnosed according to Bleulerian criteria. Follow-up occurred an average of approximately 37 years after first hospitalization. Ciompi reported that 10% of the patients never had a recurrence of a psychotic episode following initial treatment. A total of 27% of the cases were in remission. Forty-six percent showed minor or intermediate residual effects. This latter group would appear to correspond to Matson's acute–chronic type, exhibiting alternating periods of psychosis and remission. Eighteen percent were severe chronic cases. This portion of Ciompi's sample would include Matson's chronic–chronic schizophrenic type: their symptoms never show significant remission. Ciompi noted that the difficulty in locating patients for follow-up may have biased the study toward recording favorable outcomes. Bleuler (1978) reported outcomes for 208 schizophrenic patients classified as severe, moderate-severe, mild, and recovered. Outcome was reported only for those who had maintained a level of functioning that was stable for at least 5 years. Severe cases were described by Bleuler as unable even to carry on comprehensible conversations or function unsupervised. These comprised 24% of his group and are analogous to Matson's chronic–chronic group. Moderately severe cases resembled severe cases in many respects but exhibited periodic states of relative "normality" and were able to communicate. These comprised another 24% of Bleuler's group. A further 33% were rated by Bleuler as mildly disturbed. These individuals could carry on relatively normal conversations if unrelated to delusional and hallucinatory themes. These latter two groups appear to consist of acute–chronic schizophrenic cases. Bleuler judged the remaining 20% as recovered.

Similar results have been obtained in shorter-term follow-up reports. A recent study by Kolakowska et al. (1985) reported on the progress of 77 patients drawn from an original subject pool of 440 in the Oxford (England) Psychiatric Register. Patients in this group had been diagnosed as schizophrenic or schizoaffective according to Spitzer and Endicott's Research Diagnostic Criteria. Psychiatric outcome was categorized as either poor, intermediate, or good. Kolakowska et al. (1985) defined poor outcome as the existence of persistent hallucinations or delusions, moderate or severe negative symptoms, and social isolation. Twenty-five percent of their patients fell into this category. According to Matson's terminology, these would be chronic–chronic schizophrenic cases. Forty-one percent were rated as having achieved an intermediate level of outcome—residual positive or negative symptoms with some impairment of social functioning (i.e., acute–chronic schizophrenia under Matson's classification scheme). Remaining patients (34%) were rated as having achieved a good outcome—absence of delusions, hallucinations, and negative symptoms, with social functioning having recovered to approximately premorbid levels. A second study by Prudo and Blum (1987) reports results of a 5-year follow-up for English schizophrenic subjects in the IPSS survey. Psychiatrists originally assigned diagnoses using the PSE, ICD-8 criteria, and the CATEGO diagnostic program. Prudo and Blum were later able to obtain outcome data on 88 of a total of 100 patients. Classification was on the basis of four mutually exclusive categories: (1) no further episodes, (2) further episodes of less than 1 year's total duration, (3) episodes of total duration between 1 and 2-1/2 years, and (4) episodes of total duration greater than 2-1/2 years. Nineteen percent of the patients never had an additional episode. The remaining 81% suffered various levels of chronicity—30% in class 2, 10% in class 3, and 41% in class 4. Some of the last group would include what we would characterize as chronic–chronic schizophrenia. Acute–chronic schizophrenia would characterize individuals assigned to classes 2 and 3 and some individuals in class 4. Other studies, such as those by Strauss, Sirotkin, and Grisell (1974) and Kendler, Gruenberg, and Tsuang (1984), suggest that schizophrenic patients with catatonic and undifferentiated features are likely to have poorer prognoses than those with paranoid symptoms.

Adult Autism

Our present knowledge of the frequency of long-term autistic cases comes from only a handful of studies. One further drawback is that these studies have tracked their subjects only into early adulthood. It is generally agreed that the prognosis for the great majority of autistic individuals is poor. The type and intensity of impairments, as well as improvements, exhibited later in life are, however, sorely in need of further research.

All studies that we were able to find reported the frequency of autism in terms of population prevalence. Lotter (1966) conducted the earliest major epidemiological study of autism. This survey covered all children between the ages of 8 and 10 living in the county of Middlesex, England, on January 1, 1964. Lotter identified cases using the criteria of Creak et al. (1961), rating the presence or absence of 24 behaviors divided into five categories, including (1) disturbances in speech (e.g., echolalia), (2) social behavior (e.g., aloof and distant), (3) movement (e.g., toe walking), (4) auditory behavior (e.g., behaves as if deaf), and (5) ritualistic behavior (e.g., spinning objects). Lotter assigned a score from 0 (absent) to 2 (markedly present) for each behavior and classified as autistic all children scoring 32 or more. This produced a total of 32 autistic cases out of a total of 76,388 children. Lotter reported "nuclear autism" (i.e., combination of severe behavior deficiency and stereotypy) prevalent in 15 children (i.e., 2/10,000) and "non-nuclear autism" (i.e., either severe social behavior deficiency or stereotypy) in 17 children (i.e., 2.5/10,000). Approximately 69% of the autistic children had IQs below 55. Wing and Gould (1979) conducted an epidemiological survey of Camberwell, England, using local psychiatric and mental retardation service records to locate children under 15 years of age. In this study children classified as autistic had to exhibit absent or impaired social interaction, language, and stereotypes. Wing and Gould found a point prevalence rate of 4.9 per 10,000 with a point rate of 21.2 per 10,000 for social interaction impairment in general. Gillberg (1984b) found a lower prevalence rate—2 per 10,000—in an epidemiological study in Sweden using referrals from local physicians and psychiatrists. In this particular study, Gillberg used Rutter's 1978 criteria for diagnosis. Several years later, Gillberg repeated the survey (Steffenburg & Gillberg, 1986), using the same questionnaire screening procedure to locate cases and DSM-III criteria for diagnostic purposes. The results of this survey conformed more closely to those of Wing and Gould—4.7 per 10,000 children, with a 5.7:1 ratio of male to female cases. Male cases outnumber female cases overall, but the ratio appears closer at lower intellectual levels. Wing (1981), in a study of 74 children, found that the ratio of boys to girls ranged from 1.1:1 for those with an IQ below 19 to 14.2:1 for those with an IQ above 50. Gillberg (1984b) noted a similar trend. Lord and Schopler (1985) reported that more autistic females had IQs at or below 34 than above. It is estimated that between 67 and 81% of all autistic individuals are mentally retarded (Coleman & Gillberg, 1985). As many as 50% may fail to acquire speech (Rutter, 1966).

Several studies indicate that as many as 10 to 30% of the autistic population may exhibit deterioration in adolescence (Gillberg, 1984a; Rutter, 1970). Only 5 to 17% of the reported cases ever manage to function socially at near-normal levels, with approximately 39 to 54% eventually ending up in institutions (Lotter, 1978). Eisenberg (1956), in the earliest follow-up study, reported some of the most pessimistic figures. Seventy-three percent of his 63 cases (average age, 15 years) were found to be still autistic or severely impaired upon follow-up averaging 9 years. Thirty-four lived in full-time residential settings. Only 3 of 63 had managed to achieve "good" adjustment (i.e., functioning well at academic and social levels and accepted by peers, even if remaining a somewhat odd person) by the time of Eisenberg's follow-up examination. Thirty of 31 individuals who could not communicate to any extent by the age of five were still severely impaired, in contrast to 16 of 32 individuals who had some communication skills by that time. Creak (1963) reported outcome for 100 cases of "childhood psychosis" (e.g., gross social deficits, pathological preoccupation with certain objects, sustained resistance to change, language deficits, erotic intellectual impairments). Upon follow-up 5 to 15 years later, 43% were institutionalized, 40% lived at home, and 17% were rated as significantly improved (i.e., attending ordinary schools, coping with ordinary curricula or working). Rutter and his colleagues (Rutter et al, 1967; Rutter & Lockyer, 1967) looked at outcomes for children diagnosed for "infantile psychosis" (i.e., childhood psychosis, childhood schizophrenia, infantile autism). Fifty-seven of the 63 children exhibited symptoms of autism defined as (1) marked aloofness, (2) apparent lack of interest in people, (3) minimal facial expression, and (4) minimal expression of emotion. When reexamined, 16 showed no change in autistic symptoms, 6 were worse, 24 had improved, and 9 had no signs of autism (2 cases had unknown course). At follow-up, 30 of the entire group of 63 were rated as unable to lead any sort of independent existence (i.e., "very poor"). Eight of 63 were unable to lead an independent life but had achieved some social adjustment (i.e., "poor"), and 16 had made some social/educational progress but exhibited abnormal behavior or interpersonal relationships (i.e., "fair"). Eight were judged to be near normal in functioning, and 1 was rated as normal in behavior. Rutter, Greenfeld and Lockyer (1967) claimed that intelligence level, speech, severity of disorder, and amount of schooling were the best prognostic indicators.

In the United States, DeMyer and her associates (1973) conducted a follow-up for 120 autistic children with an average age of 12 and a mean follow-up of 6.1 years (minimum, 2 years). To qualify as autistic, each child had to satisfy three criteria: (1) serious emotional withdrawal, (2) noncommunicative speech or muteness, and (3) nonfunctional object use. For the purposes of analysis, DeMyer et al. (1973) divided their subjects into three groups. Twenty-one subjects were classified as high-functioning autistic persons with a mixture of communicative and noncommunicative speech as well as intellectual or perceptual motor speed near chronological age. Fifty-two subjects were moderate-functioning autistic persons with virtually no speech but at least one intellectual or perceptual motor activity near their chronological age level. Low functioning autistic individuals of which there were 47, resembled moderate-functioning autistic persons with the exception of global retardation in intellectual and perceptual-motor skills. At follow-up, 14% of the high-functioning group was residing in an institution, in contrast to 54% of the moderate group and 42% of the low-functioning group. Thirty-four percent of the moderate- and 63% of the low-functioning groups were nonverbal, whereas 29% of the high-functioning group were rated normal in social skills at follow-up. Approximately 80% of both the moderate- and low-functioning groups were rated withdrawn when reexamined (i.e., behavior ranging from intermittent attention to significant others to virtual obliviousness to humans).

Lotter, (1974), in another follow-up study, looked at the development of autistic adolescents 8 years after he first identified them in an epidemiological survey (Lotter, 1966). To measure general adjustment, Lotter (1974) defined four outcome categories. "Good" outcome applied to an adolescent leading a normal or near-normal social life and functioning satisfactorily at school or work. "Fair" outcome applied to an adolescent making social and educational progress despite significant abnormalities in behavior or interpersonal relationships. "Poor" outcome applied to a severely handicapped adolescent unable to lead an independent life but considered to have made some social adjustment and to have some potential for progress. "Very poor" outcome applied to an adolescent unable to lead any sort of independent existence. By this criteria, 14% ($n = 4$) of the follow-up group were judged to have achieved "good' outcome; 24% ($n = 7$), "fair" outcome; 14% ($n = 4$), "poor" outcome; and 48% ($n = 14$), "very poor" outcome. Of 16 children over the age of 16, only 1 was employed, and 14 were hospitalized in institutions. The remainder lived at home or attended specialized schools or training programs.

Lund (1986) estimated a prevalence rate for adult autism of 3 per 10,000 mentally retarded individuals (23/77,201) based on a random sample of 302 cases drawn from records of the Danish National Service for Mental Retardation. Of the 23 autistic individuals in this study, 11 were further diagnosed as having early childhood autism. Males constituted 12 of 23 childhood autism cases and 7 of 11 early childhood autism cases. Eighteen of 23 were in long-term residential care facilities. Since Lund drew his sample from a mental retardation register, individuals functioning above the mentally retarded level were not included in the study. In contrast, a recent study by Rumsey, Rapoport, and Sceery (1985) primarily focused on high-functioning autistic adults—9 males with Wechsler Adult Intelligence Scale verbal and performance subscale scores both in the range 81 to 126. Rumsey et al. (1985) reported that none of the individuals in this group currently met the DSM-III criteria for active autism, although the majority exhibited residual symptoms. Eighty-nine percent, for example, lacked friends, and 56% exhibited flat affect. Three of five other individuals whom the investigators interviewed, however, who had verbal IQ scores below 80 and had been diagnosed as autistic as children, still met DSM-III-R criteria for autism. These authors conducted a thorough analysis of the subjects' current psychiatric condition, and it is hoped that their study will be a model for future research projects with a larger, more representative subject population.

Although many of the earlier studies are useful for establishing at least some baseline measure of prognosis, they do not give much indication of what outcome to expect for those who are exposed to highly structured, behaviorally based education programs for extended periods of time. One recent paper by Freeman, Ritvo, Needleman, and Yokota (1985), however, reported on a longitudinal study on a group of 62 children exposed to behaviorally based programs in California. The preliminary results suggest that the improvement to be expected may be modest in many respects. Freeman et al. (1985) divided their subjects into three groups: (1) those with both verbal and performance IQs below 70, and (2) those with performance IQs above 70 and verbal IQs below 70, and (3) those with both verbal and performance IQs below 70. With a mean follow-up time of 5 years (average initial age, 3 years, 10 months), only 8 of 62 children switched to groups. In addition, Freeman et al. (1985) classified children's class placement as one of four categories: (1) normal, (2) autistic, (3) language-handicapped, and (4) educationally handicapped. Only seven children changed class placement during the follow-up time. More studies are needed at this time, but the implications of the Freeman et al. study are sobering.

General Summary

Schizophrenia occurs with a greater frequency than does autism—20 to 40 per 10,000 and, 4 to 5 per 10,000 individuals, respectively. The prognosis for schizophrenia is also substantially better. Approximately 20 to 30% of all schizophrenic persons are permanently impaired by their symptoms (Matson's chronic–chronic type), and 40 to 50% experience periodic psychotic episodes (Matson's acute–chronic type). A further 20 to 30% experience complete remission (acute schizophrenia/schizophreniform disorder). Of all individuals who are diagnosed as having infantile autism, 83 to 95% remain autistic during their lifetimes and never exhibit significant remission of their symptoms. Children with infantile autism but not mentally retarded seem to be less likely to remain autistic throughout their lifetimes; however, they constitute a minority of cases. A third distinction between schizophrenia and autism with respect to population frequency is that whereas autism is found about four times more often in males than in females, schizophrenia is equally distributed among males and females. Several long-term studies of schizophrenia have followed the course of this disorder over several decades and contributed substantially to our knowledge of outcome. Unfortunately, very few studies have followed the progress of autistic persons beyond adolescence.

CONCLUSION

It is generally accepted today that schizophrenia and autism involve neurological dysfunctions. The nature of these dysfunctions still remain uncertain despite considerable research. It has been noted for many years now that the distribution of schizophrenia cases within families suggests a genetic basis for this disorder. More recent studies of autism suggest a similar process may also be at work. The course of schizophrenia appears far more variable in nature. Persons with chronic schizophrenia can exhibit periods of apparently normal behavior only to deteriorate into psychotic states characterized by thought associations, hallucinations, and delusions. In contrast, others who have chronic schizophrenia deteriorate and never return to premorbid levels of functioning. The symptoms autistic individuals exhibit appear very early in childhood and do not fluctuate in severity to the extent that symptoms of chronic schizophrenia can. Most individuals diagnosed as autistic do not show significant remission of symptoms. Past studies suggest that 83 to 95% never significantly improve. What distinguishes those who do improve from those who do not is unclear, although higher IQs and early development of language skills are associated with better prognosis. The outlook for schizophrenia is considerably better. Twenty-five percent of all schizophrenic persons deteriorate and never recover their premorbid levels of functioning: another 50% alternate between periods of apparent lucidity and psychosis. The ratio of male to female cases of autism favors males by a factor of 4. Schizophrenia appears to afflict males and females equally.

Despite the considerable number of unanswered questions that still remain, there appears to be sufficient variation in symptomatology and course to warrant the use of the constructs of chronic schizophrenia and autism. Given the numerous classification categories and definitions that have been proposed over the years, especially with regard to schizophrenia, one may understandably look askance at the introduction of yet others. In some respects, however, classification and study of homogeneous subpopulations may be very useful in the long run. What is learned may at first apply to only a small subset of cases. The tools and conceptual insights one obtains in such study, though, may eventually elucidate factors involved in a wider range of cases. Only with further research can we tell whether chronic schizophrenia and autism are useful classification categories.

Finally, with regard to the matters of course and outcome, researchers need to collect more detailed information. Details that are especially important include the environments and treatments to which individuals are exposed. Researchers need to look at the course of individual behaviors that make up autism and schizophrenia, such as hallucinations and language disorders, rather than just the course of "autism" or "schizophrenia." Knowing that 83 to 95% of all autistic cases and 20 to 30% of all schizophrenic cases presently have poor outcomes provides only limited information, especially with schizophrenia, in which many cases may take a chronic course because the affected individuals fail to follow recommended treatment or live in overly or insufficiently stimulating environments. Additionally, it would be useful to be able to compare improvements in symptomatology achieved by different types and durations of intervention programs. Researchers and clinicians alike should not view chronic psychiatric conditions as immutable disorders. Many of today's chronic cases may be acute tomorrow, given sufficient progress in our study and treatment of these individuals. The remainder of this book will address some of the emerging strategies that are likely to prove of benefit in the treatment of these conditions.

REFERENCES

American Psychiatry Association. (1987). *Diagnostic and statistical manual of mental disorders* (Third Ed. - Revised.) Washington, DC: Author.

Angrist, B., Rotrosen, J., & Gershon, S. (1980). Differential effects of amphetamine and neuroleptics on negative versus positive symptoms in schizophrenia. *Psychopharmacology, 72,* 17–19.

Bellak, L. (1948). *Dementia praecox: The past decade's work and present status: A review and evaluation.* New York: Grune & Stratton.

Bettelheim, B. (1967). *The empty fortress.* New York: Free Press.

Bleuler, E. (1930). The physiogenic and psychogenic in schizophrenia. *American Journal of Psychiatry, 10,* 203–211.

Bleuler, M. (1978). *The schizophrenic disorders* (S. M. Clemens, Trans.). New Haven, CT: Yale University Press. (Original work published 1972).

Bridge, T. P., Canon, E., & Wyatt, R. J. (1978). Burned-out schizophrenia: Evidence for age effects on schizophrenic symptomatology. *Journal of Gerontology, 33,* 835–839.

Brown, G. W., & Birley, J. L. T . (1968). Crises and life changes and the onset of schizophrenia. *Journal of Health and Social Behavior, 9,* 203–214.

Brown, G. W., Birley, J. L. T., & Wing, J. K. (1972). Influence of family
    life on the course of schizophrenic disorders: A replication. *British
    Journal of Psychiatry, 121,* 241–258.
Brown, G. W., Bone, M., Dalison, B., & Wing, J. K. (1966). *Schizophrenia and
    social care. Maudsley monograph No. 17.* London: Oxford University Press.
Cantwell, D. P., Baker, L., & Rutter. M. (1977). Families of autistic and
    dysphasic children: I. Family life and interaction patterns. *Archives
    of General Psychiatry, 36,* 682–687.
Carlson, N. R. (1986). *Physiology of behavior* (3rd ed.). Boston: Allyn &
    Bacon.
Carlton, P. L., & Manowitz, P. (1984). Dopamine and schizophrenia: An
    analysis of the theory. *Neuroscience and Biobehavioral Reviews, 8,* 137–151.
Chess, S., Korn, S. J., & Fernandez, P. B. (1971). *Psychiatric disorders of
    children with congenital rubella.* New York: Brunner Mead.
Ciompi, L. (1980). The natural history of schizophrenia in the long term.
    British Journal of Psychiatry, 136, 413–420.
Cohen, D. J., & Johnson, W. T. (1977). Cardiovascular correlates of attention
    in normal and psychiatrically disturbed children. *Archives of General
    Psychiatry, 34,* 561–567.
Coleman, M., & Gillberg, C. (1985). *The biology of the autistic syndromes.*
    New York: Praeger.
Cooper, B. (1978). Epidemiology. In J. K. Wing (Ed.), *Schizophrenia: Towards
    a new synthesis.* New York: Academic Press.
Cox, A., Rutter, M., Newman, S., & Bartak, L. (1975). A comparative study
    of infantile autism and specific developmental receptive language
    disorder: II. Parental characteristics. *British Journal of Psychiatry, 126,*
    146–159.
Creak, E. M. (1963). Childhood psychosis: A review of 100 cases. *British
    Journal of Psychiatry, 109,* 84–89.
Creese, I., Burt, D. R., & Snyder, S. H. (1976). Dopamine receptor binding
    predicts clinical and pharmacological potencies of antischizophrenic
    drugs. *Science, 192,* 481–483.
Crow, T. J. (1980). Molecular pathology of schizophrenia: More than one
    disease process? *British Medical Journal, 280*(6207), 66–68.
Cutting, J. C. (1985). *The psychology of schizophrenia.* Edinburgh: Churchill
    Livingstone.
Dawson, G., Warrenburg, S., & Fuller, P. (1982). Cerebral lateralization
    in individuals diagnosed as autistic in early childhood. *Brain Language,
    15,* 353–368.
DeMyer, M. K., Barton, S., DeMyer, W. E., Norton, J. A., Allen, J., &
    Steele, R. (1973). Prognosis in autism: A follow-up study. *Journal of
    Autism and Childhood Schizophrenia, 3,* 199–246.

DeMyer, M. K., Pontius, W., Norton, J. A., Barton, S., Allen, J., & Steele, R. (1972). Parental practices and innate activity in normal, autistic, and brain-damaged infants. *Journal of Autism and Childhood Schizophrenia, 2,* 49–66.

Desmond, M. M., Wilson, G. S., Melnick, J. L., Singer, D. B., Zion, T. E., Rudolph, A. J., Pineda, R. G., Ziai, M. H., & Blattney, R. J. (1967). Congenital rubella encephalitis. *Journal of Pediatrics, 71,* 311–331.

Eisenberg, L., (1956). The autistic child in adolescence. *American Journal of Psychiatry, 12,* 607–612.

Essen-Moller, E. (1941). Psychiatrische Untersuchungen an einer Serie von Zwillingen. *Acta Psychiatrica et Neuralogica Scandivanica,* (Suppl. 23).

Faraone, S. V., & Tsuang, M. T. (1985). Quantitative models of the genetic transmission of schizophrenia. *Psychological Bulletin, 98,* 41–66.

Fein, D., Pennington, B., Markowitz, P., Braverman, M., & Waterhouse, L. (1986). Toward a neuropsychological model of infantile autism: Are the social deficits primary? *Journal of the American Academy of Child Psychiatry, 25,* 198–212.

Folstein, S., & Rutter, M. (1977). Infantile autism: A genetic study of 21 twin pairs. *Journal of Child Psychology and Psychiatry, 18,* 297–321.

Freeman, B. J., Ritvo, E. R., Needleman, R., & Yokota, A. (1985). The stability of cognitive and linguistic parameters in autism: A five-year prospective study. *Journal of the American Academy of Child Psychiatry, 24,* 459–464.

Friedman, E. (1969). The autistic syndrome and phenylketonuria. *Schizophrenia, 1,* 249–261.

Gillberg, C. (1983). Identical triplets with infantile autism and the Fragile X syndrome. *British Journal of Psychiatry, 143,* 256–260.

Gillberg, C. (1984a). Autistic children growing up; Problems of puberty and adolescence. *Developmental Medicine and Child Neurology, 26,* 125–129.

Gillberg, C. (1984b). Infantile autism and other childhood psychoses in a Swedish urban region. *Journal of Child Psychology and Child Psychiatry, 25,* 35–43.

Gottesman, I. I., & Shields, J. (1982). *Schizophrenia, the epigenetic puzzle.* Cambridge: Cambridge University Press.

Heston, L. L. (1966). Psychiatric disorders in foster home reared children of schizophrenic mothers. *British Journal of Psychiatry, 112,* 819–825.

Holmboe, R., & Astrup, C. (1957). A follow-up study of 255 patients with acute schizophrenia and schizophreniform psychoses. *Acta Psychiatriaca Scandinavica, 32*(Suppl. 115).

Huber, G., Gross, G., Schuttler, R., & Linz, M. (1980). Longitudinal studies of schizophrenic patients. *Schizophrenia Bulletin, 6,* 592–605.

Hutt, C., Forrest, S. J., & Richer, J. (1975). Cardiac arrhythmia and behavior in autistic children. *Acta Psychiatriaca Scandinavica, 51,* 361–372.

Johnstone, E. C., Crow, T . J., Frith, C. D., Carney, M. W. P., & Price, J. S. (1978). Mechanism of antipsychotic effect in the treatment of acute schizophrenia. *Lancet, 1,* 848–851.

Johnstone, E. C., Crow, T. J., Frith, C. D., Husband, J., & Kreel, L. (1976). Cerebral ventricular size and cognitive impairment in chronic schizophrenia. *Lancet, 2,* 924–926.

Johnstone, E. C., Crow, T. J., Frith, C. D., Stevens, M., Kreel, L., & Husband, J. (1978). The dementia of dementia praecox. *Acta Psychiatrica Scandanavica, 57,* 304–324.

Kallmann, F. J. (1946). The genetic theory of schizophrenia: An analysis of 691 schizophrenic twin index families. *American Journal of Psychiatry, 103,* 309–322.

Kanner, L. (1943). Autistic disturbances of affective contact. *Nervous Child, 3,* 217–250.

Kendler, K. S., Gruenberg, A. M., & Tsuang, M. T. (1984). Outcome of schizophrenic subtypes defined by four diagnostic systems. *Archives of General Psychiatry, 41,* 149–154.

Knobloch, H., & Pasamanick B. (1975). Some etiologic and prognostic factors in early infantile autism and psychosis. *Journal of Pediatrics, 55,* 182–191.

Kolakowska, T., Williams, A. O., Ardern, M., Reveley, M. A., Jambor, K., Gelder, M. G., & Mandelbrote, B. M. (1985). Schizophrenia with good and poor outcome; 1. Early clinical features, response to neuroleptics and signs of organic dysfunction. *British Journal of Psychiatry, 146,* 229–246.

Kootz, J. P., & Cohen, D. J. (1981). Modulation of sensory intake in autistic children. *Journal of the American Academy of Child Psychiatry, 20,* 692–701.

Kraepelin, E. (1913). *Psychiatrie (8th ed.; Vol. 3., Pt. 2). (Translated 1919 as Dementia praecox and paraphenia) Edinburgh: Livingston.*

Leff, J. (1977). International variations in the diagnosis of psychiatric illness. *British Journal of Psychiatry, 137,* 306–313.

Lord, C., & Schopler, E. (1985). Brief report: Differences in sex ratios in autism as a function of measured intelligence. *Journal of Autism and Developmental Disorders, 15,* 185–193.

Lotter, V. (1966). Epidemiology of autistic conditions in young children: I. Prevalence. *Social Psychiatry, 1,* 124–137.

Lotter, V. (1974). Social adjustment and placement of autistic children in Middlesex: A follow-up study. *Journal of Autism and Childhood Schizophrenia, 4,* 11–32.

Lotter, V. (1978). Follow-up studies. In M. Rutter & E. Schopler (Eds.), *Autism, a reappraisal of concepts and treatment*. New York: Plenum Press.

Lund, J. (1986). Behavioural symptoms and autistic psychosis in the mentally retarded adult. *Acta Psychiatrica Scandinavica, 73*, 420–428.

Machon, R. A. Mednick, S. A., & Schulsinger, F. (1983). The interaction of seasonality, place of birth, genetic risk and subsequent schizophrenia in a high-risk sample. *British Journal of Psychiatry, 143*, 383–388.

Mohler, M. S. (1952). On childhood psychosis and schizophrenia: Autistic and symbiotic psychoses. *The Psychoanalytic Study of the Child, 1*, 286–305. (Reprinted in S. I. Harrison & J. F. McDermott [Eds.], *Childhood psychopathology: An anthology of basic reading*. New York: International Universities Press.)

Matson, J. L. (1985). Biosocial theory of psychopathology: A three by three factor model. *Applied Research in Mental Retardation, 6*, 199–227.

McAdoo, W. G., & DeMyer, M. K. (1977). Research related to family factors in autism. *Journal of Pediatric Psychology, 2*, 162–166.

McAdoo, W. G., & DeMyer, M. K. (1978). Personality characteristics of parents. In M. Rutter & E. Schopler (Eds.), *Autism: A reappraisal of concepts and treatment*. New York: Plenum Press.

Meehl, P. E. (1962). Schizotaxia, schizotypy, schizophrenia. *American Psychologist, 17*, 827–838.

Niwa, W., Ohta, M., & Yamazaki, K. (1983). P300 and stimulus evaluation process in autistic subjects. *Journal of Autism and Developmental Disorders, 13*, 33–42.

Novick, B., Vaughan, H. G., Jr., Kurtzberg, D., & Simon, R. (1980). An electrophysiologic indication of auditory processing defects in autism. *Psychiatric Research, 3*, 107–114.

Ornitz, E. M. (1985). Neurophysiology of infantile autism. *Journal of the American Academy of Child Psychiatry, 24*(3), 251–262.

Parnas, J., Schulsinger, F., Teasdale, T. W., Schulsinger, H., Feldman, P. M., & Mednick, S. A. (1982). Perinatal complications and clinical outcome within the schizophrenia spectrum. *British Journal of Psychiatry, 140*, 416–420.

Prudo, R., & Blum, H. M. (1987). Five-year outcome and prognosis in schizophrenia: A report from the London Field Research Centre of the International Pilot Study of Schizophrenia. *British Journal of Psychiatry, 150*, 345–354.

Rettersol, N. (1968). Paranoid psychoses: The stability of nosological categories illustrated by a personal follow-up investigation. *British Journal of Psychiatry, 114*, 553–562.

Rimland, B. (1964). *Infantile autism*. New York: Appelton-Century-Crofts.

Ritvo, E. R., Freeman, B. J., Mason-Brothers, A., Mo., A., & Ritvo, A. M. (1985). Concordance for the syndrome of autism in 40 pairs of afflicted twins. *American Journal of Psychiatry, 142*, 174–177.

Rosenthal, D., Wender, P. H., Kety, S. S., Schulsinger, F., Welner, J., & Ostergaard, L. (1968). Schizophrenics' offspring reared in adoptive homes. In D. Rosenthal & S. S. Kety (Eds.), *The transmission of schizophrenia praecox.* Berlin: Springer.

Rumsey, J. M., Andreasen, N. C., & Rapoport, J. L. (1986). Thought, language, communication, and affective flattening in autistic adults. *Archives of General Psychiatry, 43*, 771–777.

Rumsey, J. M., Duara, R., Grady, C., Rapoport, J. L., Margolin, R. A., Rapoport, S. I., & Cutler, N. R. (1985). Brain metabolism in autism: Resting cerebral glucose utilization rates as measured with positron emission tomography. *Archives of General Psychiatry, 42*, 448–455.

Rumsey, J. M., Rapaport, J. L., & Sceery, W. R. (1985). Autistic children as adults: Psychiatric, social, and behavioral outcomes. *Journal of the American Academy of Child Psychiatry, 24*, 465–473.

Rutter, M. (1966). Prognosis: Psychotic children in adolescence and early adult life. In J. K. Wing (Ed.), *Early child autism: Clinical, educational and social aspects.* Oxford: Pergamon Press.

Rutter, M. (1970). Autistic children: Infancy to adulthood. *Seminars in Psychiatry, 2*, 435–450.

Rutter, M., Greenfeld, D., & Lockyer, L. (1967). Five to fifteen year follow-up study of infantile psychoses: II. Social and behavioural outcome. *British Journal of Psychiatry, 113*, 1183–1199.

Rutter, M., & Lockyer, L. (1967). A five to fifteen year follow-up study of infantile psychoses: I. Description of sample. *British Journal of Psychiatry, 113*, 1169–1182.

Schopler E., & Mesibov G. (1983). *Autism in adolescents and adults.* New York: Plenum Press.

Slater, E., & Cowie, V. (1971) *The genetics of mental disorder.* London: Oxford University Press.

Small, J. G. (1975). EEG and neurophysiological studies of early infantile autism. *Biological Psychiatry, 10*, 385–397.

Steffenburg, S., & Gillberg, C. (1986). Autism and autistic-like conditions in Swedish rural and urban areas: A population study. *British Journal of Psychiatry, 149*, 81–87.

Stephens, J. H., & Astrup, C. (1963). Prognosis in "process" and "non-process" schizophrenia. *American Journal of Psychiatry, 119*, 945–949.

Strauss, M. E., Sirotkin, R. A., & Grisell, J. (1974). Length of hospitalization and rate of readmission of paranoid and non paranoid schizophrenics. *Journal of Consulting and Clinical Psychology, 42*, 103–110.

Stubbs, E. G., Ritvo, E. R., & Mason-Brothers, A. (1985). Autism and shared parental HLA antigens. *Journal of the American Academy of Child Psychiatry, 24*, 182–185.

Sullivan, H. S. (1940). Conceptions of modern psychiatry: The first William Alanson White Memorial Lectures. *Psychiatry, 3*, 1–117.

Torrey, E. F., Hersh, S. P., & McCabe, K. D. (1975). Early childhood psychosis and bleeding during pregnancy: A prospective study of gravid women and their offspring. *Journal of Autism and Childhood Schizophrenia, 5*, 287–297.

Tsuang, M. T., & Vandermey, R. (1980). *Genes and the mind*. Oxford: Oxford University Press.

Vaillant, G. E. (1964). Prospective prediction of schizophrenic remission. *Archives of General Psychiatry, 11*, 509–518.

Wander, P. H., Rosenthal, D., Kety, S. S., Schulsinger, F., & Welner, J. (1974). Cross-fostering: A research strategy for clarifying the role of genetic and experiential factors in the etiology of schizophrenia. *Archives of General Psychiatry, 30*, 121–128.

Williams, A. O., Reveley, M. A., Kolakowska, T., Ardern, M., & Mandelbrote, B. M. (1985). Schizophrenia with good and poor outcome: II. Cerebral ventricular size and its clinical significance. *British Journal of Psychiatry, 147*, 239–246.

Wing, J. K. (1982). Course and prognosis of schizophrenia. In J. K. Wing & L. Wing (Eds.), *Handbook of psychiatry* (Vol. 3, pp. 33–41). Cambridge: Cambridge University Press.

Wing, L. (1981). Sex ratios in early childhood autism and related conditions. *Psychiatry Research, 5*, 129–137.

Wing, L., & Gould, J. (1979). Severe impairments of social interaction and associated abnormalities in children: Epidemiology and classification. *Journal of Autism and Developmental Disorders, 9*, 11–29.

World Health Organization. (1979). *Schizophrenia: An international follow-up study*. Chichester, England: John Wiley.

Zerbin-Rudin, E. (1972). Genetic research and the theory of schizophrenia. *International Journal of Mental Health, 1*, 42–62.

Zigler, E., & Levine, J. (1981). Age on first hospitalization of schizophrenics. *Journal of Abnormal Psychology, 90*, 458–467.

4

Treatment Programs and Social Services Delivery for Chronic Patients

Christian R. Lemmon and Janet S. St. Lawrence

Among the most disabling of all mental disorders, schizophrenia and autism intrude upon almost every aspect of an affected person's functioning. Although definitions vary, the behavioral disturbances that characterize schizophrenia appear throughout the world and across all races and cultures. Estimates suggest that between 1 and 3% of the population is affected by this disorder (Gunderson & Mosher, 1975; Keith, Gunderson, Reifman, Buschbaum, & Mosher, 1976) and approximately 50% of all hospitalized mental patients receive schizophrenic diagnoses (Curran, Monti, & Corriveau, 1982). Although the average length of hospitalization has decreased markedly in the last few decades, readmissions are frequent; 50% of persons with schizophrenia return to inpatient care within 2 years following their initial discharge (Hogarty et al., 1979; Keith et al., 1976).

Studies investigating the prevalence of autism report discrepant results. Estimates range from 0.00048% (Wing, Yeates, Brierly, & Gould, 1976) to 0.00021% (Janicki, Lubin, & Friedman, 1983). Ornitz and Ritvo (1976) suggest that reported prevalence rates underestimate the actual prevalence due to frequent misdiagnosis. Nor do estimates separate the number of children and adults affected by autism. In fact, there are very few estimates regarding the number of adults affected by autism. Janicki et al. (1983) reported that 22% of the autistic persons in their study were 22 years of age or older. The autism literature reveals a paucity of research directly investigating service delivery to autistic adults, and very little is really known about adult autism. However, as more and more individuals with autistic diagnoses reach adulthood, attention to the treatment needs of this population is increasing (Romanczyk, 1986; Schopler, 1983). Also, as more autistic adults are removed from residential institutions, the need for information has become greater (Mesibov, 1983).

Because so little attention has been given to the adult form of autism, the existing literature is largely based on speculation or generalizations from the more plentiful literatures on infantile autism, "psychotic" children, and mental retardation. Autistic children are often diagnosed as schizophrenic or mentally retarded when they reach adulthood (Bender, 1969; DeMyer et al. 1973; Fish & Ritvo, 1980; Rutter & Lockyer, 1967).

Janicki, Lubin, and Friedman (1983) report that mental retardation is the most common secondary diagnosis among autistic persons. Ninety-one percent of the autistic individuals who were administered IQ tests in their study received scores indicative of mental retardation. However, these researchers found significant differences in "activities of daily living" between the autistic adults and a comparison group of mentally retarded persons. This finding calls into question the common practice of generalizing results from nonautistic populations as though they were applicable to autistic adults. Nevertheless, until autistic adult research increases, one is left with few other choices. Limited research within adult autistic populations suggests that treatment programs designed for autistic children, schizophrenic adults, or mentally retarded children and adults are equally applicable to autistic adults. Smith and Belcher (1985) and Smith and Coleman (1986), for example, adapted treatment programs designed for other populations for use with autistic adults.

This chapter will predominantly focus on service delivery for the treatment of schizophrenia since there is very little literature on service delivery for adult autistic patients. However, the comprehensive service needs for autistic adults may be similar to those needed for schizophrenic adults. After the positive symptoms of schizophrenia have been reduced, the behavioral deficits and excesses of schizophrenia and autism are not unlike, with the possible exception of self-injurious behavior, which is more common among autistic persons. Both groups exhibit poor adaptive living skills, and their poor communication/social skills are often considered their most impairing deficits.

The frequency of institutionalization is similarly high for autistic and schizophrenic individuals, and deinstitutionalization has affected both groups. At least 50% of autistic adults are institutionalized (Lotter, 1978), not unlike the figures for adult schizophrenia. Recent research (Janicki et al., 1983) also indicates that 72% of autistic adults receive medication, suggesting that drug compliance may be equally problematic for autistic and schizophrenic populations. Behavioral treatment techniques have worked well within both populations, as have various forms of family therapy. Therefore, there seem to be some similarities in the service delivery and treatment needs of both autistic and schizophrenic adults. Finally, although many of the effective treatments that are discussed here were developed with schizophrenic patients, they may also have potential for the care and treatment of the adult autistic population.

THE "REVOLVING DOOR": FRAGMENTATION IN THE CASE SYSTEM

Since the introduction of antipsychotics there has been a dramatic decline in the number of hospitalized schizophrenic patients. Sharfstein (cited in Bellack, 1986) indicated that the number of beds in state psychiatric hospitals has been reduced from 559,000 to 138,000 since the 1950s. However, deinstitutionalization has not prevented relapse and rehospitalization. The movement away from long-term hospitalization, stabilization, and discharge, followed by relapse as the cycle repeats itself. Rehospitalizations of chronic schizophrenic patients account for about 70% of all inpatient admissions (Sharfstein, cited in Bellack, 1986).

Similar patterns are seen within the autistic adult population. Lotter (1978) suggests that 39 to 74% of autistic patients are receiving institutional care; the average is about 50%. The Janicki et al. (1983) study revealed that 38% of the autistic persons lived in an institutional setting, 62% lived at home or in a community residential program, and the likelihood of institutionalization increased with age.

The average length of stay, as well as total number of hospitalizations, increases with each rehospitalization of the schizophrenic patient. Engelhardt, Rosen, Feldman, Engelhardt, and Cohen (1982) found that patients with no previous history of hospitalization were less likely to be hospitalized (39.1%) than patients with crisis admissions only (53.5%), who in turn were less likely to be hospitalized than patients with a history of long-term hospitalization for psychiatric treatment (67.9%). These researchers indicated that the probability of release decreased tremendously once the schizophrenic patient had spent 2 years as an inpatient, and the chances of avoiding rehospitalization appeared quite poor.

What causes this revolving door of continued care? It has been suggested that the occurrence of negative symptoms, problem-solving and social skills deficits, unemployment, poor familial relationships, noncompliance with treatment procedures, poorly funded treatment programs, and the fragmentation of continued-care services all contribute to relapse and rehospitalization. Liberman, Mueser, and Wallace (1986) indicate that most schizophrenic patients whose symptomatology is under pharmacological control at the time of discharge still evinced pervasive social deficits. In other words, they are often lacking conversational, self-care, recreational, problem-solving, and money management skills, and they need help in the management of their medications, vocational rehabilitation, and social services. Finally, the schizophrenic patient may return to ill-equipped families or boarding home and even find shelter by living on the streets in major cities.

Liberman, Wallace, Vaughn, Snyder, and Rust (1980) described the deinstitutionalization process as follows:

> In most treatment settings, the question is not whether intensive psychother-
> apy, or even brief psychotherapy, is of value for schizophrenics, but rather,
> whether the schizophrenic patient will have time to brush his teeth and take
> a shower before being discharged through the hospital's "revolving door" with
> fluphenazine in his butt, a prescription in his hand, and an appointment to
> see a well-meaning but harassed aftercare worker two or three weeks later. This
> is the current practice and professional reality that must be confronted by those
> who are developing, evaluating and justifying psychosocial approaches for the
> treatment of schizophrenia. (p. 49)

Reports by LaVigna (1983) and Lovaas et al. (1973) suggest that autistic persons require continuous and lifelong behavioral treatment
programming to manage their behavioral problems. Autistic persons
have been shown to have moderate deficits in skills related to activities of daily living as well as significant communication and independent functioning skills deficits (Janicki et al., 1983). Finally, Lotter
(1978) reported that about 70% of autistic patients have severe handicaps and are unable to lead independent lives. These results suggest that autistic adults encounter many similar problems during the
deinstitutionalization process.

Schwartz, Goldfinger, Ratener, and Cutler (1983) identified three
factors that contribute to fragmentation in continued care of chronic
patient: (1) fragmentation of responsibility between the providers,
(2) fragmentation of authority between systems, and (3) fragmentation of goals and objectives. According to Talbot (cited in Cutler, 1985)
these problems result in poor care for the chronically ill, unneces-
sary competition for the highest-functioning (and most likely to pay)
patients, overutilization of expensive and restrictive settings, and
inadequate communication between elements in the mental health
system.

Often, there are too many service agencies operating independently
of one another and attempting to provide care for the discharged
patient. There is a high probability of fragmentation whenever several
agencies with different goals and values are operating simultaneously
(Cutler, 1985; Tarail, 1980). The reader is referred to Tarail (1980) for
a comprehensive discussion of the dysfunctional characteristics of
mental health systems that contribute to fragmentation.

Each of these problems plagues the treatment of chronic patients
and contributes to their relapse and rehospitalization. The absence
of solutions to these problems is costly. In 1975, the total direct and
indirect cost of schizophrenia was estimated to be $19 billion

(Gunderson & Mosher, 1975). This estimate included treatment costs, loss of productivity, public assistance payments, and research.

There is now a movement to increase and upgrade outpatient treatment of the chronic patient. Research investigating inpatient treatment continues to dominate the literature, but research investigating discharge planning, partial hospitalization or day treatment program, and case management is beginning to appear in the literature with increasing frequency.

The paucity of behavioral research on schizophrenia was highlighted in a review by Bellack (1986) and is also true for adult autism. Bellack suggests that several misconceptions contributed to the behaviorist's neglect of schizophrenia research. These include beliefs such as (1) schizophrenia does not exist; (2) schizophrenia should not be studied because it is a biological disease; (3) the disorder is adequately controlled by medication; and (4) schizophrenia is too severe for behavior therapy. Bellack discounts these assumptions and suggests that there is a place for behavioral research in the treatment of schizophrenia. Behavioral neglect of adult autism is very likely to be based upon similar views.

Just as there are many theories concerning the etiology of schizophrenia and autism, so are there numerous approaches to treatment. Some of these differences extend from the different etiological theories, whereas others are atheoretical and focus on specific behaviors and deficits. There is no general consensus as to which treatment approach is optimal. In fact, the only consensus thus far is that no single treatment is adequate for any chronic disorder and an eclectic treatment philosophy that emphasizes practical considerations is of prime important (Simpson & May, 1982).

The following discussion of service delivery models for the severely impaired patient is divided into two sections. Inpatient service delivery—including pharmacological treatment, various forms of psychotherapy, behavioral interventions, and issues involving staff development and in-service training techniques—is addressed in the first section. A second section delineates outpatient service delivery models and strategies, including issues such as patient discharge, drug maintenance, community placement, case management, the role of the family, compliance with partial hospitalization programs, drug compliance, and behavior therapies.

INPATIENT SERVICE DELIVERY
Insulin Shock and Electroconvulsive Therapy

Before neuroleptics, insulin shock and electroconvulsive therapy (ECT) were widely used in inpatient settings for the treatment of schizophrenia. Insulin shock is no longer in use, but ECT is sometimes still employed. There have been few controlled studies of its effectiveness, and the existing data are controversial. ECT may lead to more rapid results than the administration of neuroleptics provides, and it is sometimes the treatment of choice for extreme catatonic stupor or persistent paranoid delusions. However, ECT results are more temporary and maintenance is more difficult than is the case with antipsychotic medication. In most hospitals, ECT is used only as a last-resort treatment (Lehmann, 1975).

Pharmacological Treatments

Since the discovery of antipsychotic (neuroleptic) drugs in the 1950s, psychiatric treatment of schizophrenia, in particular, has changed tremendously. Until that time, the numbers of severely impaired patients in mental hospitals were growing, with no relief in sight. Straitjackets and seclusion were two of the most frequently used methods for management of the chronic inpatient. During the 1950s, chlorpromazine (Thorazine®) was synthesized in an attempt to produce a better antihistamine. However, when the drug's tranquilizing effect was discovered, it was applied to the treatment of schizophrenia.

Therapeutic Action

Researchers believed that chlorpromazine might relieve the agitation and anxiety that is often associated with schizophrenic behavior (Baldessarini, 1985). The findings that chlorpromazine and other phenothiazines actually had antipsychotic effects were not initially accepted, but for the first time large numbers of chronic patients could be discharged to live in the community. During this period, clinical evaluation concerning the efficacy of these drugs ranged from the poorly designed or controlled to reports that were scientifically and methodologically sound. As one would expect, contradictions regarding the efficacy of antipsychotic medications were abundant.

Nevertheless, clinicians found chlorpromazine to be a potent antipsychotic drug. As Baldessarini (1985) stated, "Many clinical trials have established that these agents are effective and that they are superior to agents such as barbiturates or the benzodiazepines, or to alternatives such as electroconvulsive shock or other medical or psychological therapies" (p. 409). The history of antipsychotic drug discovery and use in the treatment of schizophrenia is well documented (Caldwell, 1978). A large body of research now exists to suggest these drugs are necessary for the treatment of hospitalized schizophrenic patients in particular. These studies have been reviewed extensively elsewhere (Cole & Davis, 1969; Falloon & Liberman, 1983; Hollon & Beck, 1978; Klein & Davis, 1969; Klein, Gittleman, Quitkin, & Rifkin, 1980; Klerman, 1986; Schooler, 1978; Wallace, Donahoe, & Boone, 1986.

Chlorpromazine and the other antipsychotic drugs are primarily effective for treating the acute positive symptoms of schizophrenia (Baldessarini, 1985; Carlson, 1986; Falloon et al., 1983). Consequently, investigators have become increasingly interested in the distinction between positive and negative symptoms of this disorder. The positive symptoms, or behavioral excesses, include delusions, disordered thinking, loose associations, incoherence, hallucinations, and agitated or grossly disorganized behavior. The antipsychotics appear less effective in treating negative symptoms, sometimes termed prodromal or residual symptoms. These symptoms include social isolation or withdrawal; impairments in personal hygiene and grooming; blunted, flat, or inappropriate affect; poverty of speech; apathy; and poor judgment (Andreason & Olsen, 1982; Angrist, Rotrosen, & Gershon, 1980; Carlson, 1986; Falloon et al., 1983).

Negative symptoms are correlated with poor premorbid adjustment, poorer response to antipsychotic drug therapy, and cognitive impairment. Positive symptoms appear to be correlated with better premorbid adjustment, a better response to the antipsychotics, less cognitive impairment, and an underlying pathologic process that is neurochemical in nature (Andreason & Olsen, 1982). Carpenter, Heinrichs, and Alphs (1985) report that preoccupation with positive symptoms has resulted in a relative paucity of research investigating negative symptoms. Yet the negative symptoms of schizophrenia appear to be the most debilitating longitudinal handicap for most schizophrenic patients. These symptoms do not respond as well to antipsychotic medication, and they decrease the patients' chances of effective functioning in the community.

Carpenter et al. (1985) are among the few researchers to specifically investigate inpatient treatment of negative symptoms. They suggest it is useful to make a further distinction between primary and secondary negative symptoms, claiming that secondary negative symptoms can be effectively treated because they often coincide with exacerbations of psychosis. As patients improve, their disorganization is lifted, and they are able to interact meaningfully with others again. There may also be an increased desire to interact when there is no longer any reason to reduce external stimuli, as was the case when they were floridly psychotic. Carpenter et al. suggest that secondary negative symptoms "ebb and flow with the psychotic experience." These researchers also discuss negative symptoms that may be secondary to medication, understimulating environments, and dysphoric affect.

Administration

Individual patients differ in their responses to antipsychotic medications in terms of the type of drug to which they respond, dosage levels, and the amount of time before therapeutic effects are observed. No one drug has been shown to be significantly safer or more effective for any subgroup of patients or for any specific target symptom. Although individual patients may respond to one drug better than to another, there is no documented method upon which drug selection can be predetermined. As a result, drug selection is usually a trial-and-error process. It has been suggested that agitated or aggressive patients respond best to a drug with sedating effects, such as chlorpromazine, and that patients who appear withdrawn respond best to a drug with stimulating effects, like trifluoperazine (Stelazine®). However, this suggestion has not been supported by controlled research (Baldessarini, 1985; Kessler & Waletzky, 1981).

Kessler and Waletzky (1981) suggested that the trial-and-error process of drug selection usually operates in the following manner. If a patient has not responded to an adequate dose of antipsychotic medication after 6 weeks, he or she is given a different drug. When improvement is finally observed, an attempt is made to find the lowest dose that will continue to sustain improvement. Future dosage

and drug decisions are made according to the amount of improvement that takes place and the emergence of side effects.

The process of drug selection is simplified when the patient has
a prior history of inpatient care. The drug history should be reviewed
because patients who respond well to a particular drug will usually
do so again (Appleton, cited in Kessler & Waletzky, 1981). The drug
history should include information regarding dose, side effects, and
clinical response. This process eliminates much of the guesswork and
enables the patient to be stabilized and begin improving more quickly
(Kessler & Waletzky, 1981).

Although some acutely psychotic patients will show improvement
in 48 to 72 hrs, therapeutic effects are usually not observed until after
10 days to 3 weeks (Baldessarini, 1985; Kessler & Waletzky, 1981). Davis
and Gierl (1984) report that between 80 and 85% of patients treated
with an adequate dose of antipsychotic medication will show some
improvement within 6 to 8 weeks. More than 50% of these patients
will reveal moderate to marked improvements (Cole, 1964). Of course,
these improvements are limited to a decrease in the positive symptoms.
Negative-symptom improvement in such a short time is uncommon.
Nevertheless, this rapid improvement in positive symptoms has had
a tremendous effect on the average length of stay in an inpatient facility.
According to Bellack (1986), inpatient hospitalizations now average only
about 3 weeks. In many cases the positive symptoms are stabilized
and the patient is released.

Continuous use of antipsychotic medication after the initial stabilization of symptoms is often necessary with schizophrenic patients.
In most settings, continuation of antipsychotic medication is recommended indefinitely. Drug maintenance is supported by a number
of well-controlled studies that demonstrate the superiority of continuous medication over placebo treatment. In a review of 24 double-blind
studies of antipsychotic maintenance therapy involving over 3,000
patients, Davis (1975) found patients administered a placebo relapsed
at a higher rate than did their counterparts who were given antipsychotic medication. This finding was true across all of the studies he
reviewed. Combining the results from each of these studies, Davis
reported that 65% of the patients on placebo relapsed, whereas only
30% of patients maintained on medication relapsed. This appears to
be strong evidence for the efficacy of antipsychotic medication in the
treatment of schizophrenia.

Side Effects

The exceptions to positive benefit from continued medication are most often those who fail to comply with their medication therapy and those who drop out of the community mental health care system (Carpenter & Heinrichs, 1983). The reasons for noncompliance and dropout are addressed later in this chapter. However, one reason for poor maintenance is related to the side effects associated with continued administration of antipsychotic medication. Some side effects, such as agranulocytosis, hyperthermia, and hypertension, are extremely severe. Other side effects include akathesias, autonomic reactions, and extrapyramidal effects (Baldessarini, 1985; Falloon et al., 1983; Shapiro, 1981).

The akathesias are the most common side effects and are characterized by motor restlessness and muscle discomfort, manifested by pacing and an inability to sit still. They may be treated through administration of an antiparkinsonian drug (Cogentin®) and by lowering the neuroleptic dosage. Autonomic reactions include dizziness, blurred vision, dry mouth, urinary retention, and constipation. Other sexually specific reactions include lactation, breast enlargement, and menstrual irregularities in some women and erectile or ejaculatory difficulties in some men. Medication is often changed to haloperidol (Haldol®) in such cases because it has a lower incidence of autonomic reactions.

Extrapyramidal effects include parkinsonian side effects, acute dystonic reactions, and tardive dyskinesia. The parkinsonian effects include tremors, rigidity, trouble initiating voluntary movement, increased salivation, slurred speech, and a masklike face, among others. These symptoms are continuous and appear 2 to 3 months after drug therapy commences. Bizarre, involuntary contractions of the upper body, referred to as acute dystonic reactions, sometimes occur during the first week of treatment. These symptoms are episodic, recurring, and dose-dependent (Baldessarini, 1985; Falloon et al., 1983; Shapiro, 1981). Drug-free weekends, longer drug holidays, or the use of reduced dosages are now recommended to decrease the side effects associated with long-term drug maintenance (Carpenter & Heinrichs, 1983; Schooler & Carpenter, 1983), an issue that is discussed at length later in this chapter.

Efficacy

Despite their side effects, antipsychotic drugs are the primary inpatient treatment for schizophrenia. When compared to various other treatment regimens, the use of antipsychotic medication as a form of treatment does quite well. Unfortunately, there are no well-controlled studies in which antipsychotic medications have been compared to behavior-based treatment programs. However, there have been some well-controlled studies that compared antipsychotics and psychotherapy alone and in various combinations. At this time, these combinations have not proved to be superior to the use of medication alone.

Cole and Davis (1969) reported that 82% of the 130 controlled drug-placebo comparison studies they investigated favored drug treatment. The remaining 18% were reported to have serious methodological difficulties or problems with low-level dosages. In a review of over 100 methodologically sound studies, Klein and Davis (1969) reported that antipsychotic medications were consistently found to be superior to placebos in the treatment of schizophrenic patients. May (1976) reviewed a number of controlled studies investigating the effects of psychotherapy and antipsychotic medications. The studies that May reviewed were conducted in inpatient facilities where extensive contact from a number of mental health personnel and exposure to a number of therapeutic activities took place. There was no evidence suggesting benefit from either individual or group therapy in the inpatient treatment of schizophrenia. However, the beneficial effects of antipsychotic medications were well documented.

Hollon and Beck (1978) also reviewed a number of studies investigating the effectiveness of drugs in various schizophrenic populations. They concluded that drugs are relatively effective in chronic inpatient populations. Despite methodological flaws, various forms of psychotherapy appeared to be of little help to these patients. In addition, combinations of drugs and psychotherapy added little to drug treatments alone. Hollon and Beck (1978) also found the use of antipsychotic medications alone to be both superior to psychotherapy and equivalent to drug/psychotherapy combinations in recently admitted schizophrenic inpatients. Results concerning maintenance therapies for schizophrenic patients were more inconsistent. Overall, Hollon and Beck (1978) suggested that "there appears to be overwhelming evidence documenting the efficacy of the various anti-psychotic drugs" (p. 473).

Finally, Klerman (1986) reviewed recent research by Andrews et al. as part of the Quality Assurance Project of the Royal Australian and New Zealand College of Psychiatrists. Andrews et al. applied meta-analysis procedures to data from 600 controlled studies of schizophrenia and found the effect size for 200 studies of drug treatments and 26 studies of psychotherapy or social intervention. They found a strong effect for the drug treatments and no effect for psychotherapy.

Drug Treatment of Autism

With the discovery of chlorpromazine and other antipsychotic medications it was hoped that these drugs could be similarly used in the treatment of infantile autism. As Campbell (1978) suggests:

> It was hoped that these drugs would arrest or decrease the psychotic process in the child and that after the reduction of anxiety, hyperactivity, and/or aggressiveness he would become more amenable to special education and other treatment modalities. (p. 337)

Despite these hopes there are at present very few well-designed and well-controlled studies on pharmacological management of infantile autism. Research investigating pharmacological treatment of autistic adults is even scarcer. Nevertheless, the paucity of research in this area has not retarded the use of such medications in the treatment of childhood and adult autism. Seventy-two percent of autistic adults receive medication, and the use of medications increases significantly with age and institutional placement (Janicki et al., 1983). As the autistic child reaches adulthood, self-destructive behaviors, aggressive and agitated behaviors, sleep disturbances, and general withdrawal often become more difficult to manage without pharmacological intervention (Dalldorf, 1983; Favell, 1983; Mesibov, 1983).

The paucity of research in this area and the potentials for undesirable side effects make drug selection for the autistic adult as difficult as for the schizophrenic patient. It has also been suggested that phenothiazines may lower the seizure threshold in autistic persons (Dalldorf, 1983). Twenty-eight percent of autistic persons develop seizure disorders in adolescence of early adulthood (Rutter, as cited in Lotter, 1978). Deykin and MacMahon (1979) also concluded that autistic children are at high risk for developing seizures for the first time during adolescence. Finally, Janicki et al. (1983) found that 22% of the autistic adults in their sample had epilepsy. Anticonvulsant medication may also lead to problematic side effects such as increased irritability, drowsiness, and hyperactivity (Dalldorf, 1983).

It has been suggested that pharmacological interventions for autism be avoided until all possible environmental manipulations and behavioral treatment efforts have been exhausted (Dalldrof, 1983). As is the case with the schizophrenic disorders, research has suggested that treatment of autism by drugs alone will not be sufficient (Campbell, 1978).

Campbell (1978) and Dalldorf (1983) reviewed a number of drug studies investigating pharmacological treatment of autism. Drugs such as phenothiazines, butyrophenones, stimulants, antidepressants, lithium, minor tranquilizers, and sedative-hypnotics have shown varying therapeutic effects. However, most of these studies involved the treatment of autistic children or adolescents. The available information concerning the pharmacological treatment of autistic adults is based on generalizations from these reports and studies of adult schizophrenia and mental retardation. The reader is referred to the aforementioned reviews for a more comprehensive report on the medical management of autism.

Despite the large number of studies that consistently demonstrate the effectiveness of antipsychotic medication, this treatment is not without problems. Problems concerning side effects and the failure to alleviate negative symptomatology, previously discussed, are just two among a number of problems. A third problem, drug compliance, is discussed in the section addressing outpatient service delivery.

A fourth problem concerns relapse. The use of antipsychotic medication in the long-term maintenance treatment of schizophrenia is not as effective as its use in treating the acutely psychotic patient. Gardos and Cole (1976) indicate that 50% of schizophrenic clients either do not respond to or are helped by antipsychotic medications. Nor does antipsychotic medication prevent relapse in all patients. Davis (1975) reported that 3 to 49% of patients relapse despite continued medication. Kohen and Paul (1976) reported that 70% of schizophrenic patients are readmitted to inpatient facilities despite continued medication. Finally, Hogarty et al. (1979) reported that close to 50% of schizophrenic patients relapse within 2 years of their discharge.

Because of these problems associated with antipsychotic medication as the sole treatment, more and more researchers suggest that medication alone does not constitute optimal care. Falloon and Liberman (1983) state: "Drugs alone cannot promote the acquisition of new interpersonal skills or enhance coping behavior. Psychosocial interventions are necessary to improve social competence and to provide efficient rehabilitation of the schizophrenic patient to a functional state in the community" (p. 551). Simpson and May (1982) and Bellack (1986) arrived at similar conclusions. Therefore, the following discussion is directed to methods of behavior therapy that may or may not include the use of drugs. Although the observable behaviors of many schizophrenic and autistic patients may be controlled through chemotherapy, behavior therapy techniques may also be used. Behavior therapy may be included in the total treatment package and possibly enhances the effectiveness of antipsychotic medication.

Behavioral Treatments in Inpatient Settings

Lindsley and Skinner were among the first to employ conditioning procedures for the treatment of psychotic disorders. Interested in modifying the behavior of these patients by manipulating response-contingent reinforcements, they experimented with a large number of reinforcers and measured a wide range of responses by extending the techniques they developed with animal research. According to O'Leary and Wilson (1975), "reinforcement procedures have been the predominate means of the behavioral treatment of psychotic disorders, and have been applied to an ever-increasing range of different behaviors in an increasingly complex and sophisticated fashion" (p. 399). The goals of behavior therapy when working with a schizophrenic population are determined to a great extent by the severity of the disorder. If one starts at the beginning of treatment with a patient experiencing acute symptoms, the goals of therapy may develop in the following manner.

An immediate concern is the stabilization of psychotic behavior. This may include a reduction in hallucinations, loose associations, delusions, and other behaviors covered by the DSM-III-R diagnostic criteria. A second step may include developing more effective interpersonal and social skills, problem solving, assertiveness training, and other skills referred to collectively as social skills. Other steps may include vocational rehabilitation, family planning and training so that stress will be reduced upon reentry into the community, and drug compliance. Of course, one may deviate from these treatment steps depending on the needs of the patient.

The following summary by no means considers each and every form of therapy available for every target behavior. The reader is referred to several review articles on behavioral techniques used in the treatment of schizophrenia for a more extensive discussion (Curran et al., 1982; Hagen, 1975; Salzinger, 1981). As mentioned previously, the paucity of research specifically investigating adult autism prevents a review as comprehensive as that which is possible concerning schizophrenia. Therefore, most of the discussion will focus strictly on the behavioral treatment of schizophrenia. The discussion begins with a review of some of the earliest behavior-based research and concludes with a discussion of the more recent comprehensive behavioral service delivery models.

Reducing Delusional Behavior

A wide range of methods has been employed in inpatient settings to decrease delusional speech and increase rational talk. Rickard, Dignam, and Horner (1960) and Rickard and Dinoff (1962) used differential reinforcement procedures. Wincze, Leitenberg, and Agras (1972) compared the effects of feedback and reinforcement procedures in reducing delusional speech with 10 paranoid schizophrenic patients. Their results indicated that the feedback procedure showed some success in reducing the percentage of delusional speech for about half of the subjects, whereas the reinforcement procedures reduced delusional speech in seven of nine subjects. Liberman, Teigen, Patterson, and Baker (1973) found even more impressive results. They interviewed their subjects for four 10-min sessions each day during a baseline period. The time from the onset of the conversation to the onset of delusional speech was recorded, and discussion was terminated as soon as delusional speech began. This produced 200 to 600% increases in rational speech during the interviews, and the improvements were maintained as a reinforcement procedure was faded out. The improvement generalized from daytime to night-time conversations but did not extend to the patients' ward behaviors. A number of other behavioral treatment programs have also proved effective in reducing delusional behaviors (see Meichen-baum & Cameron, 1973; Patterson & Teigen, 1973). For example, Schaefer and Martin (1975) eliminated delusions through use of a token economy. Falloon et al. (1983) suggested that "if the total treat-ment program is focused on establishing and maintaining a wide range of skills and adaptive behavior, the chances of other reinforced behaviors supplanting delusions in the patients' repertoire are increased" (p. 576).

Reducing Hallucinations

Behavioral techniques have also been used to modify hallucinations during inpatient hospitalization. However, the fact that hallucina-tions are based on perceptions observable only to the patient makes investigation difficult other than by self-report or correlated verbal and motor behaviors such as gesturing and talking to oneself. Bucher and Fabricatore (1970) used self-administered shock to reduce the fre-quency of reported hallucinations. Despite the single-case design of this study and several possible confounding variables, operant con-trol of hallucinations was demonstrated. An interesting satiation tech-nique was introduced by Liberman, Wallace, Teigen, and Davis (1974). The researchers hypothesized that patients who verbalized their hal-lucinations (they had to listen to themselves) or listened to tapes of hallucinatory content for 30 min each day would classically condi-tion to the aversive conditions of fatigue, boredom, and satiation. Despite the single-case design, the results appeared promising. Later clinical research further documented that hallucinatory behavior could be modified with social interference and aversive procedures (Alford & Turner, 1976; Turner, Hersen, & Bellack, 1977).

Although it is not often discussed, there is controversy over decreas-ing verbal reports of delusions and hallucinations through behavioral interventions. Instead of ignoring the thoughts or perceptions, or realizing the invalidity of such experiences, patients may simply "learn" to avoid reporting such behavior. This may solve a problem for hospital staff but not for the patients affected by such experiences.

Patients may continue to be adversely affected but refrain from reporting them to avoid aversive consequences such as shocks or a more prolonged inpatient stay.

Reducing Aggressive Behaviors

Falloon et al. (1983) discuss the use of time-out procedures for the elimination of aggressive behaviors within the inpatient setting. Horn (cited in Smith & Belcher, 1985) reports that treatment of autistic adults is often interrupted by aggression, temper tantrums, self-abuse, and oppositional behaviors. Mesibov (1983) reports that aggressive and self-injurious behaviors become more intractable during adolescence and adulthood. Often, the larger size of the adult contributes to more destructive potential and to management problems associated with these behaviors.

Mesibov (1983) suggests that autistic adults become easily frustrated and that structured environments and positive reinforcement may help to reduce problematic behaviors. Differential reinforcement procedures, time-out, and relaxation training may also prove effective. Psychotropic drugs have also been used to control aggressive behaviors (Dalldorf, 1983; Favell, 1983; Mesibov, 1983). However, the results of such treatment have been inconsistent.

According to Favell (1983) the goal of treatment should be "to reduce the strength of aggression to an acceptable level" (p. 191). In other words, treatment programs should target decreases in the frequency and intensity of the aggressive behaviors. Favell further proposes that treatment programs include the following procedures:

1. A careful analysis of biological and environmental conditions and consequences which might be maintaining the individual's aggression.
2. Environmental rearrangements which ensure a safe, structured and responsive environment.
3. Systematic strengthening of appropriate alternative behavior.
4. Reduction of reinforcement for aggression.
5. Rearrangement of environmental conditions differentially associated with aggression.
6. In some cases, the inclusion of punishment for aggression itself. (pp. 191–192)

Despite numerous suggestions, little research has evaluated the treatment of aggression in autistic adults. Smith and Belcher (1985) trained five autistic adults in daily living skills despite high frequencies of aggressive behavior problems. These researchers contend that the behavioral problems were reduced through the use of a "method of redirecting the subject to the task without unduly reinforcing off-task behavior" (p. 173). Similarly, Smith and Coleman (1986) used role playing, instruction, positive reinforcement, differential reinforcement, and a response-cost procedure to reduce temper tantrums, destruction of property, and other aggressive behaviors in autistic adults.

Token Economy

A large body of research demonstrates that the behavior of patient groups may be changed by manipulating reinforcement contingencies within the inpatient setting. Despite the need for extensive staff development and monitoring, token-economy systems have worked well in such settings as inappropriate behaviors are decreased and appropriate behaviors are increased.

Ayllon and Azrin (cited in O'Leary & Wilson, 1975) were the first to employ such programs in a psychiatric setting. O'Leary and Wilson (1975) reviewed several studies that employed token economies and found that token systems prove to be a significant success as measured by increases in target behaviors, observers' ratings, and the favorable reactions of hospital staffs. Before token systems were introduced, patients were often seen as withdrawn and apathetic, but at the end of the experimental phases there were increases in the frequency with which patients left the facilities on passes, interacted socially, and adhered to hospital rules.

Curran, Monti, and Corriveau (1982) arrived at similar conclusions in their review of token systems in inpatient facilities. They suggested:

> Although many of the studies reviewed have serious methodological flaws, the mostly consistent positive results seem to support the contention that token economies can be effective in treating chronic schizophrenics . . . . It is our contention that the major advantage of a token economy is that it provides a structure and motivational system wherein patients learn new skills and coping strategies through various therapeutic interventions. (p. 450)

Model Behavioral Treatment Programs

Very little research has investigated the behavioral training of social skills, problem solving, and drug compliance within the inpatient setting. Rather, the research in these areas has been conducted with patients who have already been discharged from inpatient facilities. This makes very little sense given the frequency with which schizophrenic patients are rehospitalized. Inpatient treatment of negative symptoms through social skills training, problem solving, and medication compliance could enable the patient to function more effectively in the community after discharge. Given the current trend to limit inpatient treatment to "stabilize and discharge," it is not surprising that the treatment of negative symptoms is left to aftercare mental health systems. However, social skills training, problem solving, and drug compliance issues need to be addressed within the inpatient facility for optimal preparation of the patients before reentry into the community.

A model comprehensive inpatient service delivery program is described by Curran, Sutton, Faraone, and Guenette (1985). Their program considers biological, psychological, and social factors in the etiology and treatment of schizophrenia. Their inpatient unit has 35 beds and provides acute treatment and rehabilitative services to voluntarily committed patients. Patients progress through a series of steps designed to prepare them for discharge. As the patient proceeds through these steps, more and more is required so that by discharge patients are functioning as closely as possible to the way they would in society.

Schizophrenic patients are given antipsychotic medication and assigned to a psychologist; drug compliance is an integral part of behavioral programming before discharge. Two basic behavioral programs are employed in this facility. A social and Task-Functional Skills Training Program is designed to teach patients appropriate coping strategies to handle environmental stress. A second program is referred to as the Family Intervention Training Program. This includes education of the patient and family concerning the disorder, resolution of family guilt, the importance of drug compliance, identification of stressors, communication skills, and problem-solving techniques. Two other major strengths of this program include the time invested in educating staff about schizophrenia and behavioral treatments and the fact that patients remain under the continued care of the inpatient psychologist during the aftercare phase of the program. Such programs are a key to reducing fragmentation in the care of severely impaired patients.

A model service delivery system for autistic adolescents and adults is described by Lettick (1983). Benhaven in New Haven, Connecticut, is a day and residential program designed "with the goal of achieving optimal development in each student through maximizing the potential for independence and competence in vocational, residential, and recreational skills, and thereby avoiding custodial institutionalization in adulthood" (p. 355). The Benhaven program is behavioral and provides special education, rather than psychotherapy, to autistic individuals. Their autistic population varies considerably as many of the patients are multiply handicapped by deafness or blindness.

The Benhaven programs include a day program, residential living, family therapy and education programs, respite services, an outpatient clinic, and professional staff training and development services. In addition, Benhaven is involved in a number of ongoing research programs. As the autistic persons reach adulthood, less time is spent in formal academic programs. The focus shifts to vocational training as autistic adults are exposed to a number of vocational enterprises, such as button making, horticulture, farming, poultry raising, furniture refinishing and woodworking, and mailing services. Recreation and activity of daily living skills training are also part of the Benhaven treatment program.

Lettick (1983) places major emphasis on staff selection and development at Benhaven. Worker incentives, promotions from within, frequent staff meetings, and in-service training in behavior management techniques are just some of the factors that appear to contribute to Benhaven's success.

Staff Development

The model programs devised by Curran et al. (1985) and Lettick (1983) are commendable for their consideration of staff development, an important point that is all too often underemphasized. All of the treatment strategies outlined earlier appear quite capable of helping severely impaired patients. However, without adequately trained staff, these programs are destined to fail. In the literature on inpatient service delivery, staff training is often neglected. This situation is surprising given the 24-hr responsibility of inpatient care. Staff coordination is a necessary prerequisite for consistent treatment.

Nurses, ward technicians, psychiatric aides, and other direct-care staff have a significant impact on the patients' inpatient experience. These are the people who spend the most time interacting with patients yet receive the least education and training regarding patient care. These are the personnel who should be able to answer questions regarding patient behavior in staff meetings yet often do not understand the disorder and its accompanying characteristics. Finally, direct-care staff must be able to observe and reliably judge patient behaviors, implement treatment plans, and accurately record patients' symptomatic behaviors. In settings where behavioral treatments are designed, staff members need to understand basic reinforcement principles, including positive reinforcement, time out, extinction, and shaping, before behavioral techniques can be used effectively on the inpatient unit (Curran et al., 1982; Hagen, 1975).

Staff development is a complex and time-demanding task. Staff employees are often unmotivated, uneducated, apathetic, and resistant to change. If they do not evidence these qualities upon hiring, they are often acquired quickly as consequences of minimal pay, poor work conditions, and misunderstandings regarding their patients' behavior.

One problem encountered during staff development is resistance to change. People are most comfortable doing what is familiar. Liberman, Kuehnel, Phipps, and Cardin (1984c) suggest that asking a person to give up the patient care programs they already know and feel comfortable with so that new programs may be employed poses a number of problems. When attempting to implement a new program in an inpatient setting, Liberman and his colleagues suggest that one should take into account "focusing on adaptation rather than on adoption, slowly adding on to existing programs rather than replacing programs, and reinforcing initial change *efforts* rather than only looking toward completion and waiting to reinforce staff until results are obtained" (p. XI-12). It may be easier and more fruitful to work within the existing system, gradually adapting the existing program to the desired end.

As Liberman et al. (1984c, p. XI-13) suggest, "consciously focus on adding programs or elements of programs rather than replacing or discarding programs." Instead of redesigning the existing system, the psychologist is well advised to introduce portions of the new system one step at a time. This gives staff time to adapt and assimilate each element of the new program to what they already know, Direct-care workers cannot be expected to implement these programs without supervision. In-service training and continuing education can help staff to increase their knowledge. Yet knowledge alone is not sufficient to ensure behavioral change during their patient interactions. On the unit, the psychologist can model the behaviors and techniques described in the in-service training sessions and provide support and encouragement for the staff. Finally, the psychologist can draw from these ward experiences in later in-service training discussions.

Although very little research has been conducted investigating staff development, there have been several studies that consider instructional techniques (Paul & McInnis, 1974), and the use of positive reinforcement for staff during the training process (Kazdin & Bootzin, 1972; Panyan, Boozer, & Morris, 1970). The reader is referred to Liberman et al. (1984c) for a more comprehensive discussion regarding staff development. Future research should consider means by which direct care for severely impaired inpatients can be improved through staff development.

Patient Discharge

The average length of inpatient hospitalization is approximately 3 weeks (Bellack, 1986). The typical patient admitted to a psychiatric inpatient facility is treated on a short-term basis and then referred to a community-based aftercare treatment program. Little research has investigated when discharge from an inpatient facility is appropriate. Most commonly, the schizophrenic patient is discharged as soon as his or her positive symptoms are under control. Discharge is highly correlated with the reduction of hallucinations, delusions, and grossly disorganized behaviors. Very few studies specifically state the criteria by which a discharge decision is made, although this process should rely on nonsubjective factors such as patients' clinical and social status, community resources and placement, family conditions or living arrangements, and economic conditions. Two techniques that may be employed are the Discharge Readiness Inventory (DRI) and the Present State Examination (PSE).

The DRI was developed by Hogarty (1966), and consists of a rating scale designed to evaluate the release potential of chronic schizophrenic patients. This instrument assesses the patient's functioning across four factors, including psychosocial adequacy, belligerence (probability of aggressive behaviors), community adjustment potential, and manifest psychopathology (how much the patient's behavior reflects active hallucinations, delusions, etc.). The PSE (Wing, Cooper, & Sartorius, 1974) was developed to provide a reliable and complete description of psychopathological symptoms and behaviors. Therefore, the patient's behaviors, sensorium, and cognitive abilities are assessed using a mental status exam format.

Once the patient's clinical and social status appears adequate for discharge, community resources, placement alternatives, family conditions, and living arrangements must be evaluated. Deinstitutionalization was initiated so that treatment could take place near the home and away from large state hospitals that may foster apathy, dependency, and withdrawal. However, if patients are released from inpatient facilities to ill-equipped environments, there is little chance of avoiding relapse and subsequent rehospitalization. As Liberman et al. (1984c) suggest,

> Without sufficient community-based treatment and social support alternatives to long-term hospitalization, seriously ill individuals are either falling through the cracks of non-systems of care or are living in tenuous balance in family households that are stressed, strained, and ill-prepared for their care. (p. I-10)

Even if the patient is released to an adequate community-based treatment program, there is very little assurance that treatment will continue. Discharged patients often do not comply with their discharge referrals to community treatment resources. For example, Wolkon (1970) showed that 65% of the patients referred from psychiatric hospitals to an outpatient facility did not follow through with their referrals. In addition, many of the patients discontinued outpatient treatment after only a few sessions. When Tessler and Mason (1979) investigated compliance rates of patients referred to community clinics for aftercare, they found that 12% refused the referral altogether, 21% agreed to honor the referral but never contacted the community clinics, and 11% sought treatment immediately after discharge but failed to continue attending scheduled sessions. In other words, almost 45% of the patients in the Tessler and Mason study failed to continue treatment. In addition, a nonsignificant trend indicated that patients who continued receiving treatment on an outpatient basis were less likely to be rehospitalized. Finally, these researchers reported that 30% of the patients who did honor their referrals used the community clinics only for medication renewal and did not take part in any other treatment. It should be noted that not all of the patients in the Tessler and Mason (1979) and Wolkon (1970) studies were schizophrenic. However, these results are quite significant considering the importance of continued treatment compliance for the severely impaired patient after discharge.

A study by Caton, Goldstein, Serrano, and Bender (1984) found that comprehensive aftercare planning significantly increased treatment compliance and reduced rehospitalization rates at a 3- month follow-up. Chronic schizophrenic patients who were assigned to the experimental group in this study received individually tailored discharge planning that arranged aftercare treatment services, adequate living arrangements, economic support, and social and vocational rehabilitation before release from the inpatient facility.

OUTPATIENT TREATMENT AND SERVICE DELIVERY

One of the most significant changes in chronic patient care has been the movement toward deinstitutionalization. However, this trend is compromised by fragmentation of care and pattern of chronic rehospitalizations. The following discussion will address several issues related to deinstitutionalization: transitional housing, case management, crisis intervention, social clubs, day treatment, partial hospitalization, vocational training, and rehabilitation.

Transitional Housing

Transitional housing programs are a component in comprehensive service programs for the chronic mentally ill and are designed to aid the transition from an inpatient facility to a less restrictive environment. The major focus of these programs is on the acquisition of independent living skills within a residential setting.

These programs identify skill and resource strengths and weaknesses required for independent living and attempt to place individuals in a living environment commensurate with his or her abilities and resources. Although many patients may not be able to move beyond closely supervised living and still others may not desire to do so, an effort is made to strengthen skills and improve deficits to promote independent living in the community.

Most of these programs offer a continuum of housing alternatives ranging from highly supportive and supervised transitional housing to more independent and long-term cooperative housing. For example, Boley Manor in St. Petersburg, Florida, offers residents five housing alternatives that are graduated in their restrictiveness and treatment services. Most of these programs require that prospective patients be recommended for placement, visit their facilities, and formally apply for admission.

Transitional housing programs offer individual and group education and treatment designed to improve a wide range of independent living skills, including physical health care, personal hygiene, nutrition and meal preparation, shopping for goods and services, medication management, budget planning and money management, time management, and the use of public transportation. Movement across the various housing arrangements is determined by the patient's competence in predetermined skill areas. In addition, vocational rehabilitation services and/or help in securing disability payments are provided by these programs.

Boley Manor is one such exemplary transitional housing program. Their program includes the following services:

1. A crisis intervention unit.
2. A group home that provides close supervision and highly structured environment designed for the acquisition of basic living and social skills.
3. A halfway house designed for further acquisition services provided within the group home, with a specific focus on social skills and self-acceptance.
4. A supervised apartment program designed to provide continued counseling and support, with the added benefits and responsibilities associated with independent apartment living.
5. A satellite apartment program that serves as a final link between total independence and continued supervision before the transition process is completed.

6. Continued case management and referrals to professional and social support services.

Boley Manor appears to contribute significantly to lower recidivism rates and an increased number of patients who learn to live independently (Liberman et al., 1984c).

Total independent living for even the least intellectually impaired autistic adult appears quite rare. Therefore, transitional housing programs have not been extended to autistic adults. As Lettick (1983) states:

> Some believe that deinstitutionalization and total integration with the nonhandicapped provides the optimal environment for the autistic, and should be the only setting acceptable. If a person cannot presently function in that setting, they state, it is the fault of the community in not accommodating and providing adequately for his needs . . . such a welcoming, suitable community does not exist, to serve either as a model or proof of the validity of this belief . . . While a small portion of the autistic population may be able to function in a nonspecialized setting, the majority require a range of alternative settings, from small group homes, to local, benign, small institutions. (pp. 376–377)

Independent living is extremely rare among adult autistics because of their daily living and leisure skill deficits as well as poor social and communication skills. If placement in a facility such as the Benhaven programs (Lettick, 1983) is not possible, day treatment may provide an alternative. Janicki et al. (1983) reported that 43% of autistic adults required assistance with toileting and 46% displayed inadequate self-feeding skills. Similarly, fewer than 24% of autistic adults were capable of independent dressing or grooming. Janicki et al. reported: "Almost all autistic adults were found to be incapable of carrying out basic independence capacity functions such as using telephones, cooking, doing their own laundry, and shopping" (p. 78).

These daily living skills can be taught to autistic adults using behavioral treatment techniques. Smith and Belcher (1985) employed task analysis and shaping through "graduated schedules of assistance" to teach face washing, hair combing, tooth brushing, cleaning the sink, and cooking. The reader is referred to the Fredericks, Buckley, Baldwin, Moore, and Stremel-Campbell (1983) report for a summary of similar services provided to autistic adolescents and young adults.

Case Management

The use of case management systems can be an important component in discharge planning and avoiding fragmentation of care. Case management provides each patient with an identified person responsible for coordinating his or her care within the community's total service delivery system (Schwartz, Goldman, & Churgin, 1982). Intagliata (1982) suggests that case management is a "process or methods for ensuring that consumers (patients) are provided with whatever services they need in a coordinated, effective, and efficient manner" (p. 657). Agranoff (cited in Intagliata, 1982) suggests that comprehensive case management should include the following:

1. Assessment of client need.
2. Development of a comprehensive service plan.
3. Arranging for services to be delivered.
4. Monitoring and assessing the services delivered.
5. Evaluation and follow-up. (p. 658)

Therefore, Intagliata (1982) describes the five major functions of case management as assessment, planning, linking, monitoring, and evaluation. Case managers should be directly involved in the initial assessment of a patient's needs, ideally before the patient is discharged from an inpatient facility. In some cases, the process may begin shortly after a patient is hospitalized (Liberman, et al., 1984c). When the planning process begins well before discharge, community placements can be maximally effective immediately following discharge.

The case manager must be aware of all of the available patient resources and services and coordinate their utilization. This approach may include arranging food, shelter, clothing, income (social security benefits, disability, welfare, vocational rehabilitation, etc.), medical care, and psychological treatment (Intagliata, 1982; Schwartz et al., 1982). The case manager also monitors services and ensures that the patient actually receives these services. In other words, the case manager reduces fragmentation between the various service systems designed to treat the chronic patient and acts as a patient advocate. Finally, the case manager evaluates the patient's progress and the quality of care that patient is receiving (Intagliata, 1982).

Given the job description outlined above, it is absurd to expect paraprofessionals with limited education or training in clinical and social work to be able to perform such a role. In some areas, case management is performed by well-trained individuals or by persons supervised by such professionals. However, in most cases, paraprofessionals perform case management duties (Intagliata, 1982; Schwartz et al., 1982). This poses a problem similar to the discussion of staff development and the direct-care staff who "treat" inpatients. The case management concept is also plagued by insufficient funding. Well-trained and well-educated professionals rarely perform case management services as they are not interested in performing such duties for so little pay.

Despite the aforementioned problems, Liberman et al. (1984c) describe several comprehensive case management programs that have shown positive results. For example, rehospitalizations, psychopathology, and criminal justice contacts have been significantly reduced with sound case management programs, and patients have been able to find work and live independently.

Crisis Intervention Units

Crisis units are designed to provide services to acutely psychotic individuals on an outpatient basis. Since decompensation and rehospitalization among chronic mentally ill patients are common, such programs provide an alternative to rehospitalization. Crisis intervention units often work closely with hospital emergency room and local mental health centers to stabilize the individual before inpatient commitment becomes necessary. These programs are usually designed as day clinics with overnight housing available in family care homes, hospitals, or mental health facilities. Most of these programs also include 24-hr telephone hotlines and crisis transportation services.

Because the focus of these programs is on rapid stabilization, most patients receive some form of pharmacological treatment upon admission. The patients' medications are monitored closely, and dosages are reduced once decompensation appears under control, followed by efforts to return the patient to his or her precrisis setting or to an alternative program. If crisis intervention is insufficient or if the patient is considered to be a danger to himself and/or others, transfer to a long-term inpatient facility may begin.

The treatment provided by crisis stabilization units varies considerably across programs. However, most patients remain in these programs from 1 to 3 weeks. Discharge planning also varies but usually includes referral to an outpatient mental health facility and/or community support program and a conference with the patient's family members. In an effort to reduce noncompliance in outpatient treatment referrals, appointments with the appropriate outpatient treatment programs are scheduled and a conference with an outpatient case manager is conducted before the patient is discharged.

Liberman et al. (1984c) include descriptions of several exemplary crisis stabilization units. One such unit is the Crisis Stabilization Unit at the Baton Rouge Mental Health Center in Baton Rouge, Louisiana. This program has incorporated most of the methods and treatment programming described above. Their unit includes the following:

1. Medical supervision and medication administration—rapid tranquilization techniques as indicated.
2. Psychotherapy—individual, group, and family sessions.
3. Activity therapy.
4. Art therapy.
5. Educational health programs. (p. IV-2)

The daily schedule for patients includes medication administration, daily rounds with a multidisciplinary treatment team, recreational programs, and various forms of therapy. Patients participate in this program during the day and may be housed at a local hospital if overnight care and supervision appear necessary. The Crisis Stabilization Unit reports that about 87% of their patients are returned to their homes without long-term rehospitalization.

Social Clubs, Day Treatment, and Partial Hospitalization

Social clubs, day treatment, and partial-hospitalization facilities are also designed to reduce rehospitalization. These programs provide chronic mentally ill patients with social support and aftercare services through the use of structured activities and educational classes.

Because social isolation and poor social skills contribute to the high recidivism rates for these patients, a concentrated effort is made to provide group support from psychiatric-care workers and patient peers.

These programs usually operate 5 days per week and may offer day and/or night activities for their patients. The services vary across programs. However, most programs include some combination of services designed to increase successful community living. These may include social skills, assertiveness training, problem-solving skills, medication management and compliance, recreation and leisure activities, stress management, personal health and hygiene, independent living skills, educational services, and various forms of therapy, including art, group, family, and individual therapies. Many programs also provide transportation. Finally, these programs vary considerably in terms of the personnel who provide these services. Some are operated by professionals, such as psychiatrists, psychologists and/or social workers' others are operated by B.A.-level personnel and community volunteers.

After questioning mental health care professionals concerning necessary skills for successful community living, Wallace, Boone, Donahoe, and Foy (1985) prepared training modules for chronic mentally ill patients that included conversational skills, vocational rehabilitation, medication management, self-care skills, personal information, home finding and maintenance skills, leisure/recreational skills, food preparation, public transportation, and money management. Ideally, these skills should be taught before patient discharge, but partial-hospitalization programs can continue such training.

One exemplary program is the Social and Independent Living Program in Los Angeles, which includes all of the services mentioned above and focused particular attention on medication management. Patients are educated concerning medication's benefits, the importance of continued compliance, self-administration techniques, and the monitoring and management of side effects. The treatment program is behavior-oriented, and careful consideration is given to research design and program evaluation (Liberman et al., 1984c).

Vocational Training and Rehabilitation

Vocational training and rehabilitation programs train chronic mentally ill patients in basic vocational skills. Program goals usually include the acquisition of job skills and the development of an economically independent patient who requires less supervision. Graduation to fulltime employment, formal education, or some other job-training program is the ultimate goal of most vocational training and rehabilitation services.

Social skills, various independent-living skills, and general work habits, such as punctuality, proper dress, and personal hygiene, are usually considered necessary prerequisite skills for acceptance into these vocational rehabilitation programs. In addition, most require that prospective patients be recommended for placement in their programs, visit their facilities, and formally apply for admission before being placed in the most feasible setting. Liberman et al. (1984c) suggest that a formal assessment is typically designed "to determine the individual's vocational interests, job aptitudes, physical and emotional work capacities, work personality traits, vocational limitations, and restrictions, social and community adjustment needs, income maintenance needs, and training and employment options" (pp. IX- 22–23).

Patients receive job-skills training and are then typically employed within a sheltered program or in local businesses on a part-time basis. They receive close supervision and guidance until permanent or long-term employment appears possible. Patients also receive training designed to help them fill out applications and improve their job interviewing skills. Group meetings are usually held on a regular basis to provide support, reinforcement, and encouragement to the patients as part of the rehabilitation process. Finally, these programs often work very closely with day treatment facilities in an effort to consolidate services into a more holistic treatment program (Liberman et al., 1984c).

The Supervised Work Experience and Employment Program in Eugene, Oregon, is one such program that operates within a comprehensive rehabilitation agency serving the chronic mentally ill. Patients proceed through the following vocational training stages:

1. A prevocational stage is designed to help the patients become motivated for work and develop appropriate work habits and attitudes.
2. A work-evaluation stage includes a "career exploration class" and limited exposure to a number of different work experiences.

3. A work-adjustment stage helps the patients develop concrete career goals and gradually exposes them to more of the pressures and demands encountered in full-time employment.
4. A work-experience stage emphasizes increased "work speed, efficiency, and endurance." Wages are made contingent upon the quality and quantity of work completed, and job-finding skills are developed.
5. A transitional employment program stage includes closely supervised part-time employment within the community.
6. A job placement stage functions as a mechanism for continued supervision and follow-up services.

The patients receive encouragement, feedback, and various forms of group and individual therapy throughout the program, progressing through these stages at their own pace; some patients remain at the earlier stages indefinitely. Competence in a number of areas is required before promotion to each higher level (Liberman et al., 1984c).

Vocational training programs for autistic adults are quite similar to those designed for schizophrenic patients, However, because of their severe communication problems and high frequency of self-destructive behaviors and temper tantrums, employment opportunities for autistic adults are scarce. As Mesibov, Schopler, and Sloan (1983) indicate, these behaviors are incompatible with successful employment. It has been suggested that vocational training programs for autistic adults might include training designed specifically to help autistic adults adapt to change and comply with routine, as well as to learn the specific tasks required for successful employment (Mesibov, 1983).

In an effort to meet these goals, vocational training programs are beginning to employ a teacher-advocate (T-A) model developed by Levy (1983):

> The T-A is a professionally trained individual who is responsible for the handicapped worker's complete adjustment to the job. In this procedure the T-A's involvement and assistance is faded out as the worker becomes more competent at the job and management and fellow employees become more comfortable with the handicapped worker. (pp. 143–144)

Although the T-A model appears costly, Levy (1983) suggests that successful completion of such a program results in self-sufficient and self-supporting autistic adults.

Recent research, following Levy's (1983) suggestions has investigated methods for managing autistic adults' behavior in the job setting. Smith and Coleman (1986) reduced the frequency of aggressive and oppositional behaviors and increased work productivity through the use of closely supervised on-the-job training and behavior-management techniques. This is encouraging considering the number of autistic adolescents and adults who are chronically unemployed and financially dependent. For example, the proportion of autistic adolescents and adults reported to be employed in the studies reviewed by Lotter (1978) varied from 0% to 13%.

The Southeastern TEACCH Center in Chapel Hill, North Carolina, incorporates many of these ideas into a service delivery system for autistic adolescents and adults. One of the primary goals of this program is clients' placement in sheltered workshops; the ultimate goal involves job placement within the community (Mesibov et al., 1983).

Liberman et al. (1984c) suggested that outpatient treatment programs must offer the following services if they are to be effective:

1. Assertive outreach—this includes working with social and financial support systems and significant others for patients' needs. Because chronic mental patients have low motivation and difficulty in negotiating the system, they need flexible levels of support up to and including home treatment.
2. Individually tailored programs—staff must set realistic goals to remediate skills deficits, social and financial needs, and family burden. Training in community living skills, opportunities to improve employability, appropriate living arrangements and opportunities to develop social skills must be provided.
3. In vivo services—this means staff must be available to work with patients in real-life community settings, such as jobs, stores, and homes. This promotes transfer of learning through prompting, modeling, and reinforcement.
4. Services that build on the strengths and assets of patents.
5. Attitudes that treat patients as responsible citizens who can advocate for their needs within our political system.
6. Crisis intervention that is available round the clock.
7. Coordination and advocacy with our community agencies and resources, including the patient's family. This includes assistance in applying for entitlement programs and protection of client's rights.
8. Medical and mental health care.
9. Backup support to families, friends, and community members.
10. Case management to ensure continuous availability of appropriate forms of assistance. (pp. I-24–I-25)

Partial hospitalization and day treatment programs that include these services have been shown to be as effective as or more effective than, inpatient facilities in treating chronic schizophrenic patients. In several studies, Liberman and his colleagues instituted a behavior-oriented day treatment program (see Kuehnel, DeRisi, Liberman, & Mosk, 1984). These researchers individually tailored goals for the patients, implemented a credit incentive system similar to a token economy, and established educational workshops to help the patients reintegrate themselves into the community. A number of other model day treatment programs are outlined by Liberman et al. (1984c) and summaries of each of these programs' goals, descriptions, budgets, and other characteristics are included. Finally, the Fountain House Model of psychiatric rehabilitation (Beard, Propst, & Malamud, 1982) should be mentioned in any discussion of outpatient service delivery models. Most of the exemplary programs described by Liberman et al. (1984c) have been modeled to some extent after the Fountain House program located in New York. The Fountain House incorporates each of the outpatient service delivery models discussed above in an attempt to provide biopsychosocial services to the chronically mentally ill.

Outpatient Intervention within Service Delivery Models

Drug Maintenance and Compliance

After a patient's recovery from an acute psychotic state and before hospital discharge, a decision must be made concerning continued use of antipsychotic medication. The adverse side effects that accompany long-term use of antipsychotic medication and poor drug compliance rates after discharge have led researchers to investigate alternative medication strategies. Significant dosage reductions are feasible for some schizophrenic patients, although more research is needed to reliably identify the low-dosage responders (Kane, 1983). Kane also found that lower doses are associated with fewer side effects (involuntary movements) and improved social adjustment. A number of dose-reduction studies have been reviewed by Gardos and Cole (1976).

The second alternative to long-term drug maintenance is characterized by "drug holidays," during which medications are discontinued for an extended period of time (Carpenter & Heinrichs, 1983). Patients are stabilized and then closely followed while they are drug-free until prodromal signs of impending relapse appear. Medication is then reintroduced until the patient is restabilized, after which the medications are withdrawn once again. Results suggest that this approach can be employed without negative consequences such as extended hospitalizations, work disruption, harm to self and others, or reappearance of positive symptomatology. This "targeted" education approach produces outcomes comparable to traditional drug maintenance. Finally, Carpenter and Heinrichs's results suggest that targeted medication may lead to a significant reduction in antipsychotic medications, thus reducing the various side effects. This is important because adverse side effects are frequently implicated in drug noncompliance (Van Putten, 1974).

Schizophrenic patients are notoriously poor at complying with medication after their release from an inpatient facility. About 20% of schizophrenic inpatients and 40 to 70% of schizophrenic outpatients fail to take their medications as prescribed (Ayd, 1975). Behavior therapy techniques may potentially ameliorate such problems. For example, St. Lawrence (1981) reported increases in outpatient attendance and participation with the use of a money deposit contingency. When a "money deposit group" was compared to a "no deposit group" along such variables as attendance, in-session participation, and between-sessions self-monitoring, there were significant differences between the two groups. There is no reason that such a study could not be replicated with drug compliance as the dependent measure.

Problems that contribute to noncompliance include poor aftercare attendance, forgetfulness, adverse side effects, patient and family attitudes concerning the illness, and failure to understand the importance of drug compliance in preventing relapse (Falloon, 1984). Falloon suggests that education, cognitive structuring, and the use of reinforcers could be used to increase drug compliance.

Epstein and Cluss (1982) reviewed the research on interventions to promote drug compliance in medical illnesses. Behavioral approaches, as well as a number of nonbehavioral approaches, had only limited success. Haynes (1979) suggested that behavior therapy techniques, along with increased patient supervision and "significant other" drug administration, are the most effective approaches for increasing drug compliance in chronic mental patients.

Boczkowski, Zeichner, and DeSanto (1985) compared behavioral, psychoeducational, and control interventions on medication compliance of chronic schizophrenic outpatients. The results indicated that the behaviorally trained patients were more compliant, as measured by pill counts, than were the other groups. The researchers also found low correlation between the pill counts, significant others' ratings, and self-reports of drug compliance. This suggests that subjective ratings and self-reports of drug compliance have questionable validity. Epstein and Cluss (1982) also questioned the validity of these methods and reviewed problems associated with the self-report and pill-count methods most often used to assess drug compliance.

Another behavioral technique that may be used to increase drug compliance is suggested by the antabuse compliance research conducted by Keane and his colleagues (Keane, Foy, Nunn, & Rychtarik, 1984). Using behavioral contracting to enhance compliance in alcoholic veterans, Keane et al. (1984) reported that contracting, self-monitoring, other-monitoring, and social reinforcement in the home environment all contributed to increased compliance rates. Similar procedures could be evaluated to increase compliance among schizophrenic patients.

Researchers frequently attempt to improve drug compliance among schizophrenic individuals through patient education. Ideally, education should begin before hospital discharge (Curran et al. 1985; Kessler & Waletzky, 1981), although it is often difficult to convince patients and their families of the importance of continued drug compliance (Shapiro, 1981). Curran and his colleagues (1985) at Providence Veterans Administration Medical Center indicated that 30 to 40% of their time is spent in patient education. Given the findings cited above (Boczkowski et al., 1985; Keane et al., 1984), including family members in the educational process appears worthwhile.

Another method that has been used to increase compliance in schizophrenic patients is the use of longer-acting, injectable medication. Administration of fluphenazine decanoate (Prolixin®) has effects that may last 3 to 4 weeks (Kessler & Waletzky, 1981). The ability to treat patients with an injection every 3 weeks may reduce some compliance problems, although several attempts to examine the efficacy of this approach reveal mixed results (Hogarty et al., 1979; Kessler & Waletzky, 1981; Simpson & Lee, 1978). A number of other long-acting drugs are available in Europe and also have shown mixed results (Simpson & Lee, 1978).

Social Skills Training

Despite the use of drugs and behavioral treatments to decrease psychotic behaviors, many schizophrenic patients display poor social adjustment following their inpatient discharge because negative symptoms are still present at the time of discharge. Many of these patients leave the hospital with poor problem-solving skills and interpersonal deficits that impair adequate functioning in society. Social skills training and problem-solving training can help the patient interact more appropriately in the community and solve common everyday problems more effectively. The importance of social skills training is outlined by Bellack (1986):

> Social disability is one of the DSM-III diagnostic criteria, and poor premorbid social competence remains the best overall predictor of outcome. Inadequate social relationships is a prime contributor to the poor quality of life experienced by schizophrenics and is thought to be a significant factor in relapse. In light of these problems, remediation of social disability must be a major goal of any comprehensive intervention program. Behavior therapy offers the most effective strategy for enhancing social competence: social skills training. (p. 208)

Literature evaluating social skills training of schizophrenic patients indicates that topographical behavior and self-reports of anxiety and discomfort improve following such training. Procedures such as behavior rehearsal, dyadic interviews, conversation limitation, onward interactions, modeling, and shaping are often used to teach social skills. Christoff and Kelly (1985) suggest that social skills training should address the following:

1. Self-care.
2. Conversational skills.

3. Assertiveness skills: refusal assertiveness (saying no, standing up for rights; commendatory assertiveness (expressions of positive feelings at appropriate times, praise, appreciation, love).
4. Date initiation/heterosocial skills.
5. Job interviewing skills.

Bellack, Turner, Hersen, and Luber (1984) compared schizophrenic patients in a day hospitalization program. All patients received relaxation training, group therapy, discussion of current issues and bureaucratic systems, and training in community readjustment. In addition, a social skills group received specific skills training. Both groups showed improvement on a number of scales measuring assertiveness, social skills, and the presence of psychiatric symptoms immediately following treatment. However, at 6-month follow-up the social skills training group patients continued to improve or maintain their improvement, whereas control group patients only maintained improvement or lost them. Despite these results, the skills treatment did not affect relapse, as half of the patients in both groups were rehospitalized at least once within 12 months. Researchers suggested that their program may have been too limited and "did not adequately deal with the broad range of handicaps and life skill deficits characteristic of this population" (p. 1027).

The changes that take place when using social skills training with severely impaired patients do not occur evenly for every patient and may not be generalized to new situations. Holmes, Hansen, and St. Lawrence (1984) investigated generalization and maintenance following conversational-skills training with adult schizophrenic patients. Those experiencing conversational difficulties received group training that focused on speech content and various skills components. Training effectiveness was evaluated by behavioral ratings in dyadic unstructured conversations and in extended conversations with nonpsychiatric strangers. Improvements were maintained at 1-, 3-, and 7-month follow-up assessments.

In another study investigating generalization, Finch and Wallace (1977) studied the effectiveness of anxiety management training and behavioral rehearsal for male schizophrenic patients. It was hoped that self-evaluation procedures and homework assignments would promote generalizability for these patients. The interpersonal skills training group improved significantly compared to a control group on a number of dependent measures, including eye contact, loudness, fluency, affect, latency, content, and self-reported assertiveness. These differences were observed across both the role-play and spontaneous sessions, which indicates some limited generalizability.

Bellack, Hersen, and Turner (1976) administered social skills training to three chronic schizophrenic patients in a partial-hospitalization program. Five to seven target behaviors were identified for each patient, and those target behaviors were treated sequentially using a multiple-baseline design. Results indicated that (a) skills training was effective for two of the three patients, (b) skills generalized from trained to untrained role-play interactions, and (c) these effects continued at an 8- to 10-week follow-up.

Improved social and communication skills are also targeted in the treatment of autistic adults. A number of researchers suggest that social and interpersonal skills deficits are the primary impediments to mainstreaming adult autistic persons in society (Fredericks et al., 1983; Mesibov, 1986; Schopler & Mesibov, 1983). Kanner, Rodriguez, and Ashenden (1972) state that the most important determinant of positive outcome for autistic persons is social skill. In their study, subjects who improved their social skills were more likely to achieve greater independence during adulthood.

Target behaviors for social skills training with autistic adults vary, depending on the severity of the clients' communication and language deficits. Wing (1983) attempted to classify autistic persons into subgroups based on their social interaction, ability level, and temperament. Wing's classification system includes the "aloof group," "passive group," and "active but odd group." Target behaviors for social skills training with autistic adults often address general rules for social interaction, conversation initiation, friend making, and relationship building (Fredericks et al., 1983; Mesibov, 1986; Wing, 1983). Mesibov (1983; 1986) suggests that reducing the autistic person's tendency to exclude others, developing empathy, and increasing reciprocity are also important variables to be targeted. Finally, Mesibov (1986) suggests that the lack of positive social experiences in an autistic person's life lead to withdrawal and must be considered in the treatment design.

Mesibov (1983; 1986) designed social skills programs for autistic adults that included role playing, modeling, and the use of dyadic interviews. The clients received feedback, coaching from trained staff, and a great deal of positive reinforcement for their efforts. Clients showed improvements in their conversational initiations and maintenance, selection of relevant topics, listening skills, and eye contact. In addition, a self-report measurement reflected improved self-concept among the autistic clients. The program designed by Mesibov appears quite similar to social skills programs that have been employed with mentally retarded and schizophrenic persons and suggests that other researchers can evaluate and adapt to the autistic adult training programs that have proved effective with these two populations.

Recent research has investigated the relationship between social adjustment and patient relapse. Liberman et al. (1986) evaluated an intensive social skills training program for schizophrenic inpatients at high risk for relapse. In a pilot study, two of the three patients showed improvements in role-play performance, behavioral competence as measured by conversations with strangers, nurses' ratings of spontaneous conversations, symptomatology, social ward behavior, and self-report measures of assertiveness and social discomfort. Follow-up data revealed that two of the three patients maintained their progress 1 year postdischarge; neither patient was rehospitalized, and Present State Examination (PSE) scores revealed no psychotic symptoms.

In a second study, Liberman et al. (1986) compared social skills training with a holistic health treatment. Social skills training was based on a problem-solving model proposed by Wallace (1982). A number of outcome measures assessed patients' symptomatology, social adjustment, and problem-solving skills. Results indicated superior role-play performances at posttreatment and 9-month follow-up for the social skills group. In conversations with strangers, the social skills patients revealed significantly less hostility, mistrust, detachment, inhibition, and submission. Social adjustment ratings by relatives also reflected significant improvements. Ratings by social workers suggested improvements in employment in both groups and significant improvement in symptomatology for the social skills group. The holistic treatment patients were hospitalized twice as often as the social skills patients in the 2 years following discharge. Finally, PSE scores revealed that 50% of the social skills patients versus 79% of the holistic treatment patients evinced symptom relapse over the 2 years following discharge. Therefore, social skills training appeared to benefit the clinical course of schizophrenia (Liberman et al., 1986).

Two important aspects of the Liberman et al. (1986) study warrant further comment. Their study documented the complementary role of pharmacological treatments and social skills training to decrease rehospitalizations in schizophrenic patients. In addition, this study considered the importance of social skills training within the inpatient facility. All too often, the treatment of negative symptoms is left to outpatient or partial-hospitalization facilities. This situation may well be a major contributing factor to the high rehospitalization rates.

A review of social skills research with schizophrenic and adult autistic patients suggests that improved social adjustment may be seen in some patients. However, future research needs to attend to the suggestions of Curran et al. (1985) and Liberman et al. (1986) to treat negative symptoms of schizophrenic patients before discharge. These suggestions are also applicable to the treatment of autism. Skills maintenance across time and skill generalization to in vivo community settings also need to be more carefully assessed. Although inpatient training may enable more rapid acquisition, improved coordination with outpatient facilities may assist maintenance and generalization.

Problem-solving Training

Kelly and Lamparski (1985) suggest that schizophrenic patients lack the problem-solving skills necessary for successful independent living and outline a comprehensive treatment program to modify both social skills and problem-solving deficits in schizophrenic patients. The inability to identify that a problem exists or arrive at appropriate and workable solutions is common among schizophrenic patients. These problems contribute to the high recidivism and poor social adjustment so often experienced by these patients (D'Zurilla & Goldfried, 1971; Liberman et al., 1984b). D'Zurilla and Goldfried (1971) defined problem solving as "a behavioral process which (a) makes available a variety of response alternatives for dealing with a problematic situation and (b) increases the probability of selecting the most effective response from among these alternatives" (p. 107).

Hansen, St. Lawrence, and Christoff (1985) worked with schizophrenic outpatients who had difficulty solving interpersonal problems. The patients received group skills training in problem identification, goal definition, solution evaluation, generation of alternatives, and selection of a best solution. Each component skill increased after the introduction of training and generalized to untrained situations. Skills decreased somewhat during follow-up evaluations at 1 and 4 months but remained higher than at pretreatment.

As one might expect, the problems associated with generalization from social skills training also apply to problem-solving interventions. Kelly and Lamparski (1985) outlined suggestions to promote skill generalization. They suggest making practice scenes representative of actual situations that are problematic for the patient. They also suggest assigning homework designed to facilitate use of these skills outside sessions. Staff should reinforce improvements, practice difficult situations with the patients, and remain aware that patients may lack the prerequisite community living and social skills that are necessary to employ successfully the problem-solving skills learned in treatment sessions.

The Role of the Family

Given our current knowledge concerning stress and family interaction patterns of postdischarge adjustment and the fact that 65% of patients return to their families (Goldman, 1982), family interventions are an important research priority (Falloon, 1985; Falloon, Boyd, & McGill, 1984; Hooley, 1985; Liberman et al., 1984c; Lukoff, Snyder, Ventura, & Nuechterlein, 1984). After a patient has made progress in the inpatient setting, it is indefensible to return the patient to an environment that remains ill-equipped to deal with him or her. Schizophrenic persons face more severe problems in employment, social contacts, and unresolved family problems than do controls with less severe disorders or personality disorders (Holding, Urbanc, & Kay, 1983). Holding et al. (1983) found the family and relationship problems of schizophrenic persons were more severe and long-lasting, and the number of readmissions and total duration of rehospitalizations were greater for the schizophrenic patients. Similar findings are reported by Lukoff et al. (1984).

Vaughn and Leff (1976) reviewed a series of studies that investigated the family's influence on the course of schizophrenia. They report that the family's level of expressed emotion is highly correlated with relapse within 9 months after discharge. Schizophrenic patients who live with critical, hostile, overprotective, or emotionally overinvolved relatives [high expressed emotion (EE)] relapse significantly more often. Research investigating the EE construct was recently reviewed by Hooley (1985). She concluded that the concept was both reliable and valid. Hooley further concluded that the cumulative literature clearly documents that patients discharged to families with high emotional tension relapse at a greater rate than do patients discharged to supportive, understanding, and tolerant families or to residential care. The more disturbed a patient is at discharge, the less he or she is able to cope with the stress imposed by high-EE relatives (Anderson, 1983; cited in Hooley, 1985).

A number of researchers suggest that the families of schizophrenic patients should receive education regarding medication side effects, signs of relapse, and the importance of continuing medication (Curran et al., 1985; Kessler & Waletzky, 1981). For out patient treatment to be maximally effective, it is necessary to educate families about the patient's disorder. They should learn how to identify and predict patterns of relapse and should be encouraged to take an active role in returning patients for treatment when relapse appears imminent (Carpenter & Heinrichs, 1983; Falloon & Liberman, 1983). Bellack (1986) suggests that families of schizophrenic patients can become allies in the treatment process instead of being blamed for the disorder or ignored, as so often is the case.

Hertz and Melville (1980) found that over 90% of the families with a schizophrenic patient were able to describe signs of relapse. However, only about 70% of the patients were able to identify signs of relapse, Curran et al. (1985) suggest that it is extremely important to include a comprehensive family program in the treatment of schizophrenic patients, and their treatment program incorporates weekly or biweekly family meetings. The family sessions address educational issues, resolution of family guilt, realization of a handicap, the importance of antipsychotic medications, identification of stressors, management of disruptive behavior, and communication and problem-solving skills.

Several studies investigate the efficacy of such family involvement. Goldstein, Rodnick, Evans, May, and Steinberg (1978) compared family therapy to routine aftercare in reducing recidivism after a florid schizophrenic episode. Relapses during a 6-week controlled period and at 6-month follow-up were lowest for patients who received standard maintenance doses and family therapy (0%). By comparison, relapse rates were 48% for the low-dose-no-therapy group, 22% for the low-dose-therapy group, and 17% for the standard-dose-no-therapy group.

Liberman, Falloon, and Atchison (1984) used a behavioral, problem-solving intervention with high-EE families of young schizophrenic adults. Results indicated that the families and patients learned more information about the disorder and experienced fewer family conflicts. In addition, high-EE levels and relapse rates were reduced over those of patients exposed to holistic treatment. Comparable results were also reported by Berkowitz, Eberlein-Fries, Kulpers, and Leff (1984).

Discussion of the family's role in the treatment of chronic schizophrenic patients would be incomplete without considering the research conducted by Falloon and his colleagues (Falloon, 1985; Falloon et al., 1984). Falloon et al. (1984) authored a text on behavioral family therapy (BFT). The treatment program includes a behavioral analysis of the schizophrenic patients' families, patient and family education about schizophrenia, communication training, problem-solving training, and specific strategies for the family's management of the disorder. Detailed procedures, empirical evidence, and case examples are provided for each treatment component. A controlled outcome study comparing the effectiveness of BFT with individual supportive therapy support the efficacy of BFT. Specifically, BFT more effectively prevented exacerbations of positive symptoms and inpatient readmissions. Although exacerbations were seen in BFT group patients, these recurrences were less severe and more easily controlled than when they occurred in the comparison group. Although improvements in negative symptomatology were seen in both groups, BFT patients showed greater improvements than did the patients receiving supportive therapy. Finally, there were significant reductions in family members' distress and dissatisfaction in the families of patients assigned to BFT. Falloon et al. suggest that "a more tolerant, supportive attitude with lowered, but realistic, expectations probably contributed to a lowering of family tension in families that participated in family therapy" (p. 353). Lengthy follow-up indicated that improvements were maintained over 2 years.

In a similar study, Falloon (1985) reported fewer relapses, lower ratings of psychopathology, fewer readmissions, a trend toward fewer deficit symptoms, lower doses of antipsychotic medications, less distress and patient-related disruption in patients and family members, and improved communication, problem-solving and coping skills among the patients' families. The BFT treatment strategy offers a carefully developed and well-tested approach for community care of chronic schizophrenic patients.

Family interventions are also crucial for autistic adults. DeMyer (cited in Adams & Shaslow, 1983) describes the task of caring for an autistic person as "perpetual parenthood." Separation from one's parents is an unreachable goal for most autistic persons. The statistics that have been reported throughout this chapter concerning unemployment, social and communication skills, institutionalization, and general service needs of autistic adults all point toward continued dependence on others. Therefore, stress in the families of autistic clients is usually high.

DeMyer and Goldberg (1983) report that families must alter their life-styles drastically to accommodate the autistic person. Significant aspects of a family's life that are adversely affected include family recreation, finances, emotional, and mental health of parents and siblings, physical health of parents, and relations with friends, neighbors, relatives, and spouses. DeMyer and Goldberg also found that 100% of adolescents' parents express a need for "good" full- or part-time treatment. At the very least, families need respite care. Apparently, the need becomes greater as the autistic person ages and his or her family members become unwilling or unable to deal effectively with the affected person.

Much research has investigated treatment of the family with an autistic child. However, these issues also apply to the families of the autistic adult. It appears that these families could also benefit from BFT strategies and comprehensive family programs such as those proposed by Falloon et al. (1984) and Curran et al. (1985). Issues such as the resolution of family guilt, stressor identification, coping strategies, communication and problem-solving skills, and management of aggressive behaviors are equally relevant for the families of autistic adults as for those with autistic children. Lovaas et al. (1973) found inclusion of parents in the treatment program contributed significantly to positive outcome for autistic persons. Lovaas and his colleagues found that treatment gains were best maintained and increased at follow-up when parents were trained to continue behavior therapy techniques within the home. Since the need for continued monitoring and structured programming continues throughout the autistic person's life, comprehensive family treatment seems extremely important, if not essential.

FUTURE RESEARCH DIRECTIONS

Comprehensive service delivery systems must be developed and empirically evaluated if integrated service delivery and optimal treatment are ever to become a reality for the chronically mentally ill. Nor is it sufficient to evaluate treatment strategies in isolation, for they should be evaluated within the context of the system that provides the services. On a conceptual level, there would appear to be unique advantages and disadvantages inherent in each service delivery setting. For example, inpatient care should enable more rapid acquisition of new behavioral repertoires because greater environmental control is possible in inpatient settings and consistent consequences and coordinated treatment plans across all shifts should be feasible. However, inpatient settings may offer less opportunity to promote generalization or maintenance of newly acquired behavior. These may be better implemented in outpatient service delivery settings, where there are more opportunities to promote the use of newly acquired skills in the natural environment and for the patient to experience unorchestrated reinforcement. In addition, the day treatment program or outpatient setting should be better able to adapt the treatment in response to whatever pitfalls the patient encounters in vivo when using recently learned skills.

Continuity of care must be improved if the revolving door of patient relapse and rehospitalization is to be slowed. The existing fragmentation in service delivery needs to be replaced by consistent integrated treatments. It is not sufficient to evaluate treatment strategies in isolation. Instead, we need to begin evaluating interventions within the context of the service delivery setting.

Ideally, with comprehensive and continued care, relapses in mental functioning can be recognized quickly and treated before rehospitalization becomes necessary. Positive treatment results are maintained only as long as the patient continues to receive comprehensive treatment. As soon as patients discontinue community care, the risk of relapse increases dramatically. The literature suggests that chronic patient care must be continuous and comprehensive. In other words, these patients must receive treatment and supervision from the minute they set foot in an inpatient hospital and continue to receive such services following discharge. Ideally, treatment should begin before hospitalization becomes necessary.

Many studies have been cited demonstrating that schizophrenic symptoms may be modified through behavioral techniques. However, there is only a small amount of behavioral oriented research that has investigated the treatment of schizophrenia or autism and even less that has evaluated the optimal "fit" of interventions within the works service delivery setting. Longitudinal research designs are needed to evaluate patients' progress across service delivery settings. Monitoring patients across service delivery systems can lead to more finely honed and cost-effective care for chronically impaired adults.

REFERENCES

Adams, W., & Sheslow, D. (1983). A developmental perspective of adolescence. In E. Schopler & G. B. Mesibov (Eds.), *Autism in adolescents and adults* (pp. 11–36). New York: Plenum.

Alford, G. S., & Turner, S. M. (1976). Stimulus interference and conditioned inhibition of auditory hallucinations. *Journal of Behavior Therapy and Experimental Psychiatry, 7,* 155–160.

American Psychiatric Association. (1980). Diagnostic and statistical manual of mental disorders (3rd ed.). Washington, DC: Author.

Andreasen, N. C., & Olsen, S. (1982). Negative vs. positive schizophrenia: Definition and validation. *Archives of General Psychiatry, 39,* 789–794.

Angrist, B., Rotrosen, J., & Gershon, S. (1980). Differential effects of neuroleptics on negative versus positive symptoms in schizophrenia. *Psychopharmacology, 72,* 17–19.

Ayd, F. J. (1975). The depot fluphenazines: A reappraisal after 10 years' clinical experience. *American Journal of Psychiatry, 132,* 491–500.

Baldessaarini, R. J. (1985). Drugs and the treatment of psychiatric disorders. In A. G. Gilman, L. S. Goodman, T. W. Rall, & F. Murad (Eds.), *The pharmacological basis of therapeutics* (7th ed.). New York: Macmillan.

Beard, J. H., Propst, R., & Malamed, T. J. (1982). The Fountain House Model of psychiatric rehabilitation. *Psychosocial Rehabilitation Journal, 5,* 47–53.

Bellack, A. S. (1986). Schizophrenia: Behavior therapy's forgotten child. *Behavior Therapy, 17,* 199–214.

Bellack, A. S., Hersen, M., & Turner, S. M. (1976). Generalization effects of social skills training in chronic schizophrenics: An experimental analysis. *Behaviour Research and Therapy, 14,* 391–398.

Bellack, A. S., Turner, S. M., Hersen, M., & Luber, R. F. (1984). An examination of the efficacy of social skills training for chronic schizophrenic patients. *Hospital and Community Psychiatry, 35,* 1023–1028.

Bender, L. A. (1969). A longitudinal study of schizophrenic children with autism. *Hospital and Community Psychiatry, 20,* 230–237.

Berkowitz, R., Eberlein-Fries, R., Kulpers, L., & Leff, J. (1984). Educating relatives about schizophrenia. *Schizophrenia Bulletin, 10,* 418–429.

Boczkowski, J. A., Ziechner, A., & DeSanto, N. (1985). Neuroleptic compliance among chronic schizophrenic outpatients: An intervention outcome report. *Journal of Consulting and Clinical Psychology, 53,* 666–671.

Bucher, B., & Fabricatore, J. (1970). Use of patient-administered shock to suppress hallucinations. *Behavior Therapy, 1,* 382–385.

Caldwell, A. E. (1978). History of psychopharmacology. In W. G. Clark & J. delGuidice (Eds.), *Principles of psychopharmacology* (pp. 9–40). New York: Academic Press.

Campbell, M. (1978). Pharmacotherapy. In M. Rutter & E. Schopler (Eds.), *Autism: A reappraisal of concepts and treatment* (pp. 337–355). New York: Plenum.

Carlson, N. R. (1986). *Physiology of behavior* (3rd ed.). Boston: Allyn & Bacon.

Carpenter, W. T., & Heinrichs, D. W. (1983). Early intervention, time-limited, targeted pharmacotherapy of schizophrenia. *Schizophrenia Bulletin, 9,* 533–542.

Caton, C. L. M., Goldstein, J. M., Serrano, O., & Bender, R. (1984). The impact of discharge planning on chronic schizophrenic patients. *Hospital and Community Psychiatry, 35,* 255–262.

Christoff, K. A., & Kelly, J. A. (1985). A behavioral approach in social skills training with psychiatric patients. In L. L'Abate & M. A. Milan (Eds.), *Handbook of social skills training and research* (pp. 361–387). New York: John Wiley.

Cole, J. O. (1964). Phenothiazine treatment in acute schizophrenia. *Archives of General Psychiatry, 10,* 246–261.

Cole, J. O., & Davis, J. M. (1969). Anti-psychotic drugs. In L. Bellack & L. Loeb (Eds.), *The schizophrenic syndrome.* New York: Grune & Stratton.

Curran, J. P., Monti, P. M., & Corriveau, D. P. (1982). Treatment of schizophrenia. In A. S. Bellack, M. Hersen, & A. E. Kazdin (Eds.), *International handbook of behavior modification* (pp. 433–466). New York: Plenum.

Curran, J. P., Sutton, R. G., Faraone, S. V., & Guenette, S. (1985). Inpatient approaches. In M. Hersen & A. S. Bellack (Eds.), *Handbook of clinical behavior therapy with adults* (pp. 445–483). New York: Plenum.

Cutler, D. L. (1985). Clinical care update: The chronically mentally ill. *Community Mental Health Journal, 21,* 3–13.

Dalldorf, J. S. (1983). Medical needs of the autistic adolescent. In E. Schopler & G. B. Mesibov (Eds.), *Autism in adolescents and adults* (pp. 149–168). New York: Plenum.

Davis, J. M., & Gierl, B. (1984). Pharmacological treatment in the care of schizophrenic patients. In A. S. Bellack (Ed.), *Schizophrenia: Treatment, management, and rehabilitation* (pp. 133–174). New York: Grune & Stratton.

DeMyer, M. K., & Goldberg, R. (1983). Family needs of the autistic adolescent. In E. Schopler & G. B. Mesibov (Eds.), *Autism in adolescents and adults* (pp. 225–250). New York: Plenum.

DeMyer, M. K., Barton, S., DeMyer, W. E., Norton, J. A., Allen, J., & Steele, R. (1973). Prognosis in autism: A follow-up study. *Journal of Autism and Childhood Schizophrenia, 3,* 199–246.

Deykin, E. Y., & MacMahon, B. (1979). The incidence of seizures among children with autistic symptoms. *American Journal of Psychiatry, 136,* 1310–1312.

D'Zurilla, T. J., & Goldried, M. R. (1971). Problem solving and behavior modification. *Journal of Abnormal Psychology, 78,* 107–126.

Engelhardt, D. M., Rosen, B., Feldman, J., Engelhardt, J. Z., & Cohen, P. (1982). A 15-year followup of 646 schizophrenic patients. *Schizophrenia Bulletin, 8,* 493–503.

Epstein, L. H., & Cluss, P. A. (1982). A behavioral medicine perspective on adherence to long-term medical regiments. *Journal of Consulting and Clinical Psychology, 50,* 950–971.

Falloon, I. R. H. (1984). Developing and maintaining adherence to long-term drug-taking regimens. *Schizophrenia Bulletin, 10,* 412–417.

Falloon, I. R. H. (1985). *Family management of schizophrenia: A study of clinical, social, family, and economic benefits.* Baltimore: John Hopkins University Press.

Falloon, I. R. H., Boyd, J. L., & McGill, C. W. (1984). *Family care of schizophrenia: A problem-solving approach to the treatment of mental illness.* New York: Guilford Press.

Falloon, I. R. H., Flanagan, S., Foy, R., Lukoff, D., Marder, S., & Wittlin, B. (1983). Treatment of schizophrenia. In C. E. Walker, (Ed.), *The handbook of clinical psychology: Theory, research, and practice* (pp. 563–569). Homewood, IL: Dow Jones–Irwin.

Falloon, I. R. H., & Liberman, R. P. (1983). Interaction between drug and psychosocial therapy in schizophrenia. *Schizophrenia Bulletin, 9,* 543–554.

Favell, J. E. (1983). The management of aggressive behavior. In E. Schopler & G. B. Mesibov (Eds.), *Autism in adolescents and adults* (pp. 187–222). New York: Plenum.

Finch, B. E., & Wallace, C. J. (1977). Successful interpersonal skills training with schizophrenic inpatients. *Journal of Consulting and Clinical Psychology, 45,* 885–890.

Fish, B., & Ritvo, E. (1980). Psychoses in childhood. In J. D. Nosphpitz (Ed.), *Basic handbook of child psychiatry* (pp. 249–304). New York: Basic Books.

Fredericks, H. D., Buckley, J., Baldwin, V. L., Moore, W., & Stremel-Campbell, K. (1983). The educational needs of the autistic adolescent. In E. Schopler & G. B. Mesibov (Eds.), *Autism in adolescents and adults* (pp. 79–109). New York: Plenum.

Gardos, G., & Cole, J. O. (1976). Maintenance antipsychotic therapy: Is the cure worse than the disease? *American Journal of Psychiatry, 133,* 32–36.

Goldman, H. H. (1982). Mental illness and family burden: A public health perspective. *Hospital and Community Psychiatry, 33,* 21–27.

Goldstein, M. J., Rodnick, E. H., Evans, J. R., May, P. R. A., & Steinberg, M. R. (1978). Drug and family therapy in the aftercare of acute schizophrenics. *Archives of General Psychiatry, 35,* 1169–1177.

Gunderson, J. G., & Mosher, L. R. (1975). The cost of schizophrenia. *American Journal of Psychiatry, 132,* 1257–1264.

Hagen, R. L. (1975). Behavioral therapies and the treatment of schizophrenics. *Schizophrenia Bulletin, 1,* 70–96.

Hansen, D. J., St. Lawrence, J. S., & Christoff, K. A. (1985). Effects of interpersonal problem-solving component skills and effectiveness of solutions. *Journal of Consulting and Clinical Psychology, 53,* 167–174.

Haynes, R. B., (1979). Strategies to improve compliance with referrals, appointments and prescribed medical regimens. In R. B. Haynes, D. W. Taylor, & D. L. Sackett (Eds.), *Compliance in health care* (pp. 121–143). Baltimore: Johns Hopkins University Press.

Hartz, M. I., & Melville, C. (1980). Relapse in schizophrenia. *American Journal of Psychiatry, 137,* 801–805.

Hogarty, G. E. (1966). Discharge readiness: The components of a casework judgment. *Social Casework, 47,* 165–171.

Hogarty, G. E., Schooler, N. R., Ulrich, R., Mussare, F., Ferro, P., & Herron, E. (1979). Fluphenazine and social therapy in the aftercare of schizophrenic patients. *Archives of General Psychiatry, 36,* 1283–1294.

Holding, T. A., Urbanc, S., & Kay, D. W. (1983). Social outcome after admission for schizophrenia in Tasmania: A study of matched pairs. *Social Psychiatry, 18,* 145–152. (From *Psychological Abstracts, 72,* Abstract No. 25549)

Hollon, S., & Beck, A. T. (1978). Psychotherapy and drug therapy: Comparisons and combinations. In S. L. Garfield & A. E. Bergin (Eds.), *Handbook of psychotherapy and behavior change: An empirical analysis* (2nd ed., pp. 437–490). New York: John Wiley.

Holmes, M. R., Hansen, D. J., & St. Lawrence, J. S. (1984). Conversational skills training with aftercare patients in the community: Social validation and generalization. *Behavior Therapy, 15,* 84–100.

Hooley, J. M. (1985). Expressed emotion: A review of the critical literature. *Clinical Psychology Review, 5,* 119–139.

Intagliata, J. (1982). Improving the quality of community care for the chronically mentally disabled: The role of case management. *Schizophrenia Bulletin, 8,* 655–674.

Janicki, M. P., Lubin, R. A., & Friedman, E. (1983). Variations in characteristics and service needs of persons with autism. *Journal of Autism and Developmental Disorders, 13,* 73–85.

Kane, J. M. (1983). Low dose medication strategies in the maintenance treatment of schizophrenia. *Schizophrenia Bulletin, 9,* 528–532.

Kanner, L., Rodriguez, A., & Ashendon, B. (1972). How far can autistic children go in matters of social adaptation? *Journal of Autism & Childhood Schizophrenia, 2,* 9–33.

Kazdin, A. E., & Bootzin, R. R. (1972). The token economy: An evaluative review. *Journal of Applied Behavior Analysis, 5,* 343–372.

Keane, T. M., Foy, D. W., Nunn, B., Rychtarik, R. G. (1984). Antabuse compliance in alcoholic veterans. *Journal of Clinical Psychology, 40,* 340–344.

Keith, S., Gunderson, J., Reifman, A., Buchsbaum, S., & Mosher, L. R. (1976). Special report: Schizophrenia 1976. *Schizophrenia Bulletin, 2,* 509–565.

Kelly, J. A., & Lamparski, D. M. (1985). Outpatient treatment of schizophrenics: Social skills and problem-solving training. In M. Hersen & A. S. Bellack (Eds.), *Handbook of clinical behavior therapy with adults* (pp. 485–506), New York: Plenum.

Kessler, K. A., & Waletzky, J. P. (1981). Clinical use of antipsychotics. *American Journal of Psychiatry, 138,* 202–209.

Klein, D. F., & Davis, J. M. (1969). *Diagnosis and drug treatment of psychiatric disorders.* Baltimore: Williams & Wilkins.

Klein, D. F., Gittleman, R., Quitkin, F., & Rifkin, A. (1980). *A diagnosis on drug treatment of psychiatric disorders.* Baltimore: Williams & Wilkins.

Klerman, G. L. (1986). Drugs and psychotherapy. In S. L. Garfield & A. E. Bergin (Eds.), *Handbook of psychotherapy and behavior change* (3rd 3rd., pp. 777–818). New York: John Wiley.

Kohen, W., & Paul, G. L. (1976). Current trends and recommended changes in extended care placements of mental patients. *Schizophrenia Bulletin, 3,* 24–37.

Kuehnel, T. G., DeRisi, W. J., Liberman, R. P., & Mosk, M. D. (1984). Treatment strategies that promote deinstitutionalization of chronic mental patients. In W. P. Christian, G. T. Hannah, & T. J. Glahn (Eds.), *Programming effective human services: Strategies for institutional change and client transition* (pp. 245–265). New York: Plenum.

LaVigna, G. W. (1983). The Jay Nolan Center: A community-based program. In E. Schopler & G. B. Mesibov (Eds.), *Autism in adolescents and adults* (pp. 381–410). New York: Plenum.

Lehmann, H. E. (1975). Psychopharmacological treatment of schizophrenia. *Schizophrenia Bulletin, 2,* 27–45.

Lettick, A. L. (1983). Benhaven. In E. Schopler & G. B. Mesibov (Eds.), *Autism in adolescents and adults* (pp. 355–379). New York: Plenum.

Levy, S. (1983). School doesn't last forever: What then? Some vocational alternatives. In E. Schopler & G. B. Mesibov (Eds.), *Autism in adolescents and adults* (pp.133–148). New York: Plenum.

Liberman, R. P., Falloon, I. R. H. & Atchison, R. A. (1984a). Multiple family therapy for schizophrenia: A behavioral, problem-solving approach. *Psychosocial Rehabilitation Journal, 7,* 60–77.

Liberman, R. P., Kuehnel, T. G., Phipps, C. C., & Cardin, V. A. (1984c). *Resource book for psychiatric rehabilitation: Elements of service for the mentally ill.* Berkeley, CA: Regents of the University of California.

Liberman, R. P., Little, F., Falloon, I. R. H., Harpin, R. E., Hutchinson, W., & Stoute, B. (1984b). Social skills training with relapsing schizophrenics: An experimental analysis. *Behavior Modification, 8,* 155-179.

Liberman, R. P., Mueser, K. T., & Wallace, C. J. (1986). Social skills training for schizophrenic individuals at risk for relapse. *American Journal of Psychiatry, 143,* 523-526.

Liberman, R. P., Teigen, J., Patterson, R., & Baker, V. (1973). Reducing delusional speech in chronic paranoid schizophrenics. *Journal of Applied Behavior Analysis, 6,* 57-64.

Liberman, R. P., Wallace, C. J., Teigen, J., & Davis, J. (1974). Interventions with psychotic behaviors. In K. S. Calhoun, H. E. Adams, & K. M. Mitchell (Eds.), *Innovative treatment methods in psychopathology.* New York: John Wiley.

Liberman, R. P., Wallace, C. J., Vaughn, C. E., Snyder, K. S., & Rust, C. (1980). Social and family factors in the course of schizophrenia: Toward an interpersonal problem-solving therapy for schizophrenics and their families. In J. S. Strauss, N. Bowers, T. W. Downey, S. Fleck, S. Jackson, & I. Levine (Eds.), *The psychotherapy of schizophrenia* (pp. 21-54). New York: Plenum.

Lotter, V. (1978). Follow-up studies. M. Rutter & E. Schoplee (Eds.), *Autism: A reappraisal of concepts and treatment* (pp. 475-495). New York: Plenum.

Lovass, O. I., Koegel, R. S., Simmon, J. O., & Long, J. S. (1973). Some generalization and followup measures on autistic children in behavior therapy. *Journal of Applied Behavior Analysis, 6,* 131-165.

Lukoff, D., Snyder, K., Ventura, J., & Nuechterlein, K. H. (1984). Life events, familial stress, and coping in the developmental course of schizophrenia. *Schizophrenia Bulletin, 10,* 258-292.

Meichenbaum, D. & Cameron, R. (1973). Training schizophrenics to talk to themselves: A means of developing attentional controls. *Behavior Therapy, 4,* 515-534.

Mesibov, G. B. (1983). Current perspectives and issues in autism and adolescence. In E. Schopler & G. B. Mesibov (Eds.), *Autism in adolescents and adults* (pp. 37-53). New York: Plenum.

Mesibov, G. B. (1984). Social skills training with verbal autistic adolescents and adults: A program model. *Journal of Autism and Developmental Disorders, 14,* 395-404.

Mesibov, G. B. (1986). A cognitive program for teaching social behaviors to verbal autistic adolescents and adults. In E. Schopler & G. B. Mesibov (Eds.), *Social Behavior in Autism* (pp. 265-283). New York: Plenum.

Mesibov, G. B., Schopler, E., & Sloan, J. L. (1983). Service development for adolescents and adults in North Carolina's TEACCH program. In E. Schopler & G. B. Mesibov (Eds.), *Autism in adolescents and adults* (pp. 411–432). New York: Plenum.

O'Leary, K. D., & Wilson, G. T. (1975). *Behavior therapy: Application and outcome.* Englewood Cliffs, NJ: Prentice-Hall.

Ornitz, E., & Ritvo, E. (1976). The medical diagnosis. In E. Ritvo, B. Freeman, E. Ornitz, & P. Tanguay (Eds.). *Autism: Diagnosis current research and management.* Halliswood, NY: Spectrum Publications.

Panyan, M., Boozer, H., & Morris, N. (1970). Feedback to attendants as a reinforcer for applying operant techniques. *Journal of Applied Behavior Analysis, 3,* 1–4.

Patterson, R. L., & Teigen, J. R. (1973). Conditioning and post-hospital generalization of non-delusional responses in a chronic psychiatric patient. *Journal of Applied Behavior Analysis, 6,* 65–70.

Paul, G. L., & McInnis, T. L. (1974). Attitudinal changes associated with two approaches to training mental health technician in milieu and social-learning programs. *Journal of Consulting and Clinical Psychology, 42,* 21–33.

Rickard, H. C., Dignam, P. J., & Horner, R. F. (1960). Verbal manipulation in a psychotherapeutic relationship. *Journal of Clinical Psychology, 16,* 364–367.

Rickard, H. C., & Dinoff, M. A. (1962). A followup note on "Verbal manipulation in a psychotherapeutic relationship." *Psychological Reports, 11,* 506.

Romanczyk, R. (1986). Some thoughts on future trends in the education of individuals with autism. *The Behavior Therapist, 8,* 162–164.

Rutter, M., & Lockyer, L. (1967). A five to fifteen year follow-up study of childhood psychosis. *British Journal of Psychiatry, 113,* 1169–1182.

Salzinger, K. (1981). Remedying schizophrenic behavior. In S. M. Turner, K. S. Calhoun, & H. E. Adams (Eds.), *Handbook of clinical behavior therapy* (pp. 162–190). New York: John Wiley.

Schaefer, H. H., & Martin, P. L. (1975). *Behavioral therapy.* New York: McGraw-Hill.

Schooler, N. R. (1978). Antipsychotic drugs and psychological treatment in schizophrenia. In M. A. Lipton, A. DiMascio, & K. F. Killiam (Eds.), *Psychopharmacology: A generation of progress* (pp. 1155–1168). New York: Raven Press.

Schooler, N. R., & Carpenter, W. T. (1983). New drug treatment strategies in schizophrenia. *Schizophrenia Bulletin, 9,* 500–503.

Schopler, E. (1983). Can an adolescent or adult have autism? In E. Schopler & G. B. Mesibov (Eds.), *Autism in adolescents and adults* (pp. 3–10). New York: Plenum.

Schopler, E., & Mesibov, G. G. (Eds.). (1983). *Autism in adolescents and adults.* New York: Plenum.

Schwartz, S., Goldfinger, S., Ratener, M., & Cutler, D. (1983). The young adult patient and the care system: Fragmentation prototypes. In D. L. Curtler (Ed.), *New directions for mental health services: Effective aftercare for the 1980s.* San Francisco, CA: Jossey-Bass.

Schwartz, S. R., Goldman, H. H., & Churgin, S. (1982). Case management for the chronic mentally ill: Models and dimensions. *Hospital and Community Psychiatry, 33,* 1006–1009.

Shapiro, S. A. (1981). *Contemporary theories of schizophrenia: Review and synthesis.* New York: McGraw-Hill.

Simpson, G. M., & Lee, J. H. (1978). A ten-year review of antipsychotics. In M. A. Lipton, A. DiMascio, & D. F. Killiam (Eds.), *Psychopharmacology: A generation of progress* (pp. 1131–1137). New York: Raven Press.

Simpson, G. M., & May, P. R. (1982). Schizophrenic disorders. In J. H. Greist, J. W. Jefferson, & R. L. Spitzer (Eds.), *Treatment of mental disorders* (pp. 143–183). New York: Oxford University Press.

Smith, M. D., & Belcher, R. (1985). Teaching life skills to adults disabled by autism. *Journal of Autism and Developmental Disorders, 15,* 163–175.

Smith, M. D., & Coleman, D. (1986). Managing the behavior of adults with autism in the job setting. *Journal of Autism and Developmental Disorders, 16,* 145–154.

St. Lawrence, J. S. (1981). Efficacy of money deposit contingency on a clinical outpatient's attendance and participation in assertive training. *Journal of Behavior Therapy and Experimental Psychiatry, 12,* 237–240.

Tarail, M. (1980). Current and future issues in community mental health. *Psychiatric Quarterly, 52,* 27–38.

Tessler, R., & Mason, J. H. (1979). Continuity of care in the delivery of mental health services. *American Journal of Psychiatry, 136,* 1297–1301.

Turner, S. M., Hersen, M., & Bellack, A. S. (1977). Effects of social disruption, stimulus interference, and aversive conditioning on auditory hallucinations. *Behavior Modification, 1,* 249–258.

Van Putten, T. (1974). Why do schizophrenic patients refuse to take their drugs? *Archives of General Psychiatry, 31,* 67–72.

Vaughn, C., & Leff, J. (1976). The measurement of expressed emotion in the families of psychiatric patients. *British Journal of Social Clinical Psychology, 15,* 157–165.

Wallace, C. J. (1982). The social skills training project of the Mental Health Research Center for the Study of Schizophrenia. In J. P. Curran & P. M. Monti (Eds.), *Social skills training.* New York: Guilford Press.

Wallace, C. J., Boone, S. E., Donahoe, C. P., & Foy, D. W. (1985). The chronic mentally disabled: Independent living skills training. In D. H. Barlow

(Ed.), *Clinical handbook of psychological disorders: A step-by-step treatment manual* (pp. 462–501). New York: Guilford Press.

Wallace, C. J., Donahoe, C. P., & Boone, S. E. (1986). Schizophrenia. In M. Hersen (Ed.), *Pharmacological and behavioral treatment: An integrative approach* (pp. 357–381). New York: John Wiley.

Wincze, J. P., Leitenberg, H., & Agras, W. S. (1972). The effects of token reinforcement and feedback on the delusions verbal behavior of chronic paranoid schizophrenics. *Journal of Applied Behavior Analysis, 5,* 247–262.

Wing, J. K., Cooper, J. E., & Sartorius, N. (1974). *The measurement and classification of psychiatric symptoms.* London: Cambridge University Press.

Wing, L., Yeates, S. R. Brierly, L. M., & Gould, J. (1976). The prevalence of early chidlhood autism: A comparison of administrative and epidemiological studies. *Psychological Medicine, 15,* 215–220.

Wolkon, G. H. (1970). Characteristics of clients and continuity of care into the community. *Community Mental Health Journal, 6,* 215–221.

5

Differential Diagnosis in Chronic Schizophrenia and Adult Autism

Nirbhay N. Singh and Roger C. Katz

In a general sense, diagnosis refers to how psychological dysfunction is described and categorized. However, diagnosis may also have specific purposes, four of which have been described by Mezzich (1984, p. 4): the organization of clinical information, communication among professionals, prediction of the clinical course and selection of treatment, and etiological elucidation and theory development. To this end, a number of nosologies and diagnostic systems have been advanced in which the clinician is required to glean clinically relevant information from the client, or from an informant who knows the person well, and identify the category or categories in these systems that best describe the client's psychological dysfunction. In addition, a formal and thorough diagnosis directs our attention to the multiple determinants and probable clinical course of the dysfunctional behavior. This process can be seen as the initial stage of consultation, providing the necessary information for prognosis and treatment.

In a more general sense, diagnostic categories serve other useful functions as well. Salzinger (1981) has suggested that they provide a convenient way to find information about certain aberrant *behaviors* and to find *people* who belong to a group characterized by a single disorder. In addition, they provide ideas and insights regarding the disorder, theories of its etiology, and an appropriate course of treatment.

In this chapter we provide a brief description of current diagnostic systems, including the advantages and limitations of each, followed by sections on the diagnosis of autism and chronic schizophrenia and, finally, differential diagnosis in autism and chronic schizophrenia.

DIAGNOSTIC SYSTEMS

The three diagnostic systems currently in vogue include clinically derived, empirically derived, and behavioral diagnoses.

Clinically Derived Diagnosis

Clinically derived diagnostic systems, often referred to as the categorical or typological approach, rely on clinical observation and experience to identify discrete categories of psychological dysfunction. The assumption is that certain symptoms occur together and represent an identifiable disorder across clients.

DSM-III-R and ICD-9

The two best examples of clinically derived systems are the *Diagnostic and Statistical Manual of Mental Disorders* (DSM-III-R) (APA, 1987), and the *International Classification of Diseases* (ICD-9) (WHO, 1977). The DSM-III-R is the revised third edition of the *Diagnostic and Statistical Manual* of the American Psychiatric Association (APA, 1980), which was first published in 1952 (DSM-I) and revised in 1968 (DSM-II). Although a complete description of DSM-III-R is beyond the scope of this chapter, its important features will be addressed.

The DSM system was adopted for use in this country and is separate from the *International Classification of Diseases* (WHO, 1977), published by the World Health Organization and revised at approximately 10-year intervals. Unlike the DSM-III-R, the ICD-9 represents a compilation of more than mental disorders. It contains 17 categories, which cover the entire range of diseases and morbid conditions.

Historically, the ICD system has evoked considerable criticism among mental health workers. Much of the controversy has occurred in this country and has centered on the lack of specific diagnostic criteria, which made reliable diagnosis difficult to achieve (Kazdin, 1985). This issue eventually led to the publication of a separate volume called *Clinical Modification of the World Health Organization's International Classification of Diseases* (ICD-9-CM), which appeared in 1978 and was intended for use by clinicians and researchers in the United States. Not surprisingly, the ICD-9-CM was similar in content but not identical to the DSM-III (APA, 1980), published shortly thereafter.

The purpose of the DSM-III-R is to "provide clear descriptions of diagnostic categories in order to enable clinicians and investigators to diagnose, communicate about, study, and treat the various mental disorders" (APA, 1987, p. xxix). Like its predecessors, the current version is not meant to represent a finished product. Instead it should be regarded as a part of an ongoing process to better understand and reliably classify the known mental disorders. Future editions will appear as more information becomes available.

DSM-III-R retains the most important features of DSM-III. These are (1) a descriptive (atheoretical) approach to classification, (2) specific diagnostic criteria for each disorder, and (3) a multiaxial approach to classification.

Descriptive Classification.

Except in rare cases in which a pathophysiological cause has been clearly established (e.g., organic mental disorders), the mental disorders in DSM-III-R are described without reference to etiological factors. There is no assumption that mental disorders have an organic basis or that the listed groupings are etiologically homogeneous. Furthermore, the disorders described in the volume are not meant to be regarded as the *only* appropriate focus of professional attention nor to be explained by any particular conceptual model. The system describes clinical dysfunctions but does not attempt to explain them. As such, it is compatible with different theoretical viewpoints (Kazdin, 1985).

Multiaxial Classification.   DSM-III-R retains a multiaxial system for evaluation that was probably the most innovative change in the previous edition. The purpose of multiaxial classification is to obtain a comprehensive assessment of the patient that will facilitate treatment planning and predictions about expected outcome. It is also designed to improve interrater reliability by recording nondiagnostic information (e.g., severity of psychosocial stressors) that might aid in the understanding of the patient's problems.

Altogether five axes are listed. Axes I and II are for the mental disorders that are the focus of treatment. Most of these disorders are listed on Axis I, except the developmental disorders (e.g., mental retardation, specific developmental disorders) and personality disorders (e.g., borderline personality disorder), which are entered on Axis II. Physical problems that are pertinent to understanding or treating the patient (e.g., seizures, diabetes) are listed on Axis III. Axes IV and V are for severity of psychosocial stressors and global assessment of functioning, respectively. Estimates of these variables are based on the clinician's subjective rating.

Compatibility with ICD-9.   One of the reasons the DSM-III evolved when it did was to develop a classification system that was compatible with the already available ICD-9 (Spitzer, Williams, & Skodol, 1980). Although the two diagnostic systems are similar, they contain specific differences in content that have generated confusion among clinicians, as well as record-keeping and statistical problems. This has changed with the latest revision. All DSM-III-R diagnostic codes have been written so that they now have a corresponding ICD-9-CM code.

Advantages and Limitations of Clinically Derived Systems

Since the DSM is the main classification system used in this country and "reflects the state of the art in clinically derived diagnosis" (Kazdin, 1985, p. 13), our comments about advantages and limitations will be restricted to the DSM system.

The Advantages of DSM-III and DSM-III-R have been enumerated by various authors (Hersen & Turner, 1984; Kazdin, 1985; Nathan, 1987; Spitzer & Williams, 1985). Chief among them are the following:

1. The behavioral dysfunctions listed in DSM-III and DSM-III-R were generated from clinical experience, with an increased emphasis on empirically derived description and diagnosis. This is a far cry from earlier editions, which were based on untested assumptions derived mainly from psychodynamic theory. Moreover, many of the diagnostic categories and criteria were developed by means of rigorous field testing, which was unheard of in DSM-I and DSM-II (Taylor, 1983).
2. DSM-III and DSM-III-R provide a carefully worded definition of "mental disorder" that is based on current research findings, phenomenology, and description rather than on presumed etiology. Moreover, it is recognized that the system classifies disorders, not individuals.

In DSM-III-R each of the mental disorders is conceptualized as a clinically significant behavioral or psychological syndrome or pattern that occurs in a person and that is associated with present distress (a painful symptom) or disability (impairment in one or more important areas of functioning) or with a significantly increased risk of suffering death, pain, disability, or an important loss of freedom. In addition, this syndrome or pattern must not be merely an expectable response to a particular event, e.g., the death of a loved one. Whatever its original cause, it must currently be considered a manifestation of a behavioral, psychological, or biological dysfunction in the person. Neither deviant behavior (e.g., political, religious, or sexual) nor conflicts that a primarily between the individual and society are mental disorders unless the deviance or conflict is a symptom of a dysfunction in the person as described above. (APA, 1987, p. xxii)

3. Additional advantages have already been mentioned. They include (a) the provision of relatively clear diagnostic criteria for each specific mental disorder, (b) the multiaxial system of classification to assist in comprehensive assessment and treatment planning, and (c) evidence of improved reliability based on carefully conducted field trials (Taylor, 1983).

Although DSM-III-R represents a significant improvement over earlier versions, the current system also has limitations. For example, several writers (Hersen, 1988; Hersen & Turner, 1984; Kazdin, 1985; Nathan, 1987) have been critical of the lack of empirical support for specific diagnostic categories, especially the newer disorders that have been proposed for inclusion in DSM-III-R (e.g., self-defeating personality disorder and sadistic personality disorder). In this regard, Nathan (1987) has stated: "The new and controversial diagnoses appear to be based less on a body of substantial empirical and clinical data than on political and sociocultural considerations" (p. 205).

A perennial criticism pertains to the reliability of psychiatric diagnosis, which is only modest for certain diagnostic categories, such as the personality disorders or subgroups within major diagnostic categories (e.g., schizophrenia vs. disorganized schizophrenia) (Taylor, 1983). Reliability problems have also occurred with the rating assigned on Axes IV and V, although modifications in the revised DSM-III may help to remedy this situation (Nathan, 1987).

Empirically Derived Diagnosis

Empirically derived or multivariate approaches are fundamentally dimensional, not categorical, in nature and provide an empirical classification of behavior or clinical symptoms (Bashfield, 1984). Information on a large number of children or adults is obtained from case history data, adult informants (e.g., teachers, parents, spouses, mental health workers), or rating scales; and then statistical techniques, such as factor analysis and cluster analysis, are used to identify dimensions of covariation among signs and symptoms. Behaviors that are highly correlated constitute a factor or a syndrome. In this approach, clients are not diagnosed as having a specific disorder but are described in terms of their scores on several factors. Examples of empirically derived systems include the Behavior Problem Checklist (Quay & Peterson, 1983) and the Child Behavior Checklist (Achenbach & Edelbrock, 1983).

There are a number of reviews of factor analytic studies with children (e.g., Achenbach & Edelbrock, 1978; Quay, 1979). Quay's (1979) review shows that in spite of major differences in rating instruments, setting factors, subject samples, and methods of data analysis, four major dimensions of childhood disorder emerged in most studies: immaturity, conduct disorder, anxiety–withdrawal, and socialized-aggressive disorder. In addition, there appears to be good cross-cultural validity for two of the factors: conduct disorder and anxiety–withdrawal.

Achenbach and Edelbrock (1978) also found a convergence among a few global broad-band syndromes. They reported greater convergence on two of the broad-band syndromes: anxiety–withdrawal and conduct disorder, which they labeled as overcontrolled and undercontrolled, respectively. There was less convergence on the other two syndromes, immaturity and socialized-aggressive disorder, which they labeled as pathological detachment and learning problems, respectively. In addition, they reported considerable convergence on a large number of specific narrow-band syndromes, including aggressive, hyperactive, and schizoid syndromes and delinquent (which is akin to Quay's socialized-aggressive), anxious, depressed, social withdrawal, and somatic complaints syndromes.

Cluster analysis has not been as widely used as factor analysis in multivariate studies of children, but nonetheless, some consistent findings have emerged. For example, based on parent ratings on the Child Behavior Checklist, the following six clusters were found for boys between the ages of 6 and 11 years: schizoid–social withdrawal, depressed–social withdrawal, somatic complaints, hyperactive, and delinquent (Edelbrock & Achenbach, 1980). In addition to a number of other clusters, Soli, Nuechteriein, Garmezy, Devine, and Schaefer (1981) replicated the clusters related to aggression–delinquency, anxiety–depression, and hyperactivity in boys 4 to 15 years old. It is particularly encouraging to find overlapping clusters in the two studies, given the difference in methods, criteria for cluster analysis, and subject samples. Other studies have corroborated the clusters found in these two (e.g., Lessing, Williams, & Gil, 1982).

Finally, discriminant-function analysis has been used in an applied sense to differentiate children with different disorders or to confirm the distinction between two disorders. For example, children diagnosed with infantile autism have been differentiated from those with developmental receptive dysphasias on the basis of behavioral, language, and cognitive criteria (Bartak, Rutter, & Cox, 1977). Others have used discriminant-function analysis to differentiate children with infantile autism from those with late-onset psychosis. Kolvin, Ounsted, Richardson, and Garside (1971) confirm the distinction between school refusal and truancy in an epidemiological study, and differentially classify backward readers and retarded readers (see Yule, 1981).

Multivariate methods have also been used with adults. For example, two general factors, paranoid and nonparanoid, were found in a factor analysis of 52 symptoms in 100 hospitalized psychotic patients (Guertin, 1970). Later studies corroborated these two factors but reported the presence of additional factors (e.g., Lorr, Klett, & Cave, 1967). In addition, an analysis of the symptoms comprising these factors showed that the factors cut across traditional diagnostic categories in use at the time.

It is clear that multivariate approaches have been used to classify the symptoms or dysfunctional behaviors of both children and adults and to confirm the existence of discrete disorders. Our reading of the literature indicates that most of the past effort has been directed at providing a useful taxonomy of disorders rather than practical applications in the treatment of disordered populations. However, there is some indication that the time has come for using empirically based diagnosis as the basis of clinical interventions and that guidelines for using this approach are becoming available (e.g., Achenbach & McConaughy, 1987).

Advantages of Empirically Derived Systems

One of the major advantages of this approach is that it is based on empirical findings, and the instruments (e.g., standardized rating scales, checklists) used to derive the data are subject to continuous psychometric refinement. Increasing sophistication in the methodology used and the availability of powerful computers will lead to more sophisticated and more reliable instruments for assessing psychological dysfunction. Another advantage of this approach is that the instruments have been derived from a wide subject population and therefore are able to cover a wide range of symptoms. Indeed, a client is assessed on all of the factors that are available on a given scale. The fact that additional scales can be used means that the client's problems may be subject to even more comprehensive evaluation.

Although it is recognized that a client may meet the criteria for a number of disorders in clinically derived systems such as the DSM-III-R (APA, 1987), the guidelines for establishing the primacy of different disorders or rules for prioritizing the disorders are not clear. One of the implications of empirically based approaches is that the client will be rated on multiple syndomes or factors. However, a clear advantage is that the relationship between the different factors can be determined empirically from the client's profile data (see Achenbach, 1985). This would be helpful to the clinician in determining not only which dysfunctional behaviors need treatment but also the order in which to begin treatment.

Limitations of Empirically Derived Systems

An important limitation is that the factors derived from multivariate approaches are dependent on the types of items included in the original pool of items and the size of the sample on which the initial analysis is based. Indeed, some factors may not appear at all because items that would load on the factors have not been included in the original pool. Furthermore, it is invariably the case that low-prevalence syndromes (e.g., autism) will not be identified by this method unless the investigator biases the subject population by including large numbers of patients with low-prevalence syndromes and includes items specific to those syndromes.

Another limitation is that the primary data are obtained from rating scales and checklists that are completed either by the client or by well-informed others, usually teachers, parents, or mental health workers, and not from direct behavioral observations. Indeed, some of the items included in rating scales and checklists are difficult to define operationally for direct observation. Data from rating scales and checklists may be biased by the perceptions of the rater regarding the client's problem behavior, the psychopathology of the rater (see Griest & Wells, 1983), or other rater characteristics. In addition, whether rating scale data correlate to any significant degree with direct observation has not been determined for virtually all of the rating scales and checklists currently in use. Notable exceptions include the Child Behavior Checklist (Achenbach & Edelbrock, 1983) and the Aberrant Behavior Checklist (Aman & Singh, 1986).

Behavioral Diagnosis

Behavioral diagnosis departs from traditional diagnostic systems by focusing on an analysis of the individual client's behavior, as well as environmental controlling factors, for the purpose of understanding and modifying the dysfunctional behavior. It attempts neither to identify the "disorder," as in the clinically derived approaches, nor to assess the degree to which a person is rated on a number of factors on an empirically derived scale. In addition, behavioral diagnosis emphasizes the conditions that maintain the dysfunctional behavior rather than defining its nature or etiology (Newsome & Rincover, 1979).

The hallmark of behavioral diagnosis is the functional analysis of behavior (Ferster, 1965). Functional analysis is basically the identification of variables that maintain the behavior of interest and can be altered to bring about a change in the behavior. These variables may include setting events, other behaviors of the client, consequences of the client's behavior, and interactions of the client with the environment. Typically, only current variables maintaining the dysfunctional behavior are analyzed for the purposes of behavioral diagnosis and treatment although there are strong arguments for executing a thorough descriptive analysis of the effects of setting events as well (Singh & Repp, 1988). A microanalysis of setting events may reveal that the form and function of the client's behavior is highly consistent in specific settings but variable in others. Emphasis on situational specificity in behavioral diagnosis has led to a greater sampling of behavior in different environments, such as school, home, and clinic (Kazdin, 1979).

A number of investigators have attempted to formalize behavioral diagnosis by specifying the different components that need to be addressed (e.g., Kanfer & Saslow, 1969). One system, summarized by the acronym SORKC, emphasizes the following components: the antecedent stimuli (S) that elicit or serve as discriminative stimuli for the occurrence or dysfunctional behavior; organism (O) or client variables such as physical handicaps, biological variables, cognitions; the characteristics of the dysfunctional response (R), including its frequency, duration, and/or intensity, the contingencies (K) that maintain the behavior, such as escape and avoidance, and the consequences (C) of the response, including both positive and negative events. Of course, not all components may be relevant to given dysfunctional behaviors, but they provide the framework within which a full behavioral diagnostic workup can be undertaken.

Although behavioral diagnosis is not concerned with classification per se in the traditional psychiatric sense, attempts have been made to provide a conceptual framework for dysfunctional behaviors (see Goldfried & Davison, 1976). Three classes of behavioral dysfunction are usually delineated: *behavioral excesses, behavioral deficits,* and *stimulus control problems*. Behavioral excesses and deficits can be seen as extreme points on a continuum, with the midrange being normal or socially acceptable behavior. Thus, behaviors that are excessive in terms of frequency, duration, and/or intensity are referred to as behavioral excesses. For example, both verbal and motor stereotypy in autistic and chronic schizophrenic individuals can be characterized as behavioral excesses. Behaviors that fail to occur with sufficient frequency, duration, or intensity are referred to as behavioral deficits. For example, autistic and chronic schizophrenic individuals are often characterized by their social skills deficits. Stimulus control problems are exemplified by behaviors that are not under the appropriate control of the environment (e.g., elective mutism) or are under the control of an inappropriate stimulus (e.g., paraphilias). Thus, responding to a question is an appropriate behavior but not when the question is directed to another person.

Advantages of Behavioral Diagnosis

One of the advantages of behavioral diagnosis is that it deals with dysfunctional behavior directly rather than with classification. The approach requires a functional analysis of the problem that has direct and immediate implications for treatment selection. In addition, because treatment is based on an analysis of each client's dysfunctional behavior, the same problem in different individuals may require different treatment, depending on the SORKC analysis for each behavior of each person. The changes in the behavior of the client are monitored before, during, and after the termination of treatment, ensuring that treatment is tailored to the needs of the client and that the goals of treatment are being achieved.

Limitations of Behavioral Diagnosis

If a systematic means of classifying psychological dysfunctions is seen as important, then it is clear that it cannot be achieved through behavioral diagnosis. Lack of an adequate system of classifying behaviors means that there is no easy method of summarizing and systematically presenting the assessment and treatment information that behavioral therapists and researchers have amassed. As a result, each additional case has to be treated anew because there is no standard way of reporting such information across clinicians and researchers. As Kazdin (1983) has pointed out, the lack of standardized reporting often leads to ambiguity in interpreting the behavior therapy literature.

Another limitation of behavioral diagnosis is that its historical approach leads clinicians into eschewing such factors as chronicity and onset of the problem in favor of the current determinants of the psychological dysfunction, although these factors may have some relevance in the selection and design of the treatment. Other limitations include lack of guidelines for determining which behavior(s) should be targeted for treatment first when the client has a number of problems (Wittlieb, Eifert, Wilson, & Evans, 1978), as well as the lack of guidelines for selecting treatment after a behavioral diagnosis has been made. Although some headway has been made in selecting treatments derived from a functional analysis of the problem behavior, especially in developmentally disabled populations, the situation with regard to psychiatric problems remains to be resolved. It is important to realize that these latter problems are by no means unique to behavioral approaches.

DIAGNOSIS OF ADULT AUTISM

Since the original description of the syndrome by Kanner (1943), there have been disagreements over the diagnosis, validity, and definition of what he termed *early infantile autism*. The nature of these disagreements has been discussed extensively elsewhere (e.g., Cohen, Paul, & Volkmar, 1987; Rutter, 1970) and need not be repeated here. Our interest is in presenting the current thinking on the diagnosis of the disorder, particularly as it pertains to autistic adults. However, regardless of the diagnostic system one uses, it is clear that there is no differential diagnosis between childhood and adult autism.

In DSM-III (APA, 1980), there is provision for a "residual" category for those adults who once met the criteria for childhood autism but no longer do, even though they exhibit some residual characteristics. The assumption that autistic children somehow grow out of autism in adulthood is not supported by clinical and empirical investigations. Follow-up studies show quite clearly that few persons (less than 2%) diagnosed as having an autistic disorder during childhood ever function relatively normally as adults (DeMyer, Hingtgen, & Jackson, 1981; Wolf & Goldberg, 1986). Indeed, Cohen et al. (1987)

have stated that "most autistic children grow up to be autistic adults," and as noted in the DSM-III-R (APA, 1987), the manifestations of autism are in almost all cases lifelong. An exception to this rather bleak prognosis is the recent work of Lovaas (1987), who was able to produce significant improvement in young autistic children who were treated with an intensive (40 hr wk) behavioral intervention over a 2-year period. His results are by far the most encouraging that have been reported to date. In this chapter, autism is considered a life-span disorder and is not differentiated on the basis of age.

In the DSM-III (APA, 1980), infantile autism, childhood-onset pervasive developmental disorder, and atypical pervasive developmental disorder were grouped, together with mental retardation, on Axis I. However, the diagnostic criteria have been extensively modified in the DSM-III-R (APA, 1987). Infantile autism and childhood-onset pervasive developmental disorder have been collapsed into *autistic disorder*, and atypical pervasive developmental disorder is now termed *pervasive developmental disorder NOS* (not otherwise specified). In addition, all of the developmental disorders, including autistic disorder and pervasive developmental disorder NOS, are now coded on Axis II. The DSM-III-R diagnostic criteria for autistic disorder appear in Table 5.1.

In the ICD-9 (WHO, 1978) infantile autism is listed under "Other Psychoses" in the category "Psychoses with Origin Specific to Childhood." Other terms used to describe infantile autism in this system include childhood autism, Kanner's syndrome, and infantile psychosis. In the ICD-9, infantile autism excludes schizophrenic syndrome of childhood and disintegrative psychosis. No mention is made of adult autism, but one would assume that the same criteria would apply as long as the onset was in childhood. The ICD-9 diagnostic criteria for infantile autism appear in Table 5.2.

As noted above, because of the low prevalence rate of autism in the general population, no empirically derived systems are available for the diagnosis of this disorder. However, a few diagnostic checklists are available that may assist the clinician in a diagnostic workup. The best-known diagnostic checklist is Rimland's Diagnostic Checklist for Behavior Disturbed Children, Form E-2 (Rimland, 1964), and an expanded version, Form E-3 (Rimland, 1974). A number of other checklists used in the past for differential diagnosis have less

Table 5.1 DSM-III-R Criteria for Autistic Disorder

A. Qualitative impairment in reciprocal social interaction as manifested by
   the following:
   Marked lack of awareness of the existence or feelings of others
   No or abnormal seeking of comfort at times of distress
   No or impaired imitation
   No or abnormal social play
   Gross impairment in ability to make peer friendships

B. Qualitative impairment in verbal and nonverbal communication, and in
   imaginative activity, as manifested by the following:
   No mode of communication, such as communicative babbling, facial
      expression, gesture, mime, or spoken language
   Markedly abnormal nonverbal communication, as in the use of eye-to-
      eye gaze, facial expression, body posture, or gestures to initiate or
      modulate social interaction
   Absence of imagination activity, such as playacting of adult roles,
      fantasy characters, or animals; lack of interest in stories about
      imaginary events
   Marked abnormalities in the production of speech, including volume,
      pitch, stress, rate, rhythm, and intonation
   Marked abnormalities in the form or content of speech, including
      sterotyped and repetitive use of speech; use of "you" when "I" is
      meant; idiosyncratic use of words or phrases; or frequent irrelevant
      remarks
   Marked impairment in the ability to initiate or sustain a conversation
      with others, despite adequate speech

C. Marked restricted repertoire of activities and interests, as manifested by
   the following:
   sterotyped body movements
   Persistent preoccupation with parts of objects or attachment to unusual
      objects
   Marked distress over changes in trivial aspects of environment
   unreasonable insistence on following routines in precise detail
   Markedly restricted range of interests and a preoccupation with one
      narrow interest

D. Onset during infancy or childhood

---

[a] At least 8 of the 16 items in this list should be present and must include at least
two items from A and one each from B and C; and behavior must be
abnormal for the person's developmental level. Specify if childhood onset (after
36 months of age).

Adapted from DSM-III-R (APA 1987, pp. 38–39). Reprinted with permission from
the *Diagnostic and Statistical Manual of Mental Disorders. Third Edition, Revised.*
Copyright 1987 American Psychiatric Association.

Table 5.2 ICD-9 Criteria for Infantile Autism

1. Age of onset in the first 30 months
2. Abnormal responses in auditory and visual stimuli
3. Severe problems in receptive language
4. Delayed speech
5. Speech characterized by echolalia, reversal or pronouns, immature grammatical structure, and inability to use abstract terms
6. Impaired verbal and gestural language
7. Problems in forming social relationships
8. Ritualistic behavior and sterotyped patterns of play
9. Diminished capacity for abstract or symbolic thought and imaginative play
10. Intelligence ranges from severely subnormal to normal or above

Adapted from World Health Organization (1977).

than adequate psychometric characteristics and are useful only as rough screening devices (DeMyer, Churchill, Pontius, & Gilkey, 1971).

Although behavioral diagnosis does not rely on a standardized set of characteristics to define a disorder, investigators using a behavioral approach have nonetheless amassed a wealth of information on the features that are commonly observed in persons who have been labeled autistic. Johnson and Koegel (1982) have summarized this information into seven groups of behaviors that characterize people with autism (see Table 5.3). It must be emphasized that these behaviors are not used for the purpose of diagnosis or classification but rather are specific, observed characteristics of persons who have been labeled as autistic, using a traditional classificatory system such as DSM-III or ICD-9. In addition, not all persons with autism will exhibit behaviors from all seven groups, nor will all behaviors be exhibited at the same frequency, intensity, or duration. Indeed, only some combination of the behaviors may be observed in any given individual, and each of the behaviors may differ in frequency, intensity, and duration.

As will be clear by now, there is substantial *overall* agreement on the diagnosis of autism across the three systems. However, there is less agreement when clinicians are required to diagnose *individual* clients because there appears to be a major lack of objectivity in the

Table 5.3 Behavorial Characteristics of Persons with Autism

1. Autistic children exhibit a profound failure to relate to other people, which is often apparent from birth. They may show an absent or delayed social smile, and may not reach upwards in anticipation of being picked up. Some children fail to form emotional attachments to significant people in their environment, for example, not showing distress when their mothers leave the room. Similarily, a child might play in the vicinity of other children without interacting or participating with them.

2. Autistic children commonly show various levels of impaired or delayed language acquisition and comprehension. Many autistic children are mute and others may show echolalia. For example, a child may repeat numerous phrases or conversations heard without indication that the words convey meaning. Immature grammar, pronoun reversals, and/or inability to use abstract terms may also be apparent.

3. Many children show apparent sensory dysfunction, as if they do not see or hear some environmental events. They may exhibit under or over responsiveness to touch, light, sound, or pain. For instance, the child may not exhibit a startle response to a loud disturbance, but may respond to the sound of a candy wrapper, or may tantrum every time a siren goes by.

4. Many autistic children show inappropriate and/or flat affect. They may not display appropriate facial expressions and may not exhibit fear in dangerous situations, such as crossing the street. They may also laugh and giggle uncontrollably in the absense of any apparent eliciting stimuli, or cry inconsolably for hours.

5. Typically, autistic children will occupy themselves for hours in steroyped, repetitive self-stimulatory behaviors, which serve no apparent purpose other than providing the child with sensory input. Commonly, self-stimulatory behaviors take the form of manipulation of hands or fingers in front of the eyes, eye crossing, repetitive, meaningless vocalizations (e.g., "aeh, aeh, aeh,") suspending or spinning objects in front of the eyes, mouthing objects, hand tapping, body rocking, and other steroyped behavior. Such behaviora have been found to significantly impair learning in autistic children (Koegel & Covert, 1972).

6. Autistic children often fail to develop normal, appropriate play. They may forsake toys altogether, preferring instead to spin a lampshade or flick a light switch on and off. If they do interect with toys, they may do so in an abnormal manner. For instance, the child may arrange, stack, or sort stimuli repetitively, over and over in the same pattern, and may show extreme disruption of the pattern is altered. Or they may turn a truck over and spin the wheels rather than roll it on the ground. Social play with peers may develop spontaneously, but usually does not.

7. Finally, autistic children commonly show obsessive, ritualistic behaviors which have been characterized as a profound resistance to change in the environment or normal routines. Familiar bedtime, insistence on one type of food, one type of furniture arrangement, and particular routes to familiar places are examples of routines which, when altered even in a minor fashion, can create extreme disruptions in a child's behavior.

criteria specified in the traditional diagnostic systems. The behavioral system provides the most objective criteria that can be operationalized for observation and diagnosis. These and other problems (see Schopler, 1983) in existing classification systems have led a number of investigators to either update the systems (e.g., Rutter's [1978] update of Kanner's criteria) or advance their own criteria (e.g., Cohen et al., 1987; NSAC, 1977, 1978).

Our view is that investigators should specify the diagnostic system used to make the diagnosis of autism (e.g., DSM-III-R, NSAC, ICD-9-CM); the specific criteria that have been fulfilled; appropriate parameters of frequency, intensity, and duration of the criterion behaviors; and details of other criteria used if these are not included in the general classification system used.

DIAGNOSIS OF SCHIZOPHRENIA

Schizophrenia is one of the most serious, baffling, and common of the psychotic disorders. With a prevalence rate of between 0.6 and 3% of the population, it affects up to 7 million Americans, many of whom are completely disabled and in need of continuous care (Babigian, 1985).

Schizophrenia is diagnosed more frequently among lower socioeconomic groups and typically manifests itself during adolescence or early adulthood. It has rightfully been described as a disease of younger people. The peak age of onset for males (15 to 24 years) is about 10 years earlier than for females (24 to 35 years), although the reasons for this remain unclear. Proposed explanations have cited sex-linked cultural factors such as increased social demands on males, greater tolerance for psychopathology in females, or a combination of the two.

As with autism, the causes of schizophrenia have yet to be fully identified. However, the pendulum is currently swinging in the direction of a *diathesis*–stress interpretation (Zubin & Steinhauer, 1982). According to this view, genetic or biochemical factors represent predisposing factors that put certain individuals at risk to develop the schizophrenic phenotype. Whether this occurs, however, depends on psychosocial stressors such as poverty or family conflict. A corollary of a diathesis–stress interpretation is that schizophrenia may have multiple causes and maintaining factors. This adds to the heuristic appeal

Table 5.4 DSM-III-R Criteria for Schizophrenia

A. Presence of characteristic psychotic symptoms in the active phase either (1), (2), or (3) for at least 1 week:
   (1) Two of the following:
   Delusions
   Prominent hallucination
   Incoherence or marked loosening of associations
   Catatonic behavior
   Flat or grossly inappropriate affect
   (2) Bizarre delusions
   (3) Prominent hallucinations

B. During the course of the disturbance, functioning in such areas as work, social relations, and self-care is markedly below the highest level achieved before onset of the disturbance.

C. Schizoaffective disorder and mood disorder with psychotic features have been ruled out.

D. Continuous signs of the disturbance for at least 6 months.

E. It cannot be established that an organic factor initiated and maintained the disturbance.

F. If there is a history of autistic disorder, the additional diagnosis of schizophrenia is made only if prominent delusions or hallucinations are also present.

Adapted from DSM-III-R (APA, 1987, pp. 194–195). Reprinted with permission from the *Diagnostic and Statistical Manual of Mental Disorders. Third Edition, Revised.* Copyright 1987 American Psychiatric Association.

of the model because it allows for the integration of a broad range of clinical findings (Curran, Suttion, Faraone, & Guenette, 1985).

Schizophrenia is diagnosed as an Axis I mental disorder in DSM-III-R (APA, 1987). According to diagnostic guidelines, the defining features of the condition are (1) the presence of characteristic psychotic symptoms (e.g., delusions, hallucinations, flat affect) during the active phase of the illness, (2) deterioration from a previously higher level of adaptive functioning, and (3) continuous signs of the disorder for at least 6 months, including prodromal and residual symptoms. By definition this is a chronic condition. Criteria used for describing chronic schizophrenia in the behavioral literature have been inconsistent. We have adopted the criteria advanced by Matson (1980, p. 169), which includes the presence, for a period of 2 years or more of

Table 5.5 Types of Schizophrenia

Disorganized type
Essential features are marked incoherence and flat, inappropriate, or silly affect. Delusions of hallucinations are fragmentary rather than systematized. Associated features include oddities of behavior (facial grimacing, bizarre mannerisms), social withdrawal, and poor premorbid adjustment.

Catatonic type
The essential feature is a significant psychomotor disturbance such as stupor, negativism, rigidity, excitement, or posturing. Rapid alterations between excitement and stupor may be present. Associated features include waxy flexibility, sterotypies, mutism, and bizarre mannerisms.

Paranoid type
Essential features are prominent systematized delusions or hallucinations with presecutory or grandious content. Delusional jealousy may also be present. Associated features include unfocused anxiety, anger, argumentativeness, and violence. Impairment in functioning may be minimal if delusions or hallucinations are not acted upon. Gross disorganization of behavior, incoherence, loose associations, and flat affect are rare.

Undifferentiated type
Essential features are prominent psychotic symptoms that cannot be classified in any of the previous categories or that meet the criteria of more than one category.

Residual type
This category is used when there has been at least one episode of schizophrenia and the patient shows continuing signs of the disorder (e.g., emotional clunting, social withdrawal, eccentric behavior, loose associations) but no prominent psychotic symptoms. If delusions and hallucination are present, they are not prominent or accompanied by strong affect.

Adapted from DSM-III-R (APA, 1987, pp. 196–198) Reprinted with permission from the *Diagnostic and Statistical Manual of Mental Disorder, Third Edition Revised.* Copyright 1987 American Psychiatric Association.

the typical symptom patterns of schizophrenia used in psychiatric diagnosis (e.g., DSM-III-R); the patient having been admitted to an inpatient mental health facility several times and/or having been hospitalized for a period of at least 1 year on a single admission; and a number of deficits in adaptive behavior that are much more likely to appear with chronic patients. The DSM-III-R diagnostic criteria for schizophrenia are shown in Table 5.4.

Schizophrenia symptoms are further delineated according to *type*, of which there are five: catatonic, disorganized (sometimes called hebephrenic), paranoid, undifferentiated, and residual (see Table 5.5). The predominant clinical symptoms at the time of the most recent evaluation provides the basis for a proper diagnosis (Table 5.5). Before the type of schizophrenia is determined, the criteria for the class of schizophrenia must be satisfied.

The ICD-9 (WHO, 1978) lists "schizophrenic psychoses" under the heading of "Other Psychoses," which is separate from "Organic Psychotic Conditions." The essential clinical features of the disorder are the same in the two systems, although the ICD-9 does not specify a durational criterion for prominent psychotic symptoms of at least 6 continuous months. Consequently, the ICD-9 contains a diagnosis of "acute schizophrenic episode" that is roughly the equivalent of "schizophreniform disorder" in DSM-III-R. Otherwise, the typologies of schizophrenia in the two systems are essentially equivalent.

DIFFERENTIAL DIAGNOSIS

As clinicians and researchers we assume, with some justification, that a person's psychological dysfunction categorized on the basis of a diagnostic classificatory system will have a similar cluster of symptoms as that of another with the same disorder. In addition, we assume that a given disorder, such as chronic schizophrenia or autism, will differ in a number of clinically significant ways from other psychological or psychiatric disorders. However, because human behavior is complex and invariably multiply determined, it is likely that specific symptoms will overlap across two or more disorders or syndromes. For example, data from epidemiological studies show that some of the features of autism, but not the full syndrome, are displayed by many nonautistic persons with mental retardation (Ritvo & Freeman, 1978; Rutter & Schopler, 1987; Wing & Gould, 1979). Thus, it is essential that clinicians and researchers are able to differentially diagnose disorders reliably, particularly in the presence of overlapping symptoms.

Differential Diagnosis of Autism Disorder

Adults with autistic disorder may provide diagnostic problems to untrained individuals or inexperienced clinicians because some of the diagnostic features of autism overlap with a number of other global disorders (e.g., childhood schizophrenia, mental retardation).

Autism and Childhood Schizophrenia

Although Kanner (1943) defined autism as the earliest form of childhood schizophrenia, further research has shown conclusively that the two disorders are not related at all (Kolvin, 1971; Makita, 1966; Rutter, 1972). This is now generally accepted (Schopler, 1983), and childhood schizophrenia has not been listed as a separate diagnostic category in either the DSM-III (Cantor, Evans, & Pezzot-Pearce, 1982) or the DSM-III-R (APA, 1987). Children, including those with a diagnosis of autism, may be diagnosed as having schizophrenia if they satisfy the criteria for that disorder (e.g., delusions, hallucinations, incoherence, etc.). Age of onset is an important diagnostic variable that separates persons with autism from those with schizophrenia. For autism, the age of onset is usually before 30 months but almost never after 3 years, whereas for schizophrenia it is usually during adolescence or early childhood but rarely before the age of 5.

Autism and Mental Retardation

Although the primacy of autism over mental retardation can be established, the multiaxial diagnostic system of both the DSM-III-R and ICD-9 allows the concomitant diagnosis of autistic disorder and mental retardation. Indeed, according to Rutter (1988), approximately 75% of persons with autism also have severe intellectual handicap. Adults with autism share some common characteristics with those who have mental retardation but not autism. Diagnostic confusion may arise among those who are profoundly retarded, function below 20 months, and engage in stereotypy (Wing, Gould, Yeates, & Brierley, 1977). Although stereotypy is a common feature here, differential diagnosis would focus not on the nature of the person's stereotypy (although this would be informative) but on his or her social responsiveness. Only the nonautistic, mentally retarded person will show a clinically significant amount of social responsiveness, especially in terms of mental-age-appropriate levels of pretend play.

A number of medical differences between the two disorders have also been identified (Rutter, 1988):

1. The age of onset of seizure disorders in persons with mental retardation is usually in infancy or early childhood, whereas

in persons with autism this typically occurs in adolescence (Deykin & MacMahon, 1979; Richardson, Koller, Katz, & McLaren, 1980).

2. The neuropathology of the two disorders is different in crucial respects (Rutter, 1988).

3. The pattern of complications of pregnancy and the perinatal period is different for the two disorders. "The complications that are known to carry the greatest risk of overt brain damage are the ones most strongly connected with mental retardation, whereas this is not generally so with autism" (Rutter, 1988, p. 273). The most severe pre- and perinatal abnormalities are associated with mental retardation, and only minor abnormalities are associated with autism (Birch, Richardson, Baird, Horobin, & Illsley, 1970; Gillberg & Gillberg, 1983).

4. Autopsy studies show that only mental retardation is associated with some kind of fairly obvious brain pathology (Bauman & Kemper, 1985; Crome, 1960).

Autism, Congenital Sensory Impairments, and Developmental Language Disorders

Those with congenital or early-childhood onset of hearing or visual impairments and developmental language disorders often have problems with receptive and expressive language and articulation. However, unlike individuals with autistic disorder, who also have a severe receptive and expressive language impairment, they tend to use some sort of gesture spontaneously and appear almost eager to communicate, using whatever means possible. When taught an alternative form of communication (e.g., sign language, total communication, braille), their communication problems are quite different from those of autism. In addition, because of congenital or early-onset abnormalities, some nonautistic persons tend to engage in problem behaviors or show signs of withdrawal. Again, these tend to decrease when they are taught an alternative means of communication. Persons with autism exhibit more bizarre language than do those with developmental language disorders, and they are less likely to use gestures to communicate with others (Cox, Rutter, Newman, & Bartak, 1975). These two disorders are also differentiated on the basis of social responsiveness and imaginative play, with autistic patients displaying far less of both (Bartak, Rutter, & Cox, 1975).

Differential Diagnosis of Chronic Schizophrenia

As with autism, the diagnosis of schizophrenia may provide problems for untrained individuals or inexperienced clinicians because some of the diagnostic features of schizophrenia overlap with a number of other disorders.

Schizophrenia and Other Psychotic Conditions

A diagnosis of schizophrenia is made only when presenting psychotic symptoms cannot be attributed to organic factors (e.g., organic mental disorder or organic delusional syndrome associated with drug ingestion) or to a mood disorder such as bipolar or schizoaffective disorder. Differential diagnosis also needs to be made between brief reactive psychosis and schizophreniform disorder. The duration of psychotic symptoms (continuous for at least 6 months) is the primary criterion used to make the determination. For example, brief reactive psychosis is used to designate a psychotic condition characterized by the sudden onset of symptoms lasting from a few hours to 1 month. In schizophreniform disorder the clinical features are very similar to schizophrenia except that the duration of the illness is less than 6 months. If symptoms continue longer than that, the diagnosis is changed to schizophrenia. At this point the relationship between schizophreniform disorder and schizophrenia is unclear (APA, 1987). Because of conflicting research findings and the fact that the prognosis for persons with schizophreniform disorder is relatively good, the two disorders are classified separately.

Schizophrenia and Personality Disorders

There are a number of personality disorders in which transient psychotic symptoms may be present (e.g., schizotypal, borderline, and paranoid personality disorders). Once again, it is the short-term nature of the symptoms, followed by a return to normal functioning, that distinguishes these disorders from schizophrenia. Similarly, paranoid personality disorder is differentiated from schizophrenia, paranoid type, by the absence of prominent delusions and hallucinations as well as other oddities of behavior.

Schizophrenia and Developmental Disorders

Adults with mental retardation or autistic features may display symptoms that mimic schizophrenia, such as disturbances in communication, severe social maladjustment, and impoverished affect and cognition. If delusions and hallucinations are prominent, an additional diagnosis of schizophrenia is indicated (see "Chronic Schizophrenia and Adult Autism" below).

Schizophrenia and Mood Disorders

In the case of mood disorders with psychotic features (bipolar disorder, major depression) and schizoaffective disorders, a reliable differential diagnosis is important because of its implications for treatment selection. The task is not always easy because mood symptoms are also common in schizophrenia throughout its various phases. Much depends on the duration of the mood disturbances. If they are relatively brief in comparison to other schizophrenic symptoms, the diagnosis of schizophrenia is given. If they are not brief, the differential diagnosis is between schizoaffective disorder and mood disorder with psychotic features. The presence of psychotic symptoms for at least 2 weeks without accompanying mood symptoms suggests a schizoaffective disorder. If some but not all schizophrenic symptoms are present without a deterioration of functioning from the highest previous level, and organic factors cannot be ruled out as a causative agent, the correct diagnosis would be psychotic disorder not otherwise specified.

Chronic Schizophrenia and Adult Autism

As is the case with mentally retarded persons (Reiss, Levitan, & Szysko, 1982), adults with autism may also have a secondary diagnosis of mental illness, usually an affective disorder (Wright, 1982). Problems in differential diagnosis of chronic schizophrenia and autism may arise when clinical features of mental illness overshadow the characteristics of autism. In general, the age of onset is a major diagnostic variable that differentiates the two disorders. Autism has a much earlier age of onset, usually prior to 30 months, whereas it is usually during adolescence or early adulthood that schizophrenia is first diagnosed. In addition, persons with schizophrenia have a much higher level of language functioning and may also have irregular periods of recovery and regression, features typically not observed in persons with autism.

Social Withdrawal and Lack of Motivation

The behavior of adults with autism often seems slow and deliberate, sharing features common to psychomotor retardation in persons with chronic schizophrenia and suggestive of social withdrawal and a lack of motivation. As with autistic children, when required to perform tasks that are not meaningful or inherently interesting to them, adult autistic persons may appear to be socially withdrawn, a characteristic of chronic schizophrenia. However, on closer examination it will be obvious that this is not a general characteristic of autistic persons as they often show great interest in some tasks, usually tasks of their own choosing. Although there is no reliable method of predicting which tasks they will find engaging because of individual variations in behavior, it behooves the clinician to examine the client under a number of diverse conditions to obtain an accurate differential diagnosis.

Emotional Flattening

A feature of persons with chronic schizophrenia is that they have a flat affect; display little emotion regardless of the environment or interpersonal context; have a blank, expressionless face; appear apathetic and uninterested; and avoid looking at the speaker when spoken to (Carpenter, Sacks, Strauss, Bartak, & Rayner, 1976). In chronic schizophrenia, interpersonal interactions are often not very reinforcing because the patients display an emotional flatness—a lack of empathy, warmth, and concern for reality. These behaviors are sometimes evident in autistic adults. There are two possible reasons. One is that there is some degree of mental illness being exhibited by the person, and the other is that clinical features associated with autism are being incorrectly perceived as emotional flattening. For example, the restricted understanding and display of nonverbal communication (e.g., facial expressions, gestures) by autistic children and adults (Hermelin, 1982; Hobson, 1983; Langdell, 1978; Sigman, Ungerer, Mundy, & Sherman, 1987), as well as their monotonous vocal intonation (Ricks & Wing, 1975), can be misinterpreted as signs of emotional flattening.

Delusions and Hallucinations

There has been some speculation that the florid symptoms of chronic schizophrenia, such as delusions and hallucinations, may also be evident in autistic persons. Those with autistic disorder sometimes appear to act as if they have a thought disorder, in the sense that some of them make remarks that are out of context, carry on a conversation with themselves even in dyadic interpersonal contexts, or laugh and point at imaginary persons or things in their environment. In addition, they sometimes repeat things heard or said in the past that on the face of it may be mistaken for delusions. However, these are only instances of delayed echolalia sometimes observed in persons with autism (Newsom & Rincover, 1979). Our understanding is that there is little in the research or clinical literature to suggest that autistic adults have delusions or hallucinations. If indeed they do exhibit such behaviors, it is very likely that they will have an additional diagnosis of schizophrenia (Wolff & Chick, 1980). The person's developmental history, particularly age of onset, typical behavior patterns and current behavioral repertoire, would assist in differential diagnosis.

Ritualistic or Obsessional Behaviors

Autistic persons are characterized by their obsessive, ritualistic behaviors (Rutter, 1988) and insistence on rigid routines. These behaviors are topographically similar to those exhibited by some chronic schizophrenics. However, as noted by Wing and Attwood (1987), those with an obsessional disorder are usually aware of it and tend to resist or "struggle against their compulsions" (p. 16), but this is not the case with autistic adults.

Poverty of Speech

Persons with schizophrenia may exhibit a poverty of speech, have long lapses before responding to a question or fail to respond altogether, and have a restricted quantity of speech. These features are also evident to some extent in persons with autism who have verbal facility. However, autistic adults will display various levels of impaired or delayed language acquisition and comprehension (Johnson & Koegel, 1982). Unlike persons with schizophrenia, their language is often marked by immature grammar, pronoun reversal, and restricted use of abstract terms.

Adult Autism, Asperger's Syndrome, and Schizoid Personality

Children who display "unusual social relatedness ('autistic psychopathy') but good language competencies" (Cohen et al., 1987, p. 20) have been labeled as having Asperger's syndrome (see Wing, 1981). It has been suggested by Wolff and Barlow (1979) that Asperger's syndrome should be classified as schizoid personality. In the DSM-III-R (1987), schizoid personality disorder is defined as "a pervasive pattern of indifference to social relationships and a restricted range of emotional experience and expression, beginning by early adulthood and present in a variety of contexts" (p. 339). Those with schizoid personality disorder appear to be grossly deficient in interpersonal skills and typically withdraw when under stress. As noted by Wing and Attwood (1987), socially withdrawn persons with autism would also be classified in this category because "schizoid personality" is such a broadly defined term. However, there is no consensus that persons with Asperger's syndrome are truly autistic, and even if they were, the age of onset would differentiate those with autism from those with schizoid personality disorder.

CONCLUSIONS

It is critical that as clinicians we are able to reliably diagnose psychological dysfunction in our clients so that the most appropriate treatment is used. In this chapter we discussed three diagnostic systems and pointed out the advantages and limitations of each. Historically, behavior therapists have been very critical of psychiatric nosological schemes, particularly the DSM-I and DSM-II. However, many of the original concerns voiced by behavior therapists (e.g., reliability, validity, and utility of categories) have been adequately answered in the DSM-III and, more recently, in the DSM-III-R. Although not all concerns have been dealt with, the "emergence of DSM-III . . . has influenced all clinical practitioners, irrespective of theoretical allegiance, including behavior therapists" (Hersen & Turner, 1984, p. 485).

At present there appears to be a realization on the part of behavioral clinicians that our clients present us with complex behavior problems that may require more than what Hersen and Van Hasselt (1987) have termed narrow-band behavioral evaluation. That is, we need to use other systems to fully appreciate the diagnostic and treatment issues involved. We agree with the position taken by our behavioral colleagues (e.g., Harris & Powers, 1984; Haynes & O'Brien, 1988; Hersen, 1988; Hersen & Last, 1988, 1989; Kazdin, 1983) that psychiatric diagnosis and behavioral analysis are compatible and may indeed be necessary for adequate differential diagnosis. With regard to chronic schizophrenia and adult autism, we suggest that a two-tier diagnostic assessment may prove valuable, the first being a broad-based psychiatric diagnosis and the second a more detailed behavioral assessment of environmental events that may need modification.

REFERENCES

Achenbach, T. M. (1985). *Assessment and taxonomy of child and adolescent psychopathology*. Newbury Park, CA: Sage Publications.

Achenbach, T. M., & Edelbrock, C. (1978). The classification of child psychopathology: A review and analysis of empirical efforts. *Psychological Bulletin. 85*, 1275–1301.

Achenbach, T. M., & Edelbrock, C. (1983). *Manual for the Child Behavior Checklist and Revised Child Behavior Profile*. Burlington, VT: University of Vermont, Department of Psychiatry.

Achenbach, T. M., & McConaughy, S. H. (1987). *Empirically based assessment of child and adolescent psychopathology: Practical applications*. Newbury Park, CA: Sage Publications.

Aman, M. G., & Singh, N. N. (1986). *Aberrant behavior checklist and manual*. New York: Slosson Educational Publications.

American Psychiatric Association. (1980). *Diagnostic and statistical manual of mental disorders* (3rd ed.). Washington, DC: American Psychiatric Association.

American Psychiatric Association. (1987). *Diagnostic and statistical manual of mental disorders* (3rd ed., rev.). Washington, DC: American Psychiatric Association.

Babigian, H. (1985). Schizophrenia: Epidemiology. In A. Kaplan & B. Sadock (Eds.), *Comprehensive textbook of psychiatry*. Baltimore: Williams and Wilkins.

Bartak, L., Rutter, M., & Cox, A. (1975). A comparative study of infantile autism and specific developmental receptive language disorder: 1. The children. *British Journal of Psychiatry, 126,* 127-148.

Bartak, L., Rutter, M., & Cox, A. (1977). A comparative study of infantile autism and specific developmental receptive language disorder: III. Discriminant function analysis. *Journal of Autism and Childhood Schizophrenia, 7,* 383-396.

Bashfield, R. (1984). *The classification of psychopathology*. New York: Plenum Press.

Bauman, M., & Kemper, T. L. (1985). Histoanatomic observations of the brain in early infantile autism. *Neurology, 35,* 866-874.

Birch, H. G., Richardson, S. A., Baird, D., Horobin, G., & Illsley, R. (1970). *Mental subnormality in the community: A clinical and epidemiologic study.* Baltimore: Williams & Wilkins.

Cantor, S., Evans, J., & Pezzot-Pearce, T. (1982). Childhood schizophrenia: Present but not accounted for. *American Journal of Psychiatry, 139,* 758-762.

Carpenter, W. T., Jr., Sacks, M. H., Strauss, J. S., Bartok, J. J., & Rayner, J. (1976). Evaluating signs and symptoms: Comparisons of structured interview and clinical approaches. *British Journal of Psychiatry, 128,* 397-303.

Cohen, D. J., Paul, R., & Volkmar, F. R. (1987). Issues in the classification of pervasive developmental disorders and associated conditions. In D. J. Cohen & A. M. Donnellan (Eds.), *Handbook of autism and pervasive developmental disorders* (pp. 20-40). New York: John Wiley.

Cox, A., Rutter, M., Newman, S., & Bartak, L. (1975). A comparative study of infantile autism and specific developmental language disorder: 2. Parental characteristics. *British Journal of Psychiatry, 126,* 146-159.

Crome, L. (1960). The brain and mental retardation. *British Medical Journal, 1,* 897-904.

Curran, J., Sutton, R., Faraone, S., & Guenette, S. (1985). Inpatient approaches. In M. Hersen & A. Bellack (Eds.), *Handbook of clinical behavior therapy with adults*. New York: Plenum Press.

DeMyer, M. K., Churchill, D., Pontius, W., & Gilkey, K. (1971). A comparison of five diagnostic systems for childhood schizophrenia and infantile autism. *Journal of Autism and Childhood Schizophrenia, 1,* 175-198.

DeMyer, M. K., Hingtgen, J. N., & Jackson, R. K. (1981). Infantile autism reviewed: A decade of research. *Schizophrenia Bulletin, 7,* 388-451.

Deykin, E. Y., & MacMahon, B. (1979). The incidence of seizures among children with autistic symptoms. *American Journal of Psychiatry, 136,* 1310–1312.

Edelbrock, C. S., & Achenbach, T. M. (1980). A typology of Child Behavior Profile patterns: Distribution and correlates for disturbed children aged 6–16. *Journal of Abnormal Child Psychology, 8,* 441–470.

Ferster, C. B. (1965). Classification of behavioral pathology. In L. Krasner & L. P. Ullmann (Eds.), *Research in behavior modification.* New York: Holt, Rinehart & Winston.

Gillberg, C., & Gillberg, I. C. (1983). Infantile autism: A total population study of reduced optimality in the pre-, peri-, and neonatal period. *Journal of Autism and Developmental Disorders, 13,* 153–155.

Goldfried, M., & Davison, G. (1976). *Clinical behavior therapy.* New York: Holt, Rinehart and Winston.

Griest, D. L., & Wells, K. C. (1983). Behavioral family therapy with conduct disorders in children. *Behavior Therapy, 14,* 37–53.

Harris, S. L., & Powers, M. D. (1984). Diagnostic issues. In T. H. Ollendick & M. Hersen (Eds.), *Child behavioral assessment: Principles and procedures* (pp. 38–57). New York: Pergamon Press.

Haynes, S. N., & O'Brien, W. H. (1988). The gordian knot of DSM-III-R use: Integrating principles of behavior classification and complex causal models. *Behavioral Assessment, 10,* 95–105.

Hermelin B. (1982). Thoughts and feelings. *Australian Autism Review, 1,* 10–19.

Hersen, M. (1988). Behavioral assessment and psychiatric diagnosis. *Behavioral Assessment, 10,* 107–121.

Hersen, M., & Last, C. G. (1988). How the field has moved on. In M. Hersen & C. G. Last (Eds.), *Child behavior therapy casebook* (pp. 1–10). New York: Plenum Press.

Hersen, M., & Last, C. G. (1989). Psychiatric diagnosis and behavioral assessment in children. In C. G. Last & M. Hersen (Eds.), *Handbook of child psychiatric diagnosis.* New York: Wiley.

Hersen, M., & Turner, S. M. (1984). DSM-III and behavior therapy. In S. M. Turner & M. Hersen (Eds.), *Adult psychopathology and diagnosis* (pp. 485–502). New York: Wiley.

Hobson, R. P. (1983). The autistic child's recognition of age related features of people, animals and things. *British Journal of Developmental Psychology, 1,* 343–352.

Johnson, J., & Koegel, R. L. (1982). Behavioral assessment and curriculum development. In R. L. Koegel, A. Rincover, & A. L. Egel (Eds.), *Educating and understanding autistic children* (pp. 1–32). San Diego, CA: College-Hill Press.

Kanfer, F. H., & Saslow, G. (1969). Behavioral diagnosis. In C. M. Franks (Ed.), *Behavior therapy: Appraisal and status*. New York: McGraw-Hill.

Kanner, L. (1943). Autistic disturbances of affective contact. *Nervous Child, 2*, 217–250.

Kazdin, A. E. (1979). Situational specificity: The two-edged sword of behavioral assessment. *Behavioral Assessment, 1*, 57–75.

Kazdin, A. E. (1983). Psychiatric diagnosis, dimensions of dysfunction and child behavior therapy. *Behavior Therapy, 14*, 73–99.

Kazdin, A. E. (1985). Alternative approaches to the diagnosis of childhood disorders. In P. Bornstein & A. Kazdin (Eds.), *Handbook of clinical behaviors therapy with children* (pp. 3–43). Homewood, IL: Dorsey Press.

Koegel, R., & Covert, A. (1972). The relationship of self-stimulation to learning in autistic children. *Journal of Applied Behavior Analysis, 5*, 381–388.

Kolvin, I. (1971). Studies in the childhood psychoses: I. Diagnostic criteria and classification. *British Journal of Psychiatry, 118*, 381–384.

Kolvin, I., Ounsted, C., Richardson, L., & Garside, R. F. (1971). Studies in the childhood psychoses: III. The family and social background in childhood psychoses. *British Journal of Psychiatry, 118*, 396–402.

Langdell, T. (1978). Recognition of faces: An approach to the study of autism. *Journal of Child Psychology and Psychiatry, 19*, 255–268.

Lessing, E. E., Williams, V., & Gil, E. (1982). A cluster-analytically derived typology: Feasible alternative to clinical diagnostic classification of children? *Journal of Abnormal Child Psychology, 10*, 451–482.

Lorr, M., Klett, C. J., & Cave, R. (1967). Higher-level psychotic syndromes. *Journal of Abnormal Psychology, 72*, 74–77.

Lovaas, I. O. (1987). Behavioral treatment and normal educational and intellectual functioning in young autistic children. *Journal of Consulting and Clinical Psychology, 55*, 3–9.

Makita, K. (1966). The age of onset of childhood schizophrenia. *Folia Psychiatrica Neurologica Japonica, 20*, 111–121.

Matson, J. L. (1980). Behavior modification procedures for training chronically institutionalized schizophrenics. In M. Hersen, R. M. Eisler, & P. M. Miller (Eds.), *Progress in behavior modification* (Vol. 9, pp. 167–204). New York: Academic Press.

Mezzich, J. E. (1984). Diagnosis and classification. In S. M. Turner & M. Hersen (Eds.), *Adult psychopathology and diagnosis* (pp. 3–36). New York: John Wiley.

Nathan, P. (1987). DSM-III-R and the behavioral therapist. *The Behavior Therapist, 10*, 203–205.

National Society for Autistic Children. (1977). A short definition of autism. *NSAC Newsletter, 9*, 6.

National Society for Autistic Children. (1978). Definition of the syndrome of autism. *Journal of Autism and Childhood Schizophrenia, 8,* 162–167.

Newsom, C., & Rincover, A. (1979). Autism. In E. J. Mash & L. G. Terdal (Eds.), *Behavioral assessment of childhood disorders* (pp. 397–439). New York: John Wiley.

Quay, H. C. (1979). Classification. In H. C. Quay & J. S. Werry (Eds.), *Psychopathological disorders of childhood.* New York: John Wiley.

Quay, H. C., & Peterson, D. R. (1983). *Interim manual for the Revised Behavior Problem Checklist.* Unpublished manuscript, University of Miami and Rutgers State University.

Reiss, S., Levitan, G. W., & Szysko, J. (1982). Emotional disturbance and mental retardation: Diagnostic overshadowing. *American Journal of Mental Deficiency, 86,* 567–574.

Richardson, S. A., Koller, H., Katz, M., & McLaren, J. (1980). Seizures and epilepsy in a mentally retarded population over the first 22 years of life. *Applied Research in Mental Retardation, 1,* 123–138.

Ricks, D. M., & Wing, L. (1975). Language, communication and the use of symbols in normal and autistic children. *Journal of Autism and Childhood Schizophrenia, 5,* 191–221.

Rimland, B. (1964). *Infantile autism: The syndrome and its implications for a neural theory of behavior.* New York: Appleton-Century-Crofts.

Rimland, B. (1974). Infantile autism: Status and research. In A. Davids (Ed.), *Child personality and psychopathology* (Vol. 1). New York: John Wiley.

Ritvo, E. R., & Freeman, B. J. (1978). National Society for Autistic Children definition of the syndrome of autism. *Journal of Autism and Childhood Schizophrenia, 8,* 162–167.

Rutter, M. (1970). Autistic children: Infancy to adulthood. *Seminars in Psychiatry, 2,* 435–450.

Rutter, M. (1972). Childhood schizophrenia reconsidered. *Journal of Autism and Childhood Schizophrenia, 2,* 315–338.

Rutter, M. (1978). Diagnosis and definition of childhood autism. *Journal of Autism and Childhood Schizophrenia, 8,* 139–161.

Rutter, M. (1988). Biological basis of autism: Implications for autism. In F. J. Menolascino & J. A. Stark (Eds.), *Preventive and curative intervention in mental retardation* (pp. 265–294). Baltimore: Paul H. Brookes.

Rutter, M., & Schopler, E. (1987). Autism and pervasive developmental disorders: Concepts and diagnostic issues. In M. Rutter, A. H. Tuma, & L. Lann (Eds.), *Assessment, diagnosis and classification in child and adolescent psychopathology.* New York: Guilford.

Salzinger, K. (1981). Remedying schizophrenic behavior. In S. M. Turner, K. S. Calhoun, & H. E. Adams (Eds.), *Handbook of clinical behavior therapy* (pp. 162–190). New York: Wiley.

Schopler, E., (1983). New developments in the definition and diagnosis of autism. In B. B. Lahey & A. E. Kazdin (Eds.), *Advances in clinical child psychology* (Vol. 6. pp. 93–127). New York: Plenum Press.

Sigman, M., Ungerer, J. A., Mundy, P., & Sherman, T. (1987). Cognition in autistic children. In D. J. Cohen & Donnellan, A. M. (Eds.), *Handbook of autism and pervasive developmental disorders* (pp. 103–120). New York: John Wiley.

Singh, N. N., & Repp, A. C. (1988). Current trends in the behavioral and psychopharmacological management of problem behaviors of mentally retarded persons. *Irish Journal of Psychology, 9*, 264–285. [Special issue: Psychology and disability].

Soli, S. D., Nuechterlein, K. H., Garmezy, N., Devine, V. T., & Schaefer, S. M. (1981). A classification system for research in child psychopathology: 1. An empirical approach using factor and cluster and conjunctive decision rules. In B. A. Maher & W. B. Maher (Eds.), *Progress in experimental personality research*. New York: Academic Press.

Spitzer, R., & Williams, J. (1985). Classification in psychiatry. In A. Kaplan & B. Sadock (Eds.), *Comprehensive textbook of psychiatry*. Baltimore: Williams and Wilkens.

Spitzer, R., Williams, J., & Skodol, R. (1980). DSM III: The major achievements and an overview. *American Journal of Psychiatry, 137*, 151–164.

Taylor, B. (1983). DSM-III and behavioral assessment. *Behavioral Assessment, 5*, 5–14.

Wing, L. (1981). Asperger's sundrome: A clinical account. *Psychological Medicine, 11*, 115–129.

Wing, L., & Atwood, A. (1987). Syndromes of autism and atypical development. In D. J. Cohen & A. M. Donnellan (Eds.), *Handbook of autism and pervasive developmental disorders* (pp. 3–19). New York: John Wiley.

Wing, L., & Gould, J. (1979). Severe impairments of social interaction and associated abnormalities in children: Epidemiology and classification. *Journal of Autism and Developmental Disorders, 9*, 11–30.

Wing, L., Gould, J., Yeates, S. R., & Brierley, L. M. (1977). Symbolic play in severely mentally retarded and in autistic children. *Journal of Child Psychology and Psychiatry, 18*, 167–178.

Wittlieb, E., Eifert, G., Wilson, F. E., & Evans, I. M. (1978). Target behavior selection in recent child case reports in Behavior Therapy. *The Behavior Therapist, 1*, 15–16.

Wolf, L., & Goldberg, B. (1986). Autistic children grow up: An eight to twenty-four year followup study. *Canadian Journal of Psychiatry, 31*, 550–556.

Wolff, S., & Barlow, A. (1979). Schizoid personality in childhood: A comparative study of schizoid, autistic and normal children. *Journal of Child Psychology and Psychiatry, 20*, 29–46.

Wolff, S., & Chick, J. (1980). Schizoid personality in childhood: A controlled follow-up study. *Psychological Medicine, 10*, 85–100.

World Health Organization. (1977). *Manual of the international classification of diseases, injuries, and causes of death* (9th rev. ed.). Geneva: Author.

World Health Organization. (1978). *Mental disorders: Glossary and guide to their classification in accordance with the ninth revision of the international classification of diseases.* Geneva: Author.

Wright, E. C. (1982). The presentation of mental illness in mentally retarded adults. *British Journal of Psychiatry, 141*, 496–502.

Yule, W. (1981). The epidemiology of child psychopathology. In B. B. Lahey & A. E. Kazdin (Eds.), *Advances in clinical child psychology,* (Vol. 4, pp. 1–51). New York: Plenum Press.

Zubin, J., & Steinhauer, S. (1982). How to break the logjam in schizophrenia. *Journal of Nervous and Mental Disease, 169*, 477–492.

6

Behavioral Assessment with Chronic Schizophrenia and Autism

Laura Schreibman, N. Jennifer Oke,
and Bertram O. Ploog

Behavioral assessment has typically been defined as "the identification of meaningful response units and their controlling variables (both current, environmental, and organismic) for the purposes of understanding and altering human behavior" (Nelson & Hayes, 1979a, p. 491). In the early 1970s behavioral assessment became an area of study in its own right, and its focus broadened from a predominant concern with treatment to improving the identification and measurement of treatment goals and outcomes. This increasing interest in the area of behavioral assessment was accompanied by the appearance of numerous books (e.g., Cone & Hawkins, 1977; Hersen & Bellack, 1976; Mash & Terdal, 1976) and journals (*Behavioral Assessment* and *Journal of Behavioral Assessment*).

The purpose of this chapter is to provide an overview of the areas of behavioral assessment relevant to assessment of chronic schizophrenia and autism and to provide a framework for the use of behavioral assessment with these populations. In addition, this chapter discusses the current status of and trends in the area of meta-analysis, cost analysis, and treatment comparison; and the trend toward the increased use of computers in assessment.

TRADITIONAL ASSESSMENT

The traditional approach to assessment assumes that behavior is a function of relatively stable intrapsychic variables. Thus, behavior is viewed as a "sign" of these underlying variables (Goldfried & Kent, 1972; Nelson & Hayes, 1979b) and is important only insofar as it indicates the presence of intrapsychic problems (Hartmann, Roper, & Bradford, 1979). Because behavior is thought of as consistent across time and settings, the specific assessment situation is judged as relatively unimportant. Traditional assessment tends to utilize more indirect or global measures of behavior and makes inferences based on this information. Information gained from these assessment techniques is used primarily to diagnose and classify. For example, projective tests such as the Rorschach Inkblot Test (Rorschach, 1942) and the Thematic Apperception Test (Murray, 1943) provide ambiguous stimuli to which the client attributes meaning. The clinician uses this information to make inferences about the client's intrapsychic problems. The traditional approach assumes common histories and similar developmental courses for all individuals, given the same diagnosis, regardless of the fact that behavioral manifestations of the disorder for each individual may differ. Thus, the diagnosis, rather than specific behaviors, determines the focus of treatment for each individual within a classification (Kanfer, 1985).

The traditional approach has been criticized for several reasons (Johnson & Koegel, 1982; Schreibman & Koegel, 1981). First, for many disorders there are large differences in the characteristics displayed by individuals. Thus, the diagnostic label does not convey information about the specific characteristics or abilities of the particular individual. For example, an autistic individual may display echolalic speech or be nonverbal; a schizophrenic individual may report hallucinations and not delusions. Second, the diagnosis does not suggest an individual treatment plan; rather, diagnosis implies a common treatment. However, there is no consensus among professionals as to common treatments for specific disorders. Finally, the diagnosis does not suggest a prognosis. For example, a diagnosis of autism does not give information as to whether an individual will improve or how much improvement should be expected.

BEHAVIORAL ASSESSMENT AND ITS ADVANTAGES

In contrast to the traditional approach, the behavioral approach views behavior as a function of environment and organismic variables (Goldfried & Kent, 1972; Hartmann et al., 1979; Nelson & Hayes, 1979b). Thus, observed behavior is a representative "sample" of responding in a specific situation. Because behavior is a function of present environmental and organismic variables, behavior is consistent only if the environmental conditions are constant. If the environmental conditions are changing, then behavior is variable. Behavioral assessment places an emphasis on the use of direct methods of measuring specific behaviors. The assessment process is ongoing and is used to select target behaviors, to determine controlling variables, and to select and evaluate treatment strategies. Thus, through the use of behavioral assessment individual treatment plans can be developed. Because of its emphasis on individualized treatment, the behavioral approach has been criticized for being "excessively individualistic, low in cost effectiveness, and too narrow in the range of behavioral changes that are obtained across situations" (Kanfer, 1985, p. 9). These limitations are recognized by the field and are key issues in the area of applied behavior analysis. For example, much research is devoted to establishing techniques to enhance the generalization of behavior change.

There are three main advantages to the behavioral approach, some of which relate to these criticisms (Johnson & Koegel, 1982). First, behavioral assessment provides information on specific behaviors the individual exhibits. This is important considering the fact that both schizophrenic and autistic individuals have highly variable characteristics. Second, by determining the controlling variables of behavior a specific treatment is suggested. In addition, behavioral assessment allows continuous monitoring of treatment progress and effectiveness. Finally, prognosis can be inferred from the effectiveness of empirically derived treatment procedures. For example, behavioral techniques have been successful in establishing speech in nonverbal and echolalic autistic children. On the other hand, treatment methods have had varied success in the elimination of self-stimulatory behavior, a difficult behavior to suppress. Thus, one may conclude that the prognosis for an individual with high rates of self-stimulatory behavior might be poorer than for an individual with little or no such behavior (all else being equal).

PHASES OF BEHAVIORAL ASSESSMENT

Behavioral assessment can be divided into five separate, but not mutually exclusive, phases as follows (Cone & Hawkins, 1977; Hawkins, 1979; Johnson & Koegel, 1982):

1. Screening and evaluating general disposition: Through the use of interviews, behavior checklists, and rating scales, abilities as well as general problems and areas of difficulty are identified.
2. Defining the problem: During this phase target behaviors are selected and operationally defined, and controlling variables (both environmental and organismic) are determined.
3. Pinpointing and designing the intervention: Using the information about controlling variables, in addition to searching the experimental literature for effective treatment, appropriate interventions are designed to deal with the problem behavior.
4. Monitoring treatment progress: Throughout intervention, treatment effectiveness is monitored. This allows for reevaluation of the behavior, and if no improvement is indicated, the intervention can be redesigned.
5. Evaluating the intervention: In addition to assessment of treatment outcome, generalization and maintenance of the behavior change is also evaluated.

Hawkins (1979) conceptualized this process as a funnel strategy, in which a general description of problems and areas of difficulty is narrowed down to specific target behaviors. These target behaviors are assigned priorities, and specific treatment goals are selected. Then target behaviors are operationally defined and controlling variables determined. Treatment programs are designed on the basis of this information, and throughout intervention, treatment effectiveness is evaluated.

Screening and Evaluating General Disposition
Interviews: Autism

During the initial screening, the individual is informally observed, and parents and/or caretakers (and the individual himself, if appropriate) are interviewed to gather information and make a diagnostic evaluation (e.g., Schreibman & Charlop, 1987). Information is obtained about specific behavioral excesses and deficits. The interview includes questions concerning (1) the individual's developmental history, including the presence of apparent sensory deficits (i.e., suspected deafness or blindness) and affect during infancy; (2) social behavior, such as social responsiveness, attachment to significant others, interaction with peers, and preference to be alone; (3) speech acquisition, including the absence of speech, echolalia, and present language abilities; (4) the presence of self-stimulatory or self-injurious behaviors; (5) inappropriate emotions, such as irrational fears and tantruming or laughing for no apparent reason; (6) compulsive or ritualistic behavior the individual displays; (7) any isolated areas of skills the individual might have; and (8) behavior problems such as aggression, noncompliance, or lack of self-help skills. In addition, informal observations of the individual's behavior are also made. The client is observed informally for evidence of these same appropriate and inappropriate behaviors.

Behavior Checklists, Rating Scales, and Behavior Observation Schemes: Autism

Several behavior checklists and rating scales are used as screening measures for autism. Behavior and development, such as birth history, symptoms, and speech, are included in Rimland's Diagnostic Checklist for Behavior Disturbed Children, Form E-2 (Rimland, 1971). Questions are answered by the parent; a plus is scored for response characteristic of autism, and a minus is scored for responses not characteristic. Scores on this measure based on responses for 2,218 forms range from −42 to +45, with a score of +20 or higher indicative of autism.

The Autism Behavior Checklist is a part of the Autism Screening Instrument for Educational Planning (ASIEP) and includes behaviors from various checklists (e.g., Rimland, 1971) as well as from the diagnostic criteria of Kanner and the British Working Party (Krug, Arick, & Almond, 1981). Fifty-seven behaviors are grouped into the following areas: (1) sensory, (2) relating, (3) body and object use, (4) language, and (5) social and self-help skills. The behaviors on this scale are weighted in terms of their prediction ability. Included in this measure are sections to sample vocalizations, an interaction assessment, an educational assessment, and a measure of prognosis of learning rate.

Observation is also combined with a behavior rating scale in the Childhood Autism Rating Scale (Schopler, Reichler, DeVellis, & Daly, 1980). For this measure the diagnostic session is observed, and behavior is rated on a 4-point scale, from normal to severely abnormal, for 15 subscales. The subscales included in this measure are impairment in human relationships, imitation, inappropriate affect, bizarre use of body movement and persistence of stereotypes, peculiarities in relating to nonhuman objects, resistance to environmental change, peculiarities of visual responsiveness, peculiarities of auditory responsiveness, near receptor responsiveness, anxiety reaction, verbal communication, nonverbal communication, activity level, intellectual functioning, and general impressions. These behaviors are based on the diagnostic criteria of Kanner, the British Working Party, Rutter, and the National Society for Autistic Children (NSAC).

A measure that combines a checklist with behavioral observation is the Behavior Observation Scale for Autism or BOS (Freeman & Ritvo, 1982; Freeman, Ritvo, & Schroth, 1984; Freeman & Schroth, 1984). This measure was developed to address several limitations of previous diagnostic measures. First, these measures typically do not provide operational definitions of the behaviors on the scale to enhance interrater reliability. Second, they typically fail to assess the role of development, and finally, they do not provide profiles sufficient to differentiate "normal" and "pathological" conditions. In contrast, the BOS consists of 67 operationally defined behaviors. The child is observed in a room containing toys, and the occurrence of each behavior is recorded during nine 3-min intervals. The observation system is designed to "(1) differentiate autistic from normal and mentally retarded children, (2) identify subgroups of autistic children, and (3) develop an objective means of describing subjects in behavioral and biological research" (Freeman et al., 1984, p. 588).

Finally, Lovaas, Koegel, Simmons, and Long (1973) developed a structured observation procedure to determine behavioral deficits and excesses in autistic children. Variations of this basic format have continued to be used in various studies (e.g., Koegel, Schreibman, Johnson, O'Neill, & Dunlap, 1984; Schreibman & Britten, 1984; Schreibman, Koegel, Mills, & Burke, 1984). In the basic procedure the child is observed in the following three conditions: (1) alone in a room with age-appropriate toys, (2) in the room with an adult present who attends to the child but does not initiate any interaction, and (3) in the room with the adult present who attempts to interact with the child, converse with him or her, and make requests (e.g., "Give me the block" or "Touch your knee"). The 30-min session is scored for the occurrence of eight categories of behavior: appropriate verbal behavior (i.e., asking and answering questions, speech appropriate to the context), inappropriate vocalizations (i.e., echolalia), social nonverbal behavior (i.e., affection, compliance), self-stimulatory behavior, exploratory and appropriate play (two distinct sophistication levels of play), noncompliance, and tantrums. An operational definition for each behavior is provided. This assessment gives the clinician or researcher a profile of the individual's behavioral excesses and deficits.

Although the measures discussed above have been used primarily with autistic children, these measures can be adapted for use with adults. For example, age-appropriate materials (rather than toys) can be utilized in the observation setting. The emphasis here on children reflects the scarcity of research on measures developed for use with autistic adults.

Interviews: Schizophrenia

Two extensive structured interviews have been developed that are used frequently to assess schizophrenic individuals (Neale, Oltmanns, & Winters, 1983), the Present State Exam (Wing, Cooper, &

Sartorius, 1974), and the Schedule for Affective Disorders and Schizophrenia (Spitzer & Endicott, 1978). The Present State Exam contains over 500 questions that serve as a guide for the interviewer's assessment of the client's current status based on self-report. Also, the Present State Exam allows the interviewer to follow up with additional questions when more information is required to specify the nature and severity of the symptom. For example, an affirmative response to the question "Have you had visions or seen things other people couldn't see?" regarding visual hallucinations can be followed up with such questions as "With your eyes or in your mind?"; "What did you see?"; "Did the vision seem to arise out of a pattern on the wallpaper or a shadow?"; and "How do you explain it?" Each symptom is rated on a 3-point scale, with 0 as not present and 2 as present in severe form. In addition to the interview, direct observation of the individual's behavior, affect, and speech is also included. The interviewer rates behaviors such as agitation, mannerisms, and posturing; irritability; blunted affect; incoherence; and flight of ideas. The interviewer is provided with detailed definitions of all behaviors and symptoms.

The Schedule for Affective Disorders and Schizophrenia (Spitzer & Endicott, 1978) is a measure similarly extensive in its coverage; however, in addition to questions about the individual's current status, historical information is also gathered. This information is important in distinguishing schizophrenia from other disorders, such as autism. Symptoms are rated on either a 6-point scale of severity or the 3-point scale described for the Present State Exam. This measure is detailed and covers all of the characteristics of schizophrenia. For example, the measure not only determines the presence or absence of hallucinations but also gives information about the form and content of the hallucinations. As in the Present State Exam, operational definitions for most behaviors are given. Thus, in addition to these measures constituting excellent diagnostic tools, they also function to determine behavioral excesses and deficits displayed by the individual.

Behavior Observation Schemes and Rating Scales: Schizophrenia

Because of their widespread usefulness in identifying target behaviors and monitoring treatment programs, several observational methods have been used extensively in the assessment of schizophrenia. One such measure is the Time-Sample Behavioral Checklist (TSBC), an observational system that allows for situation-specific problem identification as well as treatment-effectiveness monitoring (Engel & Paul, 1979; Power, 1979). Sixty-nine behavioral codes are scored in the following seven categories: (1) location (e.g., own bedroom, activity area, and dining area), (2) position (e.g., sitting, lying down, and walking), (3) awake–asleep (i.e., eyes open or eyes closed), (4) facial expression (e.g., smiling, laughing, and frowning), (5) social orientation (e.g., alone, with residents, and with staff), (6) concurrent activities (e.g., talking to others, smoking, watching TV, and group activity), and (7) crazy behaviors (sic) (e.g., talking to self, verbalized delusions, repetitive and stereotypic movements, and injuring self). All behaviors are descriptively defined. For example, in the category of facial expression, the description includes whether the expression occurred in the presence or absence of a determinable external stimulus. In applying the system, the observer locates the client, observes for 2 s, and then codes the client's behavior.

The Clinical Frequencies Recording System (CFRS) is a measure similar to the TSBC (Redfield, 1979). The recording forms for this measure are divided into four areas. One form measures the utilization of facilities and services, such as visits to the barber or hairdresser. The second form is used to indicate that the client is in an inappropriate location (i.e., the client is not in the location in which a scheduled activity is occurring). "Intolerable" behaviors, including destructive and self-injurious behavior, are recorded on a third form. The record includes a complete description of the time, nature, circumstances, and consequences of the behavior. A final form is used to measure responsiveness to the treatment program, which may include a complete record of tokens earned, if applicable. The presence or absence of specified target behaviors is recorded. Target behaviors are subdivided into discrete behavioral components to measure achievement level. Both the TSBC and the CFRS are useful in that they provide a detailed description of behavioral excesses and deficits for problem identification, individualized behavioral programming, and treatment progress monitoring with greater reliability, accuracy, and sensitivity than other assessment methods (Engel & Paul, 1979).

A third measure, the Observational Record of Inpatient Behavior (ORIB), is used extensively as well but tends to be used in research involving effects of neuroleptic drugs on behavior. The ORIB is a low-inference, time-sampling measure in which the observer records the occurrence or nonoccurrence of eight behavior categories (Rosen, Sussman, Mueser, Lyons, & Davis, 1981; Rosen, Tureff, Lyons, & Davis, 1981): body activity (walking, running, jumping, and shifting), proximity, social interaction (verbal or physical interactions with another), visual activity (eye movement as opposed to a fixated stare), facial expression (laughing or smiling), participation (engaging in an ongoing activity), and idiosyncratic behavior (bizarre behavior, repetitive movements, or self-verbalizations). This measure is useful in determining the effect of psychopharmological interventions on behavior, particularly changes in activity and symptoms.

The Nurses Observation Scale for Inpatient Evaluation–30 (NOSIE-30) is a rating scale covering multiple areas of functioning that has been reported to reflect the effect of behavioral interventions (Wallace, 1981). Clients' behavior is rated by ward staff on the NOSIE-30, and scores are obtained for the following areas: social competence, social interest, personal neatness, irritability, manifest psychosis, retardation, and a composite score of total patient assets (Honigfeld, Gillis, & Klett, 1966).

A frequently used scale to assess social skills in lower-functioning schizophrenic clients is the Minimal Social Behavior Scale (MSBS) (Farina, Arenberg, & Guskin, 1957). This measure is a structured interview in which the client is presented with standard questions and contrived social situations. One situation, for example, involves the interviewer offering the client a cigarette and then searching his pockets for matches to light his own cigarette. The matches are intentionally placed close to the client. In general, the MSBS reflects changes in clients' behavior following behavioral programming (Wallace, 1981).

An enormous number of scales have been developed to measure multiple areas and specific areas of functioning in schizophrenic individuals. A brief description of a few of the most frequently used measures has been presented. Wallace (1981) provides a thorough list of these measures, and the reader is referred to that work for more extensive coverage of these assessments.

In addition to the more diagnostic and specific screening devices and scales described above, standardized measures are frequently used to measure level of functioning. For example, the Vineland Adaptive Behavior Scales (Sparrow, Balla, & Cicchetti, 1984) and the AAMD

Adaptive Behavior Scale (Nihara, Foster, Shellhaas, & Leland, 1975) are used to assess functioning, in addition to traditional IQ tests such as the Stanford-Binet Intelligence Test (Thorndike, Hagen, & Sattler, 1986) and the Wechsler Adult Intelligence Scale—Revised (Wechsler, 1981). A thorough evaluation of the individual would include such measures.

Definition of the Problem
Selection of Target Behaviors

Several issues are important in the discussion of selection of target behaviors. First, it is important for therapists, parents, caretakers, and clients to establish priorities for target behaviors. If the clients' behaviors present a danger to themselves or others, decisions about the priority of target behaviors is clear-cut. However, often the discrimination between target behaviors is much less obvious. Thus, the following guidelines have been suggested (Powers & Handleman, 1984). First, target behaviors that allow the client access to a greater number of social or individual reinforcers might be selected. Along these lines, behaviors that allow the individual access to the naturally occurring reinforcers are important to target for treatment.

Often, target behaviors are selected that are either (1) inappropriate given the client's chronological age or (2) not functional in the client's environment. Thus, it is important that the target behaviors be appropriate for the individual's chronological age even when the level of functioning may be severely impaired (Johnson & Koegel, 1982). It is more appropriate for an adult client to learn to label pictures in magazines or newspapers than in children's books. Also, the behavior should be functional, one that the client can use frequently in his or her everyday environment (Brown et al., 1979). Care should be used in selecting skills necessary to engage in activities in which the client may ultimately be involved. Thus, for autistic and schizophrenic adults, domestic, vocational, social, and leisure/recreational skills that are needed in order to function relatively independently and lead a productive life are important to target for intervention. Such skills might include learning how to shop for groceries, wash dishes, or use a stereo system. In addition, by selecting target behaviors that bring the individual into contact with the natural reinforcers in the community, are age-appropriate, and allow the individual to function in his or her environment, both generalization and social validation may be enhanced (these issues are discussed below).

Another issue in the selection of target behaviors is that an attempt should be made to increase desirable behaviors rather than only decrease unwanted behaviors. This is particularly important given the problems associated with the use of punishment. These problems include increased emotional responding, avoidance of the punishing agent, aggression directed toward the punishing agent or other nearby individuals, and modeling of aggressive behavior (Azrin & Holz, 1966). When it is necessary to use punishment to decrease a behavioral excess (as in the case of severe self-injurious behavior), it is equally important to increase an appropriate alternative behavior. Thus, rather than teaching the client merely what not to do, the client is also taught what to do instead. For example, if a client engages in self-injurious behavior when frustrated by a difficult task, in addition to the employment of punishment procedures, he or she should be taught the response "I need help" (cf., Carr & Durand, 1985).

Recently, attention has turned to the social validation of treatment objectives. Social validation refers to a methodology to examine the social acceptability of all aspects of treatment, including the selection of target behaviors, the intervention program implemented, and the evaluation of treatment outcome (Kazdin & Matson, 1981; Van Houten, 1979). Two methods have been used to examine the social validation of treatment goals and outcomes. One method, *social comparison*, involves observation of competent individuals' behavior to determine appropriate target behaviors and criterion levels for these behaviors. Social comparison is particularly useful in identifying treatment goals that involve complex or subtle skills, as in the case of conversational skills. *Subjective evaluation* is a second method of socially validating these aspects of treatment. This method uses the opinions of pertinent people in the individual's environment (e.g., parents, caretakers, and therapists) to evaluate treatment goals and outcomes.

Research in social validation has addressed the issue of treatment outcome; however, little research has been directed at socially validating treatment objectives. In an attempt to validate behavioral objectives in the treatment of autistic children, Runco and Schreibman (1987) utilized subjective evaluation to determine the importance of behaviors for the focus of treatment. Parents, teachers, and behavior therapists were asked to make judgments, using a 5-point Likert-type scale, about the importance of focus of treatment for 24 behaviors in five general areas: play behaviors (e.g., inappropriate play and repetitious, stereotyped movements), general appearance (e.g., lack of eye contact and short attention span), verbal behaviors (e.g., echolalia and unintelligible speech), interactive behaviors (e.g., controlling the situation), and noninteractive behaviors (e.g., not following instructions and demonstrating no social behaviors). Significant differences were found between all groups. Parents judged four of the five categories as more important than either of the other groups did (therapists judged interactive behaviors as more important), and teachers judged all five as less important than did the parents and behavior therapists. All groups, however, judged noninteractive behaviors as the most important focus for treatment. In summary, these groups had different views of the importance of behaviors as the focus of treatment. Thus, when making treatment decisions, it is important to get information from other relevant individuals involved in the client's life. When parents, teachers, and caretakers are involved in deciding the focus of treatment, they may also be more willing and motivated to implement or participate in treatment programs. This information may also indicate areas in which significant others need to be educated about the importance of remediating particular target behaviors.

Other studies have included the social validation of treatment goals as part of their research design. For example, Holmes, Hansen, and St. Lawrence (1984) used a social comparison technique to establish skill components for an intervention designed to teach conversational skills to psychiatric patients. Conversational skills of "normal" nonpsychiatric people in the community were used to establish four components of conversational speech in which the psychiatric patients were deficient: appropriate self-disclosing statements, conversational questions, speech acknowledgers and reinforcers, and high-interest content statements. Williams and Cuvo (1986) gathered information from landlords regarding apartment upkeep behaviors tenants were expected to perform in order to select target behaviors to train apartment upkeep skills to severely handicapped clients. In addition, examination of records kept for two federally subsidized apartment buildings for the disabled suggested that several fixtures were neglected due to tenants' skill deficits. As a result of this information, the authors selected four apartment upkeep and maintenance activities involving the air conditioner and heating unit, the electric range, the refrigerator, and electrical appliances such as the circuit box, lamps, and television.

Definition of Target Behaviors

The operational definition of target behaviors is important in order to establish baselines and later to evaluate treatment effectiveness. Operationally defining a behavior requires the precise specification of all aspects of the behavior (Johnson & Koegel, 1982; Wallace, 1981). This includes a description of the topography of the behavior, in addition to its frequency and duration. Objective measurement of the behavior requires that the description be of observable behavior rather than of hypothetical constructs such as "frustration." The definition should require as little interpretation as possible. Unclear definitions that rely on interpretation lead to error in measurement of the behavior. These errors in measurement may make it difficult to detect behavior change.

Several methods of measurement have been suggested to reliably collect data on behavior (Wallace, 1981). First, automatic assessment devices can be used to measure the behavior. For example, a voice-activated recorder could be used to measure the presence or absence of speech. Another method of measurement is to use "permanent products" as the dependent variable. Some behaviors such as soiling undergarments result in a permanent change in the physical environment. In these cases, objectively measuring the "permanent product" of the behavior is an objective and precise measurement of the occurrence of the behavior. Finally, by either narrowing or broadening the range of the description of the behavior, the discrimination (of whether or not the behavior occurred) can be made easier.

Social validation can be used to establish the validity of the definition of a target behavior (in addition to treatment goals and effectiveness). Lagomarcino, Reid, Ivancic, and Faw (1984) established the social validity of their definition of appropriate dancing by asking staff members to name retarded peers whom they would consider "good dance models" and "inappropriate dance models." These individuals were then observed to determine that the derived definition of appropriate dancing was sufficient to discriminate between those identified as "good dance models" and "inappropriate dance models." The paucity of research in the area of social validation of definitions of target behaviors suggests that additional research in this area is needed.

Identification of Controlling Variables

The final goal in defining the problem once a target behavior has been selected and operationally defined is to determine the variables controlling the behavior. By understanding or explaining the occurrence of behavior in terms of controlling variables, treatment interventions can be developed.

There are two major classes of controlling variables useful in behavioral assessment: current environmental variables (antecedents and consequences associated with the behavior) and organismic variables (individual differences produced by past learning and by physiology). In identifying the controlling variables in behavioral assessment, the acronym SORC (stimulus–organism–response–consequence) summarizes all of the necessary components (Goldfried & Sprafkin, 1976). The components have been described in numerous places, and the reader is referred to these sources for a more detailed description (e.g., Nelson & Barlow, 1981; Nelson & Hayes, 1979b; Powers & Handleman, 1984).

Current Environmental Variables: Stimulus (S).   The stimulus antecedent is a current environmental variable that precedes the behavior and exerts some control over responding. There are two types of stimulus antecedents, discriminative stimuli and elicitors. A discriminative stimulus is established as such because in the past a consequence to a response occurred in the presence of a specific stimulus; thus, the discriminative stimulus sets the stage for the response. The stimulus antecedent is an elicitor if, through classical conditioning, it results in an emotional response. Even with careful examination it may not be clear whether the stimulus antecedent is a discriminative stimulus or an elicitor, but its determination may lead to a more specific and effective intervention. In order to determine the antecedents of a behavior, a detailed description of all events prior to the behavior is necessary. This information may determine a pattern of antecedents that control behavior and thus can be used to guide intervention.

Current Environmental Variables: Consequences (C).

Responses are controlled by either reinforcing or aversive consequences. Behavioral principles define consequences functionally. Reinforcing consequences are those that increase or maintain behavior over time, whereas aversive consequences are those that decrease behavior over time. It is important to distinguish between those consequences that do and do not affect the strength of the behavior. In other words, the functional properties of the consequences must be demonstrated.

Organismic Variables (O).

Organismic variables—including biological states (i.e., hunger, fatigue, poor visual acuity, poor hearing, etc.); expectation of reward or punishment; and genetic, biochemical and neurological variables—are frequently neglected because they tend not to be amenable to change. However, they are often necessary for a complete understanding of behavior. Knowledge of these variables is frequently useful for treatment. Biological states such as hunger, fatigue, and poor hearing can be altered. Physiological variables may also be altered by the use of drugs, relaxation, and biofeedback. For example, many schizophrenic individuals are responsive to neuroleptic drugs, and these can be used in addition to behavior therapy. Thus, if organic variables exert some control over behavior, intervention should include two goals: (1) habilitation (altering behavior through the use of drugs, hearing aids, etc.) and (2) compensation for variables not amenable to alteration.

Although identification of controlling variables is important in developing a treatment program, at times attempts to identify these variables fail. Often controlling stimuli are neither simple nor intuitively obvious (Rincover & Koegel, 1975). Difficulty in identifying controlling variables may render the behavior difficult to alter. Touchette, MacDonald, and Langer (1985) demonstrated that a scatter plot can be helpful in identifying patterns of responding when a target behavior is frequent and observations do not suggest obvious controlling stimuli. By indicating that a behavior occurred at a high rate or low rate, or did not occur for an appropriate period of time (half hours, hours, etc.) all day long, a pattern of responding should emerge. For example, the scatter plot may show the behavior to be correlated with time of day, the presence of a particular person, participation in a certain activity, or numerous other variables. By altering these variables, target behaviors can be reduced or eliminated. (For several case illustrations of this technique, the reader is referred to Touchette et al., 1985.)

Determining controlling variables may also be time-consuming; thus, methods of assessing these variables that are most cost-effective need to be developed. To our knowledge only one such measure has been developed. Much research has shown that self-injurious behavior (SIB) can be maintained by several variables: positive reinforcement, negative reinforcement, and possibly self-stimulation (Carr, 1977; Demchak & Halle, 1985). Several studies (Carr & Durand, 1985; Iwata, Dorsey, Slifer, Bauman, & Richman, 1982) have used analogue situations to assess the maintaining variables of SIB; however, this approach requires highly trained staff and may take several weeks to complete. For this reason, Durand and Crimmons (1988) developed the Motivational Assessment Scale (MAS), a rating scale designed to determine the motivational variables controlling SIB. The scale consists of 16 items concerning the likelihood that the behavior will occur in a variety of situations (e.g., as a function of task difficulty or social isolation). The MAS has high interrater and test–retest reliability, and it predicted subjects' SIB in analogue situations. This measure is an alternative when formal functional analysis is not feasible to identify controlling variables.

Designing a Treatment Intervention

Once the controlling variables of the target behavior are determined, this information can be used to design an effective treatment program. By manipulating these variables (i.e., changing the antecedents or consequences of the behavior) behaviors can be reduced or eliminated. Many behavior problems have been successfully dealt with in the past, and a thorough search of the literature will reveal established treatment programs. The reader is referred to other chapters in this book that deal specifically with behavioral interventions used with autistic and schizophrenic individuals.

Outcome Assessments and Treatment Evaluation

The last phase of behavioral assessment is usually composed of various forms of outcome assessments and treatment evaluations. Such outcome assessments may consist of evaluations of treatment effectiveness (in context of assessed cost-effectiveness and cost-benefit of the treatment), replicability, and generalization of the treatment effects across time, settings, responses, and people. In addition, more recently, social validation of treatment outcome has been considered an essential part of behavioral assessment. Any of these assessments may be conducted in context of comparing two or several treatment approaches, thus providing some relative measurement standards. These assessments are by no means specific to treatment of autistic and schizophrenic clients but rather applicable to any form of behavioral assessment. In the following subsections the most important forms of outcome assessments are considered in turn.

Treatment Effectiveness

Depending on the particular information desired (or required), treatment effectiveness can be measured along various dimensions. Three major techniques of measuring treatment effectiveness, however, seem to be applicable in virtually any form of outcome assessment: graphic data, social validation, and cost analyses. (For a thorough critique and review of these techniques, see Yeaton, 1982). Each of these three techniques is discussed briefly.

Graphic Data.   Visual displays and graphs to describe treatment effects are probably the most common and oldest form of data collection in behavioral assessment. Advantages of graphic data are obvious in that a large amount of numerical data can be summarized in such a way that behavior trends, variability, frequency, and absolute level of behavior can be instantly identified. Disadvantages are that behavioral changes evident in the graph often cannot be evaluated with respect to statistical or even clinical significance, thus leaving questions unanswered. For example, does an increasing graph actually reflect a behavior change when variability within the data is taken into account (i.e., statistical significance); and if it does, is the behavior change a good indicator of how much this change is actually relevant for the client in a nonresearch context (i.e., clinical significance)? The first question can usually be answered by applying appropriate statistical tests to the data, but statistical significance in itself does not constitute clinical significance. For example, a reduction of delusional speech in a schizophrenic client by 11.3% within the time intervals when speech was assessed, or the decrease of echo-lalic responding in an autistic client from 214 to 189 occurrences per day, may well be detected as significant by a statistical test; that is, the changes can be attributed to the specific treatment. It is questionable, however, whether such changes would be detected even by people who usually interact closely with the client, or whether a treatment that brought about such changes would be considered successful by the community in which the client is living. But even numerically large treatment effects evident in the graph, as, for example, when successfully teaching a new skill, might not prove real treatment effectiveness if the client will never have the opportunity to use the newly learned skill. A means of measurement to evaluate treatment effectiveness while considering those dimensions is social validation of treatment outcome.

Social Validation of Treatment Outcome.

Social validation has already been discussed in an earlier section in a different context. Social validation was described as essential to selecting and defining relevant treatment goals. Social validation of treatment outcome, however, focuses on assessing the clinical relevance of changes produced by a certain treatment as judged by significant people and the community in which the client lives, or sometimes by the client himself. The importance of socially validating the outcome as well as the target behaviors was recognized by Woods (1984). As this author put it, "it is consistent with the empirical approach of the treatment process to validate each component stage, including the significance of the result" (p. 67). Social validation of treatment outcome is a technique to assess treatment effectiveness that has evolved in applied behavioral research only recently (Yeaton, 1982).

One of the most common procedures for social validation of treatment effectiveness is to ask persons whose judgment is considered somehow relevant to the client to rate the change in the client's target behavior on a numerical scale reflecting the various degrees of possible change (i.e., from "not at all" to "extremely"). For example, in a study by Holmes, Hansen, and St. Lawrence (1984), chronic psychiatric clients received training in conversational skills and appropriate speech content. Improvement, or treatment effectiveness, was then behaviorally rated at 1-, 3-, and 7-month follow-up by other former clients and by unfamiliar nonpsychiatric persons. Likewise, Jackson and Martin (1983) used social validation techniques to assess treatment effectiveness with a 29-year-old female chronic schizophrenic patient who had received social skills training.

Similar rating scales were used by Runco and Schreibman (1983) to socially validate treatment effectiveness with autistic children. Thirty-four parents of autistic children and 18 parents of normal children were asked to rate the behavior of four autistic children before and after behavior therapy as seen on segments of video recordings. The first type of rating scale was a 5-item Social Distance Scale evaluating willingness to visit, spend time with, or adopt a child like the one seen on the videotape. The second type of rating scale consisted of an empirically constructed set of questions assessing behaviors typically seen in autistic children, such as tantruming, social withdrawal, and self-stimulation. The treatment effectiveness was demonstrated with both measures. Parents were more willing to interact with the children after than before the treatment, and they also tended to judge the children as significantly improved on the specific behaviors.

A critique of the use of social validational techniques was provided by Yeaton (1982). First, it seems that the choice of the anchor points for the questionnaire scales plays a crucial role in the outcome of social validation, thus rendering it vulnerable to the influence of less specified factors. Also, the independence of the rater is often not guaranteed if, incidentally, he or she was sensitized to attend to a particular behavioral dimension more than to another. Third, some researchers might rely solely on social validation data. Results from social validation techniques are most meaningful if they are also ultimately compared to results obtained from alternative treatments. (The importance of comparing different treatments is discussed below.) Fourth, it might be overlooked that despite high social validity as reflected by high ratings, construct validity might be lacking. In summary, it seems advisable to conduct various measures to obtain cross-validity rather than to rely on one measure only, as is, of course, true in all research areas.

Cost Analysis.   After it has been established by social validation that the treatment effects are really relevant to the client and considered significant by the consumer of the treatment services or the community, yet another aspect is essential to establish treatment effectiveness. Any truly effective treatment still has to be considered in context of treatment costs. Although treatment cost analyses have been commonly conducted in various areas, such as emergency medical services, traffic safety, public health, and political decision making, treatment cost analyses in applied behavioral research are a relatively new approach to treatment evaluation (Yeaton, 1982). Treatment cost analysis can be broken down into two main categories: cost-effectiveness analysis and cost-benefit analysis. (For a review and discussion of cost-effectiveness and cost-benefit analyses, see Yates, 1985.) Each of these analyses provides information about how the costs of a treatment correlate with certain outcome measures. *Cost-effectiveness analyses* generally compare treatment costs (such as staff salaries, equipment and material costs, rent for facilities, etc.) in terms of monetary value to the effect size produced by the treatment. This provides a good index for comparison between two or several treatment alternatives if the emphasis is mainly on maximizing the effect size of the treatment while requiring the least amount of money. *Cost-benefit analyses*, similar to cost-effectiveness analyses, also assess treatment costs in terms of monetary value; in contrast, however, they compare those costs to financial gain or monetary output. Thus, an input-output correlation is usually assessed, both variables measured in the same monetary unit (Yates, 1985). A good example is preventive health care, where certain procedures are proposed with an initial financial investment and then compared in terms of how much money can be saved for the community by illness prevention or actually earned by reinstitution of the client's productivity. Cost-benefit analyses are essential when third-party funders or government agencies are interested in a program's monetary products. Positive findings for a cost-benefit analysis then may be the major determinant of whether a certain projects receives funding.

Four major types of benefit assessment (Yates, 1985) will be mentioned briefly. First, actual income generated for a client or community is referred to as "actual income benefit." This benefit could be in the form of a salary earned by a rehabilitated client, for example. Second, the "actual cost-savings benefit" refers to money saved by effective preventive health care. Third, the "inferred cost-saving benefit" is, for example, an estimation of money saved by some preventive procedure. Finally, the "inferred income benefits" could be an estimation of money earned, based on some nonmonetary measures such as employee productivity (Yates, 1985).

Below is a brief discussion of several studies with schizophrenic populations in which some form of cost analysis was conducted. (For a more general review of the studies utilizing cost analyses, see Yates and Newman, 1980a, 1980b.) In one study, Sharfstein and Clark (1978) emphasized the necessity of cost-effectiveness and cost-benefit analyses. According to the authors, of $36.78 billion spent in direct and indirect care for mental illness in 1974 in the United States, $32 billion was spent on long-term mental illness; therefore, careful funding policies are necessary to provide sufficient and effective care to as many mentally ill as possible. In an earlier study, Littman (1976) estimated from a cost-benefit analysis that not providing treatment to schizophrenic clients costs twice as much as treating schizophrenics, taking the clients' loss of productivity into account. Newton (1983) compared the cost-effectiveness of two treatment programs that included 28 adult schizophrenic clients. It was concluded that outpatient treatment was more effective than inpatient care because the costs were lower and the treatment could be provided for a longer time.

Our literature search did not yield any studies with autistic populations in which cost-effectiveness or cost-benefit analyses were explicitly conducted. In some studies, however, cost-effectiveness of treatment was implicitly stated, especially in the context of computerized treatment (e.g., Gardner & Breuer, 1985; Romanczyk, 1984).

Treatment Comparisons.   Another way of assessing treatment effectiveness is by comparing the outcome of two or several treatment alternatives. Kazdin (1986) discusses four advantages of comparative studies: (1) important clinical questions (i.e., treatment effectiveness) are addressed, (2) similarities and differences in the execution of treatments are revealed, (3) control procedures are provided by alternative treatment groups rather than by a no-treatment group (which alleviates some of the ethical issues of employing presumably ineffective control groups), and (4) relevant differences between alternative treatments become more evident.

Kazdin (1986) also points out five caveats of comparative studies:

1. Comparative studies may disguise other variables (such as characteristics of the therapist and the client, nature and severity of the clinical problem, etc.) that might also be responsible for differences in treatment effect because the emphasis is placed on differences of treatment.
2. The parameters of the techniques to be compared may not be well known yet; thus, conclusions drawn from comparative studies might be misleading.
3. Comparative outcome studies are often not feasible because too many alternative treatments may be available.
4. Comparative outcome studies have often failed to show differential treatment effects.
5. Some inherent differences between treatments sometimes make comparisons virtually impossible.

Kazdin also discussed other critical issues in comparative outcome research in detail, such as treatment issues (i.e., representativeness of treatment, treatment-specific ingredients, and execution of treatment), therapist factors, assessment issues (i.e., selection of outcome measures), and finally, evaluation issues (i.e., timing of follow-up assessment and experimental power to detect group differences). Keeping those caveats in mind, a sample of some more recent comparative studies with autistic and schizophrenic clients follows.

Hoult, Rosen, and Reynolds (1984), for example, compared community versus hospital treatment of psychotic clients (most of them schizophrenic). It was concluded that the community treatment did not constitute an additional burden on the community and was seen by the clients and their relatives as significantly more satisfactory and helpful. Also, the outcome was clinically superior and more cost-efficient than standard hospital treatment. Fonagy and Slade (1982) compared the effect of negative reinforcement versus punishment on auditory hallucinations in three schizophrenic clients. White noise was presented through headphones as the aversive stimulus. For two of the clients, the negative reinforcement condition was more effective in suppressing the hallucinations than was the punishment condition. Harris and Wolchik (1979) compared three strategies to decrease self-stimulatory behavior in four autistic-like boys. The three strategies used were time-out, differential reinforcement of other behavior (DRO), and overcorrection. All four boys showed a decrease in the target behavior with overcorrection; for the remaining two strategies the decrease was less pronounced. Similarly, comparing two different strategies with an alternating treatment design, Luiselli, Susskin, and McPhee (1981) assessed the effectiveness of continuous versus intermittent application of an overcorrection procedure in reducing self-injurious behavior (SIB) in an autistic child. The continuous schedule of applying overcorrection showed greater effects in decreasing SIB. Finally, Handleman and Harris (1983a) compared one-to-one instructions versus instructions given in pairs for autistic children. The four children, matched for functional level and training experience, were taught nonverbal imitation tasks. The results from this study were variable. For two children, couplet training seemed disruptive; for one child, couplet training was superior to one-to-one instruction; and for the fourth child, little difference was found between the two training techniques. In conclusion, the results indicate the effectiveness of one-to-one instruction. In addition, it was suggested that at least in some situations couplet training can be employed, depending on the "readiness of a given child," and it also might be "instrumental in weaning autistic children from highly structured teaching situations in order to approximate more normal instructional environments" (Handleman & Harris, 1983a, p. 25).

Meta-analyses

In the previous section, comparative studies were briefly discussed; these studies were designed to compare alternative treatments in terms of treatment effectiveness. Such endeavor usually necessitates a fairly complex design (such as alternating treatments design) that is not always feasible in a clinical setting, or if treatments are to be compared in a between-subject group design, time and cost efficiency often have to be sacrificed. For example, one researcher might be interested in comparing treatment A with treatment B, and another researcher might be interested in comparing treatment B with treatment C. Overall, treatment B had to be conducted twice; and in this respect, combined research effort was not maximally efficient (at least when the potentially beneficial aspects of replication are not to be considered).

In the last decade or so, meta-analysis has evolved, a new approach in outcome research that allows for analysis of already existing data and for analysis across studies conducted by different researchers. Thus, meta-analysis has great potential for making applied behavioral research more efficient. Because this form of analysis often requires the handling and accessibility of a large bulk of data, the development of meta-analysis seems to have emerged to some extent parallel with the wide availability and greater affordability of computers.

The specific methodology for conducting meta-analyses will not be discussed here because it would be beyond the scope of this chapter. Suffice it to point out that meta-analysis in general can be conceptualized as a statistical tool applied to the data of an experiment, where the overall analysis is the experiment and where each of the studies to be included in the analysis would correspond to one data point (or data from one subject) in a conventional experiment. The independent variable could be, for example, the differences in treatment approaches or design, and the dependent variable could be the differences in treatment effectiveness measured in the relevant units.

The *Journal of Consulting and Clinical Psychology* dedicated a special section in the February 1983 issue reflecting the increased importance assigned to this type of assessment. In addition, in the *Annual Review of Behavior Therapy* in 1984 and 1985, meta-analysis was critically discussed (Kendall, 1984; Kendall, 1985). Finally, the increasing importance of meta-analysis is also reflected by the growing number of entries retrieved from library reference systems dealing with this issue.

The usefulness of meta-analysis was pointed out by Strube and Hartmann (1983). The authors stated that meta-analysis allows for "(a) combining probabilities across studies, (b) estimating average effect size, (c) determining the stability of results, and (d) identifying factors that moderate the outcome of separate studies" (p. 14). Thus, meta-analysis is a valuable assessment tool to summarize cumulative research when used with caution (Burke, 1984). Fiske (1983), taking a strongly favorable stance for meta-analysis, also described the main strength of meta-analysis in providing a tool to integrate research reports generated by science.

Criticism of meta-analysis has been abundant as well. One of the criticisms can be summarized in that meta-analysis is based on a correlational model (e.g., Burke, 1984; Mintz, 1983), therefore causal implications about factors producing certain effects in treatments have to be dealt with cautiously. "Pseudo-objectivity" (Eysenck, 1984) and bias in the selection of studies are other drawbacks pointed out by researchers (e.g., Wilson & Rachman, 1983). For example, a criterion has to be established carefully for the appropriateness of inclusion or exclusion of certain studies for analysis. Finally, also in this area of research, the guideline "garbage in, garbage out" has to be considered. By conducting sophisticated statistical analyses, the false impression might be created that the outcome is highly reliable. However, individual poor-quality studies may in fact have decreased the quality of the outcome considerably (e.g., Wilson & Rachman, 1983).

In the work with schizophrenic clients some meta-analyses have been conducted. (The authors of this chapter have not found, however, any meta-analysis studies conducted with an autistic population). Parloff, London, and Wolfe (1986), for example, conducted a meta-analysis on research published between 1980 and 1984 comparing efficacy of various psychosocial therapies. Aylward, Walker, and Bettes (1984) investigated IQ levels via meta-analysis and found that both early-onset and adult-onset schizophrenia are correlated with deficits in intellectual functioning throughout the client's life; moreover, the assessed IQ seems to relate to the prognosis of the disease. And finally, Andrews (1984) used, among other sources of information, a meta-analysis of the treatment outcome literature to develop guidelines for the management of schizophrenia.

Assessment of Generalization

One major topic yet to be discussed in order to complete an overview of behavioral assessment is the generalization of treatment effects. Generalization itself, of course, is usually a goal in behavioral therapy because the emergence of generalized behavior often is clinically desirable. A treatment would hardly be considered successful if the treatment effects were so specific that the client demonstrates the improvement only in certain situations, with one or few people or for only a limited time after completion of treatment. In addition, it would probably be desirable for any treatment if training a specific behavior had some favorable side effects on behaviors not specifically trained. Consequently, there is much emphasis in the literature on how generalization can be produced (e.g., Carr, 1980; Koegel & Rincover, 1977; Stokes & Baer, 1977).

This section, however, focuses on the *assessment* of generalization, that is, how it can be determined whether (and to what extent) generalization has occurred. This is largely independent of whether or not generalization has been explicitly scheduled in a treatment program. Since the objective is to assess the occurrence of certain (generalized) behaviors, many of the techniques are identical to the ones employed to measure any behavior, as discussed in the previous sections.

It is helpful for clarity to consider briefly three aspects of generalization separately. First, *stimulus generalization* refers to treatment gains measured in a client's behavior that can be observed in various settings or situations and with a variety of people. If stimulus generalization is strong, the probability of the occurrence of a desirable behavior (or the nonoccurrence of an undesirable behavior) is equal across all appropriate stimulus settings (i.e., location, time of day, people present, etc.). For example, the treatment of an autistic child's psychotic speech, where stimulus generalization was successfully scheduled, will result in suppression of echolalia to a similar extent when the therapist, a parent, or a stranger is present. Likewise, the child's echolalia will remain suppressed when the child engages in some novel activity (such as playing with a new toy, in a novel play environment). The term *temporal generalization* is used to refer to treatment gains that maintain across time. For example, a successful treatment of a schizophrenic person's deficient social behavior, where temporal generalization was effectively scheduled, will produce a long-lasting increase of appropriate and a decrease of inappropriate social behaviors even after direct treatment has been discontinued. In this context some follow-up studies and studies that assessed maintenance of treatment goals will be mentioned. *Response generalization* produces behavior that has not been trained specifically but still occurs under certain circumstances. A child, for example, might be taught a series of nonverbal imitation tasks (e.g., raise arm, touch nose, push a button). After extended training, the child then might imitate certain behaviors of the therapist (such as buttoning a shirt) even without specific training. A response generalized from one or more specific tasks to one or more untrained tasks. In particular, single-subject strategies have been successfully applied to assess stimulus and response generalization, using multiple-baseline designs across settings and behaviors, respectively. (For a discussion of some of the critical issues in this area, see Kendall, 1981.)

What follows is a selection of studies intended to present some examples from the more recent literature on how generalization has been assessed and also to provide some framework for a discussion of some of the critical issues in the assessment of generalization. These issues are of special interest in particular with autistic individuals, who usually show very limited and impaired generalization of treatment gains (Dunlap, Koegel, & Burke, 1981).

One form of behavioral assessment of generalization (which is also still used in its basic form in our laboratory) was initially described by Lovaas et al. (1973). The child is observed in a non-treatment setting with various adults (parent, stranger, and therapist) as was described in more detail in an earlier section ("Screening and Evaluating General Disposition"). In addition to providing an initial source of information to evaluate the client's behavioral repertoire in the pretreatment phase, ongoing evaluations of this sort (e.g., once every 6 months) allow for assessment of various forms of generalization. Stimulus and response generalization could be assessed because the child was observed in a nontherapy environments, with unfamiliar people and toys that had not been used during therapy. In the Lovaas et al. study and typically in other studies using similar assessment tools (e.g., Koegel et al., 1984; Schreibman & Britten, 1984; Schreibman et al., 1984), follow-up measures were taken to assess temporal generalization.

Handleman and Harris's (1983b) study deserves mentioning because generalization across settings was explicitly scheduled and then assessed. Five autistic boys were taught answers to common questions. Teaching took place either in one classroom or in two classrooms. Generalization (quantified in terms of number of correct responses to questions) was shown to be greater when teaching took place in the two-classroom condition.

Eason, White, and Newsom (1982) conducted a study that is noteworthy because collateral treatment effects were systematically assessed and evaluated with follow-up assessments. Six autistic or autistic-like children were reinforced for appropriate play. While levels of appropriate play increased, self-stimulatory behavior decreased without being explicitly punished or extinguished. All posttests and follow-up conditions revealed that while levels of appropriate play stayed high, levels of self-stimulatory behavior remained low or negligible. This study provides a good example of the assessment of response and temporal generalization.

Often outcome studies focus on general prognosis rather than on temporal generalization of specific treatment effects. In particular, it has been thought that autistic individuals are more likely to develop schizophrenic symptoms in childhood, compared with a normal population. A long-term, systematic follow-up study by Rumsey, Rapoport, and Sceery (1985) did not support this assumption. Fourteen male autistic individuals (aged from 18 to 39 years) with well-documented histories of infantile autism were examined with various measures, such as structured interviews, parent interviews, and behavioral observations. None of the 14 clients showed schizophrenic symptoms. The symptoms observed were only those that qualified the clients for a diagnosis of autism or autism, residual state, according to the *Diagnostic and Statistical Manual of Mental Disorders* (DSM-III) (APA, 1980).

Al-Issa, Bakal, and Larkin (1975) attempted to differentiate between 60 schizophrenic and 60 normal subjects in terms of generalization gradients and peak shifts obtained from tests involving various lengths of lines. Although this study does not specifically address the issue of generalization of treatment effects, it provides some information on the basic characteristics of schizophrenic people in terms of stimulus generalization after training on a laboratory (i.e., "non-clinical") discrimination task. The results supported the notion that schizophrenic people generalized *more* than did the normal subjects. This effect, however, was limited to the positive stimulus and not evident in the responding to the negative stimulus.

Generalization of treatment outcomes with schizophrenic clients has also been investigated. In the aforementioned study by Fonagy and Slade (1982), for example, generalization of the treatment of suppressing auditory hallucinations was reported. Johnson, Rosen, and Davis (1986) assessed stimulus generalization of a treatment to induce muscle tension in schizophrenic clients. Test, Knoedler, and Allness (1985) assessed the long-term effect of treatment of almost 100 schizophrenic persons in a community support program (i.e., "Training in Community Living model"). The clients had been participating in the program for at least 2 years (some up to 6 years). It was concluded that the training produced a remarkable decrease in hospitalization of the clients. In another study, Schreibman and Carr (1978) trained one schizophrenic child (and one mentally retarded child) to answer "I don't know" to questions they previously had responded to with echolalia. By training a sufficient number of examplars, the response generalized to untrained questions and also when asked by different experimenters (stimulus generalization).

In a study by Fichter, Wallace, Liberman, and Davis (1976) a schizophrenic client's social interaction was improved by training three behaviors: voice volume, duration of speech, and holding hands and arms appropriately. A moderate degree of response generalization (increase of speech duration when not specifically trained) and a relatively high degree of stimulus generalization (increase of all three behaviors across four different conversational topics and settings) was reported. In addition, strong generalization across time was revealed at the 14-week follow-up, even with new staff members, new conversation topics, and a new setting. (Interestingly, the authors not only assessed generalization but also attempted to identify the stimulus responsible to occasion the appropriate behaviors. It seemed that the staff member's presence was a crucial factor). The treatment effects were maintained at a 1-month follow-up assessment (temporal generalization). Similarly, Bellack, Hersen, and Turner (1976) demonstrated generalization effects of social skills training in one male and two female schizophrenic clients. Target behaviors included eye contact, speech duration, appropriate intonation, response latency, and appropriate smiles. The treatment (involving instructions, feedback, and modeling) was highly effective for all three clients in that substantial changes in most target behaviors could be observed. Moreover, these behavioral changes were also evident in familiar, but untrained, and novel situations. Thus, generalization of treatment gains was successful. Finally, Matson, Zeiss, Zeiss, and Bowman (1980) also trained social skills in 12 schizophrenic clients by comparing two treatments: social skills training (presenting scripts describing scenes of appropriate social behavior involving role model prompts) and contingent attention. The results indicated that social skills training was more effective in producing an increase of target behaviors. Moreover, generalization of the treatment effects was more pronounced with social skills training. For both treatments, generalization was better for probe scenes (stimulus generalization) and less effective with untrained behaviors (response generalization).

The assessment and evaluation of treatment effects usually constitutes the final phase of behavioral assessment. In the following section issues about technical innovations that are relevant to all phases of behavioral assessment are addressed.

COMPUTER TECHNOLOGY IN BEHAVIORAL ASSESSMENT

Although it is obvious that computer technology is by no means specific to the area of behavioral assessment, nor even to psychology, it seems appropriate to include this section to provide some preliminary information about a new development in behavioral assessment. This advance has taken place over the last decade and will most certainly continue to influence behavioral assessment in the future. This is particularly true with the rapid development of microcomputers because, for the first time, computers have become affordable on a broad scale for a majority of researchers and clinicians. This section is also intended to further encourage researchers and practitioners to familiarize themselves with computer technology whenever possible because many of the newer sophisticated techniques in behavioral assessment will necessarily depend at least in part on the utilization of precise and cost-efficient computer technology.

Ready access to relevant literature is often necessary in the assessment process when, for example, a large number of available assessment tools need to be evaluated for appropriateness. As a side note it may be mentioned that a great part of the literature reviewed in this chapter was in fact retrieved by a computerized reference system ("Silverplatter," PsychLIT). This was achieved in a fraction of the time it would have taken to perform the same task by hand. It is also interesting to note that the increasing trend of involvement of computer technology is actually reflected by the entries retrieved from this system. Thus, the keywords "computerized assessment" generated only one entry for the literature reviewed for the time period of 1974 to 1981 from 1,400 different journals, but eight entries were found for the period from 1981 to 1987. Likewise, the keywords "computer and autism" generated 6 versus 27 entries, respectively, and the keywords "computer and schizophrenia" generated 84 versus 150 entries for the same time periods. The increasing influence of computers in psychological assessment is also evidenced by the fact that the *Journal of Consulting and Clinical Psychology* (December 1985) dedicated a special issue to this topic. Finally, Levitan, Willis, and Vogelgesang (1985) noted that the literature seems to suggest that mental health practitioners are only starting to appreciate the benefits of microcomputers as aids in their private practices. Typically, however, they do not fully appreciate the extent to which they depend on information as a resource for conducting their administrative and clinical duties.

In the following subsections various topics relevant to computerized behavioral assessment are touched upon briefly. Because of space limitations this will not be a complete review of the literature but rather a sample of various studies to provide some information about the development in this field.

Cost-Effectiveness

Earlier in the chapter cost-effectiveness was discussed in the context of treatment evaluations and posttreatment assessments. Here the cost factor will be considered in the context of computer technology. The development and involvement of such technology can be an essential step in decreasing expenses by reducing time spent by highly trained staff in activities that generally can be automated, such as compiling demographic information about the clients, generating standardized progress reports, and calculating numerical information needed in the assessment process. Those activities can be performed with even greater precision, in less time, when automated rather than performed individually by the staff.

The achievement of great precision and cost-efficiency in behavioral assessment by using microcomputers was addressed by Romanczyk (1984) in his paper "Micro-Computers and Behavior Therapy: A Powerful Alliance." Romanczyk's program at the psychology department of The State University New York consisted of 35 to 40 children diagnosed as autistic, psychotic, or emotionally disturbed. With growing numbers of clients a decision had to be made about how to cope with the increasing work and information load. Instead of compromising the behaviorally oriented approach in their program by being less stringent in data collection, treatment design specification, and monitoring of treatment outcome, they introduced a computerized management system. With this system staff efficiency could be increased, and much of the tedious and time-consuming administrative work load could be decreased. Also, the number of clients in the program did not have to be reduced, and the integrated staffing approach could be maintained (Romanczyk, 1984). As a result, over the course of several years a network of microcomputers providing a variety of functions was established. For example, an on-line telephone system was available to all staff members for quick retrieval of the current medical status of any of the children. Also, the planning, monitoring, evaluating, and documenting of the individualized education programs (IEPs) was largely automated by the use of the computer system. Data collection could be achieved easily, and reliability scores, frequency tables, and other data were instantaneously available. Finally, some of the direct teaching instructions for the children, such as teaching visual discriminations and mathematics, were performed by microcomputers. In evaluating the computer system, Romanczyk concluded that the time required to prepare a progress report for each child, for example, could be reduced to one hundredth of the time needed for reports generated by hand, while maintaining a higher quality standard in terms of precision and included details.

Gardner and Breuer (1985) arrived at a similar conclusion. A microcomputer assessment system was developed to assist staff in their work with developmentally disabled persons. The final outcome evaluation revealed that the cost of a comprehensive individualized assessment report of several pages (generated by nonprofessionals within 1 hr with the assistance of the computer system) was only one fourth of that of a traditional assessment report. It was also judged higher in quality by the staff, administrators, and client advocates.

Data Analysis

One of the functions performed by computers that usually comes to mind first is, of course, data analysis. Again, data analysis is not specific to behavioral assessment but is certainly an essential part of it. Also in this area, it has become more common to employ computers to perform complex data analyses such as meta-analyses, as was discussed earlier. Various authors have recently described some computer programs specifically designed to perform meta-analyses (e.g., Gorman, Primavera, & Karras, 1983; McDaniel, 1986; Mullen, 1982, 1983). Computer programs are also offered to analyze standard observational data (e.g., Deni, Szijarto, Eisler, & Fantauzzo, 1983; Dodd, Bakeman, Loeber, & Wilson, 1981) and to analyze coded videotapes (Smith, Lloyd, & Crook, 1982).

Diagnosis and Assessment of Behaviors

Another important aspect of assessment sometimes is the establishing of a valid diagnosis. The bulk of the literature in this area consists of studies in which attempts were made to detect some neurological abnormalities in autistic and schizophrenic clients. One of the earliest computerized instruments developed is computer-assisted tomography (CAT), and more recently positron emission tomography (PET) and magnetic resonance imagery (MRI). Without the involvement of computer technology none of these techniques would be possible.

On a more behavioral level of assessment many advances have been made as well. For example, Lund (1985) derived computerized psychiatric diagnoses for approximately 300 clients (including autistic and schizophrenic adults) by using, among other techniques, a behavior and skills schedule. Krause and Sprung (1980) compared normal and schizophrenic subjects in learning "conjunctive and disjunctive concepts and deductive reasoning" to develop a computer-assisted tool for diagnosis.

In a relatively early study, Tucker and Rosenberg (1975) reported an analysis of the content of schizophrenic speech. The results indicated that schizophrenic subjects could be differentiated significantly by computer analysis from nonschizophrenic and normal subjects on the basis of the free speech and dream material transcripts. Similarly, von Bender (1984) investigated speech patterns of autistic, dysphasic, and normal children (matched for age and IQ) by using a computerized digital speech processing program. Parameters analyzed were fundamental frequency, intensity, and duration of the speech segments. The speech patterns of the autistic children could easily be differentiated from the other two groups in that the intra- and intersubject variability was significantly higher for all three parameters.

Two more studies deserve mention despite the fact that the subjects in these studies were neither autistic nor schizophrenic adolescents or adults. These two studies exemplify technology that probably can be applied to various clinical populations. Pressman, Roche, Davey, and Firestone (1986) used a computer-assisted approach to study auditory perception skills in children with learning disabilities (LD). This technology might be applicable in part, for example, to assess stimulus overselectivity with auditory complex stimuli in autistic individuals as described by Reynolds, Newsom, and Lovaas (1974). With this computerized assessment tool, 92.5% of the LD children were correctly identified. Garfinkel and Klee (1983) studied children with attention deficit disorder (ADD) and exposed them to a test battery using "computerized continuous performance, progressive maze, and sequential organization tests to measure the ADD-related characteristics of vigilance, RT, impulse control, and organized planning" (p. 163). The tests were found to be sensitive to the effects of medication and reliable when compared to other behavioral measures.

Somewhat related to the diagnostic assessment is the assessment of the behavioral repertoire, including the excessive and deficient behaviors of the autistic or schizophrenic client, in that diagnostic assessment may also focus on specific behaviors. However, as discussed earlier, whereas the diagnostic assessment is aimed toward categorizing the clients rather globally for appropriate treatment directions, the assessment of the behavioral repertoire is aimed toward specifying individual treatment needs that might be independent of diagnosis. For example, Witt and Martens (1984), using computer technology, attempted to assess adaptive behaviors in mildly mentally retarded individuals. Adaptive behaviors were defined by taking various factors into account, such as cultural influences, level of independent functioning, cognitive development, and social responsibility. It seems feasible to take a similar approach for autistic and schizophrenic clients.

With the advancement of computer technology, most of the standard tests and many other tests are available in computerized form.

(Some of the tests were actually specifically designed for a computer, e.g., Brown, 1984). Computerized tests available include the Behavior Observation Checklist, the Minnesota Multiphasic Personality Inventory, the Rorschach, the Wechsler Intelligence Scale for Children—Revised (Brown, 1984) and the Stanford-Binet (Weiss, 1985). There is even a computerized DSM-III aid to facilitate application of the diagnostic criteria to client data (Swartz & Pfohl, 1981). Often the use of computers is focused on reading and summarizing the data sheets filled out by the clinician. An example is the aforementioned TSBC (Engel & Paul, 1979; Power, 1979), which also allows for convenient and efficient evaluation of the ongoing treatment.

Special Applications

One special application and its relevance to behavioral assessment has already been partly discussed in the beginning of this section: the computerized data and reference retrieval systems. Those systems are relevant in that economical scanning of already existing literature and easy access to data generated by previous studies are essential to assessment. Various authors have reported the use of such retrieval systems for conducting their studies, especially when reviewing the bulk of literature, as is necessary, for example, when conducting meta-analyses (e.g., Getsie, Langer, & Glass, 1985; Whissell, 1984).

Lambert, Intrieri, and Hollandsworth (1986) make the point that the behavior therapy literature is now so extensive that it is difficult for beginning therapists who are not yet sufficiently familiar with the literature to make use of it in their work with their clients. Consequently, to alleviate this problem, they proposed and described a reference retrieval system that presumably could be put into effect with currently available microcomputer systems. Shavalia and Delprato (1980) have suggested a similar system. Although it seems questionable now whether the actual development of a reference retrieval system for one's own use seems advisable, because commercial systems are more comprehensive and will probably be widely available to the majority of clinicians and researchers in the very near future, these two studies illustrate how important easy access to relevant literature is considered in behavioral assessment.

Another special application for computers is that of simulations. Of course, this application has been very common for the last two decades or so in cognitive science and artificial intelligence, but it has now also gained increasing importance in recent years in the area of behavioral assessment. The computer simulation studies in behavioral assessment can be grouped into two main categories. In the first group of studies, some clinical behavioral patterns are simulated by a computer with the intention to advance understanding of the real-life behaviors of certain clinical populations. Second, there are the "Monte Carlo" experiments, using artificially produced data for a computerized assessment when certain assessment techniques or parameters are tested with respect to validity, reliability, time/cost-efficiency, error estimations, and so on.

The first type of computer simulation—that is, simulating pathological behavioral patterns—is probably less common. In an early study, Tsuang, Leaverton, and Huang (1974) developed a numerical model from 30 differentiating variables to distinguish poor-prognosis paranoid schizophrenic clients from poor-prognosis nonparanoid schizophrenic clients. The minimum-size subset of three variables that yielded the highest concordance rate between the computer and the clinician consisted of age of admission, disorganized thoughts, and affect changes. Consequently, the model was successfully tested against a separate group of schizophrenic individuals. In another study Colby (1981) attempted to build a computer model simulating "the paranoid mind." The model generated response patterns that were virtually indiscriminable for those of real paranoid schizophrenic clients. The author suggested that this model might provide clinicians with a better understanding of their clients, and it might also point to specific therapeutic interventions. (For a critique of this model, see Manschreck, 1983).

In another early study, Kahn and Arbib (1973) described a computer model of autism and related psychoses. The psychopathology was conceived as a problem wherein the affected individual did not correlated present perception with past experiences. Kahn and Arbib claim that the derived theory is testable and provides directions to guide therapy approaches and research attempts in the future. Finally, Anderson (1982) described the function of computer simulations in the laboratory as a training tool for psychology students. Training can be conducted without actually depending on the "real" conditions.

Examples for "Monte Carlo" simulations are more common. Sackett, Harris, and Orr (1986) attempted to investigate the statistical power and the resistance to Type I errors ("false alarm") in conducting a meta-analysis depending on effect size, sample size, and methodological artifacts. Powell (1984a) found evidence for the inadequacy of partial interval measures by systematically varying simulated behavioral frequency, duration, and pattern with two different observation intervals. In another study, Powell (1984b) compared computer-simulated data with actual data from a 3-year-old's visual fixation on an adult person, using a modified time-sampling procedure. He concluded that the accuracy of the estimates varied as a function of the number of observations. Finally, Rojahn and Kanoy (1985) developed a procedure using computer simulations to select appropriate parameters for a time-sampling observation system. The factors analyzed included frequency, duration, and pattern of response; observe-and-record lengths; and ratios of observe to record interval lengths. They concluded that in order to avoid erroneous data, the time-sampling system to be used has to be carefully chosen. It is possible, however, to minimize measurement error by empirically selecting appropriate time-sampling intervals.

Treatment Implementation

Research has been conducted in recent years to evaluate the effectiveness of computers as teaching tools for normal persons (e.g., Bangert-Drowns, Kulik, & Kulik, 1985; Kulik, Bangert, & Williams, 1983; Kulik, Kulik, & Bangert-Drowns, 1985; Kulik, Kulik, & Cohen, 1980). However, research investigating the effectiveness of computers as treatment providers for schizophrenic and autistic individuals is still rather limited. In one early study, Colby (1973) showed the beneficial effect of producing audiovisual stimuli (i.e., visual symbols accompanied by human voice) contingent upon exploratory play with the computer keyboard in 13 of 17 nonspeaking autistic individuals. Computers have also been used to teach discrimination tasks to autistic individuals (e.g., Plienis & Romanczyk, 1985; Romanczyk, 1985). Another noteworthy study was conducted by Browning (1983). Computer-paced "reminders of appropriate verbal behavior and directions for coping with anger and difficult situations" (p. 427) were played from a tape recorder in order to enhance generalization to control severe behavior problems in autistic and schizophrenic adolescents.

Panyan (1984) reviewed computer technology for autistic students. Although some of the studies have not yet actually been conducted, several potential strategies were discussed while relating computer abilities to the learning characteristics of autistic persons. Thus, suggestions were made as to how learning problems specific to autism (such as stimulus overselectivity, inhibited generalization, perseveration, and deficient motivation) could be addressed with computer technology.

CONCLUSIONS

The emphasis on and expansion of behavioral assessment technology in the last two decades reflects both a recognition of the advantages of the approach and of the necessity to continue to refine our skills in this area. This technology is part of an evolving process, as are most technologies in the behavioral arena, and once can only speculate about how advanced our assessment capabilities will become in the future and to what new areas they will be applied. We have discussed how the behavioral assessment of severely psychopathology in chronic schizophrenia and infantile autism has been employed and how this technology has allowed us to address several aspects of treatment and evaluation. This assessment has facilitated many tremendously important advances in these areas and has indeed taken us where traditional assessment could not.

REFERENCES

Al-Issa, I., Bakal, D., & Larkin, N. (1975). Stimulus generalization and anxiety in schizophrenic and normal subjects. *British Journal of Social and Clinical Psychology, 14,* 371–378.

American Psychiatric Association. (1980). *Diagnostic and statistical manual of mental disorders* (3rd ed.). Washington, DC: Author.

Anderson, D. E. (1982). Computer simulations in the psychology laboratory. *Simulation and Games, 13,* 13–36.

Andrews, G. (1984). Treatment outlines for the management of schizophrenia: The Quality Assurance Project. *Australian and New Zealand Journal of Psychiatry, 18,* 19–38.

Aylward, E., Walker, E., & Bettes, B. (1984). Intelligence in schizophrenia: Meta-analysis of the research. *Schizophrenia Bulletin, 10,* 430–459.

Azrin, N. H., & Holz, W. C. (1966). Punishment. In W. K. Honig (Ed.), *Operant behavior: Areas of research and application* (pp. 380–447). New York: Appleton-Century-Crofts.

Bangert-Drowns, R. L., Kulik, J. A., & Kulik, C. C. (1985). Effectiveness of computer-based education in secondary schools. *Journal of Computer Based Instruction, 12,* 59–68.

Bellack, A. S., Hersen, M., & Turner, S. M. (1976). Generalization effects of social skills training in chronic schizophrenics: An experimental analysis. *Behaviour Research and Therapy, 14,* 391–398.

Brown, D. T. (1984). Automated assessment systems in school and clinical psychology: Present status and future directions. *School Psychology Review, 13,* 455–460.

Brown, L., Branston, M. B., Hamre-Nietupski, S., Pumpian, I., Certo, N., & Gruenewald, L. (1979). A strategy for developing chronological age appropriate and functional curricular content for severely handicapped adolescents and young adults. *Journal of Special Education, 13,* 81–90.

Browning, E. R. (1983). A memory pacer for improving stimulus generalization. *Journal of Autism and Developmental Disorders, 13,* 427–432.

Burke, M. J. (1984). Validity generalization: A review and critique of the correlational model. *Personnel Psychology, 37,* 93–115.

Carr, E. G. (1977). The motivation of self-injurious behavior: A review of some hypotheses. *Psychological Bulletin, 84,* 800–816.

Carr, E. G. (1980). Generalization of treatment effects following educational intervention with autistic children and youth. In B. Wilcox & A. Thompson (Eds.), *Critical issues in educating autistic children and youth* (pp. 118–134). Washington, DC: U.S. Office of Special Education.

Carr, E. G., & Durand, V. M. (1985). Reducing behavior problems through functional communication training. *Journal of Applied Behavior Analysis, 18,* 111–126.

Colby, K. M. (1973). The rationale for computer-based treatment of language difficulties in nonspeaking autistic children. *Journal of Autism and Childhood Schizophrenia, 3,* 254–260.

Colby, K. M. (1981). Modeling a paranoid mind. *The Brain and Behavioral Sciences, 4,* 515–560.

Cone, J. D., & Hawkins, R. P. (1977). *Behavioral assessment: New directions in clinical psychology.* New York: Brunner/Mazel.

Demchak, M. A., & Halle, J. W. (1985). Motivational assessment: A potential means of enhancing treatment success of self-injurious individuals. *Education and Treatment of the Mentally Retarded, 20,* 25–38.

Deni, R., Szijarto, K., Eisler, A., & Fantauzzo, C. (1983). BASIC programs for observational research using the TRS-80 Model 100 portable and Model 4 computers. *Behavior Research Methods and Instrumentation, 15,* 616.

Dodd, P. W., Bakeman, R., Loeber, R., & Wilson, S. C. (1981). JOINT and SEQU: FORTRAN routines for the analysis of observational data. *Behavior Research Methods and Instrumentation, 13,* 686–687.

Dunlap, G., Koegel, R. L., & Burke, J. C. (1981). Educational implications of stimulus overselectivity in autistic children. *Exceptional Education Quarterly, 2,* 37–49.

Durand, V. M., & Crimmins, D. B. (1988). Identifying the variables maintaining self-injurious behavior. *Journal of Autism and Developmental Disorders, 1,* 99–117.

Eason, L. J., White, M., & Newsom, C. (1982). Generalized reduction of self-stimulatory behavior: An effect of teaching appropriate play to autistic children. *Analysis and Intervention in Developmental Disabilities, 2,* 157–169.

Engel, K. L., & Paul, G. L. (1979). Systems use to objectify program evaluation, clinical, and management decisions. *Journal of Behavioral Assessment, 1,* 221–238.

Eysenck, H. J. (1984). Meta-analysis: An abuse of research integration. *Journal of Special Education, 18,* 41–59.

Farina, A., Arenberg, D., & Guskin, S. (1957). A scale for measuring minimal social behavior. *Journal of Consulting Psychology, 21,* 265–268.

Fichter, M. M., Wallace, C. J., Liberman, R. P., & Davis, J. R. (1976). Improving social interaction in a chronic psychotic using discriminated avoidance ("nagging"): Experimental analysis and generalization. *Journal of Applied Behavior Analysis, 9,* 377–386.

Fiske, D. W. (1983). The meta-analytic revolution in outcome research. *Journal of Consulting and Clinical Psychology, 51,* 65–70.

Fonagy, P., & Slade, P. D. (1982). Punishment versus negative reinforcement in the aversive conditioning of auditory hallucinations. *Behaviour Research and Therapy, 20,* 483–492.

Freeman, B. J., & Ritvo, E. (1982). The syndrome of autism: A critical review of diagnostic systems and follow-up studies and the theoretical background of the Behavior Observation Scale. In P. Karoly (Ed.), *Advances in child behavior analusis and therapy* (pp. 1–39). Toronto: D. C. Heath.

Freeman, B. J., Ritvo, E. R., & Schroth, P. C. (1984). Behavior assessment of the syndrome of autism: Behavior Observation System. *Journal of the American Academy of Child Psychiatry, 23,* 588–594.

Freeman, B. J., & Schroth, P. C. (1984). The development of the Behavioral Observation System (BOS) for autism. *Behavioral Assessment, 6,* 177–187.

Gardner, J. M., & Breuer, A. (1985). Reliability and validity of a microcomputer assessment system for developmentally disabled persons. *Education and Training of the Mentally Retarded, 20,* 209–213.

Garfinkel, B. D., & Klee, S. H. (1983). A computerized assessment battery for attention deficits. *Psychiatric Hospital, 14,* 163–166.

Getsie, R. L., Langer, P., & Glass, G. V. (1985). Meta-analysis of the effect of type and combination of feedback on children's discrimination learning. *Review of Educational Research, 55,* 9–22.

Goldfried, M. R., & Kent, R. N. (1972). Traditional versus behavioral personality assessment: A comparison of methodological and theoretical assumptions. *Psychological Bulletin, 77,* 409–420.

Goldfried, M. R., & Sprafkin, J. N. (1976). Behavioral personality assessment. In J. T. Spence, R. C. Carson, & J. W. Thibaut (Eds.), *Behavioral approaches to therapy.* Morristown, NJ: General Learning Press.

Gorman, B. S., Primavera, L. H., & Karras, A. (1983). A microcomputer program package for metaanalysis. *Behavior Research Methods and Instrumentation, 15,* 617.

Handleman, J. S., & Harris, S. L. (1983a). A comparison of one-to-one versus couplet instruction with autistic children. *Behavioral Disorders, 9,* 22–26.

Handleman, J. S., & Harris, S. L. (1983b). Generalization across instructional settings by autistic children. *Child and Family Behavior Therapy, 5,* 73–83.

Harris, S. L., & Wolchik, S. A. (1979). Suppression of self-stimulation: Three alternative strategies. *Journal of Applied Behavior Analysis, 12,* 185–198.

Hartmann, D. P., Roper, B. L., & Bradford, D. C. (1979). Some relationships between behavioral and traditional assessment. *Journal of Behavioral Assessment, 1,* 3–21.

Hawkins, R. P. (1979). The functions of assessment: Implications for selection and development of devices for assessing repertoires in clinical, educational, and other settings. *Journal of Applied Behavior Analysis, 12,* 501–516.

Hersen, M., & Bellack, A. S. (1976). *Behavioral assessment: A practical handbook.* New York: Pergamon.

Holmes, M. R., Hansen, D. J., & St. Lawrence, J. S. (1984). Conversation skills training with aftercare patients in the community: Social validation and generalization. *Behavior Therapy, 15,* 84–100.

Honigfeld, G., Gillis, R. O., & Klett, C. J. (1966). NOSIE-30: A treatment-sensitive ward behavior scale. *Psychological Reports, 19,* 180–182.

Hoult, J., Rosen, A., & Reynolds, I. (1984). Community oriented treatment compared to psychiatric hospital oriented treatment. *Social Science and Medicine, 18,* 1005–1010.

Iwata, B. A., Dorsey, M. F., Slifer, K. J., Bauman, K. E., & Richman, G. S. (1982). Toward a functional analysis of self-injury. *Analysis and Intervention in Developmental Disabilities, 2,* 3–20.

Jackson, H. J., & Martin, R. (1983). Remedying social skills deficits in a chronic schizophrenic-retarded person. *Australia and New Zealand Journal of Developmental Disabilities, 9,* 55–63.

Johnson, J., & Koegel, R. L. (1982). Behavioral assessment and curriculum development. In R. L. Koegel, A. Rincover, & A. L. Egel (Eds.), *Educating and understanding autistic children* (pp. 1–32). Houston, TX: College Hill Press.

Johnson, P. B., Rosen, A. J., & Davis, J. M. (1986). Maintenance of induced muscle tension, stimulus generalization performance, and schizophrenia. *Journal of Clinical Psychology, 42,* 54–62.

Kahn, R. M., & Arbib, M. A. (1973). A cybernetic approach to childhood psychosis. *Journal of Autism and Childhood Schizophrenia, 3,* 261–273.

Kanfer, F. H. (1985). Target selection for clinical change programs. *Behavioral Assessment, 7,* 7–20.

Kazdin, A. E. (1986). Comparative outcome studies of psychotherapy: Methodological issues and strategies. *Journal of Consulting and Clinical Psychology, 54,* 95–105.

Kazdin, A. E., & Matson, J. L. (1981). Social validation in mental retardation. *Applied Research in Mental Retardation, 2,* 39–53.

Kendall, P. C. (1981). Assessing generalization and the single-subject strategies. *Behavior Modification, 5,* 307–319.

Kendall, P. C. (1984). Behavioral assessment and methodology. In G. T. Wilson, C. M. Franks, K. D. Brownell, & P. C. Kendal (Eds.), *Annual review of behavior therapy: Theory and practice* (pp. 39–94). New York: Guilford.

Kendall, P. C. (1985). Behavioral assessment and methodology. In C. M. Franks, G. T. Wilson, P. C. Kendall, & K. D. Brownell (Eds.), *Annual review of behavior therapy: Theory and practice* (pp. 47–86). New York: Guilford.

Koegel, R. L., & Rincover, A. (1977). Research on the difference between generalization and maintenance in extra-therapy responding. *Journal of Applied Behavior Analysis, 10,* 1–12.

Koegel, R. L., Schreibman, L., Johnson, J., O'Neill, R. E., & Dunlap, G. (1984). Collateral effects of parent training on families with autistic children. In R. F. Dangel & R. A. Polster (Eds.), *Parent training foundations of research and practice* (pp. 358–378). New York: Guilford.

Krause, W., & Sprung, L. (1980). Experimental analyses of cognitive processes as a basis for a computer-aided diagnostic process for schizophrenic thought disorders. *Zeitschrift fur Psychologies, 188,* 57–73.

Krug, D. A., Arick, J. R., & Almond, P. J. (1981). Autism Screening Instrument for Educational Planning: Background and development. In J. E. Gilliam (Ed.), *Autism: Diagnosis, instructions, management, and research*. Springfield, IL: Charles C. Thomas.

Kulik, C. C., Kulik, J. A., & Cohen, P. A. (1980). Instructional technology and college teaching. *Teaching of Psychology, 7*, 199–205.

Kulik, J. A., Bangert, R. L., & Williams, G. W. (1983). Effects of computer-based teaching on secondary school students. *Journal of Educational Psychology, 75*, 19–26.

Kulik, J. A., Kulik, C. C., & Bangert-Drowns, R. L. (1985). Effectiveness of computer-based education in elementary schools. *Computers in Human Behavior, 1*, 59–74.

Lagomarcino, A., Reid, D. H., Ivancic, M. T., & Faw, G. D. (1984). Leisure-dance instruction for severely and profoundly retarded persons: Teaching an intermediate community-living skill. *Journal of Applied Behavior Analysis, 17*, 71–84.

Lambert, M. E., Intrieri, R. C., & Hollandsworth, J. G. (1986). Development of a computerized reference retrieval system: A behavior therapy training tool. *Journal of Behavior Therapy and Experimental Psychiatry, 17*, 167–169.

Levitan, K. B., Willis, E. A., & Vogelgesang, J. (1985). Microcomputers and the individual practitioner: A review of the literature in psychology and psychiatry. *Computers in Human Services, 1*, 65–84.

Littman, S. K. (1976). Schizophrenia and rehabilitation. *Canada's Mental Health, 24*, 10–12.

Lovaas, O. I., Koegel, R. L., Simmons, J. Q., & Long, J. S. (1973). Some generalizations and follow-up measures on autistic children in behavior therapy. *Journal of Applied Behavior Analysis, 6*, 131–166.

Luiselli, J. K., Suskin, L., & McPhee, D. F. (1981). Continuous and intermittent application of overcorrection in a self-injurious autistic child: Alternating treatments design analysis. *Journal of Behavior Therapy and Experimental Psychiatry, 12*, 355–358.

Lund, J. (1985). The prevalence of psychiatric morbidity in mentally retarded adults. *Acta Psychiatrica Scandinavica, 72*, 563–570.

M⁹REF⁵ anschreck, T. C. (1983). Modeling a paranoid mind: A narrower interpretation of the results. *Behavioral and Brain Sciences, 6*, 340–341.

Mash, E. J., & Terdal, L. G. (1976). *Behavior therapy assessment*. New York: Springer Publishing Co.

Matson, J. L., Zeiss, R. A., & Bowman, W. (1980). A comparison of social skills training and contingent attention to improve behavioural deficits of chronic psychiatric patients. *British Journal of Social and Clinical Psychology, 19*, 57–64.

McDaniel, M. A. (1986). Computer programs for calculating meta-analysis statistics. *Educational and Psychological Measurement, 46*, 175–177.

Mintz, J. (1983). Integrating research evidence: A commentary on meta-analysis. *Journal of Consulting and Clinical Psychology, 51*, 71–75.

Mullen, B. (1983). A BASIC program for metaanalysis of effect sizes using r, BESD, and d. *Behavior Research Methods and Instrumentation, 15*, 392–393.

Murray, H. A. (1943). *Thematic Apperception Test.* Cambridge, MA: Harvard University Press.

Neale, J. M., Oltmanns, T. F., & Winters, K. C. (1983). Recent developments in the assessment and conceptualization of schizophrenia. *Behavioral Assessment, 5*, 33–54.

Nelson, R. O., & Barlow, D. H. (1981). Behavioral assessment: Basic strategies and initial procedures. In D. Barlow (Ed.), *Behavioral assessment of adult disorders* (pp. 13–43). New York: Guilford.

Nelson, R. O., & Hayes, S. C. (1979a). The nature of behavioral assessment: A commentary. *Journal of Applied Behavior Analysis, 12*, 491–500.

Nelson, R. O., & Hayes, S. C. (1979b). Some current dimensions of behavioral assessment. *Behavioral Assessment, 1*, 1–16.

Newton, P. A. (1983). An evaluation of the cost effectiveness of day hospitalization for black male schizophrenics. *Journal of the National Medical Association, 75*, 273–285.

Nihara, K., Foster, R., Shellhaas, M., & Leland, H. (1975). *AAMD Adaptive Behavior Scale, 1975 revision manual.* Washington, DC: American Association of Mental Deficiency.

Panyan, M. V. (1984). Computer technology for autistic students. *Journal of Autism and Developmental Disorders, 14*, 375–382.

Parloff, M. B., London, P., & Wolfe, B. (1986). Individual psychotherapy and behavior change. *Annual Review of Psychology, 37*, 321–349.

Plienis, A., & Romanczyk, R. G. (1985). Analyses of performance, behavior, and predictors for severely disturbed children: A comparison of adult vs. computer instruction. *Analysis and Intervention in Developmental Disabilities, 5*, 345–356.

Powell, J. (1984a). On the misrepresentation of behavioral realities by a widely practiced direct observation procedure: Partial interval (one-zero) sampling. *Behavioral Assessment, 6*, 209–219.

Powell, J. (1984b). Some empirical justification for a modest proposal regarding data acquisition via intermittent direct observation. *Journal of Behavioral Assessment, 6*, 71–80.

Power, C. T. (1979). The Time-Sample Behavioral Checklist: Observational assessment of patient functioning. *Journal of Behavioral Assessment, 1*, 199–210.

Powers, M. D., & Handleman, J. S. (1984). General issues in the behavioral assessment of severe developmental disabilities. In M. Powers & J. Handleman, *Behavioral assessment of severe developmental disabilities* (pp. 25–54). Rockville, MD: Aspen.

Pressman, E., Roche, D., Davey, J., & Firestone, P. (1986). Patterns of auditory perception skills in children with learning disabilities: A computer-assisted approach. *Journal of Learning Disabilities, 19,* 485–488.

Redfield, J. (1979). Clinical Frequencies Recording System: Standardizing staff observations by event recording. *Journal of Behavioral Assessment, 1,* 211–219.

Reynolds, B. S., Newsom, C. D., & Lovaas, O. I. (1974). Auditory overselectivity in autistic children. *Journal of Abnormal Child Psychology, 2,* 253–263.

Rimland, B. (1971). The differentiation of childhood psychoses: An analysis of checklists for 2,218 psychotic children. *Journal of Autism and Childhood Schizophrenia, 1,* 161–174.

Rincover, A., & Koegel, R. L. (1975). Setting generality and stimulus control in autistic children. *Journal of Applied Behavior Analysis, 8,* 235–246.

Rojahn, J., & Kanoy, R. C. (1985). Toward an empirically based parameter selection for time-sampling observation systems. *Journal of Psychopathology and Behavioral Assessment, 7,* 99–120.

Romanczyk, R. G. (1984). Micro-computers and behavior therapy: A powerful alliance. *Behavior Therapist, 7,* 59–64.

Rorschach, H. (1942). *Psychodiagnostics: A diagnostic test based on perception* (4th ed.). New York: Grune & Stratton.

Rosen, A. J., Sussman, S., Mueser, K. T., Lyons, J. S., & Davis, J. M. (1981). Behavioral assessment of psychiatric inpatients and normal controls across different environmental contexts. *Journal of Behavioral Assessment, 3,* 25–36.

Rosen, A. J., Tureff, S. E., Lyons, J. S., & Davis, J. M. (1981). Pharmacotherapy of schizophrenia and affective disorders: Behavioral assessment of psychiatric medications. *Journal of Behavioral Assessment, 3,* 133–148.

Rumsey, J. M., Rapoport, J. L., & Sceery, W. R. (1985). Autistic children as adults: Psychiatric, social, and behavioral outcomes. *Journal of the American Academy of Child Psychiatry, 24,* 465–473.

Runco, M. A., & Schreibman, L. (1983). Parental judgment of behavior therapy efficacy with autistic children: A social validation. *Journal of Autism and Developmental Disorders, 13,* 237–248.

Runco, M. A., & Schreibman, L. (1987). Brief report: Socially validating behavioral objectives in the treatment of autistic children. *Journal of Autism and Developmental Disorders, 17,* 141–147.

Sackett, P. R., Harris, M. M., & Orr, J. M. (1986). On seeking moderator variables in the meta-analysis of correlational data: A Monte Carlo investigation of statistical power and resistance to Type I error. *Journal of Applied Psychology, 71,* 302–310.

Schopler, E., Reichler, R. J., DeVellis, R. F., & Daly, K. (1980). Toward objective classification of childhood autism: Childhood Autism Rating Scale (CARS). *Journal of Autism and Developmental Disorders, 10,* 91–103.

Schreibman, L., & Britten, K. R. (1984). Training parents as therapists for autistic children: Rationale, techniques, and results. In W. P. Christian, G. T. Hannah, & T. J. Glahn (Eds.), *Programming Effective Human Services* (pp. 295–314). New York: Plenum Press.

Schreibman, L., & Carr, E. G. (1978). Elimination of echolalic responding to questions through the training of a generalized verbal response. *Journal of Applied Behavior Analysis, 11,* 453–463.

Schreibman, L., & Charlop, M. H. (1987). Autism. In V. B. Van Hasselt & M. Hersen (Eds.), *Psychological evaluation of the developmental and physically disabled* (pp. 155–177). New York: Plenum.

Schreibman, L., & Koegel, R. L. (1980). A guideline for planning behavior modification programs for autistic children. In S. Turner, K. Calhoun, & H. Adams (Eds.), *Handbook of clinical behavior therapy* (pp. 500–526). New York: John Wiley.

Schreibman, L., Koegel, R. L., Mills, D. L., & Burke, J. C. (1984). Training parent-child interactions. In E. Schopler & G. B. Mesibov (Eds.), *The effects of autism on the family* (pp. 187–205). New York: Plenum Press.

Sharfstein, S. S., & Clark, H. W. (1978). Economics and the chronic mental patient. *Schizophrenia Bulletin, 4,* 399–414.

Shavalia, T. L., & Delprato, D. J. (1980). A computerized reference system for behavior therapy outcome studies. *Journal of Behavior Therapy and Experimental Psychiatry, 11,* 113–115.

Smith, C., Lloyd, B., & Crook, C. (1982). Instrumentation and software report: Computer-assisted coding of videotape material. *Current Psychological Research, 2,* 289–292.

Sparrow, S. S., Balla, D. A., & Cicchetti, D. V. (1984). *Vineland Adaptive Behavior Scales: A revision of the Vineland Social Maturity Scale by Edgar A. Doll.* Circle Pines, MN: American Guidance Service.

Spitzer, R. L., & Endicott, J. (1978). *Schedule for affective disorders and schizophrenia (SADS)* (3rd ed.). New York: Biometrics Research.

Stokes, T. F., & Baer, D. M. (1977). An implicit technology of generalization. *Journal of Applied Behavior Analysis, 10,* 349–367.

Strube, M. J., & Hartmann, D. P. (1983). Meta-analysis: Techniques, applications, and functions. *Journal of Consulting and Clinical Psychology, 51,* 14–27.

Swartz, C. M., & Pfohl, B. (1981). A learning aid for DSM-III: Computerized prompting of diagnostic criteria. *Journal of Clinical Psychiatry, 42,* 359–361.

Test, M. A., Knoedler, W. H., & Allness, D. J. (1985). The long-term treatment of young schizophrenics in a community support program. *New Directions for Mental Health Services, 26,* 17–27.

Thorndike, R. L., Hagen, E. P., & Sattler, J. M. (1986). *Stanford-Binet Intelligence Scale* (4th ed.). Burlington, MA: Riverside.

Touchette, P. E., MacDonald, R. F., & Langer, S. N. (1985). A scatter plot for identifying stimulus control of problem behavior. *Journal of Applied Behavior Analysis, 18,* 343–351.

Tsuang, M. T., Leaverton, P. E., & Huang, K. S. (1974). Criteria for subtyping poor prognosis schizophrenia: A numerical model for differentiating paranoid from non-paranoid schizophrenia. *Journal of Psychiatric Research, 10,* 189–197.

Tucker, G. J., & Rosenberg, S. D. (1975). Computer content analysis of schizophrenic speech: A preliminary report. *American Journal of Psychiatry, 132,* 611–616.

Van Houten, R. (1979). Social validation: The evolution of standards of competency for target behaviors. *Journal of Applied Behavior Analysis, 12,* 581–591.

von Bender, U. (1984). *Untersuchungen zur Intonation autistischer, sprachentwicklungsgestorter und sprachunauffalliger Kinder.* Unpublished doctoral dissertation. Max Planck Institut fur Psychiatrie, Munchen.

Wallace, C. J. (1981). Assessment of psychotic behavior. In M. Hersen & A. S. Bellack (Eds.), *Behavioral assessment: A practical handbook* (pp. 328–388). New York: Pergamon.

Wechsler, D. (1981). *Wechsler Adult Intelligence Scale—Revised manual.* New York: Psychological Corporation.

Weiss, D. J. (1985). Adaptive testing by computer. *Journal of Consulting and Clinical Psychology, 53,* 774–789.

Whissell, C. M. (1984). Emotion: A classification of current literature. *Perceptual and Motor Skills, 59,* 599–609.

Williams, G. E., & Cuvo, A. J. (1986). Training apartment upkeep skills to rehabilitation clients: A comparison of task analytic strategies. *Journal of Applied Behavior Analysis, 19,* 39–51.

Wilson, G. T., & Rachman, S. J. (1983). Meta-analysis and the evaluation of psychotherapy outcome: Limitations and liabilities. *Journal of Consulting and Clinical Psychology, 51,* 54–64.

Wing, J. K., Cooper, J. E., & Sartorius, N. (1974). *The measurement and classification of psychiatric symptoms.* London: Cambridge University Press.

Witt, J. C., & Martens, B. K. (1984). Adaptive behavior: Tests and assessment issues. [Special issue: Computers in school psychology]. *School Psychology Review, 13,* 478–484.

Woods, T. S. (1984). Social validation: Its implications for practitioners of applied behavior analysis serving the developmental disabled. *Scandinavian Journal of Behaviour Therapy, 13,* 67–84.

Yates, B. T. (1985). Cost-effectiveness analysis and cost-benefit analysis: An introduction. *Behavioral Assessment, 7,* 207–234.

Yates, B. T., & Newman, F. L. (1980a). Approaches to cost-effectiveness and cost-benefit analysis of psychotherapy. In G. VandenBos (Ed.), *Psychotherapy: Practice, research, policy* (pp. 103–162). Beverly Hills, CA: Sage.

Yates, B. T., & Newman, F. L. (1980b). Findings of cost-effectiveness and cost-benefit analysis of psychotherapy. In G. VandenBos (ed.), *Psychotherapy: Practice, research, policy* (pp. 163–185). Beverly Hills, CA: Sage.

Yeaton, W. H. (1982). A critique of the effectiveness of applied behavior analysis research. *Advances in Behavior Research and Therapy, 4,* 75–96.

7

Operant Learning Methods with Chronic Schizophrenia and Autism: Aberrant Behavior

V. Mark Durand and Edward G. Carr

The historical roots of operant treatment research with humans lie in work with persons with autism and chronic schizophrenia. For example, Ferster (1961) conducted landmark experimental research with children with autism that served to influence decades of treatment research with this population (e.g., Lovaas, Koegel, Simmons, & Stevens, 1973). Similarly, workers such as Lindsley and Skinner pioneered the application of operant conditioning principles for severe clinical problems observed among persons with chronic schizophrenia (Kazdin, 1978). In many ways, the early history of behavior modification is the history of the treatment of problem behavior among individuals with autism and schizophrenia.

Bizarre, chaotic, and unsettling, aberrant behaviors are typically the focus of clinical intervention efforts with persons exhibiting autism and chronic schizophrenia. The behaviors of concern for those who live with and provide services for people with schizophrenia and autism are surprisingly consistent across these two diagnostic groups. These individuals often engage in such aberrant behaviors as aggression (i.e., hitting and striking out at others), self-injurious behavior (i.e., a variety of behaviors producing physical injury to the clients themselves), repetitive, stereotyped behavior (e.g., rocking, hand twirling, and head weaving), compulsive, ritualistic behavior (e.g., hoarding, stacking of objects), and various forms of bizarre, psychotic speech (e.g., echolalia, delusional speech) (Durand & Carr, 1987a; Hersen & Bellack, 1978; Paul & Lentz, 1977). In this chapter we discuss operant treatment approaches that have focused on eliminating or reducing the frequency of these behaviors.

Although persons who are diagnosed as having infantile autism or chronic schizophrenia engage in many of the same problem behaviors, the respective treatment literatures for these two groups are quite disparate. Operant approaches to the treatment of persons with autism dominate the research literature. In fact, it can be confidently argued that operant treatment of the problems associated with autism is the treatment of choice (e.g., Durand & Carr, 1987a; Gaylord-Ross & Holvoet, 1985). However, despite having similar historical roots, treatment of persons with chronic schizophrenia is *not* dominated by operant approaches. Bellack (1986) has referred to the field of schizophrenia as "behavior therapy's forgotten child" because it has ceased to be a major area of clinical work and research for many behavior therapists.

One reason for the disparity in research on problem behavior may involve the way problem behavior is conceptualized. For autism, problem behavior is typically considered part of the disorder. Although the third edition of the *Diagnostic and Statistical Manual* of the American Psychiatric Association (DSM-III) (APA, 1980) included only peculiar speech patterns (e.g., delayed echolalia, metaphorical language) in its criteria for a diagnosis of infantile autism, the revised manual (DSM-III-R) (APA, 1987) includes such behaviors as stereotyped body movements, head banging, and "marked distress" as criteria. Additionally, many writers include behaviors such as self-injury and other stereotyped behavior as associated features of autism (e.g., Cohen, Paul, & Volkmar, 1987; Lovaas et al., 1973). Thus, one reason that workers in the field of autism have frequently studies problematic behavior may be that these behaviors are at least implicitly considered part of autism.

In contrast, workers in the field of schizophrenia do not consider behaviors such as self-injury, aggression, or stereotyped behavior as symptomatic of this disorder. DSM-III and DSM-III-R include only verbal forms of aberrant behavior (e.g., bizarre delusions, incoherence) as symptomatic of schizophrenia. Writing and clinical work in schizophrenia does not reflect that these aberrant motor behaviors may be part of the disorder. An interesting quote by Curran, Sutton, Faraone, and Guenette (1985) perhaps sums up this disparity most clearly.

> For example, family members are told that violence cannot be tolerated and are urged to call the police if such behavior is exhibited. Similarly, families are told not to argue with or confront paranoid thinking but rather to take a benign, indifferent attitude toward it and accept it as part of the illness. (p. 470)

Thus, aggression (violence) is dealt with in a supposedly nontherapeutic manner because it is apparently not part of the "illness," but paranoid verbal behavior is to be tolerated and accepted because it is symptomatic of schizophrenia (clearly, some would argue that the "therapy" was being given to the violent behavior). This disparity in the conceptualization of problem behavior between the two fields may explain the different emphasis the research literatures have taken toward these behaviors.

ASSUMPTIONS

Certain basic assumptions are made throughout this chapter. Our first assumption is that the research on children and adolescents with autism is generalizable to adults. This is necessitated by the dearth of treatment research on adults with autism. Therefore, our conclusions about the treatment of aberrant behavior in persons with autism will be based mostly on research with children and adolescents and should be qualified by this limitation. However, it is our expectation that future treatment efforts with adults exhibiting this disorder will parallel findings with younger persons. It is important to note that most problematic behavior exhibited by children with autism does not appear to dissipate with time and, for many children, can become more serious following puberty (Gillberg & Steffenburg, 1987). Finally, where gaps in the treatment literature exist, we will discuss related research with persons exhibiting other developmental disorders (e.g., severe retardation).

The second assumption made in this chapter is that aberrant behavior should be the target of treatment. Although this may seem to be an obvious assumption, an argument can be made that behaviors such as aggression, self-injury, and rocking are aberrant in form but not in function. In other words, hitting another person (the behavior's form) may be aberrant; however, trying to get some-one's attention (the behavior's function) is not. This has led some to argue against the treatment of some forms of problem behavior because they appear to be adaptive responses for many individuals.

Concern for reducing or eliminating these forms of aberrant behavior comes from overwhelming evidence that these behaviors are detrimental to long-term positive outcomes for persons with autism and chronic schizophrenia. For example, experimental work with persons with autism has shown that behaviors such as aggression, self-injury, and other, stereotyped behaviors can interfere with habilitation efforts (e.g., Carr, Newsom, & Binkoff, 1980; Koegel & Covert, 1972). Aberrant behavior appears to be a major obstacle to placing persons in work settings (Hayes, 1987; Rutter, 1978) and community residences (Scheerenberger, 1981). It has been shown that the characteristic of persons with severe developmental disabilities most related to return to institutional settings is the presence of aggression (Scheerenberger, 1981). Similarly, the occurrence of bizarre behavior on the part of persons with chronic schizophrenia is typi-cally identified as a major reason for rehospitalization (Arthur, Ell-sworth, & Kroeker, 1968; Davis, Dinitz, & Pasamanick, 1972; Pasama-nick, Scarpitti, & Dinitz, 1967; Paul & Lentz, 1977; Sanders, Smith, & Weinman, 1967).

An additional assumption is that behavioral (operant) treatment of aberrant behavior is the intervention of choice. There is consider-able evidence that traditional forms of psychotherapy are ineffective with persons with autism (Kanner & Eisenberg, 1955) and with per-sons exhibiting chronic schizophrenia (Paul & Lentz, 1977). In addi-tion, there is equivocal support for medical treatment of these behaviors. For persons with autism, research with drug treatments has demonstrated only modest reductions in the frequency of such behaviors as aggression and self-injury (Beckwith, Couk, & Schumacher, 1986; Durand, 1982; Singh & Millichamp, 1985). Medical treatment is highly prevalent for persons with chronic schizophrenia. However, as many as 50% of these persons may not benefit from the use of psychotropic medication (Gardos & Cole, 1976), and a relapse is high among those who do respond positively to such medications (hogarty, Schooler, & Ulrich, 1979). Thus, there appears to be a significant proportion of persons with autism and schizophrenia who do not benefit from traditional psychotherapy or current medical treatments.

Finally, we will adopt a functional view of problematic behavior in this chapter (Baer, 1981; Ferster, 1965; Holland, 1978; Skinner, 1953). In other words, severe behavior problems are looked upon as reasonable adaptations by the persons exhibiting these behaviors to the limitations of their environment and their own abilities (Carr & Durand, 1985b; Durand & Crimmins, 1988). Thus, these behaviors do not occur in a vacuum but instead serve to elicit certain responses from their external (e.g., social attention, escape from work, tangibles) or internal (e.g., sensory feedback) environments. This conceptualization will guide our review of the extant literature on problematic behavior.

TREATMENT RESEARCH

Consistent with the functional view of problem behavior adopted in this chapter, we will discuss separately prescriptive and nonprescriptive approaches to treatment. Most of the treatment literature has been nonprescriptive; in other words, no attempt is made to assess the variables maintaining problem behavior or to use this information to design treatments. Prescriptive treatment research (i.e., using information on maintaining variables to design treatments) has received increased attention in recent years, and these studies will be discussed separately.

DANGEROUS BEHAVIOR

In this section we review operant treatment research with behaviors considered harmful or dangerous to the clients or others. These behaviors include physical aggression (e.g., hitting, pushing, kicking others), self-injurious behavior (e.g., head banging, face slapping), and tantrums (e.g., violent yelling and screaming, property destruction). These behaviors are typically of greatest concern to society and result in the allocation of an inordinate amount of clinical effort. Although typically discussed and reviewed separately, behaviors such as aggression, tantrums, and self-injury may be usefully conceptualized together. In recent reviews of research on problem behavior, it has been pointed out that these forms (e.g., hitting others, screaming, hand biting) may share common functions (Carr, 1977; Durand & Carr, 1985; Evans & Meyer, 1985; Gaylord-Ross, 1980). Therefore, although these behaviors differ in topography (i.e., form), they do not appear to be maintained by similar consequences (i.e., functions) and will, therefore, be considered together in this review.

Nonprescriptive Interventions

Planned Ignoring

This procedure involves the removal of social attention contingent upon instances of problem behavior (Hall & Hall, 1980). Research on planned ignoring is distinguished from research on extinction (where no reinforcers are present for the behavior) (Zeiler, 1977) because there is rarely an independent demonstration in planned ignoring studies that social attention serves as a reinforcer for the target behavior (i.e., it is not used prescriptively). A number of studies with persons displaying autism and chronic schizophrenia have demonstrated the effectiveness of this type of intervention in reducing such behaviors as tantrums (e.g., Wolf, Risley, & Mees, 1964), aggression (Martin & Foxx, 1973), and self-injurious behavior (e.g., Cox & Klinge, 1976; Lovaas, Freitag, Gold, & Kassorla, 1965). Cox and Klinge (1976), for example, evaluated the effectiveness of planned ignoring on the self-injurious behaviors exhibited by one young woman (e.g., pulling out her hair, cutting her wrists, burning her head). They found that withholding social attention resulted in significant reductions in these behaviors. In contrast, other investigators have not been successful in using planned ignoring to reduce problem behavior (e.g., Martin & Iagulli, 1974).

The occasional failure of planned ignoring to treat problem behavior may be directly tied to the nonprescriptive use of these procedures. Thus, if an individual's problem behavior is being maintained by social attention, then one may predict the success of planned ignoring. However, if the problem behavior is maintained by variables other than social attention (e.g., sensory consequences, escape from tasks), then this procedure would be predictably ineffective. In a study consistent with this hypothesis, Solnick, Rincover, and Peterson (1977) found that the tantrums, self-injurious behaviors, and spitting exhibited by two individuals increased following contingent removal of attention. These behaviors may have served as escape responses (i.e., responses that remove the person from aversive academic demands) or as a means of gaining access to sensory input (i.e., through stereotyped behavior). Thus, this procedure may have served as a reinforcer by removing demands and/or allowing contingent access to sensory consequences and therefore caused an increase in these dangerous behaviors.

Differential Reinforcement Procedures

Perhaps the most widely used nonaversive intervention for problem behavior involves some form of differential reinforcement technique. Differential reinforcement of other behavior (DRO) involves reinforcing an individual for a period of time in which no instances of the problem behavior has occurred (Homer & Peterson, 1980). DRO procedures have been used extensively with people with autism and schizophrenia and have effectively reduced aggression (e.g., Ayllon & Michael, 1959; Vukelich & Hake, 1971), tantrums (e.g., Bostow & Bailey, 1969), and self-injurious behavior (e.g., Ragain & Anson, 1976), although such procedures have not always been effective (e.g., Corte, Wolfe, & Locke, 1971).

Another version of this technique, differential reinforcement of incompatible behavior (DRI), involves the reinforcement of behaviors that are physically incompatible with the target behavior. For example, one study (Lovaas et al., 1965) attempted to reduce self-injurious behavior in one girl by reinforcing hand clapping. This approach was attempted because it was felt that hand clapping was incompatible with her head banging. The frequency of hand clapping increased following reinforcement, and the frequency of head banging decreased.

Numerous other studies have demonstrated the effectiveness of DRI procedures with other behaviors such as aggression (Repp & Deitz, 1974). Again, however, DRI procedures have not always been successful in reducing problematic behavior (e.g., Measel & Alfieri, 1976).

One limitation of DRO procedures is the lack of instruction. No specific skills are prescribed by this procedure. Thus, it may be difficult for clients to discriminate just what they *should* be doing during the DRO interval. A second limitation of these procedures is related to the reinforcers used. It is assumed in these studies that such stimuli as praise and foods are reinforcers. However, the reinforcing nature of these stimuli are rarely assessed prior to their use. An exception to this is exemplified in a study by Favell, McGimsey, and Jones (1978), who determined that access to arm restraints was reinforcing for a 27-year-old woman with a long history of self-injury. They found that contingently providing her with restraints for periods of time during which she did not display self-injury resulted in significant reductions in this behavior.

An additional problem inherent in DRI procedures is the lack of guidelines for selecting alternative behaviors (Voeltz, Evans, Derer, & Hanashiro, 1983). Typically, caregivers have attempted to teach *physically* incompatible behaviors (e.g., hands in pockets) without a consideration of the role or function the problem behavior serves for the client. This nonprescriptive approach to using differential reinforcement procedures may also account for the occasional failures reported in the literature.

Contingent Negative Consequences

To date, the most common type of intervention for severe behavior problems reported in the research literature has been the contingent application of negative consequences. The rationale for the use of these procedures involves the process of punishment; in other words, if a behavior is followed by an aversive stimulus, the frequency of that behavior should be reduced in the future. No knowledge of the function of a particular behavior is assumed.

A plethora of negative consequences have been tried in efforts to reduce the behavior problems exhibited by persons with autism and schizophrenia, including time-out from positive reinforcement (Cayner & Kiland, 1974; Wolf et al., 1964), contingent restraint (Azrin, Besalel,

& Wisotzek, 1982), overcorrection (Johnson, Baumeister, Penland, & Inwald, 1982; Matson & Stephens, 1977), and contingent electric shock (Corte, Wolf, & Locke, 1971; Tate & Baroff, 1966). A study by Foxx and colleagues is prototypical of such research. Foxx, McMorrow, Bittle, and Bechtel (1986) describe the treatment of severe aggression exhibited by one 20-year-old man. Among other procedures, these investigators employed contingent electric shock and found an immediate reduction in aggression. Additionally, a follow-up observation 15 months after this intervention showed that aggression remained greatly reduced. These results are typical for several reasons.

First, when successful, the application of extremely aversive stimuli (e.g., electric shock) results in immediate and dramatic reductions in problem behavior (Carr & Lovaas, 1983). Second, however, there are rarely reports of complete and long-term suppression (Guess, Helmstetter, Turnbull, & Knowlton, 1987; Murphy & Wilson, 1981). In the present example, this man continued to require the application of electric shock over a year later. Thus, someone was required to provide the aversive stimulus wherever he went and will continue to for an indeterminate amount of time. This factor is a major limitation of the use of contingent negative consequences because it may limit the environments in which such treated persons can live (i.e., the person may need constant one-to-one attention from highly trained staff). And because such procedures are routinely rated as unacceptable by caregivers (Pickering & Morgan, 1985; Singh, Watson, & Winton, 1987), they may be unwilling to apply such treatments consistently (Foxx & Livesay, 1984). Third, the functional nature of this man's aggression was not considered in designing treatment. The use of contingent negative consequences alone suffers from the same limitations as the nonaversive procedures described above, namely, that there is no consideration of the function of the student's problematic behavior in treatment design.

When used to treat dangerous behavior, contingent negative consequences share an additional limitation of the nonaversive procedures; that is, occasional reports of ineffectiveness. Failure to observe clinically significant results has been reported with procedures such as overcorrection (e.g., Rapoff, Altman, & Christophersen, 1980) and electric shock (e.g., Anderson, Dancis, & Alpert, 1978; Romanczyk & Goren, 1975).

Prescriptive Interventions

Extinction

Recall that extinction was distinguished from planned ignoring because most of the latter studies did not independently assess the role of social attention as a reinforcer. Few studies have assessed the reinforcers maintaining problematic behavior and then contingently removed these stimuli to reduce their frequency. In one exception, Durand (1984) assessed the variables maintaining the problematic behavior of a number of individuals and selected six persons whose behaviors appeared to be maintained by social attention. It was found that contingent removal of attention resulted in quick and reliable suppression of their behavior problems. In a related study, Carr et al. (1980) reported that escape from academic demands was maintaining the aggressive behavior of their subject. These investigators confined the subject to a chair during tasks, thus not letting him escape work by being aggressive (i.e., escape extinction). This form of extinction resulted in dramatic reductions in aggression. Finally, Rincover and Devany (1982) treated the self-injurious behaviors of three individuals whose problem behaviors were presumably maintained by their sensory consequences (i.e., tactile input). By preventing the subjects from receiving tactile input through their self-injury (through various protective padding devices), they substantially reduced these behaviors. In fact, this treatment (referred to as sensory extinction) was more effective for reducing self-injurious behavior with one subject than was a contingent negative consequence (i.e., vinegar sprayed into his mouth). These studies stand in contrast to the majority of the treatment research, which has not assessed the function of problem behavior prior to treatment.

Stimulus Control Procedures

Efforts to rearrange or remove stimuli that are reliably associated with problem behavior will be referred to as stimulus-control procedures (Gaylord-Ross, 1980; Meyer & Evans, 1986). For example, Touchette and colleagues (Touchette, MacDonald, & Langer, 1985) have used their "scatter plot" data sheet to identify the situations and times of day in which problem behavior is most likely to occur. Similarly, they also identify those situations associated with low rates of problem behavior and attempt to replicate the settings. For one student, aggression was less frequent during the morning. Intervention, therefore, involved replicating the morning activities in the afternoon. This simple activity change resulted in significant reductions in aggression. A 12-month follow-up observation after the gradual reintroduction of the afternoon activities showed no increases in problematic behavior. In addition to molar modifications in activities as described above, other workers have examined the effects of more molecular changes in activities that are related to problem behavior, such as task variation (Winterling, Dunlap, & O'Neill, 1987) and errorless learning techniques (Weeks & Gaylord-Ross, 1981), and have demonstrated clinically significant reductions in problem behaviors as a result of these minor environmental manipulations.

Carr and Newsom (1985) describe the treatment of escape-maintained tantrums in three persons with developmental disabilities. They provided strongly preferred reinforcers (i.e., special foods) contingent upon task compliance. The rationale for this intervention is that since the task setting is less aversive when these reinforcers are present, the clients should not have to escape the situation through tantrums. These researchers found that escape-maintained tantrums were reduced to near zero levels when highly preferred foods were introduced as task reinforcers. Similar results with this procedure have been observed with other behavior problems (e.g., Carr et al., 1980; Russo, Cataldo, & Cushing, 1981). Researchers are only just beginning to explore the value of stimulus control procedures for the treatment of severe behavior problems.

Teaching Functionally Equivalent Behaviors

An additional approach to the application of a functional model of behavior to the treatment of severe behavior problems is teaching functionally equivalent, alternative behavior (Carr & Durand, 1985b; Donnellan, Mirenda, Mesaros, & Fassbender, 1984; Durand, 1986; Evans & Meyer, 1985). This involves the analysis of the function of the problem behavior (e.g., attention-getting) and the teaching of a more appropriate form that serves the same function (e.g., verbal requests for attention). A number of studies have been conducted that demonstrate the value of this procedure in reducing severe behavior problems (e.g., Carr & Durand, 1985a; Durand, 1984; Durand & Kishi, 1987; Horner & Budd, 1985; Smith, 1985; Smith & Coleman, 1986). In one example, Durand and Kishi (1987) assessed the function of the severe behavior problems of five adults with multiple handicaps (deaf and blind and severe/profound retardation) through the use of a rating scale, the Motivation Assessment Scale (Durand & Crimmins, 1988). On the basis of this information (i.e., that these behaviors were maintained by escape, social attention, and their tangible consequences), these individuals were taught to communicate nonverbally requests that were equivalent to the assessed functions of their behavior problems (e.g., requests for assistance, requests for attention, and requests for tangibles). This intervention resulted in significant improvements in their problematic behavior (severe self-injury and aggression). Smith (1985) treated one 18-year-old male with autism who presumably engaged in aggression to obtain tangible reinforcers (i.e., food). Teaching him to request favorite foods resulted in dramatic improvements in the number of his aggressive episodes.

In a related study, Favell, McGimsey, and Schell (1982) worked with individuals engaging in self-injurious behavior maintained by sensory consequences. These researchers taught the individuals to manipulate toys that provided equivalent sensory input and found that self-injurious behavior was substantially reduced. Thus, providing these individuals with a more appropriate way of obtaining their preferred reinforcers (i.e., through toy play rather than through self-injury) resulted in clinically significant improvements in the dangerous behaviors. Teaching functionally equivalent alternative behaviors is an intervention strategy that holds much promise for the treatment of severe behavior problems.

STEREOTYPED MOTOR BEHAVIOR

Of additional concern to those who live and work with individuals with autism and chronic schizophrenia are repetitive and bizarre motor behaviors. These behaviors are observed in a variety of forms, including rocking, hand flapping, body posturing, hand wringing, and other compulsive or ritualistic types of behaviors. Although these behaviors do not pose an immediate physical risk to the clients or to others, they can hinder efforts at placement in community settings. Such behaviors can be stigmatizing, and attempts to interrupt them can often lead to more severe problems (e.g., self-injury, aggression). It is important to note that stereotyped behaviors should not always be the target for treatment. Although such behaviors can inhibit learning in some individuals (Koegel & Covert, 1972), this is not true for all persons exhibiting stereotyped behavior (Chock & Glahn, 1983). Preliminary longitudinal observations suggest that stereotyped behaviors in young children may change in form over time to resemble more acceptable, albeit idiosyncratic, behavior (Epstein, Taubman, & Lovaas, 1985) Efforts should therefore be made to document, prior to implementation, the necessity of using any intervention for such behavior.

Nonprescriptive Interventions

Planned Ignoring

Contingently removing social attention for stereotyped motor behavior has generally been ineffective in reducing these responses. Even when planned ignoring has been extended over prolonged periods of time, little reduction has been observed (Romanczyk, Gordon, Crimmins, Wenzel, & Kistner, 1980). The ineffectiveness of such an intervention is generally attributed to the nonsocial function these behaviors appear to serve (Baumeister & Forehand, 1973; Berkson, 1983; Lovaas, Newsom, & Hickman, 1987; Romanczyk, Kistner, & Plienis, 1982). Thus, many writers agree that stereotyped motor behaviors may serve to provide individuals with sensory input. Although this may not be true for all persons who engage in stereotyped behavior (Durand & Carr, 1987b), the self-reinforcing nature of these responses for most individuals may account for the relative ineffectiveness of planned ignoring treatments.

Differential Reinforcement Procedures

Variations of differential reinforcement procedures have been employed in a large number of treatment studies (e.g., Baumeister & Forehand, 1971; Harris & Wolchik, 1979; Repp, Deitz, & Speir, 1974; Tierny, McGuire, & Walton, 1979). A number of these studies have evaluated the effects of DRO procedures alone (e.g., Horner, 1980; Repp, Deitz, & Deitz, 1976; Repp et al., 1974). Horner (1980), for example, found that stereotyped behaviors partially reduced by introducing toys into the environment could be further reduced by DRO procedures.

Barton, Brulle, and Repp (1986) have examined the relative effectiveness of whole-interval DRO (delivering reinforcement if the target behavior does not occur throughout an entire interval) versus momentary DRO (reinforcement is delivered if the target behavior does not occur at the moment of observation) in reducing stereotyped motor behaviors. They found that both DRO procedures resulted in significant reductions in the stereotyped responses of seven individuals. This study points out the potential effectiveness of DRO procedures and our relative lack of knowledge concerning the necessary treatment parameters for a successful DRO program (Repp, Barton, & Brulle, 1983). In an excellent review of treatment research, LaGrow and Repp (1984) observe that DRO procedures are most effective with moderately high rates of stereotyped behavior if the DRO interval length is sufficiently short to allow multiple instances of reinforcement.

Using a variation of the DRO procedure, Carroccio, Latham, and Carroccio (1976) assessed the effects of a DRL schedule (differential reinforcement of low rates of behavior) on the stereotyped head/face touching of a 40-year-old man with chronic schizophrenia. Access to a guitar was provided for decreasing rates of this behavior, resulting in significant reductions in head/face touching.

DRI procedures alone have also been successfully employed to reduce stereotyped motor behavior in a number of studies (e.g., Baumeister & Forehand, 1971; Brawley, Harris, Allen, Fleming, & Peterson, 1969; Eason, White, & Newsom, 1982; Favell, 1973; Jorgenson, 1971; Lovaas, Litrownik, & Mann, 1971). For example, Favell (1973) found that teaching toy play (e.g., playing with a ball, push toy, or pegboard) resulted in significant decreases in repetitive motor movements exhibited by three institutionalized males.

Despite the success of differential reinforcement procedures in significantly reducing stereotyped motor behavior in a large number of studies, there have also been a number of investigations that have not observed such positive results (e.g., Barrett, Matson, Shapiro, & Ollendick, 1981; Cavalier & Ferretti, 1980; Foxx & Azrin, 1973; Harris & Wolchik, 1979). It is difficult to interpret the results of these latter studies. As we have mentioned before, although there is a relative lack of knowledge concerning appropriate differential reinforcement procedure parameters, several recommendations have been made in the literature (e.g., interval length, frequency of target behavior).

Studies failing to find effects rarely investigate more than one set of parameters (i.e., various reinforcers, several reinforcement schedules). Thus, it is difficult to say whether the differential reinforcement *procedures* were not working in these studies or that the most effective parameters were not explored. Additionally, as we mentioned in the section on dangerous behavior, limitations in the procedures themselves (e.g., physical vs. functional incompatibility of the responses) may account for these divergent findings.

Contingent Negative Consequences

The literature on the use of various negative consequences for stereotyped motor behavior parallels that of dangerous behavior. A plethora of contingent negative consequences have been employed to reduce stereotyped behavior, including electric shock (e.g., Baumeister & Forehand, 1972; Lovaas, Schaeffer, & Simmons, 1965), slaps to the hand (e.g., Koegel & Covert, 1972; Koegel, Firestone, Kramme, & Dunlap, 1974), physical restraint (e.g., Luiselli, Reisman, Helfen, & pemberton, 1976), and overcorrection (e.g., Azrin, Kaplan, & Foxx, 1973; Coleman, Whitman, & Johnson, 1979; Rollings, Baumeister, & Baumeister, 1977). However, despite the success observed in using these procedures, one must question the use of contingent negative consequences as a treatment for stereotyped motor behavior. First, these procedures are extremely restrictive, often involving pain or discomfort; they can be expensive (Hill & Spreat, 1987) and are subject to abuse. Second, as we mentioned above, it is not clear that these behaviors always warrant intervention. Third, a recent meta-analytic review of the prescriptive treatment literature (Gorman-Smith & Matson, 1985) suggests that in some cases reinforcement-based procedures (e.g., DRO) may be more effective than contingent negative consequences (e.g., overcorrection). These observations (along with occasional reports of undesirable side effects when using contingent negative consequences—e.g., Mayhew & Harris, 1978) argue against the use of these procedures for stereotyped motor behavior.

Prescriptive Interventions

Extinctions

Based on the conceptualization that many individuals engage in stereotyped motor behavior to again access to pleasurable sensory consequences, Rincover and colleagues (Rincover, 1978; Rincover, Cook, Peoples, & Packard, 1979) have attempted to remove these consequences in a procedure termed sensory extinction. In one experiment (Rincover, 1978), the plate spinning exhibited by a person with autism was presumed to be maintained by its auditory feedback. Treatment involved carpeting the surface of a table to attenuate this feedback, resulting in significant reductions in stereotyped plate spinning. Similar results have been observed for such behaviors as object mouthing and stereotypic eye gazing (e.g., Maag, Wolchik, Rutherford, & Parks, 1986).

Stimulus Control Procedures

A number of studies have attempted to rearrange or remove the stimuli associated with stereotyped motor behavior as a behavior reduction technique. One of these studies (Dunlap, Dyer, & Koegel, 1983) assessed intertrial interval duration and its relationship to stereotyped behavior. This study found that introducing short intertrial intervals (1–2 s) for students with autism resulted in much less stereotyped behavior than was seen with long intertrial intervals (5 or more seconds) for the same students. A variety of studies have documented that stereotyped motor behavior can be significantly reduced by increasing the opportunities for individuals to manipulate objects (e.g., Berkson & Mason, 1963; Davenport & Berkson, 1963; Guess & Rutherford, 1967; Horner, 1980). For example, Guess and Rutherford (1967) found that for persons with retardation and visual impairments, providing objects that produced a variety of sounds reduced stereotyped responses by half. Other studies, however, have not replicated these results (Baumeister & Forehand, 1970; Hutt & Hutt, 1965). Hutt and Hutt (1965), for example, found that presenting toy blocks to their subjects increased rates of stereotyped motor responses.

Several factors may account for these discrepant results. For some individuals, providing certain objects to manipulate may allow the person to receive the same or similar sensory input as is provided by their stereotyped behavior (e.g., a toy that creates visual sensory input may serve the same function as flapping one's hand in front of a light). In this way, providing objects to manipulate may resemble providing opportunities to engage in functionally equivalent responses. Thus, in the Hutt and Hutt (1965) study, for example, the blocks may not have provided sensory feedback equivalent to the subjects' stereotyped behavior. Also, just making objects available does not ensure that clients have the skills or the inclination to manipulate them properly. For example, Eason et al. (1982) found that *teaching* appropriate toy play skills resulted in significant reductions in stereotyped motor behavior for their subjects. This and other studies (e.g., Azrin et al., 1973; Favell, 1973) suggest that just providing opportunities for alternative behaviors may not be sufficient for clients who do not have the skills or are not sufficiently motivated to manipulate objects. Finally, Durand and Carr (1987b) have recently shown that for some individuals, stereotyped behavior can acquire social functions (e.g., to escape academic demands). Thus, providing objects to manipulate may be viewed by some as similar to academic demands, thereby increasing rates of stereotyped behavior. Consistent with the latter explanation of these discrepant results, Mace, Browder, and Lin (1987) observed that their subject engaged in more stereotyped mouthing during difficult activities. By introducing a prompt hierarchy to reduce the difficulty of the tasks, they observed significant decreases in mouthing.

One antecedent intervention has recently been investigated as a treatment for stereotyped behavior. A few investigators have assessed the effects of exercise on subsequent rates of behaviors such as body rocking, hand flapping, and object spinning (e.g., Bachman & Fuqua, 1983; Kern, Koegel, Dyer, Blew, & Fenton, 1982; Watters & Watters, 1980). Results have consistently shown moderate reductions in these behaviors following increased physical activity (e.g., jogging).

Teaching Functionally Equivalent Behaviors

A number of studies have found that teaching toy play can lead to reduced levels of stereotyped behavior (e.g., Azrin et al., 1973; Eason et al., 1982; Favell, 1973). A limitation of these studies is that there is no assessment of the function of the stereotyped behavior exhibited by the subjects. Thus, it is not clear that (1) these behaviors functioned to gain access to specific sensory input or (2) the types of toys these individuals were taught to play with provided alternative access to this sensory input. Research needs to be conducted that, first, uses an assessment methodology to determine the sensory function of these behaviors (e.g., sensory extinction) and, second, demonstrates that teaching subjects to manipulate objects providing alternative sensory consequences will reduce stereotyped motor behavior. One example of this type of research (Rincover et al., 1979) demonstrated that for three of four subjects with autism, significant reductions in stereotyped behavior were observed during toy play that matched the function of their behavior. Additional work in this area is recommended to validate this type of treatment.

As we noted previously, some individuals appear to engage in stereotyped motor behavior for social reasons. For these individuals, then, functionally equivalent responses would include behavior that elicits specific social reactions by others (as opposed to producing specific sensory feedback). Following this reasoning, Durand and Carr (1987b) determined that the rocking and hand flapping of four individuals were maintained by escape from unpleasant situations. Using this information, these subjects were taught assistance-seeking responses (e.g., saying the phrase "Help me") during difficult tasks. This treatment resulted in significant reductions in stereotyped motor behavior for all four individuals. Although few studies have examined the efficacy of teaching functionally equivalent behavior as a treatment for stereotyped motor responses, this approach warrants further investigation given the nonaversive and constructive nature of this procedure.

PECULIAR SPEECH

Peculiar speech patterns are characteristic of both autism and chronic schizophrenia. In the approximately 50% of children with autism who have speech, it typically consists of such forms as immediate and/or delayed echolalia, metaphorical language, and pronominal reversal. In persons with chronic schizophrenia, peculiar speech patterns include verbal reports of bizarre delusions and hallucinations, incoherence, and loosening of associations. Although the forms of these bizarre speech patterns have typically been considered quite different between these two diagnostic groups, peculiar speech forms may be more similar for adults with autism and adults with schizophrenia. Obsessive speech (e.g., repeating questions over and over again), loosening of associations, preoccupation with particular topics, and semantic concreteness have been reported among adults with autism

(Paul, 1987; Rutter & Garmezy, 1983). To date, however, there is no systematic research on these peculiar speech patterns seen in adults with autism.

Discussed in this section is the operant treatment of peculiar speech patterns including the *verbal reports* of delusions and hallucinations. These symptoms of schizophrenia are usually considered disorders of cognition (e.g., delusional beliefs) (Winters & Neale, 1983). In other words, delusional speech and hallucinatory behavior are only the overt signs of the private events occurring within the individual. However, behavioral treatment research with delusions and hallucinations has focused on the overt behavior consisting of their verbal reports and has, in general, not addressed the covert aspects of these disorders. This emphasis on the overt aspects of hallucinations and delusions to the exclusion of the "cognitive" processes involved has been criticized (e.g., Marzillier & Birchwood, 1981). Others, however, have recognized the possible functional nature of these behaviors (Layng & Andronis, 1984). Thus, verbal reports of hallucinations and delusions may come to acquire sensory and/or social functions through the cumulative impact of their consequences (Durand & Crimmins, 1987).

Nonprescriptive Interventions

Planned Ignoring

As observed with stereotyped motor behavior, few studies have documented successful treatment of peculiar speech with planned ignoring. In one of the earliest behavioral studies of hallucinatory behavior, Lindsley (1963) observed groups of persons with chronic schizophrenia for thousands of hours in various experimental and hospital settings. He noted that even when there was no apparent social reinforcement for hallucinatory behaviors for prolonged periods of time, individuals continued to behave as if they were experiencing auditory hallucinations. Lindsley interpreted these findings to suggest that hallucinations (unlike other psychotic-like behavior) did not serve an environmental function and was part of the "psychotic" syndrome. In a similar investigation, Lovaas and colleagues (Lovaas, Varni, Koegel, & Lorsch, 1977) observed both children with autism and children without developmental disabilities for a number of hours while they were alone and found that verbal behavior for both groups was maintained without social consequences. Thus, the peculiar speech patterns of the children with autism (e.g., delayed echolalia) and the presumably normal speech patterns of the children without autism appeared to be maintained by the sensory feedback they produced. Like the sensory-maintained dangerous behavior and stereotyped motor behavior discussed previously, many of the peculiar speech patterns observed among persons with autism and schizophrenia may be maintained by sensory consequences (i.e., the auditory input may be self-reinforcing) and will therefore be unaffected by the removal of social stimuli (i.e., planned ignoring).

Differential Reinforcement Procedures

A plethora of studies have demonstrated the successful treatment of peculiar speech patterns using variations of differential reinforcement procedures. Among persons with autism, differential reinforcement procedures have effectively reduced stereotyped vocalizations (e.g., Haring, Breen, Pitts-Conway, & Gaylord-Ross, 1986), echolalia (e.g., McMorrow & Foxx, 1986; McMorrow, Foxx, Faw, & Bittle, 1987; Risley & Wolf, 1967; Wolf et al., 1964), and bizarre speech (e.g., Stephens, Matson, Westmoreland, & Kulpa, 1981; Varni, Russo, & Cataldo, 1978). Similarly, differential reinforcement procedures have been demonstrated to reduce hallucinatory behavior (e.g., Rutner & Bugle, 1969) and delusional speech (e.g., Ayllon & Michael, 1959; Kennedy, 1964; Liberman, Teigen, Patterson, & Baker, 1973; Patterson & Teigen, 1973; Rickard, Dignam, & Horner, 1960; Rickard & Dinoff, 1962; Wincze, Leitenberg, & Agras, 1972) among persons with chronic schizophrenia. In one study, Anderson and Alpert (1974) found that a DRI procedure (i.e., reinforcing work efficiency) was more effective in reducing reports of visual hallucinations by a 26-year-old male than a self-administered contingent electric shock program.

Despite the initial success of such programs to reduce peculiar speech patterns, a failure of these results to generalize to new situations over time has been an often-cited problem. For example, Wincze and colleagues (Wincze et al., 1972) found that although delusional verbal behavior was significantly reduced through their program, independent psychiatrists were unable to detect changes in the subjects' delusional speech. Few studies have successfully demonstrated long-term generalized reductions in peculiar speech patterns with differential reinforcement procedures.

Contingent Negative Consequences

In contrast to the literature on dangerous behavior, relatively few studies have investigated the effectiveness of contingent negative consequences on peculiar speech. One study used a time-out procedure (Haynes & Geddy, 1973) to reduce hallucinatory behavior. In addition, several studies have demonstrated reductions in hallucinatory behavior among persons with chronic schizophrenia through the use of self-administered shock (e.g., Alford & Turner, 1976; Bucher & Fabricatore, 1970; Turner, Hersen, & Bellack, 1977). In one of the few experiments using a group design to investigate aberrant behavior, Weingaertner (1971) studied the hallucinations of 45 males with chronic schizophrenia. One group was given a shock device and was asked to administer shocks to themselves if they experienced hallucinations. A second group was given the same instructions; however, their device did not deliver shocks. Finally, a third group acted as a control. In general, all three groups reported reduced hallucinations, with the experimental group and the placebo group demonstrating the most improvement. These results suggest that the contingent electric shock was not necessary for the observed reductions in hallucinations and that social influences may have been involved.

Only one study was found that employed a contingent negative consequence for echolalia speech. Goren, Romanczyk, and Harris (1977) evaluated the use of a verbal reprimand ("No") and holding the subject's head to the side for 10 s on the echolalic responding of two autistic children. They found that, in general, echolalic responses were reduced for both subjects but that punishment had a generalized suppressive effect on the appropriate and inappropriate speech of the second subject. These results suggest that contingent negative consequences may not be an appropriate treatment approach for echolalia.

Prescriptive Interventions

Extinction

There have been relatively few studies of extinction in particular and prescriptive treatments in general for peculiar speech patterns. One early study of peculiar speech among persons with schizophrenia demonstrated the effectiveness of extinction (Ayllon & Haughton, 1964). The subjects in this study were three women who all had extensive histories of psychiatric hospitalizations and who engaged in a variety of peculiar speech patterns including delusional talking (e.g., "I'm the queen") and unsubstantiated somatic complaints (e.g., "I can't hear"). The authors found that listening, paying attention to, and showing interest in these behaviors substantially increased their frequency, although ignoring them (extinction) resulted in almost complete suppression. Thus, the investigators demonstrated that these peculiar speech patterns may have been maintained by their social consequences (i.e., attention from staff) and by removing this attention these presumably psychotic speech patterns could be reduced.

In a second study of extinction, Aiken and Salzberg (1984) used a sensory extinction procedure on the stereotyped sounds produced by two individuals with autism. These researchers hypothesized that the peculiar and disruptive vocalizations were being maintained by their auditory feedback, and therefore they employed noncontingent white noise in an attempt to mask this feedback. They found that the stereotyped sounds exhibited by the two individuals were substantially reduced with the introduction of white noise when, presumably, the vocalizations no longer provided reinforcing auditory input.

The preceding two studies illustrate several important points. First, just as has been demonstrated with dangerous behavior and stereotyped motor behavior, the peculiar speech patterns of different individuals may serve different functions. Thus, peculiar speech can serve both social (e.g., social attention) and nonsocial (e.g., sensory) functions within and between individuals. Second, again as we have observed previously, depending on the function of the particular behavior, different treatments may be effective for different individuals. Ignoring was an effective treatment for the attention-getting delusional talking exhibited by the subjects in Ayllon and Haughton (1964). However, this procedure (i.e., removing attention) would be predictably ineffective as a treatment for the sensory-maintained stereotyped sounds observed in the subjects in Aiken and Salzberg (1984).

Stimulus Control Procedures

A recent study examined the efficacy of one stimulus control procedure on the stereotyped vocalizations of persons with chronic schizophrenia. Wong and colleagues (1987) conceptualized the high-rate mumbling and self-talk exhibited by two males as being maintained by their sensory consequences. The authors observed that these stereotyped vocalizations were substantially reduced by introducing recreational activities (e.g., reading, working with leather), and they hypothesized that these activities competed with the self-reinforcing nature of the vocalizations. Other studies have observed substantial reductions in hallucinatory and delusional speech by engaging subjects in social conversations (e.g., Alford, Fleece, & Rothblum, 1982; Turner et al., 1977) and by providing access to a television or radio (Magen, 1983).

Although some success has been observed using stimulus-control procedures to reduce the peculiar speech of persons with chronic schizophrenia, no comparable literature exists for persons exhibiting autism. A number of avenues of research on the peculiar speech patterns of individuals with autism seem to be worthy of investigation. For example, a replication of the type of intervention used by Wong et al. (1987) may be effective with the type of sensory-maintained vocalizations observed in the subjects in the study by Aiken and Salzberg (1984). Also, other investigators have observed that behaviors such as echolalia and psychotic speech can serve social functions such as escape from unpleasant situations (e.g., Charlop, 1986; Durand & Crimmins, 1987; Goren et al., 1977). This suggests that such stimulus changes as errorless learning procedures and intertrial-interval manipulations may reduce these peculiar speech patterns in task-related situations, just as they have with dangerous behavior (e.g., Weeks & Gaylord-Ross, 1981; Winterling et al., 1987).

Teaching Functionally Equivalent Behaviors

Durand and Crimmins (1987) applied the logic of teaching functionally equivalent behaviors, effectively applied with dangerous and stereotyped behavior, to the treatment of psychotic speech. They found that the peculiar speech (phrases such as "parachute now" and "fried eggs on your head") of one male with autism appeared to be maintained by its ability to remove him from unpleasant situations. Therefore, he was taught to say "Help me" when faced with a difficult situation, in an effort to reduce the unpleasantness of such things as academic tasks. Teaching him this functionally equivalent response (i.e., saying "Help me," which elicited trainer prompts that, in turn, presumably reduced the aversiveness of the training situation) resulted in significant reductions in psychotic speech at implementation and at a 6-month follow-up. Thus, this socially mediated peculiar speech pattern was effectively treated by teaching an alternative assistance-seeking response. Similar results have been observed with echolalic speech among persons with autism (e.g., Carr, Schreibman, & Lovaas, 1975; Schreibman & Carr, 1978). No equivalent research has been conducted on the hallucinatory or delusional speech of persons with chronic schizophrenia, although social functions have been hypothesized to play a part in the maintenance of these responses as well (Layng & Andronis, 1984).

SUMMARY AND CONCLUSIONS

A surprising degree of consistency was observed in this review of treatment research, across both diagnostic category and behavioral topography. In general, most of the behavioral treatments evaluated have been successful in initially reducing aberrant behavior among persons with autism and chronic schizophrenia. The nonprescriptive approach, including differential reinforcement procedures and contingent negative consequences, has repeatedly been demonstrated to produce timely reductions in the frequency of problematic behavior. However, two caveats are in order. First, planned ignoring, when used without a prior assessment of a behavior's function, appears to be an inconsistent and relatively ineffective treatment procedure for most forms of problem behavior. And second, evidence was presented that may argue against the use of contingent negative consequences with stereotyped motor behavior and peculiar speech.

Research using a prescriptive approach to treatment (which has received increased empirical support in recent years) has documented reductions in aberrant behavior comparable to those observed with differential reinforcement procedures and contingent negative consequences. A growing number of studies using extinction, stimulus-control procedures, and the teaching of functionally equivalent behaviors have demonstrated their successful application for the treatment of dangerous behavior and stereotyped motor behavior. Far fewer studies have applied these treatments to peculiar speech patterns, and therefore, conclusions about the effectiveness of prescriptive treatments with these behaviors await convincing demonstration. The use of prescriptive treatment to reduce peculiar speech is an area for future investigation.

Previous reviews of the operant treatment literature have emphasized the effectiveness of nonprescriptive approaches in reducing aberrant behavior observed among persons with autism and chronic schizophrenia (e.g., Favell et al., 1982; LaGrow & Repp, 1984; Paul & Lentz, 1977). More recently, there has been an increased emphasis by some researchers on including consideration of a behavior's function in the design of treatments, and the present review appears to validate this prescriptive approach as a viable alternative to nonprescriptive interventions. Both approaches to the treatment of aberrant behavior appear to result in clinically significant improvements that are unmatched by any documented nonbehavioral attempts at treatment. It is important to note, however, that it would be premature for workers using behavioral treatments with problematic behavior to be too self-congratulatory. A number of critical issues remain unresolved in this field, precluding conclusions that are overly optimistic for the ultimate outcome of persons who exhibit aberrant behavior.

CRITICAL ISSUES
The Technology of Assessment

A major obstacle to the routine inclusion of a functional analysis prior to treatment design is our relatively unsophisticated assessment technology. Despite routine and frequent admonitions by behavior analysts to incorporate the results of functional analyses in treatment decisions (e.g., Ferster, 1965; Kanfer & Saslow, 1969; Skinner, 1953; Sulzer-Azaroff & Mayer, 1977), there has been relatively little research or specific instruction to guide clinicians in performing these assessments.

Most often, clinicians, educators, and others are advised to observe clients and list the antecedents and consequences of the behavior of interest (e.g., Bijou, Peterson, & Ault, 1968). The problem with this approach is that it provides few guidelines to the observer as to which of the myriad of stimuli that serve as antecedents and consequences are important. More specific guidelines are available in recent work with analogue assessments (e.g., Carr & Durand, 1985b; Durand & Carr, 1987b; Iwata, Dorsey, Slifer, Bauman, & Richman, 1982). Finally, rating scales are being developed that may serve as an alternative or adjunct to more formal functional analyses (e.g., Durand & Crimmins, 1988).

It is imperative that we provide explicit guidelines for clinicians and other service providers who are concerned with conducting functional analyses of problematic behavior. Only then will we see a general acceptance of this crucial aspect of treatment design by those who are responsible for the daily treatment of persons exhibiting aberrant behavior. Until our assessment technology advances beyond its current state, we will continue to see trial-and-error implementation of various negative consequences as the predominant treatment strategy for aberrant behavior.

The Contexts of Treatment

Seldom discussed in the treatment literature are the implications of the contexts in which these interventions are applied. For example, does the successful outcome of a treatment depend, in part, on *where* the intervention is conducted? Are some treatments more successful when carried out in segregated, institutional settings, others more successful in integrated, community-based settings? This particular example is and will continue to be a critical question, given the increasing numbers of individuals who are being placed in small homelike settings in their community. The majority of the treatment research conducted to date has been carried out in large institutional environments (Guess et al., 1987) and thus may have limited applicability for persons living in noninstitutional settings.

Using contingent negative consequences as one example, the implementation of procedures such as overcorrection, water sprays, and physical restraint are commonplace in many large facilities. However, these types of interactions (e.g., holding a person on the floor or moving a person's arms over the head and to the side) are rarely observed in the community. And as we have frequently observed, many staff people are reluctant to carry out such programs when they are outside treatment facilities. Therefore, some interventions, because of their limited acceptability, may not be practical in some settings.

In contrast, attempts to teach and reinforce behavior that is incompatible with aberrant behavior may be more difficult in institutional settings. Whether because of size or because of treatment philosophy, it has been our experience (along with that of others) that institutional settings often discourage appropriate behavior among residents (e.g., Durand & Kishi, 1987; Paul & Lentz, 1977). Using nonaversive intervention strategies may be more successful in community settings, where appropriate behaviors are more likely to be noticed and encouraged through natural communities of reinforcement (Stokes & Baer, 1977).

A related issue has to do with the political contexts in which treatment occurs. For example, at the time of this review, a major controversy over the use of some of the more aversive negative consequences (e.g., contingent electric shock) with persons with severe developmental disabilities resurfaced within the professional community (for a discussion of these issues see, Axelrod, 1987; Bailey, 1987; Durand, 1987; Snell, 1987). It is clear that the use of such treatments with persons who cannot provide informed consent is highly controversial, and clinicians must be aware of all aspects of this issue and weigh them prior to recommending interventions using contingent negative consequences.

Evaluating Outcomes

The final issue confronting those who are involved in the treatment of aberrant behavior is evaluation. The question here is not *whether* outcomes of treatment should be evaluated (most responsible clinicians regard this as an essential aspect of treatment) but *how* outcomes should be evaluated (Evans & Meyer, 1987). Several aspects of evaluation are discussed below, including design and measurement issues and criteria for evaluating success.

Design and Measurement

The predominant method of evaluating research on the treatment of aberrant behavior has been single-subject methodology. The strengths of this approach include the ability to study the nature of the intervention process and potential outcomes. However, it is difficult to make general statements about the effectiveness of various intervention strategies without studies using larger numbers of subjects. Despite the fact that this criticism has been made before (e.g., Lovaas, 1982), few group comparison studies exist. This lack of larger-sample studies may be because of the relative rarity of these disorders among persons in a particular geographic area and/or because of the clinical complexities involved with treating a large number of persons with aberrant behavior at the same time. Group comparisons may not be feasible outside multisite collaborative studies.

One suggested alternative would be for scientist-practitioners to conduct clinical replication series (Barlow, Hayes, & Nelson, 1984). A clinical replication involves the use of a specific treatment or treatment package with a relatively large number of clients exhibiting common behavioral problems. During this process, "the practitioner observes and records successes and failures, analyzing, the reasons for these individual variations (p. 58)." Such a strategy incorporates the strengths of single-subject design and allows for empirical generalizations about our treatments.

In addition to using single-subject designs, researchers in this area almost exclusively rely on individually developed dependent variables. Thus, observational measures of idiosyncratically defined behaviors (e.g., aggression defined as hitting, slapping, or kicking another person) are developed for each study and used to assess treatment effectiveness. Idiosyncratic definitions of aberrant behavior can be useful in monitoring the effects of treatment on a particular individual; however, using these measures limits comparisons across subjects and studies. Investigators using idiosyncratic definitions are often observing different behaviors, occurring at different degrees of intensity. Including data from standardized measures such as the Maladaptive Behavior Subscale of the Vineland Adaptive Behavior Scale (Sparrow, Balla, & Cicchetti, 1984), in addition to behavioral definitions, would provide information about aberrant behavior among similar populations and would facilitate comparisons across studies.

Criteria for Evaluating Success

As we have discussed above, many of the behavioral interventions used to treat aberrant behavior have been demonstrated to reduce these problematic responses. However, a critical assessment of the overall impact of these interventions on the lives of our clients leads us to qualify our enthusiasm. It can almost be said that "everything works, and nothing works" when it comes to treating aberrant behavior. Again, most of the treatments reviewed were generally successful in *initially* reducing these behaviors. Yet to date there has not been a large-scale demonstration that any treatment strategy can reliably reduce aberrant behavior for prolonged periods of time (Foxx & Livesay, 1984; Paul & Lentz, 1977).

The value of the prescriptive approach to treatment (particularly teaching functionally equivalent behavior) may lie in its ability to facilitate generalization and maintenance of treatment gains. The goal of teaching functionally equivalent behaviors, for example, is to provide an individual with behaviors (e.g., asking for favorite tangibles) that will continue to be reinforced in a variety of settings, with a variety of persons, and over time. Successful generalization and maintenance of such responses should, in turn, assure generalization and maintenance of reductions in aberrant behavior. Our technology for teaching adaptive responses that generalize and maintain over time is quite advanced when compared to our behavior reduction technology (Stokes & Baer, 1977) and should allow us to provide more effective interventions.

In conclusion, we would like to echo the sentiments articulated in the preface of a book by Cohen and Donnellan (1987): "Be skeptical about ideology and about any practitioner's enthusiastic claims for 'remarkable success' " (p. xviii). To this we would also add that the success of the field is attributable, in part, to its optimism. There continue to be clinicians and researchers who are indefatigable in their efforts to develop successful interventions for aberrant behavior. This crucial area in the fields of autism and chronic schizophrenia will continue to need enthusiastic and idealistic individuals to advance our knowledge and our ability to provide more independent lives for our clients. It is our hope that workers in this field will not become discouraged by our relative lack of success but will be motivated by this challenge.

REFERENCES

Aiken, J. M., & Salzberg, C. L. (1984). The effects of a sensory extinction procedure on stereotypic sounds of two autistic children. *Journal of Autism and Developmental Disorders, 14,* 291–299.

Alford, G. S., Fleece, L., & Rothblum, E. (1982). Hallucinatory-delusional verbalizations: Modification in a chronic schizophrenic by self-control and cognitive restructuring. *Behavior Modification, 6,* 421–435.

Alford, G. S., & Turner, S. M. (1976). Stimulus interference and conditioned inhibition of auditory hallucinations. *Journal of Behavior Therapy and Experimental Psychiatry, 7,* 155–160.

American Psychiatric Association (1980). *Diagnostic and statistical manual of mental disorders* (3rd ed.). Washington, DC: Author.

American Psychiatric Association (1987). *Diagnostic and statistical manual of mental disorders* $1(3rd ed., rev.). Washington, DC: Author.

Anderson, L. T., & Alpert, M. (1974). Operant analysis of hallucinatory frequency in a hospitalized schizophrenic. Journal of Behavior Therapy and Experimental Psychiatry, 5, 13–18.

Anderson, L., Dancis, J., & Alpert, M. (1978). Behavioral contingencies and self-mutilation in Lesch-Nyhan disease. *Journal of Consulting and Clinical Psychology, 46,* 529–536.

Arthur, G., Ellsworth, R. B., & Kroeker, D. (1968). Readmission of released mental patients: A research study. *Social Work, 13,* 78–84.

Axelrod, S. (1987). Doing it without arrows [Review of *Alternatives to punishment: Solving behavior problems with non-aversive strategies*]. *The Behavior Analyst, 10,* 243–251.

Ayllon, T., & Haughton, E. (1964). Modification of symptomatic verbal behavior of mental patients. *Behaviour Research and Therapy, 2,* 87–97.

Ayllon, T., & Michael, J. (1959). The psychiatric nurse as a behavioral engineer. *Journal of the Experimental Analysis of Behavior, 2,* 323–334.

Azrin, N. H., Besalel, V. A., & Wisotzek, I. E. (1982). Treatment of self-injury by a reinforcement plus interruption procedure. *Analysis and Intervention in Developmental Disabilities, 2,* 105–113.

Azrin, N. H., Kaplan, S. J., & Foxx, R. M. (1973). Autism reversal: Eliminating stereotypic self-stimulation of retarded individuals. *American Journal of Mental Deficiency, 78,* 241–248.

Bachman, J. E., & Fuqua, W. (1983). Management of inappropriate behaviors of trainable mentally impaired students using antecedent exercise. *Journal of Applied Behavior Analysis, 16,* 477–484.

Baer, D. M. (1981). The imposition of structure on behavior and the demolition of behavioral structures. In D. J. Bernstein (Ed.), *Response struc-*

ture and organization: 1981 Nebraska Symposium on Motivation (pp. 217–254). Lincoln, NE: University of Nebraska Press.

Bailey, J. S. (1987). Misguided alternatives [Review of *Alternatives to punishment: Solving behavior problems with non-aversive strategies*]. *Contemporary Psychology, 32,* 571–572.

Barlow, D. H., Hayes, S. C., & Nelson, R. O. (1984). *The scientist practitioner.* New York: Pergamon Press.

Barrett, R. P., Matson, J. L., Shapiro, E. S., & Ollendick, T. H. (1981). A comparison of punishment and DRO procedures for treating stereotypic behavior of mentally retarded children. *Applied Research in Mental Retardation, 2,* 247–256.

Barton, L. E., Brulle, A. R., & Repp, A. C. (1986). Maintenance of therapeutic change by momentary DRO. *Journal of Applied Behavior Analysis, 19,* 277–282.

Baumeister, A. A., & Forehand, R. (1970). Social facilitation of body rocking in severely retarded patients. *Journal of Clinical Psychology, 26,* 303–305.

Baumeister, A. A., & Forehand, R. (1971). Effects of extinction of an instrumental response on stereotyped body rocking in severe retardates. *Psychological Record, 21,* 235–240.

Baumeister, A. A., & Forehand, R. (1972). Effects of contingent shock and verbal command on body rocking of retardates. *Journal of Clinical Psychology, 28,* 586–590.

Baumeister, A. A., & Forehand, R. (1973). Stereotyped acts. In N. R. Ellis (Ed.), *International review of research in mental retardation* (Vol. 6, pp. 55–96). New York: Academic Press.

Beckwith, B. E., Couk, D. I., & Schumacher, K. (1986). Failure of naloxone to reduce self-injurious behavior in two developmentally disabled females. *Applied Research in Mental Retardation, 7,* 183–188.

Bellack, A. S. (1986). Schizophrenia: Behavior therapy's forgotten child. *Behavior Therapy, 17,* 199–214.

Berkson, G. (1983). Repetitive stereotyped behaviors. *American Journal of Mental Deficiency, 88,* 239–246.

Berkson, G., & Mason, W. (1963). Stereotyped movements of mental defectives: III. Situation effects. *American Journal of Mental Deficiency, 68,* 409–412.

Bijou, S. W., Peterson, R. F., & Ault, M. H. (1968). A method to integrate descriptive and experimental field studies at the level of data and empirical concepts. *Journal of Applied Behavior Analysis, 1,* 175–191.

Bostow, D. E., & Bailey, J. B. (1969). Modifications of severe disruptive and aggressive behavior using brief timeout and reinforcement procedures. *Journal of Applied Behavior Analysis, 2,* 31–37.

Brawley, E. R., Harris, R. R., Allen, K. E., Fleming, R. S., & Peterson, R. F. (1969). Behavior modification of an autistic child. *Behavioral Science*, 14, 87–97.

Bucher, B., & Fabricatore, J. (1970). Use of patient-administered shock to suppress hallucinations. *Behavior Therapy*, 1, 382–385.

Carr, E. G. (1977). The motivation of self-injurious behavior: A review of some hypotheses. *Psychological Bulletin*, 84, 800–816.

Carr, E. G., & Durand, V. M. (1985a). Reducing behavior problems through functional communication training. *Journal of Applied Behavior Analysis*, 18, 111–126.

Carr, E. G., & Durand, V. M. (1985b). The social-communicative basis of severe behavior problems in children. In S. Reiss & R. R. Bootzin (Eds.), *Theoretical issues in behavior therapy* (pp. 219–254). New York: Academic Press.

Carr, E. G., & Lovaas, O. I. (1983). Contingent electric shock as a treatment for severe behavior problems. In S. Axelrod & J. Apsche (Eds.), *The effects of punishment on human behavior* (pp. 221–245). New York: Academic Press.

Carr, E. G., & Newsom, C. D. (1985). Demand-related tantrums: Conceptualization and treatment. *Behavior Modification*, 9, 403–426.

Carr, E. G., Newsom, C. D., & Binkoff, J. A. (1980). Escape as a factor in the aggressive behavior of two retarded children. *Journal of Applied Behavior Analysis*, 13, 101–117.

Carr, E. G., Schreibman, L., & Lovaas, O. I. (1975). Control of echolalic speech in psychotic children. *Journal of Abnormal Child Psychology*, 3, 331–351.

Carroccio, D. F., Latham, S., & Carroccio, B. B. (1976). Rate-contingent guitar rental to decelerate stereotyped head/face-touching of an adult male psychiatric patient. *Behavior Therapy*, 7, 104–109.

Cavalier, A. R., & Ferretti, R. P. (1980). Stereotyped behavior, alternative behavior and collateral effects: A comparison of four intervention procedures. *Journal of Mental Deficiency Research*, 24, 219.

Cayner, J. J., & Kiland, J. R. (1974). Use of brief time out with three schizophrenic patients. *Journal of Behavior Therapy and Experimental Psychiatry*, 5, 141–145.

Charlop, M. H. (1986). Setting effects on the occurrence of autistic children's immediate echolalia. *Journal of Autism and Developmental Disorders*, 16, 473–483.

Chock, P. N., & Glahn, T. J. (1983). Learning and self-stimulation in mute and echolalic autistic children. *Journal of Autism and Developmental Disorders*, 13, 365–381.

Cohen, D. J., & Donnellan, A. M. (1987). *Handbook of autism and pervasive developmental disorders*. New York: John Wiley.

Cohen, D. J., Paul, R., & Volkmar, F. R. (1987). Issues in the classification of pervasive developmental disorders and associated conditions. In D. J. Cohen, & A. M. Donnellan (Eds.), *Handbook of autism and pervasive developmental disorders* (pp. 20–40). New York: John Wiley.

Coleman, R. S., Whitman, T. L., & Johnson, M. R. (1979). Suppression of self-stimulatory behavior of a profoundly retarded boy across staff and settings: An assessment of situational generalization. *Behavior Therapy, 10,* 266–280.

Corte, H. E., Wolf, M. M., & Locke, B. J. (1971). A comparison of procedures for eliminating self-injurious behavior of retarded adolescents. *Journal of Applied Behavior Analysis, 4,* 201–213.

Cox, M. D., & Klinge, V. (1976). Treatment and management of a case of self-burning. *Behaviour Research and Therapy, 14,* 382–385.

Curran, J. P., Sutton, R. G., Faraone, S. V., & Guenette, S. (1985). Inpatient approaches. In M. Hersen & A. S. Bellack (Eds.), *Handbook of clinical behavior therapy with adults* (pp. 445–483). New York: Plenum Press.

Davenport, R. K., & Berkson, G. (1963). Stereotyped movements of mental defectives: II. Effects of novel objects. *American Journal of Mental Deficiency, 67,* 879–882.

Davis, A. E., Dinitz, S., & Pasamanick, B. (1972). The prevention of hospitalization in schizophrenia: Five years after an experimental program. *American Journal of Orthopsychiatry, 42,* 375–388.

Donnellan, A. M., Mirenda, P. L., Mesaros, R. A., & Fassbender, L. L. (1984). Analyzing the communicative functions of aberrant behavior. *Journal of the Association for Persons with Severe Handicaps, 9,* 201–212.

Dunlap, G., Dyer, K., & Koegel, R. L. (1983). Autistic self-stimulation and intertrial interval duration. *American Journal of Mental Deficiency, 88,* 194–202.

Durand, V. M. (1982). A behavioral/pharmacological intervention for the treatment of severe self-injurious behavior. *Journal of Autism and Developmental Disorders, 12,* 243–251.

Durand, V. M. (1984). *Attention-getting problem behavior: Analysis and intervention.* Unpublished doctoral dissertation. SUNY, Stony Brook, NY.

Durand, V. M. (1986). Self-injurious behavior as intentional communication. In K. D. Gadow (Ed.), Advances in learning and behavioral disabilities (Vol. 5, pp. 141–155). Greenwich, CT: JAI Press.

Durand, V. M. (1987). Look homeward angel: A call to return to our (functional) roots. *The Behavior Analyst, 10,* 299–302.

Durand, V. M., & Carr, E. G. (1985). Self-injurious behavior: Motivating conditions and guidelines for treatment. *School Psychology Review, 14,* 171–176.

Durand, V. M., & Carr, E. G. (1987a). Autism. In V. B. Van Hasselt, P. S. Strain, & M. Hersen (Eds), *Handbook of developmental and physical disabilities* (pp. 195–214). New York: Pergamon Press.

Durand, V. M., & Carr, E. G. (1987b). Social influences on "self-stimulatory" behavior: Analysis and treatment application. *Journal of Applied Behavior Analysis, 20,* 119–132.

Durand, V. M., & Crimmins, D. B. (1987). Assessment and treatment of psychotic speech in an autistic child. *Journal of Autism and Developmental Disorders, 17,* 17–28.

Durand, V. M., & Crimmins, D. B. (1988). Identifying the variables maintaining self-injurious behavior. *Journal of Autism and Developmental Disorders, 18,* 99–117.

Durand, V. M., & Kishi, G. (1987). Reducing severe behavior problems among persons with dual sensory impairments: An evaluation of a technical assistance model. *Journal of the Association for Persons with Severe Handicaps, 12,* 2–10.

Eason, L. J., White, M. J., & Newsom, C. (1982). Generalized reduction of self-stimulatory behavior: An effect of teaching appropriate play to autistic children. *Analysis and Intervention in Developmental Disabilities, 2,* 157–169.

Epstein, L., Taubman, M. T., & Lovaas, O. I. (1985). Changes in self-stimulatory behavior with treatment. *Journal of Abnormal Child Psychology, 13,* 281–294.

Evans, I. M., & Meyer, L. H. (1985). *An educative approach to behavior problems.* Baltimore: Paul H. Brookes.

Evans, I. M., & Meyer, L. H. (1987). Moving to educational validity: A reply to Test, Spooner, and Cooke. *Journal of the Association for Persons with Severe Handicaps, 12,* 103–106.

Favell, J. E. (1973). Reduction of stereotypes by reinforcement of toy play. *Mental Retardation, 11,* 21–23.

Favell, J. E., McGimsey, J. F., & Jones, M. L. (1978). The use of physical restraint in the treatment of self-injury and as positive reinforcement. *Journal of Applied Behavior Analysis, 11,* 225–241.

Favell, J. E., McGimsey, J. F., & Schell, R. M. (1982). Treatment of self-injury by providing alternate sensory activities. *Analysis and Intervention in Developmental Disabilities, 2,* 83–104.

Ferster, C. B. (1961). Positive reinforcement and behavioral deficits of autistic children. *Child Development, 32,* 437–456.

Ferster, C. B. (1965). Classification of behavioral pathology. In L. Krasner & L. P. Ullmann (Eds.), *Research in behavior modification* (pp. 6–26). New York: Holt, Rinehart, & Winston.

Foxx, R. M., & Azrin, N. H. (1973). The elimination of autistic self-stimulatory behavior by overcorrection. *Journal of Applied Behavior Analysis, 6*, 1–14.

Foxx, R. M., & Livesay, J. (1984). Maintenance of response suppression following overcorrection: A 10-year retrospective examination of eight cases. *Analysis and Intervention in Developmental Disabilities, 4*, 65–79.

Foxx, R. M., McMorrow, M. J., Bittle, R. G., & Bechtel, D. R. (1986). The successful treatment of a dually-diagnosed deaf man's aggression with a program that included contingent electric shock. *Behavior Therapy, 17*, 170–186.

Gardos, G., & Cole, J. O. (1976). Maintenance antipsychotic therapy: Is the cure worse than the disease? *American Journal of Psychiatry, 133*, 32–36.

Gaylord-Ross, R. (1980). A decision model for the treatment of aberrant behavior in applied settings. In W. Sailor, B. Wilcox, & L. Brown (Eds.), *Methods of instruction for severely handicapped students* (pp. 135–157). Baltimore: Paul H. Brookes.

Gaylord-Ross, R., & Holvoet, J. F. (1985). *Strategies for educating students with severe handicaps*, Boston: Little, Brown.

Gillberg, C., & Steffenburg, S. (1987). Outcome and prognostic factors in infantile autism and similar conditions: A population-based study of 46 cases followed through puberty. *Journal of Autism and Developmental Disorders, 17*, 273–287.

Goren, E. R., Romanczyk, R. G., & Harris, S. L. (1977). A functional analysis of echolalic speech: The effects of antecedent and consequent events. *Behavior Modification, 1*, 481–498.

Gorman-Smith, D., & Matson, J. L. (1985). A review of treatment research for self-injurious and stereotyped responding. *Journal of Mental Deficiency Research, 29*, 295–308/

Guess, D., Helmstetter, E., Turnbull, H. R., III, & Knowlton, S. (1987). *Use of aversive procedures with persons who are disabled: A historical review and critical analysis* (TASH Monograph Series, No. 2). Seattle: TASH.

Guess, D., & Rutherford, G. (1967). Experimental attempts to reduce stereotyping among blind retardates. *American Journal of Mental Deficiency, 71*, 984–986.

Hall, R. V., & Hall, M. C. (1980). *How to use planned ignoring*. Lawrence, KS: H & H Enterprises.

Haring, T. G., Breen, C., Pitts-Conway, V., & Gaylord-Ross, R. (1986). Use of differential reinforcement of other behavior during dyadic instruction to reduce stereotyped behavior of autistic students. *American Journal of Mental Deficiency, 90*, 694–702.

Harris, S. L., & Wolchik, S. A. (1979). Suppression of self-stimulation: Three alternative strategies. *Journal of Applied Behavior Analysis, 12*, 185–198.

Hayes, R. P. (1987). Training for work. In D. J. Cohen & A. M. Donnellan (Eds.), *Handbook of autism and pervasive developmental disorders* (pp. 360–370). New York: John Wiley.

Haynes, S. T., & Geddy, P. (1973). Suppression of psychotic hallucinations through time-out. *Behavior Therapy, 4,* 123–127.

Hersen, M., & Bellack, A. S. (1978). Chronic psychiatric patients: Individual behavioral approaches. In M. Hersen & A. S. Bellack (Eds.), *Behavior therapy in the psychiatric setting* (pp. 128–168). Baltimore: Williams and Wilkins.

Hill, J., & Spreat, S. (1987). Staff injury rates associated with the implementation of contingent restraint. *Mental Retardation, 25,* 141–145.

Hogarty, G. E., Schooler, N. R., & Ulrich, R. (1979). Fluphenazine and social therapy in the aftercare of schizophrenic patients. *Archives of General Psychiatry, 36,* 1283–1294.

Holland, J. G. (1978). Behaviorism: Part of the problem or part of the solution? *Journal of Applied Behavior Analysis, 11,* 163–174.

Homer, A. L., & Peterson, L. (1980). Differential reinforcement of other behavior: A preferred response elimination procedure. *Behavior Therapy, 11,* 449–471.

Horner, R. D. (1980). The effects of an environmental "enrichment" program on the behavior of institutionalized profoundly retarded children. *Journal of Applied Behavior Analysis, 13,* 473–492.

Horner, R. H., & Budd, C. M. (1985). Acquisition of manual sign use: Collateral reduction of maladaptive behavior, and factors limiting generalization. *Education and Training of the Mentally Retarded, 20,* 39–47.

Hutt, C., & Hutt, S. (1965). Effects of environmental complexity on stereotyped behavior of children. *Animal Behavior, 13,* 1–4.

Iwata, B. A., Dorsey, M. F., Slifer, K. J., Bauman, K. E., & Richman, G. S. (1982). Toward a functional analysis of self-injury. *Analysis and Intervention in Developmental Disabilities, 2,* 3–20.

Johnson, W. L., Baumeister, A. A., Penland, M. J., & Inwald, C. (1982). Experimental analysis of self-injurious, stereotypic, and collateral behavior of retarded persons: Effects of overcorrection and reinforcement of alternative responding. *Analysis and Intervention in Developmental Disabilities, 2,* 41–66.

Jorgenson, J. (1971). Effect of contingent preferred music in reducing two stereotyped behaviors of a profoundly retarded child. *Journal of Music Therapy, 8,* 139–145.

Kanfer, F. H., & Saslow, G. (1969). Behavioral diagnosis. In C. M. Franks (Ed.), *Behavior therapy: Appraisal and status* (pp. 417–444). New York: McGraw-Hill.

Kanner, L., & Eisenberg, L. (1955). Notes on the follow-up studies of autistic children. In P. Hoch & J. Zubin (Eds.), *Psychopathology of childhood* (pp. 227–239). New York: Grune and Stratton.

Kazdin, A. E. (1978). *History of behavior modification: Experimental foundations of contemporary research*. Baltimore: University Park.

Kennedy, T. (1964). Treatment of chronic schizophrenia by behavior therapy. *Behaviour Research and Therapy, 2,* 1–6.

Kern, L., Koegel, R. L., Dyer, K., Blew, P. A., & Fenton, L. R. (1982). The effects of physical exercise on self-stimulation and appropriate responding in autistic children. *Journal of Autism and Developmental Disorders, 12,* 399–419.

Koegel, R. L., & Covert, A. (1972). The relationship of self-stimulation to learning in autistic children. *Journal of Applied Behavior Analysis, 5,* 381–387.

Koegel, R. L., Firestone, P. B., Kramme, K. W., & Dunlap, G. (1974). Increasing spontaneous play by suppressing self-stimulation in autistic children. *Journal of Applied Behavior Analysis, 7,* 521–528.

LaGrow, S. J., & Repp, A. C. (1984). Stereotypic responding: A review of intervention research. *American Journal of Mental Deficiency, 88,* 595–609.

Layng, T. V. J., & Andronis, P. T. (1984). Toward a functional analysis of delusional speech and hallucinatory behavior. *The Behavior Analyst, 7,* 139–156.

Liberman, R., Teigen, J., Patterson, R., & Baker, V. (1973). Reducing delusional speech in chronic paranoid schizophrenics. *Journal of Applied Behavior Analysis, 6,* 57–67.

Lindsley, O. R. (1963). Direct measurement and functional definition of vocal hallucinatory symptoms. *Journal of Nervous and Mental Disorders, 136,* 293–297.

Lovaas, O. I. (1982). Comments on self-destructive behaviors. *Analysis and Intervention in Developmental Disabilities, 2,* 115–124.

Lovaas, O. I., Freitag, G., Gold, V. J., & Kassoria, I. C. (1965). Experimental studies in childhood schizophrenia: Analysis of self-destructive behavior. *Journal of Experimental Child Psychology, 2,* 67–84.

Lovaas, O. I., Koegel, R., Simmons, J. Q., & Stevens, J. (1973). Some generalization and follow-up measures on autistic children in behavior therapy. *Journal of Applied Behavior Analysis, 6,* 131–166.

Lovaas, O. I., Litrownik, A., & Mann, R. (1971). Response latencies to auditory stimuli in autistic children engaged in self-stimulatory behavior. *Behaviour Research and Therapy, 9,* 39–49.

Lovaas, O. I., Newsom, C., & Hickman, C, (1987). Self-stimulatory behavior and perceptual reinforcement. *Journal of Applied Behavior Analysis, 20,* 45–68.

Lovaas, O. I., Schaeffer, B., & Simmons, J. Q. (1965). Experimental studies in childhood schizophrenia: Building social behavior by use of electric shock. *Journal of Experimental Research in Personality, 1,* 99–109.

Lovaas, O. I., Varni, J. W., Koegel, R. L., & Lorsch, N. (1977). Some observations on the nonextinguishability of children's speech. *Child Development, 48,* 1121–1127.

Luiselli, J. K., Reisman, J., Helfen, C. S., & Pemberton, B. W. (1976). Control of self-stimulatory behavior of an autistic child through brief physical restraint. *School Applications of Learning Theory, 9,* 3–13.

Maag, J. W., Wolchik, S. A., Rutherford, R. B., & Parks, B. T. (1986). Response covariation on self-stimulatory behaviors during sensory extinction procedures. *Journal of Autism and Developmental Disorders, 16,* 119–132.

Mace, F. C., Browder, D. M., & Lin, Y. (1987). Analysis of demand conditions associated with stereotypy. *Journal of Behavior Therapy and Experimental Psychiatry, 18,* 25–31.

Magen, J. (1983). Increasing external stimuli to ameliorate hallucinations. *American Journal of Psychiatry, 140,* 269–270.

Martin, J. A., & Iagulli, D. M. (1974). Elimination of middle-of-the-night tantrums in a blind, retarded child. *Behavior Therapy, 5,* 420–422.

Martin, P. L., & Foxx, R. M. (1973). Victim control of the aggression of an institutionalized retardate. *Journal of Behavior Therapy and Experimental Psychiatry, 4,* 161–165.

Marzillier, J. S., & Birchwood, M. J. (1981). Behavioral treatment of cognitive disorders. In L. Michelson, M. Hersen, & S. Turner (Eds.), *Future perspectives in behavior therapy* (pp. 131–159). New York: Plenum Press.

Matson, J. L., & Stephens, R. M. (1977). Overcorrection of aggressive behavior in a chronic psychiatric patient. *Behavior Modification, 1,* 559–564.

Mayhew, G. L., & Harris, F. C. (1978). Some negative side effects of a punishment procedure for stereotyped behavior. *Journal of Behavior Therapy and Experimental Psychiatry, 9,* 245–251.

McMorrow, M. J., & Foxx, R. M. (1986). Some direct and generalized effects of replacing an autistic man's echolalia with correct responses to questions. *Journal of Applied Behavior Analysis, 19,* 289–297.

McMorrow, M. J., Foxx, R. M., Faw, G. D., & Bittle, R. G. (1987). Cues-pause-point language training: Teaching echolalics functional use of their verbal labeling repertoires. *Journal of Applied Behavior Analysis, 20,* 11–22.

Measel, C. J., & Alfieri, P. A. (1976). Treatment of self-injurious behavior by a combination of reinforcement for incompatible behavior and overcorrection. *American Journal of Mental Deficiency, 81,* 147–153.

Meyer, L. H., & Evans, I. M. (1986). Modification of excess behavior: An adaptive and functional approach for educational and community contexts. In R. H. Horner, L. H. Meyer, & H. D. Fredericks (Eds.), *Education of learners with severe handicaps: Exemplary service strategies.* Baltimore: Paul H. Brookes.

Murphy, G. H., & Wilson, B. (1981). Long-term outcome of contingent shock treatment for self-injurious behavior. In P. Mittler (Ed.), *Frontiers of knowledge in mental retardation* (pp. 303–311). London: IASSMD.

Pasamanick, B., Scarpitti, F. R., & Dinitz, S. (1967). *Schizophrenics in the community.* New York: Appleton-Century-Crofts.

Patterson, R., & Teigen, J. (1973). Conditioning and post-hospitalization generalization of nondelusional responses in a chronic psychotic patient. *Journal of Applied Behavior Analysis, 6,* 65–70.

Paul, G. L., & Lentz, R. J. (1977). *Psychosocial treatment of chronic mental patients: Milieu versus social-training programs.* Cambridge. MA: Harvary University.

Paul, R. (1987). Natural history. In D. J. Cohen & A. M. Donnellan (Eds.), *Handbook of autism and pervasive developmental disorders* (pp. 121–130). New York: John Wiley.

Pickering, D., & Morgan, S. B. (1985). Parental ratings of treatments of self-injurious behavior. *Journal of Autism and Developmental Disorders, 15,* 303–314.

Ragain, R. D., & Anson, J. E. (1976). The control of self-mutilating behavior with positive reinforcement. *Mental Retardation, 14,* 22–25.

Rapoff, M. A., Altman, K., & Christophersen, E. R. (1980). Suppression of self-injurious behavior: Determining the least restrictive alternative. *Journal of Mental Deficiency Research, 24,* 37.

Repp, A. C., Barton, L. E., & Brulle, A. R. (1983). A comparison of two procedures for programming the differential reinforcement of other behaviors. *Journal of Applied Behavior Analysis, 16,* 435–445.

Repp, A. C., & Deitz, S. M. (1974). Reducing aggressive and self-injurious behavior in institutionalized retarded children through reinforcement of other behaviors. *Journal of Applied Behavior Analysis, 7,* 313–325.

Repp, A. C., Deitz, S. M., & Deitz, D. E. D. (1976). Reducing inappropriate behaviors in classrooms and in individual sessions through DRO schedules of reinforcement. *Mental Retardation, 14,* 11–15.

Repp, A. C., Deitz, S. M., & Speir, N. C. (1974). Reducing stereotypic responding of retarded persons by the differential reinforcement of other behavior. *American Journal of Mental Deficiency, 79,* 279–284.

Rickard, H. C., Dignam, P. J., & Horner, R. F. (1960). Verbal manipulation in a psychotherapeutic relationship. *Journal of Clinical Psychology, 16,* 364–367.

Rickard, H. C., & Dinoff, M. (1962). A follow-up note on "verbal manipulation in a psychotherapeutic relationship." *Psychological Reports, 11,* 506.

Rincover, A. (1978). Sensory extinction: A procedure for eliminating self-stimulatory behavior in psychotic children. *Journal of Abnormal Child Psychology, 6,* 299–310.

Rincover, A., Cook, R., Peoples, A., & Packard, D. (1979). Sensory extinction and sensory reinforcement principles for programming multiple adaptive behavior changes. *Journal of Applied Behavior Analysis, 12,* 221–233.

Rincover, A., & Devany, J. (1982). The application of sensory extinction procedures to self-injury. *Analysis and Intervention in Developmental Disabilities, 2,* 67–81.

Risley, T., & Wolf, M. (1967). Establishing functional speech in echolalic children. *Behaviour Research and Therapy, 5,* 73–88.

Rollings, J. P., Baumeister, A. A., & Baumeister, A. A. (1977). The use of overcorrection procedures to eliminate the stereotyped behaviors of retarded individuals: An analysis of collateral behaviors and generalization of suppressive effects. *Behavior Modification, 1,* 29–46.

Romanczyk, R. G., Gordon, W. C., Crimmins, D. B., Wenzel, A. M., & Kistner, J. A. (1980). Childhood psychosis and 24-hour rhythms: A behavioral and psychophysiological analysis. *Chronobiologia, 7,* 1–14.

Romanczyk, R. G., & Goren, E. R. (1975). Severe self-injurious behavior: The problem of clinical control. *Journal of Consulting and Clinical Psychology, 43,* 730–739.

Romanczyk, R. G., Kistner, J. A., & Plienis, A. (1982). Self-stimulatory and self-injurious behavior: Etiology and treatment. In J. J. Steffen & P. Karoly (Eds.), *Advances in child behavioral analysis and therapy: Autism and severe psychopathology* (pp. 189–254). Lexington, MA: Lexington Books.

Russo, D. C., Cataldo, M. F., & Cushing, P. J. (1981). Compliance training and behavioral covariation in the treatment of multiple behavior problems. *Journal of Applied Behavior Analysis, 14,* 209–222.

Rutner, I. T., & Bugle, C. (1969). An experimental procedure for the modification of psychotic behavior. *Journal of Consulting and Clinical Psychology, 33,* 651–653.

Rutter, M. (1978). Diagnosis and definition of childhood autism. *Journal of Autism and Childhood Schizophrenia, 8,* 139–161.

Rutter, M., & Garmezy, N. (1983). Developmental psychopathology. In E. M. Hetherington (Ed.), *Socialization, personality, and social development: Vol. 4. Mussen's handbook of child psychology* (4th ed., pp. 775–911). New York: Wiley.

Sanders, R., Smith, R. S., & Weinman, B. S. (1967). *Chronic psychosis and recovery*. San Francisco, CA: Jossey-Bass.

Scheerenberger, R. C. (1981). Deinstitutionalization: Trends and difficulties. In R. H. Bruininks, C. E. Meyers, B. B. Sigford, & K. C. Lakin (Eds.), *Deinstitutionalization and community adjustment of mentally retarded people* (pp. 3–13). (Monograph No. 4). Washington, DC: American Association on Mental Deficiency.

Schreibman, L., & Carr, E. G. (1978). Elimination of echolalic responding to questions through the training of a generalized verbal response. *Journal of Applied Behavior Analysis, 11,* 453–463.

Singh, N. N., & Millichamp, C. J. (1985). Pharmacological treatment of self-injurious behavior in mentally retarded persons. *Journal of Autism and Developmental Disorders, 15,* 257–267.

Singh, N. N., Watson, J. E., & Winton, A. S. W. (1987). Parents' acceptability ratings of alternative treatments for use with mentally retarded children. *Behavior Modification, 11,* 17–26.

Skinner, B. F. (1953). *Science and human behavior.* New York: Macmillan.

Smith, M. D. (1985). Managing the aggressive and self-injurious behavior of adults disabled by autism. *Journal of the Association for Persons with Severe Handicaps, 10,* 228–232.

Smith, M. D., & Coleman, D. (1986). Managing the behavior of adults with autism in the job setting. *Journal of Autism and Developmental Disorders, 16,* 145–154.

Snell, M. E. (1987). In response to Saul Axelrod's review of *Alternatives to punishment. The Behavior Analyst, 10,* 295–297.

Solnick, J. V., Rincover, A., & Peterson, C. R. (1977). Some determinants of the reinforcing and punishing effects of timeout. *Journal of Applied Behavior Analysis, 10,* 415–424.

Sparrow, S. S., Balla, D. A., & Cicchetti, D. V. (1984). *Vineland Adaptive Behavior Scales.* Circle Pines, MN: American Guidance Service.

Stephens, R. M., Matson, J. L., Westmoreland, T., & Kulpa, J. (1981). Modification of psychotic speech with mentally retarded patients. *Journal of Mental Deficiency Research, 25,* 187–197.

Stokes, T. F., & Baer, D. M. (1977). An implicit technology of generalization. *Journal of Applied Behavior Analysis, 10,* 349–367.

Sulzer-Azaroff, B., & Mayer, G. R. (1977). *Applying behavior analysis procedures with children and youth.* New York: Holt, Rinehart, & Winston.

Tate, B. G., & Baroff, G. S. (1966). Aversive control of self-injurious behavior in psychotic boy. *Behavior Research and Therapy, 4,* 281–287.

Tierney, I. R., McGuire, R. J., & Walton, H. J. (1979). Reduction of stereotyped body-rocking using variable time reinforcement: Practical and theoretical limitations. *Journal of Mental Deficiency Research, 23,* 175.

Touchette, P. E., MacDonald, R. F., & Langer, S. N. (1985). A scatter plot for identifying stimulus control of problem behavior. *Journal of Applied Behavior Analysis, 18,* 343–351.

Turner, S. M., Hersen, M., & Bellack, A. S. (1977). Effects of social disruption, stimulus interference and aversive conditioning on auditory hallucinations. *Behavior Modification, 1,* 249–258.

Varni, J. W., Russo, D. C., & Cataldo, M. F. (1978). Assessment and modification of delusional speech in an 11-year-old child: A comparative analysis of behavior therapy and stimulant drug effects. *Journal of Behavior Therapy and Experimental Psychiatry, 9,* 377–380.

Voeltz, L. M., Evans, I. M., Derer, K. R., & Hanashiro, R. (1983). Targeting excess behavior for change: A clinical decision model for selecting priority goals in educational contexts. *Child and Family Behavior Therapy, 5,* 17–35.

Vukelich, R., & Hake, D. F. (1971). Reduction of dangerously aggressive behavior in a severely retarded resident through a combination of positive reinforcement procedures. *Journal of Applied Behavior Analysis, 4,* 215–225.

Watters, R. G., & Watters, W. E. (1980). Decreasing self-stimulatory behavior with physical exercise in a group of autistic boys. *Journal of Autism and Developmental Disorders, 4,* 379–387.

Weeks, M., & Gaylord-Ross, R. (1981). Task difficulty and aberrant behavior in severely handicapped students. *Journal of Applied Behavior Analysis, 14,* 449–463.

Weingaertner, A. H. (1971). Self-administered aversive stimulation with hallucinatory hospitalized schizophrenics. *Journal of Consulting and Clinical Psychology, 36,* 422–429.

Wincze, J. P., Leitenberg, H., & Agras, W. S. (1972). The effects of token reinforcement and feedback on delusional verbal behavior of chronic paranoid schizophrenics. *Journal of Applied Behavior Analysis, 5,* 247–262.

Winterling, V., Dunlap, G., & O'Neill, R. E. (1987). The influence of task variation on the aberrant behaviors of autistic students. *Education and Treatment of Children, 10,* 105–119.

Winters, K. C., & Neale, J. M. (1983). Delusions and delusional thinking in psychotics: A review of the literature. *Clinical Psychology Review, 3,* 227–253.

Wolf, M. M., Risley, T. R., & Mees, H. (1964). Application of operant conditioning procedures to the behavior problems of an autistic child. *Behaviour Research and Therapy, 1,* 305–312.

Wong, S. E., Terranova, M. D., Bowen, L., Zarate, R., Massel, H. K., & Liberman, R. P. (1987). Providing independent recreational activities to reduce stereotyped vocalizations in chronic schizophrenics. *Journal of Applied Behavior Analysis, 20,* 77–81.

Zeiler, M. (1977). Schedules of reinforcement: The controlling variables. In W. K. Honig & J. E. R. Staddon (Eds.), *Handbook of operant behavior* (pp. 201–232). Englewood Cliffs, NJ: Prentice-Hall.

8

Social Learning Treatment for Chronic Schizophrenia and Autism

Kim T. Mueser and Alan S. Bellack

Schizophrenia and autism have a negative impact on a range of adaptive functioning, including the ability to care for oneself, obtaining and keeping employment, use of leisure time, and interpersonal relationships. Although the characteristic symptoms of schizophrenia—hallucinations, delusions, disturbances in affect (incongruent or flattened affect, anhedonia) and motor behavior (agitation, catatonia, stereotypes—fluctuate between exacerbations and remissions, impairments in social functioning are the hallmark of the illness. Modern diagnostic criteria for schizophrenia reflect the importance of social dysfunction among schizophrenics. For example, to meet the criteria for schizophrenia according to DSM-III-R (American Psychiatric Association, 1987), patients need not have any one specific symptom, yet evidence must be present of "deterioration from a previous level of functioning in such areas of work, of social relations, and self-care" (p. 189). Poor social competence in childhood may predate the onset of schizophrenic illness (Lewine, Watt, Prentky, & Fryer, 1980), and the attainment of social milestones in adolescence and early adulthood (e.g., sexual experience, independent employment) are important prognostic indicators of the outcome of schizophrenia (Phillips, 1968; Zigler & Glick, 1986).

Advances in the pharmacological treatment of schizophrenia have served to highlight the social problems of this population. Neuroleptic drugs have a potent effect on both the positive (delusions, hallucinations, bizarre behavior) and negative (withdrawal, psychomotor retardation, blunted affect) symptoms of schizophrenia (Goldberg, 1985; Meltzer, 1985). However, these medications cannot improve the social competence of patients who have never developed adequate social skills (as with autistic individuals) or who have lost use of their skills over years of disuse in unresponsive environments. Nor can they improve the impoverished quality of life experienced by most schizophrenic and autistic patients (Diamond, 1985; Lehman, 1983).

The widespread use of neuroleptic drugs for schizophrenic patients, both to treat acute symptomatology and to reduce the chances of relapse, has shifted the focus of treatment for most patients from long-term inpatient care to outpatient care. Despite the clinical efficacy of these medications, they can impose debilitating side effects (Johnson, 1985; Van Putten & May, 1978) and do not prevent relapse for all patients. Within 1 year following discharge from a psychiatric hospital, approximately 40% of all schizophrenic patients will have an exacerbation of their symptoms (Hogarty et al., 1979), and over 3 years up to 75% will have to return to the hospital (Talbott, 1981). The increase in patients' tenure in the community, coupled with severe interpersonal and functional deficits in life skills that are unaffected by medications, has led to poor community adjustment (Goldstrom & Manderscheid, 1981; Sylph, Ross, & Kedward, 1978) and to social rejection (Kirk & Therrien, 1975) of patients with varying degrees of residual symptomatology. Large numbers of schizophrenic and autistic patients in the community populate substandard living facilities with inadequate social supports or are homeless (Cordes, 1984), and their visible presence on the streets is viewed as stigmatizing to some communities. The increased visibility of socially deficient schizophrenic patients in the community and the reduced need for institutionalization has shifted the goals of treatment from isolation and containment to the active building of new repertoires of social skills.

Improving the social and living skills of schizophrenic patients promises not only to better their impoverished quality of life and acceptance in the community but may also facilitate their community survival and lower risk of symptom exacerbations. The social adjustment of patients is correlated with their level of symptoms (Casey, Tyrer, & Platt, 1985), indicating that adequate social functioning may reduce susceptibility to psychosis. Social adjustment has been repeatedly found to be a potent predictor of symptom exacerbation, rehospitalization, and long-term outcome (Linn, Klett, & Coffey, 1982; Phillips & Zigler, 1961; Presly, Grubb, & Semple, 1982; Strauss & Carpenter, 1974). The superior outcomes of socially competent schizophrenic persons may be the result, in part, of their ability to effectively manage noxious stressors such as life events and negative ambient emotion. Thus, modern skills-based treatments for schizophrenia strive to maximize community tenure and prevent symptom relapses by enhancing social functioning and lowering environmental stress.

STRESS-VULNERABILITY–COPING-SKILLS MODEL OF SCHIZOPHRENIA

Social skills interventions are guided by the stress-vulnerability–coping-skills model of schizophrenia (Zubin & Spring, 1977). According to this model, the emergence of schiophrenic symptoms results from the combined influences of psychobiological vulnerability and environmental stress. Vulnerability is thought to be determined largely by genetic and developmental factors, although it can also be influenced by drug abuse. Psychobiological vulnerability may be reflected by indices such as genetic loading (Gottesman, 1968), information-processing capacity (Nuechterlein & Dawson, 1984), autonomic reactivity (Dawson & Nuechterlein, 1984), and schizotypal personality. Stressors are environmental events or contingencies that impact negatively upon an individual, such as life events (Rabkin, 1980), negative ambient family emotion (Koenigsberg & Handley, 1986), or an unstructured, impoverished environment (Rosen, Sussman, Mueser, Lyons, & Davis, 1981; Wing & Brown, 1970; Wing & Freudenberg, 1961; Wong et al., 1985). The greater an individual's vulnerability, the less stress he needs to be exposed to for his schizophrenic symptoms to appear.

The impact of environmental stressors on biological vulnerability is mediated by a person's coping or social skills. Coping skills are those skills that enable an individual to obtain instrumental or socioemotional goals that maximize both the quantity and quality of time spent in the community. Such skills include the ability to perceive relevant social stimuli (e.g., facial expression) and situational parameters, to identify problems and generate and evaluate effective solutions, to use appropriate verbal and nonverbal behaviors during interpersonal encounters, and to apply basic self-care skills (e.g., personal hygiene, grooming). Coping skills can either minimize the negative effect of a stressor on the individual or enable the person to diminish or remove the source of the stress itself. In addition to the patient's coping skills, the social support of other people in the environment can mediate the effects of stress on vulnerability. The social support and social skills of significant others can diminish or remove sources of stress impinging on the patient, or facilitate the patient's own coping skills.

The implications of this model for the treatment of schizophrenia are depicted in Figure 8.1. Neuroleptic medications are assumed to lower psychobiological vulnerability directly, without affecting either the individual's coping skills or environmental stress. When someone's vulnerability is stable, increases in schizophrenic symptomatology are caused by the balance between coping skills and environmental stress. As the stress to which a patient is exposed increases, so does the likelihood that his schizophrenic symptoms will emerge or worsen. The main effect of social skills training is to improve coping skills and social support linkages, although some reduction in environmental stress may be expected. Conversely, behavioral family therapy focuses primarily on lowering environmental stress while also building the coping skills of the patient and his family members. The influences of vulnerability, stress, and coping skills combine to determine the multidimensional outcome of schizophrenia (Strauss & Carpenter, 1974, 1977): symptoms, time in the hospital, and social and vocational functioning. The present

TREATMENT

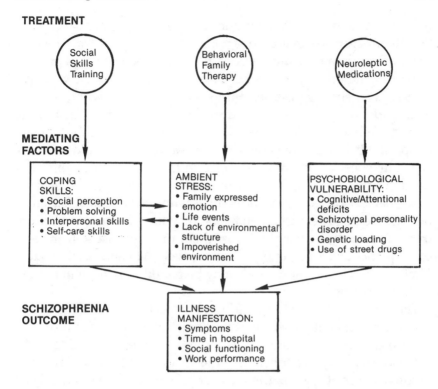

Figure 8.1 Treatment implications for the stress–vulnerability–coping-skills model of schizophrenia. Social skills training and behavioral family therapy impact on coping skills and ambient stress to improve the multidimensional outcome of schizophrenia. Neuroleptic medications reduce vulnerability to the illness.

chapter reviews recent research and clinical procedures for these two psychosocial treatment approaches: social skills training and behavioral family therapy.

SOCIAL SKILLS TRAINING
The Nature of Social Skill

The term *social skill* has been used very loosely in the behavioral literature, and there is no one uniform definition. However, there are several core parameters that seem to be widely accepted. First, as implied by the word *skill*, it is generally agreed that effective social functioning depends on a specific set of learned or learnable abilities. In our everyday interactions with others we tend to create somewhat overgeneralized impressions based on the overall pattern or impact of the other person's behavior. Thus, we may view people as assertive, shy, aggressive, humorous, and so on without being able to identify precisely what they do to merit that label. But the impact we have on each other depends on the form and intensity of specific behaviors, such as the way we make or avoid eye contact, our speech content, and voice inflection. Furthermore, it is assumed that the majority of these specific behaviors are learned or learnable. Consequently, individuals with social skills deficits may not have learned requisite behaviors, may have learned to perform them incorrectly, or may have lost them through disuse (e.g., as a consequence of a long period of social isolation, hospitalization, etc.). Similarly, unskilled individuals may be taught to behave in a more effective manner.

The second commonly agreed upon aspect of social skills is that they are situationally specific. Few, if any, behaviors are appropriate in all situations. There are explicit or implicit rules governing social behavior that vary as a function of the sex of the partners in an interaction, their relationship, the number of people involved, the focus of the interaction, the time and place of the interaction, and so on. For example, one may pat the buttocks of a spouse at home or a same-sex athlete during a competition but not of a co-worker of either sex. Jokes about death may be acceptable at a party but not at a funeral or with someone who has just lost a loved one. It should also be underscored that social rules vary substantially across cultures. In light of the situational variability of skilled behavior, it should not be surprising that no one is uniformly skillful or uniformly unskilled. All but the most severely impaired autistic patients are able to perform adequately in some situations.

Social Skill versus Social Competence

There has been considerable controversy in the literature about how broadly the term *social skills* should be defined (Curran, 1979; McFall, 1982). Some writers have used the term in reference to the overall level or quality of performance in social situations. From this perspective social skills training can be viewed as any intervention designed to improve social functioning. We prefer a narrower definition, in which social skill is distinguished from social competence. The former refers to a relatively specific set of abilities that contribute to effective performance in social situations. Social skills are necessary but not sufficient for effective performance. Social competence refers to the overall ability of the individual to achieve his or her goals in social interactions. Social competence is a function of a number of factors in addition to social skills. As indicated in Table 8.1, social performance can be affected by cognitive factors, affective states, environmental factos, and biological limitations. For example, schizophrenic persons with negative syndrome are avolitional: they have little motivation to engage in social interactions. Such patients tend to learn social skills when exposed to training but frequently fail to use the skills spontaneously in the environment. Many unassertive patients do not respond to assertion training because they cannot determine when they are being taken advantage of (and when to use the skills); either they do not adequately attend to the environment or they somehow fail to acknowledge mistreatment. Individuals with very low thresholds for anger and aggression sometimes do poorly in conventional skills training programs because they become enraged with

Table 8.1 Factors That Can Affect Social Performance

Social skill deficits

Cognitive factors
  Goals
  Expectancies
  Self-efficacy

Affective states
  Anxiety
  Depression
  Anger

Environmental factors
  Cultural mores
  Lack of reinforcement
  Lack of resources (e.g., money)
  Isolation

Biological factors
  Attentional impairments
  Negative symptoms
  Medication side effects

minimal provocation and thus do not have the control to apply more modulated forms of assertion. The distinction between social impairment based on skill deficits and impairment based on other factors has important implications for treatment. Social skills training can be expected to be effective in remediating skill deficiencies, but it may not improve social competence if nonskill factors play an important role in the impairment. With schizophrenic and autistic patients in particular it is important to consider the range of factors that may affect behavior and to integrate social skills training with a comprehensive intervention program.

Components of Social Skills

As indicated above, social skills consist of a set of specific behavioral components. The most important of these components are involved in the expression or communication of one's thoughts, feelings, and desires. Generally, the most critical parameter is speech content: the ability to put our ideas into words and communicate in intelligible sentences. Schizophrenic and autistic patients have particular difficulty in generating appropriate speech content. They have well-documented disorders in thinking that interfere with the organization and structure of their speech (Andreason, 1979; Hotchkiss & Harvey, 1986). But even when their thought pathology is controlled, they are difficult to understand because they do not supply adequate linkages between speech clauses (Harvey, 1983; Rutter, 1985). For example, they tend to intermingle references to personal concerns or remote topics without explaining the connection (Harrow & Miller, 1980). These patients also frequently have a paucity of material to talk about, as they are relatively isolated from society. They cannot share experiences from work or school, comment on current events, movies, and so on because they do not participate in these activities. In general, speech form and content are important targets for training.

Paralinguistic features refer to the manner in which the person speaks, including rate and pace of speech, voice tone and pitch, and volume. The "meaning" of a statement can be altered dramatically as a function of how it is spoken. A simple phrase such as "I love you" can be a statement of affection, a question, an annoyed affirmation, a joke, or a sarcastic retort. Schizophrenics often fail to provide proper inflection to their messages and seem especially poor at communicating affective tone.

A third category of expressive behavior is composed of nonverbal responses, including proxemics, kinesics, eye contact or gaze, and facial expression (Harper, Wiens, & Matarazzo, 1978). Proxemics refers to interpersonal distance: how near or far from each other people station themselves. Interpersonal distance is related to many important aspects of interactions, including dominance, intimacy, and level of formality. For example, moving away from a partner can be a sign of submission or fear, and formal interactions (e.g., business meetings) take place at greater distances than romantic or social interactions. Kinesics refers to the way we move our bodies during interactions and includes such things as head nods, hand gestures, and nervous or "autistic" movements (e.g., rubbing one's body or biting one's nails). Schizophrenics frequently seem ill at ease in social situations, as manifested by postural rigidity and/or nervous movements and gestures.

Eye contact or gaze pertains to the way in which we use our eyes during interactions. Our eyes have historically been thought to be "windows of the soul," implying that they contain a great deal of information about our feelings and thoughts. For example, assertion, dominance, anger, and affection are often associated with direct eye-to-eye gaze; lying, submissiveness, fear and boredom are associated with failure to maintain direct eye contact. Facial expression is generally thought to be the most important vehicle for communicating emotion. Subtle changes in the mouth, eyebrows, and facial muscles can communicate joy, anger, sadness, or confusion, without any verbalization whatsoever. Schizophrenic persons often are unable to maintain direct eye contact, and they frequently have a relatively wooden or unexpressive facial countenance. Consequently, both aspects of nonverbal behavior are important targets in social skills training programs.

Expressive behaviors account for only one side of social interactions: sending messages transmitted by the partner. Effective social performance requires that one attend to the cues emitted by the interpersonal partner and translate or decode them in the context of the situation (Morrison & Bellack, 1981). Liberman (1982) has referred to these two aspects of social behavior as receiving skills and processing skills, respectively. In light of their well-documented attentional impairments (Neuchterlein & Dawson, 1984), it is not surprising that schizophrenic individuals fail both to attend to critical social cues and to interpret cues accurately. They may also have neurological dysfunctions that impede their ability to perceive and/or process certain cues even when they are paying attention. For example, research suggests that they have marked impairments in the ability to identify affect from facial expressions, especially negative affect (Morrison & Bellack, 1987).

Assessment of Social Skills

In our experience the majority of schizophrenic and autistic patients can profit from social skills training. However, some patients have adequate skills when other symptoms of the disorder are in remission, whereas others seemingly do not respond well to the intervention. Moreover, there is considerable variation in the precise pattern of deficits manifested by those patients who are good candidates for skills training. Therefore, it is vital to conduct a careful assessment before assigning a patient to a skills program. We customarily organize our assessment around four questions, which are organized hierarchically in a decision tree. The questions seek progressively more specific information, ranging from the general applicability of skills training to the specific behaviors that should be targeted.

1. Does the patient have an interpersonal dysfunction? As indicated above, most schizophrenic persons doe have social impairments, but a significant minority are reasonably well skilled between episodes. Deficits seem to worsen with chronicity, and younger patients often retain more skills than do their older peers. The existence of an interpersonal impairment can be determined by a number of relatively general strategies. Interviews with the patient can provide information about his perceptions of how he relates with others, but many patients with marked impairments will deny (or be unaware of) any difficulties. The interview is often more useful as a source of observational data (e.g., how does the patient behave during the interaction). Interview with significant others and with staff members who know the patient are generally more informative. It is also helpful to observe the patient interacting with other patients in the program.

2. Is the dysfunction associated with a skill deficit? We have previously indicated that social competence can be affected by a variety of factors other than social skill and that skills training may not be appropriate for nonskill problems. Unfortunately, there is no definitive test to determine the nature or cause of social impairments. We can only provide a number of guidelines to help in drawing inferences. First, social skills are situationally specific, and people tend to manifest differential patterns of strengths and deficits across situations. Consequently, a global pattern of social dysfunction suggests that nonskill factors are involved. Second, in the absence of skills training, skills deficits should be relatively stable. Some improvement can be expected as the patient recovers from an acute episode, but there should not be marked shifts in overall social competence or in the pattern of deficits between episodes. A patient who exhibits adequate skills on an intermittent basis probably has the skills in her repertoire, and performance is affected by other factors (e.g., delusions).

Three nonskill factors that require special mention are negative symptoms, depression, and medication side effects. All three are quite common among schizophrenic patients and have the capacity to impair social functioning. They can decrease the overall level of motivation and behavioral output, produce an anergic countenance and blunted effect, and restrict bodily movements. Neuroleptics can also induce disconcerting movements. At this point it is unclear whether or not social skills training can be effective in patients with marked negative symptoms or depression. We believe the training can be useful, but it must be supplemented with effective pharmacotherapy and a systematic program to modify the patient's environment and reinforce use of the skills (e.g., a token economy). Conversely, skills training is unlikely to remediate medication side effects.

3. Under what circumstances does the dysfunction occur? Once it is determined that the patient has skill deficits, the situational context of the deficits must be determined. For example, chronic patients tend to be unassertive, but they have been found to be differentially assertive with males and females, strangers and acquaintances, and in the expression of positive and negative feelings (Eisler, Hersen, Miller, & Blanchard, 1975; Hersen, Bellack, & Turner, 1978). The liter-

ature on expressed emotion (Hooley, 1985) indicates that many schizophrenic persons have considerable difficulty in dealing with criticism and hostility from significant others, but it is not clear if they have difficulty responding to these stimuli from other people as well. In addition, these general tendencies are not true of all schizophrenic individuals. Thus, it is essential to tailor the training curriculum to the specific deficits of the patients involved and not apply the same content to all patients. The most useful strategies for determining appropriate training areas are interviews and observation (as discussed above in regard to question 1) and role-play tests, which will be discussed in the following section.

4. What is the specific nature of the patient's skill deficits? We have previously indicated that social skill consists of a variety of specific behavioral components. It should be apparent by now that not all patients with deficits in a specific area (e.g., assertion with relatives) will manifest precisely the same pattern of dysfunction. Some individuals might have adequate speech content but fail to provide adequate emphasis with paralinguistic and nonverbal components. Others might manifest the opposite pattern, and still others might have difficulties in a different subset of components. Consequently, it is necessary to determine exactly which behaviors to target in training.

The only valid and reliable way to assess specific skills is direct observation. An extensive discussion of the pros and cons of the various options for conducting observations is beyond the scope of this chapter (see Bellack, 1979, 1983). The majority of alternatives are either impractical in most settings or have questionable utility and validity for most behaviors of clinical relevance. Despite their shortcomings, we recommend role-play tests as a cost-effective strategy that is useful i most clinical and research settings (Bellack, Hersen, & Turner, 1978, 1979). Subjects generally perform more skillfully in role-play interactions than when faced with comparable situations in the natural environment, as role playing does not generate high levels of affect or provide real consequences. But role playing does provide a good indication of the individual's skill repertoire. If a patient can perform effectively in role play, one can assume that the behavior is in her repertoire, whether or not she can employ it effectively in the environment. Conversely, poor role-play performance probably indicates that she does not have the skill in her repertoire. Role playing has a number of other added benefits that make it quite useful: it is inexpensive, it can be easily modified to represent most relevant social situations, and the interactions can be recorded for subsequent evaluation of specific response components.

Skills Training Procedures

Social skills training is a highly structured intervention in which patients are taught to perform new behaviors. It is similar to programs for teaching motoric skills, such as playing a musical instrument or sport, in that it emphasizes demonstration and rehearsal rather than discussion and insight. Several aspects of the intervention make it especially suited for schizophrenic patients. It breaks down complex behaviors into small units and proceeds in a gradual, hierarchical fashion from easy to difficult behaviors. Progress is tailored to the needs and limitations of the individual, assuring success for all participants and avoiding the frustration that results from unrealistic demands and failure. There is an emphasis on extended practice and overlearning so that responses can be performed automatically, even in stressful circumstances or when cognition is impaired. Training also focuses on pragmatic skills that can enhance daily living, rather than particularly frightening issues or unreachable goals.

Format

Skills training in schizophrenia is generally conducted in a small-group format. The group setting is cost-efficient, allows patients to learn from other group members and practice new skills with them, and permits participants an opportunity to "relax" for brief periods within sessions when they are feeling too much pressure and/or are excessively distracted. The last factor is important for many patients who cannot tolerate the intensity of a 1-hr session.

In our experience the optimal group size is 6 to 10 patients. Larger groups present a number of problems that diminish the effectiveness of the program. First, it is essential that patients have ample opportunity to practice new behaviors during sessions, and the opportunity for practice decreases as the number of participants increases. Second, the larger the group, the less the likelihood that the curriculum will be appropriate for all members. Third, most patients will have residual psychotic symptoms and attentional difficulties, and it becomes progressively more difficult to keep all patients attentive and nondisruptive as the numbers increase beyond 8 to 10.

The training does not require doctoral-level clinicians. It can be conducted effectively by bachelor's- or master's-degree level staff, nurses, and nurses aides. There are three requirements: (a) experience working with severely disturbed patients; (b) understanding and agreement with the structured behavioral approach (i.e., does not feel obliged to develop insight and/or allow patients to discuss other problems at length during training sessions); and (c) ability to be reinforcing, especially in the face of slow progress. It is generally helpful to employ co-therapists so that they can alternate responsibility for segments of each session, use one another as models for appropriate behavior, and subdivide the group to provide focalized training for patients who are either more or less advanced in a particular skill area.

Training is customarily conducted 3 to 5 times per week for 1 to 1½ hr. The precise schedule will often be determined by pragmatic factors in the clinical setting. However, there is considerable regression between sessions in the best of circumstances, and it is counterproductive to conduct fewer than three sessions per week (or to permit individual patients to attend irregularly). The duration of training depends on the amount of material that is to be covered and the rate of progress of participants. We organize our training programs around circumscribed skill repertoires, such as assertiveness, conversation skills, job interview skills, dating skills, medication management, and deflecting negative affect. Each repertoire is divided into segments, and a curriculum unit is developed for the primary elements required for effective responding in each segment. This is illustrated for assertiveness in Tables 8.2 and 8.3. Specific response components (e.g., eye contact, voice volume) are taught in the context of each segment, rather than in the abstract. The material in Tables 8.2 and 8.3 was developed for work with a chronic population attending a day treatment program. It takes about 1 month to complete. Naturally, a less handicapped population could proceed more quickly and/or focus on more complex aspects of assertiveness. However, the two most common errors made by new trainers are to provide too little practice and to underestimate how difficult it is for these patients to learn the skills. Hence, it is advisable to break down the

Table 8.2 Curriculum for Teaching Assertion Skills

Positive assertion
  Offering compliments
  Expressing affection
  Expressing approval and praise
  Making apologies

Negative assertion (standing up for one's rights)
  Refusing unreasonable requests
  Requesting new behavior from others
  Compromise and negotiation
  Expressing disapproval and annoyance

Table 8.3 Steps in Asking a Favor

1. Get the other person's attention; e.g., say "Excuse me," make eye contact.

2. Give a reason for the favor; e.g., explain the situation, your problem or needs.

3. Say what you would like the person to do; e.g., "Could you please . . ."

4. Thank the person for his/her help.

curriculum into smaller units and proceed much more slowly than seems necessary. It is easier to speed up progress or add more difficult material when patients are bored than to slow down and backtrack after they have experienced a good deal of frustration and failure.

Optimally, patients should be assigned to a group on the basis of similar training needs. But this is not always possible. At the very least, all participants should have deficits in the primary skill repertoire to be targeted. Patients with different skill levels or deficits in different response components can be managed in the same group by using them as role models in areas of strength and by subdividing the group for focalized practice after some general training for the group as a whole. The one combination that does not seem to work well is mixing "young chronic" (ages 18–30) patients with older chronic patients. The former characteristically have unreasonably high expectations about what they can accomplish, deny their illness, and resent the slow pace and modest goals required by the older patients. As a result, they tend to act out in sessions and attend erratically. Skills training is appropriate for these patients, but it must be administered in the context of their particular needs (e.g., more time needs to be spent on goal setting, the limitations imposed by the illness, etc.).

Techniques

It is essential that the trainer(s) enter each session with a relatively structured plan. The syllabus details the content to be covered in each session (e.g., initiating conversations with strangers). It is also necessary for the trainer to identify a set of interpersonal scenarios that the participants can role-play during the session. These scenarios, which are analogous to the scenarios employed in role-play tests, provide the core around which training is organized. They represent situations the patients might encounter in the everyday environment in which they could use the targeted skills. Three to four scenarios are required for each session so as to provide some generality to the training. As training progresses, patients are invited to develop their own scenarios based on situations they have experienced. However, the trainer should have a set prepared for each session.

Training proceeds by teaching each of the response elements of a particular skill one at a time, in order of increasing difficulty. The training initially focuses on one scenario and then is repeated for other scenarios developed for the topic. Thus, patients might first be taught how to start a conversation with a familiar person in a day treatment center waiting room, then with a familiar person at a bus stop, and so on. Once that skill is mastered, they could be taught how to start a conversation with a stranger or how to end a conversation with a familiar person, and so on. The training process entails five elements: instructions, modeling, role play, feedback and positive reinforcement, and homework.

The first step is to provide *instructions* about how the target behavior is to be performed. Instructions should always be simple and relatively brief, and they should emphasize what the patient should do rather than what he should not do. For example: "The first step in starting a conversation is to get the other person's attention. In order to do that you should look at her face, say 'Excuse me,' and wait to see if she looks back at you." The instructions should then be repeated by the trainer, after which one of the patients is asked to repeat them. It is very helpful to have the instructions written on a blackboard so that patients can refer to them and/or to provide the patients with handouts they can take home.

The next step is for the trainer to *model* the correct response. A relevant scenario is described to the group, and the trainer then enacts the behavior with a co-trainer or group member. The modeling display should be brief and should focus narrowly on the targeted behavior so as not to confuse patients with extraneous response parameters. Patients are prompted to attend to the relevant components both before and after the modeled display (e.g., "Watch the way I nod my head when he speaks"). It will generally be desirable (necessary) to repeat the enactment as well.

The heart of the training process is *role playing*. After watching the trainer model the behavior, patients are then required to enact it with one of the trainers. Once again, a relevant scenario is described, the patient is directed to the blackboard or handout and asked to identify the requisite components, and he is them prompted to perform the behavior. Depending on the quality of the performance, the patient would be requested to repeat the role two to four times, with feedback and reinforcement (see below) interspersed between trials. Each of the other group members would then take a turn. It is important for each patient to perform at least two repetitions no matter how skillful the response, as the first trial often involves parroting of the trainer. Conversely, it is not advisable to conduct more than four trials in succession, no matter how poor the response, as patients become frustrated and other group members become bored and distracted. Patients experiencing difficulty can be given further practice after their peers have had an opportunity to role-play or can be taken aside by one of the therapists for more individualized coaching. After most patients have shown some progress in role play with the trainer, they are requested to role-play with one another. With more complex behaviors or when more extended interactions are being taught, patients can be paired off, with the trainer circulating among the pairs to provide feedback and give added instruction.

Patients are given feedback and reinforcement after each role-play trial. The feedback should be specific to the behaviors targeted and should be couched in positive terms: "That was nice, Fred. I liked the way you looked at him when you spoke. Let's try it again, and this time remember to speak a little louder." Patients appear to be hypersensitive to criticism and negative feedback. Thus, it is important to avoid negatives, such as telling the patient what she did wrong or what she should not do in subsequent trials. After observing the trainer in the first few sessions, group members will become aware of the appropriate way to provide positive feedback. At that point, they should be asked to comment on one another's performance. This teaches them to express positive feelings (which they almost all fail to do otherwise) and helps keep them attentive and involved while their peers are rehearsing.

Regardless of how well the patient performs in sessions, there is little likelihood of achieving transfer of training if the behavior is not practiced in vivo between sessions. Consequently, *homework* should be assigned at the conclusion of each session. Homework assignments should be designed to assure compliance and success. They should be highly likely to secure reinforcement from the environment; that requires that the behavior be well within the patient's skill level and that the other person in the interaction is likely to be cooperative. For example, a patient who has just learned to to request other people to change their behavior should not be directed to confront a hostile parent. The assignments should also be very specific as to when, where, and what should be done. An assignment of the form "So you will all try to start a conversation with someone this week, OK?" is not apt to be successful. A more desirable approach would be the following: "I would like you all to start a conversation with someone this week. Fred, can you think of a situation in which you will be able to start a conversation? No? How about in the cafeteria during lunch? OK. Which day do you think you can do it? Tuesday? Good. Here is a notecard. Why don't you write it down to help you remember." The assignments should be reviewed at the beginning of the next session. Patients who complied should be reinforced for effort. Those who failed to attempt the assignment should simply be encouraged to try again; they should not be criticized.

Additional Considerations

The elements described above comprise the basis of social skills training. If employed appropriately, they will be effective with the majority of patients. However, as implied in our earlier discussion about the multiplicity of factors that can impair social functioning, there are additional techniques that may be required with some patients. Space does not permit a full discussion of all possible alternatives, but we would like to briefly highlight one that has been developed by Wallace and Liberman (1985) for work with severely impaired patients. Often, such patients fail to attend adequately to the social environment and/or are unable to process adequately the information they have received. As a result, they cannot determine when to employ the behaviors they have learned in training. In an effort to develop receiving and processing skills, Wallace and Liberman have built a series of prompts and feedback into the role-play process. After each role-play enactment, patients are asked a series of questions concerning the nature of the interaction and then are prompted to clarify their own goals or intentions. The former includes such queries as the following: Who is in the scene? What did he say? What was he feeling? The second set of questions include the following: What was your short-term goal? What was your long-term goal? What did you do to achieve your goal? In both cases, patients are reinforced for task-relevant answers and taught how to seek clarification when they are uncertain. Similarly, they are given help in formulating possible response alternatives and in the decision making required to develop choices and goals. Their behavioral responses are then guided to be consistent with the task demands of the situation and their goals for the interaction. Although there are no data to document that these particular additions enhance the effects of the basic social skills training techniques, a package combining both procedures has proved highly effective with a very chronic population.

The literature documents that social skills training procedures are effective in teaching patients new skills, that the skills are reasonably well maintained, and that they are associated with decreased frequency of relapse (Bellack, Turner, Hersen, & Luber, 1984; Hogarty et al., 1986; Wallace and Liberman, 1985). However, considerable questions remain as to the extent to which patients use the new behaviors in their day-to-day interactions and whether the targeted skills actually improve their quality of life. We cannot provide empirical data to support our hypotheses, but we believe there are three aspects of current practice that may limit the value of the training and that need to be addressed in the future:

1. The content of training is generally based on the values and beliefs of the clinical team, rather than on the explicit goals and desires

of the patients. As a result, we may not teach the skills patients want to learn or need to learn. We previously referred to this issue in regard to young chronic patients. We are unlikely to get generalization or clinical significance without learning more about which behaviors are vital and enlisting the cooperation of patients in establishing syllabi.

2. We generally confine our interventions to the clinic, despite volumes of evidence with other interventions that behaviors do not generalize unless they are systematically prompted and reinforced in the natural environment. It is essential that we integrate clinic-based training with environmental management, such as by conducting training in the environment (e.g., in the evening and on weekends) and by teaching parents and board-and-care home operators how to reinforce targeted behaviors.

3. We are generally dealing with very severe and long-standing deficits in populations that have significant difficulties in attention and learning. Yet we tend to approach training as if a few trials over a few weeks will be sufficient. To the contrary, we believe that training must involve dozens (or hundreds) of trials over months and years. We must be prepared to work with our patients more extensively over longer periods of time than has been our custom. Behavior therapy has always been promoted as a relatively rapid intervention. That is definitely not the case with schizophrenic and autistic patients.

BEHAVIORAL FAMILY THERAPY

As neuroleptic medications have increased the proportion of time schizophrenics spend in the community, families have assumed a major role as the primary caregivers for patients between hospitalizations. Although the family has long been recognized as a potentially powerful rehabilitative force in the patient's life (e.g., Evans, Bullard, & Solomon, 1961), early research suggested that schizophrenic persons living with the nuclear family had a worse prognosis than those with other living arrangements. Freeman and Simmons (1958, 1959) found that schizophrenic patients who returned from the hospital to spouses functioned at a higher level than patients who returned to parental homes, although the living arrangement did not differentially affect the role of readmission to the hospital. In a retrospective study, Brown, Carstairs, and Topping (1958) found that patients who returned to the homes of either parents *or* wives had higher rehospitalization rates than patients who went to siblings or more distant relatives or to lodges. A later study replicated the lower rehospitalization rate for schizophrenic persons living with their siblings than for those living with parents and wives (Brow, Monck, Carstairs, & Wing, 1962). Similarly, living with one's nuclear family has been found to be associated with higher rates of relapse for schizophrenic persons that living with an extended family (El-Islam, 1979).

Systematic studies of family factors related to the outcome of schizophrenia have found that negative ambient emotion can have a deleterious effect on the course of the illness. High expressed emotion (EE) is defined as critical comments, hostility, or emotional overinvolvement elicited during a semistructured interview (the Camberwell Family Interview) with a relative of a patient who has recently been hospitalized (Brown & Rutter, 1966; Rutter & Brown, 1966). High level of EE in family members is hypothesized to reflect a stressful emotional environment for a stabilized schizophrenic patient, increasing the risk of subsequent relapse by a factor of 2 to 3 compared to low EE (Brown, Birley, & Wing, 1972; Karno et al., 1987; Vaughn & Leff, 1976; Vaughn, Snyder, Jones, Freeman, & Falloon, 1984). In addition, the predictive relationship between EE and outcome among schizophrenic patients cannot be accounted for by other indices, such as premorbid social functioning or symptomatology (e.g., Miklowitz, Goldstein, & Falloon, 1983). Recent studies of problem-solving behavior during family interactions have provided cross-validation for the EE construct by demonstrating that high-EE parents are more critical and intrusive toward their schizophrenic offspring than are low-EE parents (Miklowitz, Goldstein, Falloon, & Doane, 1984; Strachan, Goldstein, & Miklowitz, 1986; Strachan, Leff, Goldstein, Doane, & Burtt, 1986). This research has shifted a major goal of family interventions for schizophrenia from the modification of "communication deviance" (Bateson, Jackson, Haley, & Weakland, 1956), which was hypothesized to cause the illness itself, to the reduction of ambient stress in order to lower the risk of symptom exacerbation.

The negative affective climate in some families of schizophrenic patients both predisposes these patients to relapses and reflects the stress experienced by family members, whose coping efforts may be overwhelmed by problems associated with the patient's illness. The impact of schizophrenia on objective burden (e.g., loss of income, separation from children) and subjective burden of the family can be substantial (Hoenig, 1974; Hoenig & Hamilton, 1966). Creer (1978) extensively interviewed 80 relatives of schizophrenic patients and reported that the problems experienced fell into three major categories:

1. Distress caused by the patient's symptoms and social deficits.
2. Anxiety and burnout experienced by family members.
3. Disruptions in the relative's own social networks.

The residual symptoms of schizophrenia are visibly evident in many patients living at home and can cause distress and challenge the coping skills of relatives. Although both positive and negative symptoms may be present in varying degrees in the course of schizophrenia, negative symptoms tend to resolve more slowly and are more stable over time (Crow, 1980; Pogue-Geile & Harrow, 1984, 1985; but see Lindenmayer, Kay, & Friedman, 1986). In addition, relatives are less likely to recognize symptoms such as anhedonia, apathy, motor-retardation, blunted affect, and social withdrawal as due to the illness, compared to delusions and hallucinations. These symptoms in many chronic schizophrenic patients are frequently interpreted by relatives as signs of laziness and inferior moral character (Leff & Vaughn, 1985). Concerned family members may respond to such distressing behaviors by actively trying to change them, either by venting their anger and criticizing the patient or by intensifying their involvement and concern with the patient's life.

Intervention Procedures

Several different approaches to family therapy for schizophrenia that attempt to modify the emotional climate have recently been developed (Falloon, Boyd, & McGill, 1984; Hogarty et al., 1986; Goldstein, Rodnick, Evans, May, & Steinberg, 1978; Leff, Kuipers, Berkowitz, & Sturgeon, 1985). The family therapy approach described here is based on a behavioral perspective that combines didactic education with skills training in a semistructured format. The treatment can be divided into five sequential stages, although material from each stage is repeated as needed throughout the course of treatment: family assessment, education about schizophrenia or autism, communication skills training, problem-solving training, and special problems.

Behavioral family therapy is conducted in the home when possible to enhance the generalization of newly acquired skills into the family's natural environment and to observe the physical surroundings and family organization that serve as a backdrop for problem-solving efforts. Meeting with the family in their own home conveys directly to the family the therapist's concern and involvement, stemming possible family resistance to therapy (Liberman, 1981). Resistance to family therapy may be particularly strong among families who have been blamed for causing the patient to become schizophrenic (Appleton, 1974; Terkelson, 1983). In engaging such families, who may resent and resist efforts of professionals in the mental health community, effort is expended before treatment or early in therapy to dispel the myth that families cause schizophrenia and to educate them about the alternative stress-vulnerability–coping-skills model of schizophrenia.

Family Assessment

Behavioral assessment of the family, as in individual behavioral therapy, is an ongoing process that both precedes and is interwoven throughout treatment. The goals of assessment are to identify (1) the assets and deficits of individual members of the family as a whole and (2) the role that specific problem behaviors play in the functioning of the family. Information for assessment is obtained through individual interviews, observing family members interact while participating in family sessions, and noting the performance of family members on specific problem-solving tasks.

During the individual interviews, conducted with each member of the family, their understanding of schizophrenia or autism and perceptions of its burden are assessed. Short-term goals relevant to each individual's needs, rather than only patient-oriented goals, are formulated for all participating family members during the individual interviews, and they are reviewed and revised routinely during therapy. Problem-solving assessments in which family members attempt to solve a problem together in the absence of the therapist are conducted before therapy and throughout treatment to track the acquisition of problem-solving skills taught in the sessions. The use of communication skills by each member during treatment sessions, both prompted in role plays and spontaneous, are recorded by the therapist to monitor the learning of these skills, which are critical to successful family problem solving.

Education about Schizophrenia and Autism

During the educational sessions the ill relative is encouraged to take the role of the "expert" and to describe to the family his experience with the symptoms. The impact of the illness on the patient and his relatives is elicited, and problems of management are discussed. Frequently, family members who have been living with a chronic patient for years have never openly discussed the illness with him and are relieved when they can do so in the family sessions without having any negative consequences on the patient.

Common misconceptions about the causes of schizophrenia and autism are refuted, such as people with the illness having a "split personality" or being violent people. Families learn about how schizophrenia or autism is diagnosed, the characteristic signs and symptoms, its prevalence and course, genetic and biological theories, and the role of stress in triggering symptom exacerbations in vulnerable persons. Patients and family members are taught to recognize the prodromal signs of relapse. The effects of neurolepic medications in reducing acute symptoms and prevention of relapses are emphasized, as are the negative effects of street drugs and excessive alcohol consumption. Side effects of neuroleptic medication are explained, and the use of side-effect medications and coping strategies are reviewed. The availability and appropriate utilization of community resources, such as psychiatric hospitals, day treatment centers, vocational programs, supervised living arrangements, and social agencies are addressed, depending upon the individual family's needs. This material is covered in the first three or four sessions, using didactic presentation, discussion, posters, and handouts.

Communication Skills Training

Good communication skills are assumed to be necessary prerequisites for family problem solving because they enable family members to discuss potentially stressful issues with a minimum of negative affect. Communication skills training strives to lower family tensions by teaching attentive listening skills, effective ways for expressing positive and negative feelings, and making positive requests for changes in behavior. Training in these behaviors emphasizes direct, brief verbal communications with another person that specify a behavior of the other person (either commenting on a behavior or requesting one) and that express the speaker's feeling about that behavior. The initial phase focuses on empathic listening and the expression of positive feelings through prompting mutually reinforcing behavior. The goal of this phase of treatment is to create a warm milieu where family members are able to recognize and reward specific positive behavior in one another.

Training in communication skills is conducted using the same procedures employed in social skills training: providing a rationale for the importance of the skill, modeling, role playing, coaching, social reinforcement and corrective feedback, repeated role playing, and homework assignments. For example, when expressing negative feelings, four steps are learned:

1. Look at the person and speak firmly.
2. Say exactly what they did that upset you.
3. Tell them how it made you feel.
4. Tell them how the person might prevent this from happening in the future.

Communication deficits are assessed in an ongoing fashion within each family, with targeted skills training being systematically applied throughout the therapy.

Problem-solving Training

One hypothesis regarding the heightened stress sensitivity of schizophrenic persons is that they lack adequate problem-solving skills to cope effectively with tension, conflict, or stressors. The main tenet of behavioral family therapy is that improvements in family problem-solving skills will lessen the ambient stress in the family by improving members' ability to attain personal goals and buffer the noxious effects of exogenous stressors. Training in problem solving consists of teaching a set of sequential steps for resolving problems that minimizes negative emotional undercurrents while maximizing the identification, evaluation, and implementation of optimal solutions. The steps of problem solving include the following:

1. Define the problem to everyone's satisfaction.
2. Brainstorm a list of potential solutions to the problem.
3. Evaluate the advantages and disadvantages of each solution.
4. Choose the best solution or combination of solutions. Compromise between solutions if necessary.
5. Formulate a plan for how to implement the solution.
6. Review progress on implementing the solution and reinforce approximations toward attaining the goal.

All problem-solving efforts by family members are recorded on problem-solving sheets, which are kept in a folder accessible to all family members, in order to monitor progress toward achieving family goals. During training, family members take turns "chairing" the family discussion. In addition to leading the discussion, the chairman records the definition of the problem, alternative solutions, and the steps for implementing the solutions. Early in problem-solving training the therapist demonstrates the different steps by chairing the sessions and recording the progress made. This role is gradually relinquished to family members as the therapist progressively gives the family responsibility for conducting its own problem-solving sessions. As the therapist fades his role as chairman of problem-solving discussions, family members become more active in solving their own problems together, and weekly family problem-solving meetings are held between therapy sessions. Crises are handled by using the problem-solving approach, with the therapist stepping in to chair the session if the family's skills are not sufficient or if the problem is too difficult. The end goal of behavioral family therapy is for families to conduct their own weekly problem-solving sessions in the absence of the therapist and for these sessions to focus on removing current stressors and achieving individual and family goals.

Special Problems

When family members have acquired good problem-solving skills, attention turns to working on special problems that remain and have not responded to family problem solving. This involves teaching a wide range of behavioral techniques, depending on the nature of the problem, such as contingency contracting for mutually desired behavior changes, cognitive–behavioral modification for depression or anxiety, social skills training for social inadequacy, token economy programs for enhancing constructive daily activity, and relaxation and/or exposure treatments for anxiety problems. Usually, the entire family is involved in implementing these strategies and monitoring their effects, although in some cases the therapist can work with one member individually.

Evaluation of Behavioral Family Therapy

The effects of behavioral family therapy on the outcome of recently hospitalized schizophrenic patients has been reported in a well-controlled study conducted by Falloon and his colleagues (Falloon, 1985; Falloon et al., 1985). Treatment was provided in the context of a comprehensive outpatient treatment program, and the study compared home-based behavioral family therapy with individual therapy and management.

Thirty-six schizophrenic patients who were discharged from psychiatric inpatient facilities to high-EE families were randomly assigned to either 9 months of behavioral family therapy or equally intensive individual therapy. After the intensive-therapy phase, individuals and their families were provided with case management, crisis intervention services, and therapy as necessary, and thorough assessments were made at the end of the second year. Individual therapy was done at the clinic and employed a goal-oriented behavioral approach that focused on improving the patient's skills in anticipating and coping with a range of environmental stressors. Strategies were applied on the basis of individual need and included social skills training, anxiety and depression management, cognitive restructuring, and relaxation training. In addition to participating in individual or family therapy, all patients were maintained on neuroleptic medications by physicians who were blind to their treatment assignment; they had access to therapists for crisis intervention, received rehabilitation counseling, and had good continuity of care.

The results strongly favored the family over the individual treatment. After 9 months and at the 2-year follow-up, patients who received family treatment had significantly fewer hospitalizations, spent less time in the hospital, experienced fewer major exacerbations in schizophrenic symptoms and episodes of depression, and required fewer emergency crisis sessions than did patients who received individual therapy. Although few patients in either treatment group showed a complete remission of all symptoms, patients in the family group tended to exhibit more stable and lower levels of mainly neurotic symptoms. Behavioral disturbances, such as poor self-care, unusual behavior, and poor medication compliance, showed strengths for the family approach, although gains for individually treated patients lessened this difference at 2 years.

Patients receiving the family intervention also improved more in their social and vocational adjustment. Over the 2-year period, family-treated patients spent an average of 12.6 months engaged in work or training activities, compared to 7.2 months for individually treated patients. Similarly, the social role performance of patients, based on the report of family members, favored the family over the individual treatment.

These differences in the course, severity, and social outcome of schizophrenic patients could not be accounted for by medication compliance. Compliance was closely monitored by monthly neuroleptic blood level assays. Family-treated patients were actually prescribed *lower* doses of neuroleptics to control their systems than were individually treated patients. This finding raises the possibility that behavioral family therapy may lower the ambient stress to which a patient is exposed, reducing the amount of neuroleptic medication required to control symptoms and prevent exacerbations.

Improvements in family functioning were also more evident for the family-treated patients than for the individually treated patients (Falloon & Pederson, 1985). Coping efforts of family members receiving family therapy were more effective than in families where the patient received individual therapy. Families that received therapy also showed less disruption of family members' activities, better physical and emotional health, fewer negative attitudes expressed toward the patient, and less subjective burden attributed to the patient. In an assessment of problem-solving skill during a structured 10-min family discussion of a problem, families that had received therapy made more problem-solving statements than did the families of individually treated patients, suggesting that family problem-solving ability may be an important skill mediating the effects of behavioral family therapy. Consistent with the improved prognoses of patients who returned to families engaged in therapy, these families showed significant decreases in their level of tense and intrusive communication, compared to slight worsening in communication for families of individually treated patients.

The family treatment resulted in greater therapeutic gains than did individual treatment for both the patients and their families. A cost-benefit analysis calculated over the 2-year period revealed that although the direct cost of delivering the family therapy was slightly more than that of the individual therapy, the indirect costs of care (e.g., hospitalization) were much greater for individually treated patients. Overall, therefore, the family approach cost "society" less than half as much as the individual treatment.

Future Directions

The National Institute of Mental Health (NIMH) is currently conducting a study to replicate and extend the positive results reported by Falloon et al. (1985). In addition to providing behavioral family therapy for 1 year and case management for a second year for half of all of the patients, all families in the project are invited to attend an educational workshop about schizophrenia based on Anderson and associates' (1986) approach and to participate in monthly multiple-family support groups. The NIMH study is also comparing three different strategies for prescribing prophylactic neuroleptic medication to schizophrenic, schizoaffective, and schizophreniform patients: standard dose; low-dose neuroleptic maintenance treatment, in which approximately one fifth of the standard dose is given (Kane, Woerner, & Sarantakos, 1986; Van Putten & Marder, 1986) and targeted neuroleptic intervention, in which medication is given only when early warning signs of the illness appear (Carpenter, 1986). The results of this study will provide further validation for the efficacy of behavioral family therapy. The study will also yield data indicating whether patients who receive this type of treatment can be maintained on lower doses of neuroleptics than patients who receive standard case management and whose families receive education about schizophrenia without skills training.

Future research should address whether improvements in problem-solving skill among families who receive behavioral family therapy are correlated with clinical changes in the patient, since the main assumption of this intervention is that family problem-solving skill acts as a buffer to stress. Additional questions include whether a home-based treatment can be delivered with equal efficacy in the clinic. Finally, research is needed to examine why schizophrenic persons are so sensitive to and unable to effectively manage interpersonal stress such as expressed emotion. Although the literature on expressed emotion, reviewed previously shows the clear negative impact of ambient emotion on the course of schizophrenia, and perhaps autism as well, the specific nature of patients' interpersonal skill deficits in these situations has not been examined. The identification of skill deficits in negative emotion situations, as well as parental behaviors that pose special problems to patients, could lead to skills training that would improve patients' ability to handle these difficult situations.

CONCLUSION

In this chapter we have reviewed treatments for schizophrenia and autism that attempt to improve the outcome of the illness by enhancing the social skills of patients and their family members. Skills training interventions are based on the stress-vulnerability–coping-skills model of schizophrenia, which postulates that symptom increases in a medication-compliant patient are the consequence of environmental stressors, whose effects can be mediated by a patient's social skill. These data may also have implications for adult autism and other chronic mental health problems and warrant investigation. Individual social skills training reduces patients' risk for symptomatic relapses and improves their social functioning, possibly because it enables them to successfully identify and eliminate noxious stressors and to attain instrumental and interpersonal goals necessary for community survival. Behavioral family therapy also improves the outcome of schizophrenic persons by lowering ambient family stress and improving the problem-solving capacity of the family as a whole. Although the efficacy of these treatment approaches has received empirical support in controlled clinical studies, future research is needed to determine the specific role of skills acquisition in effecting the improved outcome.

REFERENCES

American Psychiatric Association (1987). *Diagnostic and statistical manual of mental disorders* (3rd ed. revised). Washington, DC: Author.

Anderson, C. M., Reiss, D. J., & Hogarty, G. E. (1986). *Schizophrenia and the family*. New York: Guilford.

Andreasen, N. C. (1979). Thought, language, and communication disorders: II. Diagnostic significance. *Archives of General Psychiatry, 36*, 1325–1330.

Appleton, W. S. (1974). Mistreatment of patients' families by psychiatrists. *American Journal of Psychiatry, 131*, 655–657.

Bateson, G., Jackson, D. D., Jaley, J., & Weakland, J. (1956). Toward a theory of schizophrenia. *Behavioral Science, 1*, 251–264.

Bellack, A. S. (1979). A critical appraisal of strategies for assessing social skill. *Behavioral Assessment, 1*, 157–176.

Bellack, A. S. (1983). Recurrent problems in the behavioral assessment of social skill. *Behaviour Research and Therapy, 21*, 29–42.

Bellack, A. S., Hersen, M., & Turner, S. M. (1978). Role play tests for assessing social skills: Are they valid? *Behavior Therapy, 9*, 448–461.

Bellack, A. S., Hersen, M., & Turner, S. M. (1979). The relationship of role playing and knowledge of appropriate behavior to assertion in the natural environment. *Journal of Consulting and Clinical Psychology, 47*, 670–678.

Bellack, A. S., Turner, S. M., Hersen, M., & Luber, R. F. (1984). An examination of the efficacy of social skills training for chronic schizophrenic patients. *Hospital and Community Psychiatry, 35*, 1023–1028.

Brown, G. W., Birley, J. L. T., & Wing, J. K. (1972). Influence of family life on the course of schizophrenic disorders: A replication. *British Journal of Psychiatry, 121*, 241–258.

Brown, G. W., Carstairs, G. M., & Topping, G. (1958). The post hospital adjustment of chronic mental patients. *Lancet, 2*, 685–689.

Brown, G. W., Monck, E. M., Carstairs, G. M., & Wing, J. K. (1962). Influence of family life on the course of schizophrenic illness. *British Journal of Preventive and Social Medicine, 16*, 55–68.

Brown, G. W., & Rutter, M. (1966). The measurement of family activities and relationships. A methodological study. *Human Relations, 19*, 241–263.

Carpenter, W., Jr. (1986). Early targeted pharmacotherapeutic intervention in schizophrenia. *Journal of Clinical Psychiatry, 47* (Suppl.), 23–29.

Casey, P. R., Tyrer, P. J., & Platt, S. T. (1985). The relationship between social functioning and psychiatric symptomatology in primary care. *Social Psychiatry, 20*, 5–9.

Cordes, C. (1984). The plight of the homeless mentally ill. *APA Monitor,* 15, 1–13.

Creer, C. (1978). Social work with patients and their families. In J. K. Wing (Ed.), *Schizophrenia: Towards a new synthesis* (pp. 233–251). London: Academic.

Crow, T. J. (1980). Molecular pathology of schizophrenia: More than one disease process. *British Medical Journal, 280,* 66–68.

Curran, J. P. (1979). Pandora's box reopened? The assessment of social skills. *Journal of Behavioral Assessment, 1,* 55–72.

Dawson, M. E., & Neuchterlein, K. H. (1984). Psychophysiological dysfunctions in the development course of schizophrenic disorders. *Schizophrenia Bulletin, 10,* 204–232.

Diamond, R. (1985). Drugs and the quality of life: The patient's point of view. *Journal of Clinical Psychology, 46,* 29–35.

Eisler, R. M., Hersen, M., Miller, P. M., & Blanchard, E. B. (1975). Situational determinants of assertive behaviors. *Journal of Consulting and Clinical Psychology, 43,* 330–340.

ElIslam, M. F. (1979). A better outlook for schizophrenics living in extended families. *British Journal of Psychiatry, 135,* 343–347.

Evans, A. S., Bullard, D. M., & Solomon, M. H. (1961). The family as a potential resource in the rehabilitation of the chronic schizophrenic patient: A study of 60 patients and their families. *American Journal of Psychiatry, 117,* 1075–1083.

Falloon, I. R. H. (1985). *Family management of schizophrenia: A study of clinical, social, family, and economic benefits.* Baltimore, MD: Johns Hopkins University Press.

Falloon, I. R. H., Boyd, J. L., & McGill, C. W. (1984). *Family care of schizophrenia.* New York: Guilford.

Falloon, I. R. H., Boyd, J. L., McGill, C. W., Ranzani, J., Moss, H. B., Gilderman, A. M., & Simpson, G. M. (1985). Family management in the prevention of morbidity of schizophrenia: Clinical outcome of a two year longitudinal study. *Archives of General Psychiatry, 42,* 887–896.

Falloon, I. R. H., & Pederson, J. (1985). Family management in the prevention of morbidity of schizophrenia: The adjustment of the family. *British Journal of Psychiatry, 147,* 156–163.

Freeman, H. W., & Simmons, O. G. (1958). Mental patients in community family setting and performance level. *American Sociological Review, 23,* 147–154.

Freeman, H. E., & Simmons, O. G. (1959). Social integration of former mental patients. *International Journal of Social Psychiatry, 4,* 264–271.

Goldberg, S. C. (1985). Negative and deficit symptoms in schizophrenia do respond to neuroleptics. *Schizophrenia Bulletin, 11,* 453–456.

Goldstein, M. J., Rodnick, E. H., Evans, J. R., May, P. R. A., & Steinberg, M. R. (1978). Drug and family therapy in the aftercare of acute schizophrenics. *Archives of General Psychiatry, 35,* 1169–1177.

Goldstrom, I., & Mandersheid, R. (1981). The chronically mentally ill: A descriptive analysis from the uniform data instrument. *Community Support Services Journal, 2,* 4–9.

Gottesman, I. I. (1968). Severity/concordance and diagnostic refinement in the Maudsley-Bethlem schizophrenic twin study. In D. Rosenthal & S. S. Kety (Eds.), *The transmission of schizophrenia* (pp. 37–48). New York: Pergamon.

Harper, R. G., Wiens, A. N., & Matarazzo, J. D. (1978). *Nonverbal communication: The state of the art.* New York: John Wiley.

Harrow, M., & Miller, J. G. (1980). Schizophrenic thought disorders and impaired perspective. *Journal of Abnormal Psychology, 89,* 717–727.

Harvey, P. D. (1983). Speech competence in manic and schizophrenic psychoses: The association between clinically rated thought disorder and cohesion and reference performance. *Journal of Abnormal Psychology, 92,* 368–377.

Hersen, M., Bellack, A. S., & Turner, S. M. (1978). Assessment of assertiveness in female psychiatric patients: Motor and autonomic measures. *Journal of Behavior Therapy and Experimental Psychiatry, 9,* 11–16.

Hoenig, J. (1974). The schizophrenic comes home. *Acta Psychiatrica Scandinavica, 30,* 297–308.

Hoenig, J., & Hamilton, M. W. (1966). The schizophrenic patient in the community and his effect on the household. *International Journal of Social Psychiatry, 12,* 165–176.

Hogarty, G. E., Schooler, N. R., Ulrich, R. F., Mussare, F., Ferro, P., & Herron, E. (1979). Fluphenazine and social therapy in the aftercare of schizophrenic patients: Relapse analyses of a two-year controlled study of fluphenazine decanoate and fluphenazine hydrochloride. *Archives of General Psychiatry, 36,* 1283–1294.

Hooley, J. (1985). Expressed emotion: A review of the critical literature. *Clinical Psychology Review, 5,* 119–139.

Hotchkiss, A. P. & Harvey, P. D. (1986). Linguistic analyses of speech disorder in psychosis. *Clinical Psychology Review, 6,* 155–175.

Johnson, D. A. W. (1985). Antipsychotic medication: Clinical guidelines for maintenance therapy. *Journal of Clinical Psychiatry, 46,* 6–15.

Kane, J. M., Woerner, M., & Sarantakos, S. (1986). Depot neuroleptics: A comparative review of standard, intermediate, and low-dose regimens. *Journal of Clinical Psychiatry, 47* (Suppl.), 30–33.

Karno, M., Jenkins, J. H., De La Selva, A., Santana, F., Telles, C., Lopez, S., & Mintz, J. (1987). Expressed emotion and schizophrenic outcome among Mexican-American families. *Journal of Nervous and Mental Disease, 175*, 143–151.

Kirk, S. A., & Therrien, M. E. (1975). Community mental health myths and the fate of former hospitalized patients. *Psychiatry, 38*, 209–217.

Koenigsberg, H. W., & Handley, R. (1986). Expressed emotion: From predictive index to clinical construct. *American Journal of Psychiatry, 143*, 1361–1373.

Leff, J., Kuipers, L., Berkowitz, R., & Sturgeon, D. (1985). A controlled trial of social intervention in the families of schizophrenic patients: Two year follow-up. *British Journal of Psychiatry, 146*, 594–600.

Leff, J., & Vaughn, C. J. (1985). *Expressed emotion in families.* New York: Guilford.

Lehman, A. (1983). The well-being of chronic mental patients. *Archives of General Psychiatry, 40*, 369–373.

Lewine, R. R. J., Watt, N. F., Prentky, R. A., & Fryer, J. H. (1980). Childhood social competence in functionally disordered psychiatric patients and normals. *Journal of Abnormal Psychology, 89*, 132–138.

Liberman, R. P. (1981). Managing resistance to behavioral family therapy. In A. S. Gurman (Ed.), *Questions and answers in the practice of family therapy* (Vol. 1, pp. 186–194). New York: Brunner/Maze.

Liberman, R. P. (1982). Assessment of social skills. *Schizophrenia Bulletin, 8*, 62–84.

Lindenmayer, J., Kay, S. R., & Friedman, C. (1986). Negative and positive schizophrenic syndromes after the acute phase: A prospective follow-up. *Comprehensive Psychiatry, 27*, 276–286.

Linn, M. W., Klett, C. J., & Coffey, E. M. (1982). Relapse of psychiatric patients in foster care. *American Journal of Psychiatry, 139*, 778–783.

McFall, R. M. (1982). A review and reformulation of the concept of social skills. *Behavioral Assessment, 4*, 1–33.

Meltzer, H. Y. (1985). Dopamine and negative symptoms in schizophrenia: Critique of the type I-II hypothesis. In M. Alpert (Ed.), *Controversies in schizophrenia* (pp. 110–136). New York: Guilford.

Miklowitz, D. J., Goldstein, M. J., & Falloon, I. R. H. (1983). Premorbid and symptomatic characteristics of schizophrenics from families with high and low expressed emotions. *Journal of Abnormal Psychology, 92*, 357–367.

Miklowitz, D. J., Goldstein, M. J., Falloon, I. R. H., & Doane, J. A. (1984). Interactional correlates of expressed emotion in the families of schizophrenics. *British Journal of Psychiatry, 144*, 482–487.

Morrison, R. L. M., & Bellack, A. S. (1987). The social functioning of schizophrenic patients: Clinical and research issues. *Schizophrenia Bulletin, 13*, 715–725.

Morrison, R. L. M., & Bellack, A. S. (1981). The role of social perception in social skill. *Behaviour Therapy, 12*, 69-79.

Neuchterlein, K. H., & Dawson, M. E. (1984). A heuristic vulnerability/stress model of schizophrenic episodes. *Schizophrenia Bulletin, 10*, 300-312.

Phillips, L. (1968). *Human adaptation and its failures.* New York: Academic.

Phillips, L., & Zigler, E. (1961). Social competence: The action-thought parameter and vicariousness in normal and pathological behavior. *Journal of Abnormal and Social Psychology, 63*, 137-146.

Pogue-Geile, M. F., & Harrow, M. (1985). Negative symptoms in schizophrenia: Their longitudinal course and prognostic importance. *Schizophrenia Bulletin, 11*, 427-439.

Pogue-Geile, M. F., & Harrow, M. (1984). Negative and positive symptoms in schizophrenia and depression: A followup. *Schizophrenia Bulletin, 10*, 371-387.

Presley, A. S., Grubb, A. B., & Semple, D. (1982). Predictors of successful rehabilitation in long stay patients. *Acta Psychiatrica Scandinavica, 66*, 83-88.

Rabkin, R. G. (1980). Stressful life events and schizophrenia: A review of the research literature. *Psychological Bulletin, 87*, 408-425.

Rosen, A. J., Sussman, S., Mueser, K. T., Lyons, J. S., & Davis, J. M. (1981). Behavioral assessment of psychiatric inpatients and normal controls across different environmental contexts. *Journal of Behavioral Assessment, 3*, 25-36.

Rutter, D. R. (1985). Language in schizophrenia the structure of monologues and conversation. *British Journal of Psychiatry, 146*, 399-404.

Rutter, M., & Brown, G. W. (1966). The reliability and validity of measures of family life and relationships in families containing a psychiatric patient. *Social Psychiatry, 1*, 38-53.

Strachan, A. M., Goldstein, M. J., & Miklowitz, D. J. (1986). Do relatives express expressed emotion? In M. J. Goldstein, I. Hand, & K. Halweg (Eds.), *Treatment of schizophrenia: Family assessment and intervention* (pp. 51-58). Berlin: Springer-Verlag.

Strachan, A. M., Leff, J. P., Goldstein, M. J., Doane, J. A., & Burtt, C. (1986). Emotional attitudes and direct communication in the families of schizophrenics: A cross-national replication. *British Journal of Psychiatry, 149*, 279-287.

Strauss, J. S., & Carpenter, W. T., Jr. (1974). Prediction of outcome in schizophrenia: II. Relationships between predictor and outcome variables. *Archives of General Psychiatry, 30*, 429-434.

Strauss, J. S., & Carpenter, W. T., Jr. (1977). Prediction of outcome in schizophrenia: III. Five year outcome and its predictors. A report from The International Pilot Study of Schizophrenia. *Archives of General Psychiatry, 34*, 159-163.

Slyph, J. A., Ross, H. E., & Kedwaod, H. B. (1978). Social disability in chronic psychiatric patients. *American Journal of Psychiatry, 134,* 1391–1394.

Talbott, J. A. (1981). *The chronic mentally ill.* New York: Human Sciences Press.

Terkelsen, K. G. (1983). Schizophrenia and the family: II. Adverse effects of family therapy. *Family Process, 22,* 191–200.

Van Putten, T., & Marder, S. (1986). Low dose treatment strategies. *Journal of Clinical Psychiatry, 47* (Suppl.), 12–16.

Van Putten, T., & May, P. R. A. (1978). Akinetic depression in schizophrenia. *Archives of General Psychiatry, 35,* 1101–1107.

Vaughn, C. E., Snyder, K. S., Jones, S., Freeman, W. B., & Falloon, I. R. H. (1984). Family factors in schizophrenic relapse. *Archives of General Psychiatry, 41,* 1169–1177.

Wallace, C. J., & Liberman, R. P. (1985). Social skills training for patients with schizophrenia: A controlled clinical trail. *Psychiatry Research, 14,* 239–247.

Wing, J. K., & Brown, G. W. (1970). *Institutionalization and schizophrenia.* London: Cambridge University Press.

Wing, J. K., & Freudenberg, R. K. (1961). The response of severely ill chronic schizophrenic patients to social stimulation. *American Journal of Psychiatry, 118,* 311–322.

Wong, S. E., Terranova, M. D., Bowen, L., Zarete, T., Massel, H. K., & Liberman, R. P. (1987). Providing independent recreational activities to reduce stereotypic vocalizations in chronic schizophrenics. *Journal of Applied Behavior Analysis, 20,* 77–81.

Zigler, E., & Glick, M. (1986). *A developmental approach to adult psychopathology.* New York: John Wiley.

Zubin, J., & Spring, B. (1977). Vulnerability—a new view of schizophrenia. *Journal of Abnormal Psychology, 86,* 103–126.

9

Treatment Overview and Description of Psychotherapy

Ramasamy Manikam

Schizophrenia and autism constitute two severely disabling disorders that afflict millions of people. The cost is considerable to family members, educators, clinicians, and society in general. In recent decades, psychology has made progress in assessment and treatment, but much remains to be accomplished. Although the number of individuals hospitalized for schizophrenia has decreased with the advent of antipsychotic medication and the movement toward deinstitutionalization and community treatment, the rate of admissions has actually increased as a result of multiple admissions via relapses (Paul, 1986). Today two thirds of hospitalized patients are classified as chronic, and 50% of those are considered schizophrenic (Fuoco & Tyson, 1986). Even less has been accomplished in the treatment of autism. It is estimated that only 5 to 17% of all children diagnosed with autism ever achieve normal social functioning (Lotter, 1975). At the same time, there has been little work specifically concerned with autistic adults.

Although professionals can agree on the seriousness of these disorders, there is much controversy concerning issues of controlling variables, diagnosis, and treatment. The purpose of this book is to synthesize materials pertaining to two disorders that until now have been dealt with in isolation despite overlap in symptoms and treatment. Other chapters in this volume explore the similarities and differences between chronic schizophrenia and adult autism; thus, they will be mentioned only briefly here. Among the most noticeable similarities are deficits in motivation, expression of emotion, social skills, and adaptive behavior. Differences, on the other hand, exist with regard to such factors as stability of symptoms (more stable in autism), presence of hallucinations and delusions (absent or much less prominent in autism), age of onset (much later in schizophrenia), and intelligence level (higher prevalence of mental retardation in autism).

The present chapter is a discussion of psychotherapy and milieu therapy in the treatment of chronic schizophrenia and adult autism. Psychotherapy has fallen into disfavor in recent years, especially in the treatment of severe psychiatric disorders for reasons which will be discussed later in this chapter. However, focusing on the issue of psychotherapy brings to the forefront many of the differences between schizophrenia and autism in general, especially with regard to the nature of cognitive and emotional impairments. An attempt will be made to define the construct of psychotherapy, which encompasses everything from Freudian psychoanalysis to Rogerian client-centered therapy. Subsequent sections cover the use of psychotherapy specifically in the treatment of schizophrenia and autism. The chapter concludes with an evaluation of the contributions of psychotherapy.

DEFINING PSYCHOTHERAPIES

To discuss the value of psychotherapy in the treatment of chronic schizophrenia and adult autism, it is important to be clear about definitions and terms, in particular, psychotherapy, chronicity, and level of treatment outcome.

Psychotherapy is a generic term for numerous approaches to the treatment of psychological problems by psychological means. In all, there are said to be more than 250 psychotherapies (Herink, 1980), and the number is still growing (Wojceichowski, 1985). Psychotherapy has been variously defined (Hinsie & Campbell, 1970; Close, 1966; Cowen, 1955). Most definitions, however, emphasize the therapist–patient relationship as the main theme. One comprehensive definition is that of Szymanski (1980):

> Psychotherapy is a treatment procedure performed by a trained mental health professional through the application of psychologically based verbal and nonverbal means within the context of a relationship with the patient or client and with definite goals of improving the patient's coping abilities and/or ameliorating psychopathological symptoms. (p. 132)

Goldstein, Heller, and Sechrest's (1966) definition was based on the assumption that change can occur only when the process of learning is meaningful. They defined psychotherapy as follows:

> Whatever else it is, psychotherapy must be considered a learning enterprise. We need not specify too narrowly just what is to be learned in psychotherapy; it may be specific behaviors of a whole new outlook in life, but it cannot be denied that the intended outcome of psychotherapy is a change in an individual that can only be termed a manifestation of learning. (p. 213)

Although no single definition of psychotherapy will be satisfactory to all, one might identify the following general themes in most psychotherapies: (1) cure through intellectual insight into problems (psychoanalysis, (2) improvement in functioning through the benefits of the therapist–client relationship (Rogerian and psychodynamic therapies), and (3) the therapist as a model of appropriate behaviors (milieu therapy and psychoeducational therapy). Of course, the value of a therapy cannot be based on its intention to help, as expressed by its definition, but on what is accomplished. Treatment in the analytical and dynamically oriented therapies is viewed as largely a private matter between client and therapist and does not lend itself to standardization. Assuming that the irrational client is able to relate his deep-rooted conflict, and the meaning attached to the words by the patient is the same as that understood by the therapist, the interpretation and ensuing help or guidance would still rest upon the individual therapist. In addition, because the treatment effect is largely seen as a therapist–patient relationship, the effect of nonspecific factors (Shapiro, 1975) needs to be evaluated. Herbert (1987), for example, pointed out that "many processes of change that take place in psychodynamic therapies are somewhat mysterious and invisible to the patient or client" (p. 292). There are a multitude of metaphors that psychodynamic therapists use to connect with their clients. How does one account for their effectiveness? It is hardly possible to compare psychotherapists, within or between therapies. In comparing psychotherapy issues between different therapy orientations, the only choice is client change variables.

Moreover, merely showing that a procedure eliminates symptoms, although important, is inadequate in the overall evaluation of a treatment. Other factors, such as length of treatment, cost, side effects, and overall functioning, need to be considered in the equation before a treatment procedure is accepted as the most appropriate for a given situation.

The Issue of Chronicity

There is not total agreement in the literature on the definition of "chronic" when applied to mental patients (Toews & Barnes, 1986). For the most part, distinguishing the chronic patient from the acute patient is done simply by the duration of illness. Matson (1980) has stated that the typical criteria used in defining chronic schizophrenia are length and number of admissions reported, nature of adaptive skills, and intensity and frequency of delusions and hallucinations. Dimensions other than duration can be important in delivering comprehensive treatment. Minkoff (1979) defined chronicity in three dimensions: diagnosis, duration, and disability. Chronic patients develop impairment (organic dysfunctioning), disability (poor daily living skills) and handicap (socially imposed barriers resulting from the individual's impairment and disability). Gruenberg (1982) stated that whenever impairment is reduced, the disability is reduced. Toews and Barnes (1986) have recently developed a comprehensive definition that integrates the disease with the environment:

> . . . chronic patients are persons suffering from a mental or emotional disorder that is long term and produces serious psychological difficulties that sharply limit

their ability to interact with their environment in such a way as to sustain themselves and/or relate completely to others. (p.3)

Treatment Outcome

With regard to treatment outcome, this can mean anything from simple discharge from the hospital (deinstitutionalization) or normalization (successful integration into and acceptance by the community) to total cure (elimination of the disease). Treatment outcome for chronic schizophrenic and adult autistic patients might best be characterized as normalization. Many of the problems with psychotherapy arise from the lack of specificity with regard to treatment outcome. For example, assessment and diagnosis has typically been used more as a means of showing pretreatment and posttreatment changes rather than guiding treatment by psychotherapists. The same treatment techniques are used regardless of the patient's specific diagnostic category. Kovacs and Paulauskas (1896), in their review on traditional psychotherapies stated: "Authors used presenting problems and clinical (as opposed to diagnostic criteria) constructs to describe their patients. And even when the relevant information was provided, there were rarely any details as to how and by whom the diagnoses were ascertained" (p. 514).

There have been few references to the use of psychotherapy for autism. Moreover, studies on autism more often focused on etiology and assessment than on treatment. Autism was identified in 1943 by Kanner. He called it early infantile autism because of its onset in the early part of life. Four decades have passed, but there is a great paucity of literature on this condition in the adult population. It is hard to find books specifically addressing adult autism. The few follow-up studies carried out to date (Creak, 1963; Kanner, 1971; Rutter, 1970) indicate that about 60% of autistic children are unable to lead a functional life in society. However, recent investigations suggest that characteristics of autism change somewhat over age, with a decrease in activity level, stereotypic movement, and fewer compulsive and ritualistic behaviors (Schopler, 1981; Wing, 1983). It is difficult to explain the lack of research in this chronic condition. The first book written on the adult autistic patient appeared only recently (Schopler & Mesibov, 1983).

One reason for this state of affairs with adults may be lack of differential diagnosis between autistic and mentally retarded clients. Because mentally retarded and autistic individuals share some behavioral characteristics, such as stereotyped and self-injurious behavior, qualitatively poor speech, and poor intellectual ability, many autistic individuals could have been treated as evincing mental retardation rather than autism. In fact, it is estimated that 70% of autistic children have intellectual functioning in the mentally retarded range (APA, 1987). Further, the intellectual functioning of these children has been found to be stable over time, failing to rise with age-related improvements in clinical symptoms (Rutter, 1983).

PSYCHOTHERAPIES
Psychoanalysis

Psychoanalysis, which has traditionally been a driving force in the psychotherapy movement, has addressed the treatment of schizophrenia and autism with considerable trepidation and ambivalence. Freud (1940) cautioned against the use of psychoanalysis in treating schizophrenia, reasoning that because the schizophrenic patient has lost touch with reality he would be precluded from the benefits of psychoanalysis. But Sullivan (1962) attributed many of the abnormal behaviors of chronic schizophrenia to hospitalization. Sullivan applied a modified form of Freudian psychoanalysis with schizophrenic patients. The catalyst of treatment was, however, attributed to the therapist's attitude. This makes studying effectiveness troubling because it involves many factors that cannot be standardized. The major unanswered question regards the ability of the chronic patient to reliably and validly verbalize repressed emotions, to make connections, and to understand interpretations.

The results with psychoanalytic treatment of schizophrenia have not been remarkable. In an early review Knight (1941) found more failures with psychotic patients than with patients having other disorders. He found the highest success rate for organic neuroses and organic conditions (78%), followed by psychoneuroses (63.2%), character disorder (56.6%), sexual disorders (46.5%), and psychoses (25%). Seventy-five percent of the sample under psychoanalytic treatment for psychoses had no change or worsened. Rachman and Wilson (1980) found this low rate across all reported studies using psychoanalytic techniques with psychotic patients. For example, 7 of 29 patients at the Berlin Psychoanalytic Institute, 1 of 15 patients at the London Psychoanalytic Clinic, 2 of 6 patients at the Chicago Institute, 14 of 31 patients at the Menninger Clinic improved with psychoanalytic treatment (p. 108). The ratio between those who improved and those who did not was low. Statistically, these rates do not seem to be greater than chance occurrence.

Psychoanalysis with autistic individuals appears to have been even less promising. There is hardly any work done with adults, and what little is done with infantile autism has not proved beneficial. The early literature on autism by Kanner, Bettleheim, Mahler, and others focused on how the parents perceived autism. These authors proposed that parents' emotional coldness permanently hindered the emotional development to their children (Bettelheim, 1967). Bettelheim (1974) has done some work using the psychodynamic approach with autistic children and their families. He postulated that it was the cold and rejecting nature of the parents that resulted in their children being autistic. This hypothesis has proved incorrect (DeMyer, 1979; Rutter, 1983). Less emphasis was placed on developing treatment programs within a psychotherapy framework. There have been few references in the literature on psychotherapy with autistic persons. Given the paucity of literature on adult autism, therapeutic techniques and treatment modalities dealing with psychotherapy of infantile autism and mental retardation provide the nearest model. Schopler (1981), in fact, has stated that knowledge accrued from children with autism can be extended to adolescents and adults. Again, one is forced to reckon with the fact that most of the analytical studies were fraught with methodological problems that made acceptance of the conclusions difficult.

Other Psychodynamic Therapies

As mentioned earlier, there are hundreds of dynamic therapies. However, most of them have themes in common. Most variations of the analytic theme emphasize different phases in the analytic continuum. The main unifying factor among all of the dynamic therapies is their heavy reliance on the patient–therapist relationship. Only the major therapies, which have a strong structure and relevance (by way of application) to the schizophrenic and autistic population, will be addressed in this chapter.

Psychodynamic therapy has been shown to be of little benefit with children (Werry, 1972). G. W. Brown (1960), Creak (1962), and Rutter (1966) have all indicated that treatment through psychodynamic methods did not show better outcome than no treatment. The failures of psychotherapy in the treatment of autism mirror information on mental retardation. This situation is understandable because most autistic persons are mentally retarded. A strong emphasis has been placed on IQ and prognosis. Individuals with IQ below 50 showed poor outcome, whereas those with an IQ of 70 or more showed good adjustment in later life (Rutter, 1977), demonstrating a positive correlation between improvement and higher level of intellectual functioning.

Rogerian Client-Centered Therapy

Carl Rogers viewed psychodynamic therapies as insufficient, resulting in his development of client-centered therapy in the 1940's. His premise was that man is basically good and can be trusted to control his own life. Rogers claimed the way to the maladjusted individual is through unconditional positive regard as a means of realizing his or her self-actualizing tendencies. In his view the therapist must allow the patient to explore and experience the incongruencies between self-concept and the experiencing self. A fundamental element of therapy would be to enable the patient to reduce defenses. Rogers postulated three essential ingredients for therapy: genuineness, acceptance, and empathic understanding (Rogers, 1980). He argued that these conditions were necessary and sufficient for therapy to take place, thus emphasizing the therapist–client relationship (Rogers, 1957). In fact, this one aspect of stating a necessary and sufficient condition as therapeutic sets Rogerian therapy apart from most other psychotherapies because other psychotherapies cannot identify the therapeutic components. Nevertheless, the very essence of the Rogerian claim has been disputed by others (Traux & Carkhuff, 1967).

Rogers and his colleagues applied this therapeutic technique to schizophrenic patients through the Wisconsin Schizophrenia Study (Rogers, Gendlin, Kiesler, & Traux, 1967). This project lasted years with three groups of patients (chronic, acute, and normal). They found the need for greater therapist involvement and indicated that psychotherapy did not produce significantly better results than for controls. Rogerian therapy has not been demonstrated to be efficacious with patients of other ailments, such as neurosis, and little has been done to empirically validate this method with chronic schizophrenia and adult autistic groups. The lack of verbal and relatively normal thinking processes of individuals with chronic schizophrenia and adult autism, discussed in this volume, may make this approach unworkable.

Existentialism-based Psychotherapy

Existentialism-based psychotherapy has not developed a single set of assumptions or approaches. Rather, divergent methods to understand and aid people are used. Existential psychotherapists see human behavior as the product of deterministic factors such as biology, culture, and indeterministic factors such as environmental events. Most existential psychotherapists emphasize freedom and responsibility . Although there have been many who have delved in existentialism, Rollo May is perhaps the most visible leader. He emphasizes the integrative aspects of existentialism, biological, environmental, and phenomenological (May, 1968). The therapist was to help the patient foster self-awareness, assume responsibility, and piece together the divided personality (May, 1958; Ruffin, 1984). The work of the therapist is seen as authenticity, openness, and the sharing of oneself. In fact, unlike other therapies that speak of helping the patient, existential psychotherapy sees change occurring in both the client and therapist as a result of interaction (Carpenter, Fishel, George, & Gould, 1977). There is very little evidence on the efficacy of existential therapeutic modalities with any form of maladaptiveness, let alone with schizophrenic and autistic individuals. Few studies have appeared concerning schizophrenia. The little information that appeared is mainly analogue reports rather than well-controlled experimental studies (Biswanger, 1952). No reports on the use of existentialism-based psychotherapy in treating autism have been published.

Gestalt Therapy

Gestalt therapy's founder and best-known advocate was Fredreck S. Perls. Perls rejected the notion that human beings are controlled by external or internal factors, rather that they are responsible for themselves and their lives. Gestalt therapy is seen as a noninterpretive, phenomentological, existentially based therapy focusing on the here-and-now phenomena of the person's existence (Simkin, 1979). In the case of the schizophrenic patient, Gestalt therapists proposed that the individual cannot understand and differentiate the figure from the ground and that severely disturbed patients are out of touch with reality and unable to distinguish reality from fantasy and hallucinations. Gestalt therapists set out to assist the individual to integrate himself and to attain his holistic self. Gestalt therapy methods vary; most often treatment is conducted in groups. There are many techniques, and each is presented in a game form developed for a particular individual in a given situation. Nevertheless, the main emphasis is on forcing the client to confront the areas that he avoids and resists and to make the client work through the impasse that will lead to a resolution (Allen, 1986). In Serok and Zemet (1983) we see the results of the use of Gestalt therapy with schizophrenic patients. They treated nine experimental and eight control subjects over a 2½-month period. Significant increases were reported in reality differentiation and perception for treatment subjects as opposed to the control group subjects. However, subjects were also treated simultaneously by a variety of other techniques. The authors were unable to operationalize the actual process that went on during treatment using Gestalt therapy. Moreover, one has to question the wisdom of using outcome measures such as the Rorschach test. The authors state a number of disturbed behaviors diminished over time, but they failed to quantify them. Once again, the difficulty of trying to measure and quantify the process and outcome variables of psychotherapies is apparent. However, there may be some promise for this procedure with highly verbal schizophrenic patients. Further research is needed. No studies on the effects of Gestalt therapy or autism have been reported.

Cognitive Therapy

Cognitive therapy refers to psychological approaches that place emphasis on the strictures and processes of the mind (Toskala, 1986). There is interest on the part of cognitive therapists in working with schizophrenic clients because it is believed that the schizophrenic person's deficiency is diminished. Cognitive mediators are considered to be salient between overt symptoms and underlying biological abnormality (Hemsley, 1985). There are many paradigms of cognitive therapy; however, they all can be said to deal with faulty processing and mental representation (Toskala, 1986). The therapists do not align themselves to any one specific interventions (Hollon & Beck, 1979). Cognitive therapies also utilize behavioral concepts. The covert conditioning model regards private events as covert forms of observable behaviors (Homme, 1965). This situation would parallel principles of classical and operant conditioning (Kazdin, 1977).

There are many representative models of cognitive therapy, of which the three best known are Ellis's rational–emotive therapy (RET), Beck's cognitive therapy, and Meichenbaum's self-instructional training (SIT). Ellis's RET rests on the hypothesis that people's thoughts influence their emotions and behaviors and that their behaviors are based on the interpretations they place on their experiences (Ostby, 1986). Cognitive restructuring through didactic educational approaches, forcing the clients to dispute and change their irrational, self-defeating beliefs (Toskala, 1986), is the fundamental strategy employed. Beck's cognitive therapy gets the client to discover inaccurate thoughts and to make personal discoveries through questions and hypothesis testing. Meichenbaum's SIT emphasizes coping skills and stress inoculation. The presumption of cognitive therapists in the case of schizophrenia specifically is that the schizophrenic person's symptoms result from incorrect interpretations of auditory and perceptual stimuli (Hemsley, 1976).

Few studies using cognitive therapy with schizophrenic persons have been published. For the few papers that exist, the dependent variables selected to evaluate treatment outcome—improving information organization and segmentation of information (Schwartz-Place & Gilmore, 1980), attention and language (Meichenbaum & Cameron, 1973), digit symbol and auditory distraction task (Margolis & Shemberg, 1976)—seems to be largely unrelated to the disease process. Unfortunately, cognitive therapy has not been carried out with autistic adults, so its efficacy with this population is still open to question. What little has been postulated is theoretical rather than empirically derived.

Family Therapy

Family therapy, which was once in the forefront in treatments for schizophrenia and autism, has dwindled in influence because of the emphasis on biological markers, drug therapies, and behavior management therapies. However, two new issues have brought about renewed interest in family therapy: the vulnerability view of schizophrenia (Zubin & Spring, 1977) and the role of expressed emotion in relapse (Hooley, 1985). These two aspects of treatment brought about the need to work with family members and educate them on how to deal with the schizophrenic individual in order to minimize stress and to eliminate hostility and intrusiveness. Both factors have been implicated in relapse (Anderson, 1983; Goldstein, 1981; Vaughn, Snyder, Freeman, Jones, & Falloon, 1984). A number of studies have reported the relationship between expressed emotion and relapse. Patients returning to live with relatives exhibiting expressed emotion had a higher relapse rate than did those returning to relatives with low expressed emotion (Vaughn & Leff, 1976); and discharged patients sent to live with their relatives had a higher relapse rate than did those who lived on their own (Brown, Bone, Dalinson, & Wing, 1966). Three major advantages are attributed to family therapy: boosting the support network for the impaired patient, reduction in stress level in the management of the patient, and home-based education leading to generalization and maintenance (Wong, Massel, Mosk, & Liberman, 1986). Although there are a number of published studies using family therapy with schizophrenic patients (Goldstein, 1984; Jackson & Weakland, 1961), the problem of evaluating the efficacy of these studies remains because of lack of controls.

Hogarty and associates (1986) carried out a controlled study of family therapy, social skills training, and maintenance chemotherapy in the aftercare treatment of schizophrenic patients. Patients from households with high expressed emotion were randomly assigned to a 2-year aftercare study. The groups were (1) family treatment and medication, (2) social skills training and medication, (3) a combination of the above, and (4) drug-treated condition. The control group received individualized maintenance chemotherapy. Results indicated that the group that received the combination of family treatment, social skills training, and medication had the lowest relapse rate, followed by the family treatment and medication group and the social skills training and medication group. The group on medication alone had the highest relapse rate. The authors did point out, however, that the study indicated the delay of relapse rather than prevention of relapse. This study points strongly to multimodal therapy of schizophrenia patients.

Group Therapy

The advent of short hospital stays, attributable to the deinstitution-alization process, has struck a blow to the long-term analytic and dynamic therapies. Traditionally, dynamic therapies do not have a place with schizophrenic and autistic persons. A group setting would not be conducive to bringing forth the deep-rooted feelings of the patient. Rather, as Mosher and Gunderson (1979) have pointed out, a number of individuals were allowed to explore, play with infantile objects, know their bodies, and develop friends and social skills rather than to facilitate insight into personal problems. Studies that purport-edly used group therapy have reported success (Kanas, 1985). However, there are many logistics that need to be taken into consider-ation in conducting group therapy. Homogeneity of the sample— similarities of behavioral excesses and various groups. In general, insight-oriented therapies have not been very effective with the schizophrenic and autistic populations. The interaction-oriented ther-apies have been shown to be more effective.

Milieu Therapy

No discussion of psychotherapy interventions would be complete without mentioning milieu therapy, which is generally defined as ther-apy through environmental management and/or manipulation. The term was first coined by Bettelheim and Sylvester (1948) to imply environmental management within a hospital setting to promote the patients' social rehabilitation. The premise was that a setting that cre-ates a better social context would improve the course of functional psychoses (Wing, 1978). There is overwhelming evidence document-ing the debilitating effects of long-term hospitalization. Barton (1959) and Goffman (1961) characterized the syndrome as one of apathy, lack of expression, lack of interest and initiative, and, most of all, deterio-ration in personal habits. Wing (1961) found that the longer the stay in the hospital, the more unfavorable the patient's attitude toward dis-charge. Wing and Brown (1961) reported that individuals in hospitals that implemented social rehabilitation showed less clinical disturbance, compared to those in hospitals where social rehabilitation service was not in place or was slow to develop. Wing and Brown (1970) thus con-cluded that the morbidity shown by long-stay schizophrenic patients is a result of their environment.

Among the primary goals of milieu therapy as originally conceived was the reorganization of the institutional ward to foster group interactions (Osmond, 1975). Patient's are made aware that they are to be responsible for and to aid their more seriously impaired peers. In this way the stage is set for the patients to interact not only with other schizophrenic patients but also with healthy individuals. It was hoped that the stimulating and exciting environment would draw the individual from isolation and withdrawal, away from reflecting upon himself and directed to things outside himself. This then would create a position to establish contact and form a relationship between therapist and patient.

The conceptual theory described above is complex when put into practice. Despite its presumed efficacy, demonstrated evidence of outcome research using milieu therapy is inconclusive, with as many successes as failures. The Massachusetts Mental Health Center carried out a controlled comparison study in which a group of chronic schizophrenic patients who had been hospitalized for 10 years or more were moved to a therapeutic atmosphere while the rest of the group remained at the nontherapeutic setting. The study reported that none of the patients in the active milieu improved after 6 months of treatment. In contrast, Hamilton (1963) treated a group of chronic male and female schizophrenic patients with an average of 18 years in custodial settings. Milieu therapy was administered for 17 weeks. Activities consisted of occupational therapy, group therapy, recreational therapy, and a stimulating environment. He reported that behavioral ratings by psychiatrists were said to have shown a significant difference between control and treatment group only in the male patients. It was speculated that the change in men was attributable to female nursing personnel, indicating a sex-by-treatment interaction. There are a number of unexplained areas in the study that limit understanding and make replication difficult. What were the stimulating environmental components, and what aspects of the female nurses were controlling factors for the change?

Another program that included a full complement of milieu therapy components was conducted by Miller (1954), who had 38 chronic women patients in an open ward for more than a year. Each patient had an individual treatment program, including activity outside the ward for the better part of the day with opportunities for socialization and recreational activities. Seating arrangements were varied, and speakers were brought in. Better-adjusted patients had weekly bus rides. Supervising personnel were said to have been positive and supportive. Their program resulted in 14 patients leaving the hospital during the year and eventually becoming self-supporting. This study also lacks detail and clarity as to who the speakers were and what topics were presented. Such details may help in pinpointing therapeutic elements of a treatment and aid replication.

Studies such as that of Greenblatt, Solomon, and Evans (1965) have also reported that milieu therapy accounted for therapeutic effects. Their study, conducted at the Boston State Hospital Center, involved the treatment of chronic schizophrenic patients in intensive milieu therapy. Patients were entered into drug and no-drug therapy groups. Sanders, Smith, and Weinman (1967) also treated chronic patients in a milieu therapy program, conducted at the Philadelphia State Hospital. The focus of their therapy was one of structure and social interaction. Their results indicated that greater improvement was realized in the setting with structure in comparison to one with less or no structure.

The early milieu programs have today given way to more systematic treatments that incorporate the principles of behavior modification and social learning to shape appropriate behavior. In an extensive and well-controlled study carried out by Paul and Lentz (1977), social learning (classical conditioning, shaping, prompting, response cost, time-out), milieu therapy (communication, positive expectations, problem solving), and traditional therapies (chemotherapy, psychotherapy, custodial care) were compared. Their data led them to conclude that social learning therapy was superior to milieu therapy and traditional hospital custodial care. However, milieu therapy was superior to traditional hospital treatment. Patients in routine hospital treatment failed to evince perceptible improvement. Interestingly, posttreatment differences were maintained even after 18 months. Social learning therapy not only resulted in greater improvement and longer maintenance but was also the most cost-efficient.

Although milieu therapy with autistic persons has been suggested by some (Goldfarb, Mintz, & Strook, 1969), no studies have appeared. Milieu therapy seems to have a great potential not only for reducing institutionalization but also for ameliorating the individual's pathology and, more important, preparing the individual for life outside the hospital. However, studies on milieu therapy carried out to date have

fallen short because of many oversights. One main factor is staff training. In fact, shortcomings in many studies can be attributed to staff
inadequacies (Birrell & Henderson, 1986). No study has been reported
on staff training, monitoring of staff, of modification of programs
according to developments taking place in implemented programs.
This situation makes it difficult to determine the adequacy of milieu
therapy. Further, the procedures used in milieu therapy may differ
markedly. We need to learn what factors are most effective and under
what conditions.

Just because something is good does not automatically translate
into more is better. There is some evidence that certain patients do
not improve but rather react poorly to an over-stimulating environment (Ciompi, 1983; Goldberg & Rubin, 1964). This factor, the toxic
milieu (Cole, 1967), could result in negative outcomes (Hemsley, 1978;
Schooler & Spohn, 1982; Wing, 1975). Given the heterogeneity of
the disease and marked interindividual differences, such a finding
is not surprising. However, further study needs to be carried out
to identify exactly what kinds of patients act or react to various
environments. Day (1981) outlined four types of environments that
may be problematic for schizophrenic patients. They are (1) cogni-
tively confusing environments, (2) emotionally critical or intrusive
environments, (3) overly demanding environments, and (4) threaten-
ing or demoralizing physical environments (p. 78). The same assumptions can be applied to the hospital milieu.

Treatment Integrity

A major issue in determining the optimal value of psychotherapy is
treatment integrity, defined as the degree to which the intervention
plan has been implemented as designed. It is naive to assume that
interventions are fully implemented from paper to the practice setting with total accuracy. This issue has not been addressed fully in
the area of psychotherapy. In 30 articles randomly surveyed, none
discussed training of caretakers who were to implement the procedure or, in the case of direct therapy, training of the therapist. No
mention was made of documentation of frequency and duration of
the sessions or of the type of patient–therapist interaction that took
place. Thus, comparison of therapies becomes meaningless because
comparisons may be made between a well-executed therapy and one

that was well planned but poorly executed, or even one that was not implemented. As Birrell and Henderson (1986), in talking of token economy stated, the major causes for failure are lack of consistency among staff and administrative difficulties. Such failures are not new and have been a frequent pitfall. Until meticulous attention is given to the various aspects discussed above, the uncertainty of psychotherapy effects with schizophrenic and autistic populations will never be satisfactorily resolved. It is hoped that future psychotherapy research will address some of these issues.

Treatment Outcome Studies

Judgment of the efficacy of any treatment procedure should be based on social validity (Wolf, 1978). The treatment should be useful, meaningful, and patient-oriented; statistical significance alone is not sufficient. Outcome research for psychotherapy remains a morass of confusion, controversy, and misunderstanding. Numerous authors have pointed out the weaknesses of reported studies in their lack of methodological rigor (Eysenk, 1985; Hartman, Roper, & Gelfand, 1977; Rachman & Wilson, 1983). Eysenck's (1952) study pointed out the lack of effectiveness of traditional psychotherapy. Later, Levitt (1957) reported that psychotherapy is no more effective than no treatment. These two studies raised more controversy than could have been imagined. Meltzoff and Kornreich (1970) reacted to Eysneck and reported in their findings that psychotherapy showed greater improvement than no treatment (Bergin, 1971). Smith and Glass (1977), in their more recent meta-analytical study, reported that psychotherapy was effective. The literature is replete with arguments and counterarguments about the fairness of the measures, the adequacy of the samples, the validity of the diagnosis, the appropriateness of various analyses, and the conclusions drawn. Eysenck (1985), in a rejoinder, identified what he considered flaws in the psychotherapy reviews. For example, he referred to meta-analysis as meta-silliness.

Meta-analysis is good only in explaining the average effect size. However, much that happens during therapy—namely, the process, the integrity of implementation, and other procedural factors—cannot be explained through meta-analysis. Shapiro and Shapiro (1982), in their review of 143 studies, have pointed out the many inadequacies in those studies. Rachman and Wilson (1983) have eloquently discussed the many limitations and liabilities of meta-analysis. The only way to adequately tackle the issue of the efficacy of psychotherapy is through properly planned and executed studies with direct comparisons of treatments and using matched subjects. To date, few studies of this type have appeared.

Summary

The evaluation of psychotherapy—or of any intervention, for that matter—must deal with three distinct phases: input, process, and outcome. What goes into the therapy via input is the first phase. The various studies published do not adequately describe the very essence of the therapeutic program, especially in the case of the dynamically oriented therapies. This problem is perhaps intrinsic to the therapeutic modality itself. Therapists use what their patients tell them as a basis for going on; therefore, it is not possible to outline the program completely before treatment. The behaviorally oriented treatments can be planned ahead with more accuracy because, although they are symptom-oriented, they are not patient- or therapist-dependent.

What happens during the therapy process is another aspect that needs to be considered. Here again psychodynamically oriented therapy has had difficulty in defining what goes on during therapy. There are no standard verbal responses that are used by the therapist to a given patient's verbal behavior, and although this meets the tenets of this approach, it is hard to quantify. Therapists feel that it is a dynamic interaction between patient and therapist that cannot be standardized. On the other hand, behavioral strategies do not involve much personal involvement by the therapist. Instead, specific steps of the program are implemented by the therapist, or by the client.

Outcome is the end result of the process of treatment. Two main areas can be studied: the social and psychological aspects of the patient. Absence of symptoms is one of the main dependent variables used in most outcome studies of psychotherapy. However, as often pointed out, absence of symptoms is not always a good indicator of therapeutic outcome because of the possibility of spontaneous remission of symptoms; or, as Malan (1973) pointed out, symptoms can be reduced by factors such as environmental change or by the patient's new but nevertheless maladaptive way of handling the situation, which has nothing to do with the therapy. Weissman (1984) suggested that evaluating treatment outcome could best be left in the hands of those who have nothing to do with treatment and have no commitment to the treatments being compared.

Comprehensive treatment evaluation should include dependent variables selected from three domains: physical, social, and psychological. All three of these areas also evince direct effects on the target behaviors treated as well as on untargeted behaviors changed through treatment.

What then should be the future direction for treatment of schizophrenia and autism? In the case of autism there is an urgent need for improved diagnostic specificity and a need for expanded work with adult autistic individuals; at present this seems to be a neglected group. Second, it is time for therapists to drop biases toward other orientations and embark upon a cooperative venture in using combined therapies with autistic and schizophrenic individuals. A common code of research methodology to study the effects of various modalities needs to be developed. In this respect, a manual of procedures and methodologies acceptable to various professional camps and based on empirical findings would be most meaningful.

REFERENCES

Allen, H. A. (1986). A Gestalt perspective. In T. F. Rigger, D. R. Maki, & A. W. Wolf (Eds.), *Applied rehabilitation in counseling* (pp. 148–157). New York: Springer Publishing Co.

American Psychiatric Association (1987). *Diagnostic and statistical manual of mental disorders* (3rd ed. rev.). Washington, DC: Author.

Anderson, C. (1983). A psycho-educational model of family treatment for schizophrenia. In H. Stierlin, L. C. Wynne, & M. Wirsching (Eds.), *Psychosocial intervention in schizophrenia* (pp. 48–62). New York: Springer Publishing Co.

Barton, C. (1959). *Institutional neurosis*. Bristol: J. Wright & Sons, Ltd.

Bergin, A. E. (1971). The evaluation of therapeutic outcomes. In S. L. Garfield & A. E. Bergin (Eds.), *Handbook of psychotherapy and behavior change* (pp. 217–270). New York: Wiley

Bettelheim, B. (1967). *The empty fortress: Infantile autism and the birth of the self*. Now York: Free Press.

Bettelheim, B. (1974). *A home for the heart*. New York: Alfred Knopf.

Bettelheim, B. & Sylvester, E. (1948). A therapeutic milieu. *American Journal of Orthopsychiatry, 18,* 191–206.

Birrell, J., & Henderson, M. (1986). The psychological approach. In C. Hume & I. Pullen (Eds.), *Rehabilitation in psychiatry.* (pp. 108–125). New York: Churchill Livingstone.

Biswanger, L. (1960). Existential analysis, psychiatry, schizophrenia. *Journal of Existential Psychiatry, 1,* 157-165.

Brown, G. W., (1960). Length of hospital stay and schizophrenia: A review of statistical studies. *Acta Psychiatrica Neurologia Scnandinavica, 35,* 414–430.

Brown, G. W., Bone, M., Dalison, B., & Wing, J. K. (1966). *Schizophrenia and social care.* Maudsley Monograph No. 17, (pp. 53-66). London: Oxford University Press.

Brown, J. (1960). Prognosis from presenting symptoms of preschool children with atypical development. *American Journal of Orthopsychiatry, 30,* 382–390.

Carpenter, W. L., Fishel, A., George, S., & Gould, F. (1977). *Health instruction packages: Humanistic nursing-nurse patient relationship.* Los Angeles: League for innovation in the Community Colleges.

Ciompi, L. (1983). How to improve the treatment of schizophrenics: A multicausal illness concept and its therapeutic consequences. In H. Stierlin, L. C. Wynne, & M. Wirsching (Eds.), *Psychosocial intervention in schizophrenia.* New York: Springer-Verlag.

Close, H. T. (1966) Psychotherapy. *Voices, 2,* 79–81.

Cole, J. O. (1967). Long term treatment of chronic schizophrenia: A lack of controls. *International Journal of Psychiatry, 4,* 116–128.

Cowen, E. L. (1955). Psychotherpy and play technique with the exceptional child. In W. H. Gurkshawk (Ed.), *Psychology of exceptional children and youth* (pp. 520–575). Englewood Cliffs, Prentice Hall.

Creak, M. (1964). Juvenile psychosis and mental deficiency. In B. W. Richards (Ed.), *Proceedings, London Conference of Scientific Studies of Mental Deficiencies* (Vol. 2.). Dangenham, England: May and Baker.

Creak, M. (1963). Childhood psychosis: A review of 100 cases. *British Journal of Psychiatry. 109,* 84–89.

Creak, M. (1964). Schizophrenic syndrome in childhood: Further progress of a working party. *Developmental Medicine in Child Neurology, 6,* 530-535.

Day, R. (1981). Life events and schizophrenia: The triggering hypothesis. *Acta Psychiatrica Scandinavica 64,* 97–122.

DeMyer, M. K. (1979). *Parents and children in autism.* Washington, DC: Victor H. Winston & Sons.

Eysenck, H. J. (1952). The effects of psychotherapy: An evaluation. *Journal of Consulting Psychology, 16,* 319–324.

Eysenck, H. J. (1985). Studying the effects of psychotherapy. In R. N. Gaind (Eds.), *Current themes in psychiatry*, vol. 4, (pp. 123–141). New York: Medical and Scientific Books.

Fish, B. (1976). Pharmacotherapy for autistic and schizophrenic children. In E. R. Ritvo, B. J. Freeman, E. M. Ornitz, & O. E. Tanguay (Eds.), *Autism: Diagnosis, current research and management* (pp. 107–120). New York: Spectrum.

Freud, S. (1940). *An outline of psychoanalysis*. New York: Norton.

Fuoco, F. J., & Tyson, W. M. (1986). Behavior therapy in residential programs for psychiatric clients. In F. J. Fuoco & W. P. Christian (Ed.), *Behavior analysis and therapy in residential programs* (pp. 231–259). New York: Van Nostrand Reinhold.

Goffman, E. (1961). *Asylums: Essays of the social situations of mental patients and other inmates*. New York: Doubleday.

Goldberg, A., & Rubin, B. (1964). Recovery of patients during periods of supposed neglect. *British Journal of Medical Psychology, 37*, 266–272.

Goldfarb, W., Mintz, I., & Strook, K. W. (1969). *A time to heal, corrective socialization: A treatment approach to childhood schizophrenia*. New York: International Universities Press.

Goldstein, A. (1984). *Psychological skill training: Structured learning technique*. New York: Pergamon Press.

Goldstein, A. P., Heller, K., & Sechrest, L. B. (1966). *Psychotherapy and the psychology of behavior change*. New York: Wiley.

Greenblatt, M., Solomon, M., & Evans, A. S. (1965). *Drugs and social therapy in chronic schizophrenia*. Springfield, Il: Charles C. Thomas.

Gruenberg, E. M. (1982). Social breakdown in young adults: Keeping crises from becoming chronic. In B. Pepper & H. Ryglewicz (Eds.), *The young adult chronic patient*. Washington, DC: Jossey-Bass.

Hamilton, V. (1963). Size constancy and cue responsiveness in psychosis. *British Journal of Psychology, 54*, 25-39.

Hartmann, D. P., Roper, B. L., & Gelfand, D. M. (1977). In B. B. Lahey & A. E. Kazdin (Eds.), *Advances in clinical child psychology* (pp. 1–46). New York: Plenum Press.

Hemsley, D. R. (1976). Problems in the interpretation of cognitive abnormalities in schizophrenia. *British Journal of Psychiatry, 129*, 332-335.

Hemsley, D. R. (1978). Limitations of operant procedures in the modification of schizophrenic functioning: The possible relevance of studies of cognitive disturbance. *Behavior Analysis and Modification, 2* 165–173.

Hemsley, D. R. (1985). Schizophrenia. In B. P. Bradley & C. Thompson (Eds.), *Psychological applications in psychiatry* (pp.95–117). New York: John Wiley & Sons.

Herbert, M. (1987). *Conduct disorders of children and adolescence: A social learning perspective.* New York: John Wiley & Sons.

Hinsie, L. E., & Campbell, R. J. (1970). *Psychiatric dictionary.* New York: Oxford University Press.

Hogarty, G. E., & Anderson, C. M., Reiss, D. J., Kornblith, S. J., Greenwald, P. D., Javna, C. D., Madonia, M. J., & Epics Schizophrenia Research Group, (1986). Family psychoeducation, social skills training, and maintenance chemotherapy in the aftercare treatment of schizophrenia. *Archives of General Psychiatry, 43,* 633–642.

Hollon, S. D., & Beck, A. T. (1979). Cognitive therapy of depression. In P. C. Kendall & S. D. Hollon (Eds.), *Cognitive-behavioral interventions: Theory research and procedures* (pp.153-204). New York: Academic Press.

Homme, L. E. (1965). Perspectives in psychology: Controls of coverants, the operants of the mind. *Psychological Record, 24,* 501–511.

Hooley J. M. (1985). Expressed emotions: A review of the critical literature. *Clinical Psychology Review, 5,* 119–139.

Journal of Speech and Hearing Disorders, 25, 8–12.

Jackson, D. D., & Weakland, J. H. (1961). Cojoint family therapy: Some considerations on theory, technique, and results. *Psychiatry, 24*(Supp. 2), 30–45.

Kanas, N. (1985). Inpatient and outpatient group therapy for schizophrenic patients. *American Journal of Psychotherapy, 39*(3), 431–439.

Kanner, L. (1971). Follow-up study of eleven autistic children originally reported in 1943. *Journal of Autism and Childhood Schizophrenia, 1,* 119–145.

Kazdin, A. E. (1977). Assessing the clinical or applied significance of behavior change through validation. *Behavior Modification, 1,* 427–452.

Kazdin, A. E. (1982). Methodology of psychotherapy outcome research: Recent developments and remaining limitations. In J. H. Harvey, & M. M. Parks, *Psychotherapy research and behavior change* (151-193). Washington, DC. : American Psychological Association.

Knight, R. P. (1941). Evaluation of the results of psychoanalytic therapy. *American Journal of Psychiatry, 98,* 434–446.

Kovaks, M., & Paulauskas, S. (1986). The traditional psychotherapies. In H. C. Quay & J. S. Werry (Eds.), *Psychopathological disorders of childhood* (pp.496–522). New York: John Wiley & Sons.

Levitt, E. E. (1957). The results of psychotherapy with children: An evaluation. *Journal of Consulting Psychology, 21,* 189–196.

Lotter, V. (1975). Social adjustment and placement of autistic children in Middlesex: A follow-up study. *Journal of Autistic and Childhood Schizophrenia, 4,* 11–32.

Malan, D. H. (1973). The outcome problem in psychotherapy research; a historical review. *Archives of General Psychiatry, 29,* 719–729.

Margolis, R. B., & Shemberg, K. M. (1976). Cognitive instruction in process and reactive schizophrenia: A failure to replicate. *Behavior Therapy, 7,* 668-671.

Matson, J. L. (1980). Behavior modification procedures for training chronically institutionalized schizophrenics. *Progress in Behavior Modification, 9,* 167-204.

Matson, J. L. (1984). Psychotherapy with persons who are mentally retarded. *Mental Retardation, 22,* 170-175.

May, P. R. A. (1968). *Treatment of schizophrenia.* New York: Science House.

Meltzoff, J., & Kornreich, M. (1970). *Research in psychotherapy.* New York: Atherton.

Meichenbaum, D. H., & Cameron, R. (1973). Training schizophrenics to talk to themselves: A means of developing attentional controls. *Behavior Therapy, 4,* 515-534.

Miller, D. H. (1954). The rehabilitation of chronic open-ward neuropsychiatric patients. *Psychiatry, 17,* 347.

Mosher, L. R.,& Gunderson, J. G. (1979). Group, family, milieu and community support systems treatment for schizophrenia. In L. Bellak (Ed.), *The disorders of the schizophrenic syndrome.* New York: Basic.

Ostby, S. S. (1986). A rational-emotive perspective. In T. F. Riggar, D. R. Maki, & A. W. Wolf (Eds.), *Applied rehabilitation counseling* (pp. 167-175). New York: Springer Publishing Co.

Paul, G. L. (1969). Chronic mental patient: Current status, future directions. *Psychological Bulletin, 71,* 81-94.

Paul, G. L. (1986). Net relative cost of the maximum potential utility assessment paradigm. In G. L. Paul (Ed.), *Assessment in residential treatment settings* (part 1, pp 165-189). Champaign, IL: Research Press.

Paul G. L., & Lentz, R. (1977). *Psychosocial treatment of chronic mental patients.* London: Harvard University Press.

Rachman, S. J., & Wilson, G. T. (1980). *The effects of psychological therapy* (2nd ed.). New York: Pergamon Press.

Rogers, C. R. (1957). The necessary and sufficient conditions of therapeutic personality change. *Journal of Consulting Psychology, 21,* 95-103.

Rogers, C. R. (1980). *A way of being.* Boston: Houghton Mifflin.

Rogers, C. R., Gendlin, E. T., Kiessler, C., & Truax, C. B. (1967). *The therapeutic relationship and its impact: A study of psychotherapy with schizophrenics.* Madison: University of Wisconsin Press.

Ruffin, J. E. (1984). The anxiety of meaninglessness. *Journal of Counseling and Development, 63,* 40-42.

Rutter, M. (1966). Behavioral and cognitive characteristics of a series of psychotic children. In J. K. Wing (Ed.). *Early childhood autism: Clinical, educational, and social aspects* (pp. 55-81). New York: Pergamon Press.

Rutter, M. (1970). Autistic children: Infancy to adulthood. *Seminars in Psychiatry, 2,* 435–450.

Rutter, M. (1977). Speech patterning in recently admitted and chronic long-stay schizophrenic patients. *British Journal of Social and Clinical Psychology, 16,* 47-55.

Rutter, M. (1983). Cognitive defects in the pathogenesis of autism. *Journal of Child Psychology and Psychiatry, 24,* 513–531.

Sanders, R., Smith, R. S. & Weinman, B. S. (1967). *Chronic psychosis and recovery.* San Francisco: Jossey-Bass.

Schooler, C., & Spohn, H. (1982). Social dysfunction and treatment failure in schizophrenia. *Schizophrenia Bulletin, 8,* 85–98.

Schopler, E. (1981). Autism in adolescence and adulthood. In *Proceedings of the 1981 International Conference on Autism* (pp. 16–22). Washington DC: National Society for Children and Adult Autism.

Schopler, E., & Mesibov, G. B. (Eds.). (1983). *Autism in adolescents and adults.* New York: Plenum Press.

Schwartz-Place, E. J., & Gilmore, G. C/ (1980). Perceptual organization in schizophrenia. *Journal of Abnormal Psychology, 89,* 409–418.

Serok, S., & Zemet, R. M. (1983). An experiment of gestalt group therapy with hospitalized schizophrenics.

Shapiro, D. A. (1975). Some implications of psychotherapy research for clinical psychology. *British Journal of Medical Psychology, 48,* 199–206.

Shapiro, D. A., & Shapiro, D. (1982). Meta-analysis of comparative therapy outcome studies: A replication and refinement. *Psychological Bulletin, 92*(3), 581–604.

Simkin, J. (1979). Gestalt therapy. In R. Corsini (Ed.), *Current psychotherapies* (2nd ed., pp. 273-301). Itasca, IL: Peacock.

Smith, M. L. & Glass, G. V. (1977). Meta-analysis of psychotherapy outcome studies. *American Psychologist, 32,* 752-760.

Sullivan, H. S. (1962). Peculiarity of thought in schizophrenia. In H. S. Sullivan (Ed.), *Schizophrenia as a human process* (pp. 4-16). New York: W. W. Norton.

Szymanski, L. L. (1980). Individual psychotherapy with retarded persons. In S. Szymanski & P. E. Tanguay (Eds.) *Emotional disorders of mentally retarded persons* (pp. 132-147. Baltimore: University Park Press.

Toews, J., & Barnes, G. (1986, June). The chronic mental patient and community, psychiatry: A system in trouble. *Canada's Mental Health,* 2–16.

Toskala, A. (1986). The development of cognitive therapy. *Scandinavian Journal of Behavior Therapy, 15,* 143–162.

Truax, C., & Carkhuff, R. (1967). *Toward effective counselling and psychotherapy.* Chicago: Aldine Press.

Vaughn, C., & Leff, J. P. (1976). The influence of family and social factors on the course of psychiatric illness. *British Journal of Psychiatry, 129,* 125–137.

Vaughn, C, E., Snyder, K. S., Jones, S., Freeman, W. B., & Falloon, I. R. H. (1984). Family factors in schizophrenic relapse: A California replication of the British research on expressed emotion. *Archives of General Psychiatry, 41,* 1169–1177.

Weissman, M. M. (1979). The psychological treatment of depression. *Archives of General Psychiatry, 36,* 1261–1269.

Werry, J. S. (1972). Childhood psychosis. In H. C. Quay & J. S. Werry, (Eds.), *Psychopathological disorders of childhood* (pp. 173–233). New York: Wiley.

Wing, J. K. (1961). A simple and reliable sub-classification of chronic schizophrenia. *Journal of Mental Science, 107,* 862–875.

Wing, J. (1975). Impairments in schizophrenia. In R. Wirt, G. Winokur, & M. Roff (Eds.), *Life history research in psychopathology* (vol. 4, pp. 236–269). Minneapolis, MN: University of Minnesota Press.

Wing, J. (1978). Social influences on the course of schizophrenia. In L. C. Wynne, R. L. Cromwell. & S. Matthysse (Eds.), *The nature of schizophrenia: New approaches to research and treatment* (pp. 185–200). New York: John Wiley & Sons.

Wing, J. K. (1983). Standardized methods of classification of mental disorders. In T. Helgason (Ed.), *Methodology in evaluation of psychiatric treatment* (pp. 81–92). New York: Cambridge University Press.

Wing, J. K., & Brown, G. W. (1961). Social treatment of schizophrenia: A comparative study of three mental hospitals. *Journal of Mental Science, 107,* 847–861.

Wing, J. K., & Brown, G. W. (1970). *Institutionalism and schizophrenia: A comparative study on three mental hospitals 1960–1968.* London: Cambridge University Press.

Wojciechowski, F. L. (1985). Outcome research strategies in psychotherapy: From anecdotal case reports to double blind research. In M. A. van Kalmthout Cas Schaap & f. L. Wojciechowski (Eds.), *Common factors in psychotherapy* (pp. 123–142). Berwyn: Swits North America.

Wolf, M. M. (1978). Social validity: A case for subjective measurement of how behavioral analysis is finding its heart. *Journal of Applied behavior Analysis, 11,* 302–214.

Wong, S. E., Massed, H. K., Mosk, M. D., & Liberman, R. P. (1986). Behavioral approaches to the treatment of schizophrenia. In G. D. Burrows, T. R. Norman, & G. Rubenstein (Eds.), *Handbook of studies on schizophrenia: 2. Management and research* (pp. 75–95). New York: Elsevier.

Zubin, J., & Spring, B. (1977). Vulnerability: A new view of schizophrenia. *Journal of Abnormal Psychology, 86,* 103–126.

Index